UNIVERSAL BANKING

Universal Banking

International Comparisons and Theoretical Perspectives

JORDI CANALS

CLARENDON PRESS • OXFORD
1997

Oxford University Press, Great Clarendon Street, Oxford OX2 6DP
Oxford New York
Athens Auckland Bangkok Bogota Bombay
Buenos Aires Calcutta Cape Town Dar es Salaam
Delhi Florence Hong Kong Istanbul Karachi
Kuala Lumpur Madras Madrid Melbourne
Mexico City Nairobi Paris Singapore
Taipei Tokyo Toronto
and associated companies in
Berlin Ibadan

Oxford is a trade mark of Oxford University Press

Published in the United States by
Oxford University Press Inc., New York

British Library Cataloguing in Publication Data
Data available

Library of Congress Cataloging in Publication Data
Canals, Jordi.
Universal banking : international comparisons and theoretical perspectives / Jordi Canals.
Includes bibliographical references and index.
1. Universal banks. I. Title.
HG1601.C26 1997 332.1—dc20 96–34856
ISBN 0–19–877506–7
ISBN 0–19–877505–9 (Pbk)

Typeset by Graphicraft Typesetters Ltd., Hong Kong
Printed in Great Britain by
Biddles Ltd., Guildford & King's Lynn

To my parents

Contents

List of Figures

List of Tables

Introduction

The drastic changes that have occurred in the banking industry in many industrial countries over the past two decades have had a tremendous impact on financial intermediaries.

The deregulation and disintermediation processes, the globalization of financial markets, the emergence of new competitors, and the introduction and application of new information technologies in the banking industry have led to profound changes in its structure, increased competition, and squeezed margins. As a result, banks are reconsidering their traditional ways of competing and are seeking to redefine their strategy and organization.

One of the challenges facing banks in the major industrial countries is the growing importance of capital markets which, with the emergence of new financial instruments, are replacing some of the banks' traditional functions as financial intermediaries.

The banks' response to these challenges has been varied. Some have opted for concentrating on the traditional retail business, others for controlling part of the transactions that take place in the capital markets. Finally, some banks are following the financial markets in their globalization process, seeking to internationalize their activities, either alone or in alliance with other banks. However well the banks following these strategies may do, it can be safely said that nothing is as it was in the banking industry.

This book tries to make a contribution in three areas regarding universal banks in industrial countries. First, many banks have figured out that the only way to survive in this changing industry is to become universal banks by integrating different financial businesses. This strategy has manifested itself in several decisions: diversification into other financial activities, diversification into non-banking or non-financial activities, mergers and acquisitions, internationalization of activities, and, finally, the adoption of new organizational structures that enable a response to a quickly changing market. We will discuss the challenges and risks that universal banks face in their diversification process, and suggest ways of handling the increasing complexity. Moreover, the analysis of the advantages of universal banks over specialist institutions is developed from the viewpoint of banks, not from the more usual perspective of non-financial firms or the growth rate of a country. For that purpose, we will adopt the approach of considering what a universal bank's corporate strategy should be and problems of its implementation.

Second, we will discuss the relationship between banks and financial markets in this context of deregulation and disintermediation. The questions we want to address are: Will financial markets capture all the financial intermediation activity? Can banks play a role in the increasingly sophisticated world of financial markets? Will banks exert control over financial markets?

Third, we will look at the role of banks in financing and influencing non-financial companies in industrial countries from the viewpoint of banks themselves, not from the perspective of companies. The particular model developed in each country in the past decades has a clear effect in banks' strategy and performance. We will discuss the nature and evolution of universal banking in three countries: Germany, Spain, and Japan. Although the universal bank model seems to be the dominant one in all three countries, the differences in each country's financial system single out a number of distinctive features.

The methodology we will use will be primarily inductive. We will combine academic contributions from the fields of industrial economics, strategic management and finance with the detailed study of real cases, mainly of European and North American banks. Some chapters (for instance, Chapters 4, 5, and 10) present a blend of theory, formal models, and real cases. Consequently, this book should be useful to both students and professionals of the financial system. The banks studied in detail include the following: Argentaria, Banc One, Banco Santander, Banco Popular, Banesto, Bankers Trust, Bankinter, Bank of America, Barclays, BBV, BCH, Chase Manhattan, Citibank, Crédit Lyonnais, Deutsche Bank, HSBC, Midland, Mitsubishi, Morgan Grenfell, Nationsbank, Prudential, Shearson Lehman, and S. G. Warburg.

This book is addressed both at scholars and managers who work in the financial services industry. It has been written in a non-technical way, although in some sections (Chapters 4 and 5, for instance) certain banks' decisions are modelled following a more formal pattern.

The structure of this book is as follows (see Fig I.1). Chapter 1 briefly discusses the profound transformations that have taken place in the international financial system in the last twenty years and the innovations that have had most significance for the banking business, and their impact on the banks' performance.

In particular, we ask whether these changes are transforming the nature of banking activities, and, if so, how banks should adapt to the new circumstances. In this chapter, our conceptual approach will be functional: we will seek to analyse the tasks and functions that a bank should be carrying out and its real possibilities of achieving success in an environment of stiffening competition.

This chapter also introduces the notion of financial model. By financial model, we mean the unique configuration adopted by the financial system in a particular country, paying particular attention to the roles and relative weight of the banks and capital markets. At one extreme, there are countries where bank financing predominates. At the other extreme, there are a few countries where financial markets play a greater role in financial activity.

Chapter 2 discusses in greater detail the various models that have emerged for the organization of the financial system. First, we will discuss the model based on financial markets as a means of channelling flows between saving and

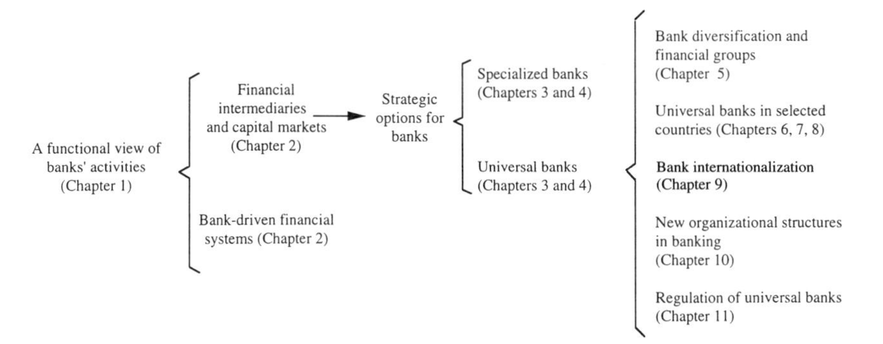

FIG. I.1 *Conceptual framework of the book*

investment. The second model is based on the pre-eminent role played by banks and other financial intermediaries. Unlike the first model in the bank-driven model financial markets play a much less prominent role in financing real investment. However, these two models, which are both deeply embedded in various countries, are not static but are presently undergoing a major process of mutation or change. This process seems to be tending to bring the two models closer together rather than differentiate or separate them.

Chapter 3 analyses, from a historical viewpoint, one of the banks' major strategic options at the present time: their transformation into universal banks. In the course of this analysis, we will briefly review the main arguments used in the United States—where commercial banks and capital markets were separated in 1933—with regard to the desirability of abandoning the universal banking model and separating commercial banking from investment banking.

However, the arguments used against universal banks in the United States, based on partial data, are not unequivocal. In fact, the banks that combined commercial banking with investment banking generally came out better from the crisis than those banks that confined their business to pure commercial banking. Therefore, looking at the issue in terms of profitability, number of banks failing, or solvency, the arguments do not support a separation of activities.

After discussing the separation of commercial banking from investment banking in the United States, Chapter 4 introduces the main arguments used to evaluate the theoretical and practical advantages and disadvantages of the universal bank system *vis-à-vis* specialized banks, from the banks' viewpoint.

The various arguments we will discuss—some of which have been extensively aired in the debates on the financial system or on public policy regarding the universal banks—are not fully conclusive in establishing the superiority of one bank model over the other. This chapter also presents a short discussion on mergers and acquisitions in the banking industry.

Chapter 5 will discuss two issues related to universal banks. The first is the diversification of the universal banks' activities towards other financial services.

Among the advantages of the diversification of activities, we will discuss—using real-life cases—the potential economies of scope between different financial services and the possibility of solving the capital markets' alleged information problems. We will then analyse a special case of universal banking: that in which the bank not only is involved in corporate lending, but also acts as shareholder. This is the situation in which the bank starts up a group of industrial or services companies whose core is the bank itself.

The next three chapters will discuss how the different role of universal banks, specialized banks, and financial markets has helped shape three financial models with some similarities but also with significant differences. These are the cases of Germany, Spain, and Japan. The reason why we have chosen these countries is that their respective financial models all have a common denominator: the major role played by bank financing in non-financial companies and the dominant presence of universal banks. It seems that the latter feature is slowly but surely gaining ground in many countries and an analysis from three different outlooks may be beneficial.

Chapter 6 analyses the German model. The widely held opinion that the presence of banks in German industrial corporations is highly important and positive for the country as a whole is based on a series of assumptions on bank financing and banks' control in non-financial firms. In this chapter, we will examine the validity of those arguments, using a detailed empirical analysis.

The Japanese model is analysed in Chapter 7. After outlining the main features of the Japanese financial system and its differences from the German system, we will discuss the role and importance of universal banks in Japan. In particular, we will analyse the concept of the main bank, its special relationships with non-financial companies, within business groups known as 'keiretsu', and their role within the framework of a financial system in which financial markets will play an increasingly important role.

Chapter 8 discusses the Spanish financial model. One cannot understand the involvement of banks in financing non-financial companies in Spain in the 1980s and 1990s without discussing two conditions that determine the framework within which the bank system operates in Spain: heightened competition within the industry and a situation of economic recession until 1984 and later between 1991 and 1993.

In general, we point out that relations between banks and non-financial companies in Spain are closer to the German model. The reasons for this are the significant weight of banks in the financing of companies and the smaller presence of some banks as leading shareholders of large companies. However, the Spanish model departs from the German model in one respect: the long-term bank debt of Spanish companies comprises only a small proportion of total bank debt.

After discussing the advantages and disadvantages of universal banks and their relative positioning in the three countries, in Chapter 9 we will analyse in certain depth another critical strategic decision for the banks: the internationalization of its activities. The globalization of the international financial system driven by financial markets seems to be also pushing the banks in this direction. After examining the various reasons in favour of or against bank internationalization, we will introduce a conceptual model that explains the internationalization of banks, based on both theory and real cases.

In Chapter 10, we will address a new critical issue for banks, particularly the universal banks: their organizational design. In particular, we will focus on multidivisional organizations and the model that has already been popularized as federated banking, based upon a federal organizational structure. None of the organizational solutions we describe is ideal for restructuring financial groups and adapting them to the new competitive situation. Each of these solutions could be applied with varying degrees of success depending on the bank group's history, the dominant styles and cultures, the resources available, and the weight of each of its business units.

Chapter 11 discusses the challenges that the financial regulators of industrial nations now face as a result of financial innovation and changes in the strategy of financial intermediaries. Generally speaking, the need for commercial banks to enter new businesses, given the decreasing importance of traditional financial intermediation, has led to a review of the means for regulating bank activity. This review has affected—and continues to affect—the separation of the classic financial intermediation activity from other activities, primarily securities trading and interests acquired by banks in other companies, whether these be financial companies—for example, insurance companies—or non-financial companies—other industrial or services companies.

Chapter 12 presents both a summary of the main conclusions and some final reflections on the management of universal banks and their role in a modern financial system.

Many colleagues and bank managers contributed to this book with their time dedicated to the author and their valuable comments and suggestions. In particular, I want to thank for their many comments on specific chapters and sections of the book Eduard Ballarín (IESE), Jordi Gual (IESE), David T. Llewellyn (Loughborough University), Joan Enric Ricart (IESE), and Rafael Termes (IESE). Dwight Crane (Harvard University), Sam Hayes (Harvard University), and Don Lessard (MIT) also provided useful comments on some of the ideas discussed here. All remaining errors are the responsibility of the author.

Eulàlia Escolà and Carmina Valiente helped the author in editing efficiently the different drafts of the book.

IESE's International Center on Financial Research (CIIF) also contributed to this project. Special thanks go to Carlos Cavallé, Rafael Termes, Natalia Centenera, and all the sponsoring companies.

I also want to thank David Musson and María Cifuentes. David Musson (Oxford University Press) played a key role in shaping the content of the book and encouraging the author through the process. María Cifuentes (Alianza Editorial) was very enthusiastic about the book from its inception and made possible quick publication of its Spanish version.

A special thank you goes to Jenni Scott and the rest of her team at Oxford University Press for their outstanding editorial help.

Barcelona, December 1995

1

The Transformation of the Banking Industry and the Theory of Financial Intermediation

1. CRISIS AND CHANGE IN THE BANKING INDUSTRY

The 1980s and early 1990s have witnessed major structural changes in the world economy. The globalization of markets and finance, the creation of regional economic blocks such as the European Union (EU) or the North American Free Trade Area (NAFTA), the emergence of newly industrialized countries in Asia or Latin America, the introduction of new technologies in product design and manufacturing, or new forms of firms' organization are just some of the main features of the new international economic order that is emerging.

The majority of the sectors in industrial countries have suffered, to a greater or less extent, the consequences of these dramatic changes: increased competition, squeezed margins, and a brutal pressure to cut prices and quickly develop and bring to market new products with shorter life cycles.

Many observers agree that the banking industry is one of the sectors that has been hardest hit by the effects of these changes. In addition, the banking industry has been subjected to the competitive forces of deregulation in activities and prices, so that the rivalry is perhaps even more intense than in other industries which had already been exposed several years before to the winds of domestic and foreign competition.

1.1. The banking crisis in the 1990s

The combination of these developments has had a direct impact on the banks' performance. Table 1.1 provides information on the growth and profitability of the banking industry in several industrial countries during recent years. Table 1.2 provides information on the banking industry in Spain between 1975 and 1994. Table 1.3 provides more detailed information on a number of Spanish bank groups.

The rapid fall in financial margins in the EU is remarkable. This drop in financial margins or net interest income is a direct result of the increased rivalry both in attracting deposits and in granting loans to solvent companies.[1]

[1] Gual (1994) provides a detailed discussion of the decline in financial margins in the banking industry. In particular, he stresses the decreased spread between the return on banks' lending investments and the cost of deposits.

TABLE 1.1 *Banking industry: return on assets* (before taxes) (%)

Country	Years							
	1986	1987	1988	1989	1990	1991	1992	1993
France	0.35	0.35	0.38	0.29	0.25	0.29	0.23	−0.03
Germany	0.81	0.60	0.73	0.70	0.63	0.58	0.51	0.55
Italy	1.20	0.82	0.91	1.09	1.18	1.03	0.92	0.99
Spain	0.81	1.00	1.36	1.58	1.53	1.56	1.23	0.91
Great Britain	1.19	0.28	1.51	0.81	0.71	0.41	0.44	0.75

Source: OECD.

TABLE 1.2 *Spanish banking industry: economic performance* (return on assets) (%)

	Mean 1975–1979	Mean 1980–1984	1987	1992	1993	1994
Banks						
Net interest income	3.96	4.00	3.96	3.35	2.82	2.63
Gross margin	4.34	4.82	4.72	4.28	3.86	3.10
Operating expenses	3.17	3.15	2.67	2.74	2.30	2.12
Personnel expenses	2.20	2.16	1.72	1.68	1.41	1.30
Result before tax	0.94	0.67	1.02	1.06	0.88	0.65
Savings banks						
Net interest income	3.45	4.79	5.38	4.04	3.85	3.69
Gross margin	3.60	4.99	5.63	4.52	4.46	4.21
Operating expenses	2.65	3.34	3.19	2.91	2.78	2.69
Personnel expenses	2.22	2.18	1.87	1.74	1.67	1.65
Result before tax	0.87	1.00	1.34	1.05	0.97	0.92

Source: Bank of Spain.

This rivalry is happening not only at the interbank level, that is, rivalry with other banks, but also with other financial institutions (insurance companies, savings banks, stock market, capital markets, etc.) and non-financial organizations (department stores, automobile companies, building contractors, etc.).

As a result of this fall in banking profitability, some banks have recently embarked on major diversification projects, playing an active role in certain industrial or services businesses, with varying degrees of success. The economic recession of 1992–3, however, was pernicious for several banks that were highly involved in business projects with a high degree of financial risk, as the recent crises of Banesto or Crédit Lyonnais have shown.

It is interesting to compare the changes in the profitability of the banking industry (banks and savings banks) with other sectors of the economy. Table 1.4 shows the various rates of return for the period 1989–92 (Gual, 1994) and

TABLE 1.3 *Spanish banking industry: return on assets (%)*

	BBV Group							Santander Group						
	1994	1993	1992	1991	1990	1989	1988	1994	1993	1992	1991	1990	1989	1988
Financial revenue	8.13	10.81	10.92	11.18	11.87	11.62	10.85	8.39*	11.10	11.47	12.36	12.26	11.86	11.11
Financial costs	5.42	7.97	7.78	7.81	7.73	6.97	5.98	5.98	8.10	8.09	8.78	8.29	7.50	6.32
Financial margin	2.71	2.83	3.14	3.37	4.14	4.65	4.87	2.41	3.00	3.38	3.58	3.97	4.36	4.79
Fees	0.92	0.90	0.95	0.89	0.81	0.71	0.82	0.86	0.93	1.15	1.03	0.93	1.01	1.09
Gross margin	3.59	3.74	4.09	4.26	4.95	5.36	5.69	3.37	3.94	4.53	4.61	4.90	5.37	5.88
Operating expenses	2.15	2.25	2.51	2.65	2.71	2.70	2.75	2.29	2.23	2.50	2.64	2.38	2.43	2.43
Operating margin	1.44	1.49	1.58	1.60	2.24	2.66	2.94	0.82	1.70	2.03	1.97	3.52	2.94	3.45
Pretax income	0.92	1.05	1.18	1.58	1.80	1.91	1.84	1.17	1.43	1.67	1.65	2.36	2.14	2.02
Net income	0.69	0.79	0.82	1.15	1.36	1.36	1.34	0.82	0.96	1.10	1.07	1.70	1.44	1.33

	Popular Group							BCH Group		
	1994	1993	1992	1991	1990	1989	1988	1994	1993	1992
Financial revenue	10.02	12.56	12.79	12.96	13.14	11.83	12.86	8.86	10.50	10.95
Financial costs	4.65	6.72	6.86	7.15	6.75	5.87	6.47	6.07	7.65	7.59
Financial margin	5.37	5.84	5.93	5.81	6.39	5.96	6.39	2.85	2.85	3.36
Fees	1.37	1.64	1.54	1.52	0.88	0.82	0.89	0.83	0.82	0.87
Gross margin	6.74	7.48	7.47	7.33	7.27	6.78	7.28	2.57	3.67	4.23
Operating expenses	3.02	3.12	3.17	3.01	2.80	3.36	3.62	2.55	2.61	2.90
Operating margin	3.72	4.36	4.30	4.32	4.47	3.42	3.66	0.91	1.06	1.33
Pretax income	2.88	3.18	3.26	3.24	2.89	2.69	2.47	0.43	0.76	0.91
Net income	1.97	2.08	2.12	2.01	1.84	1.73	1.65	0.34	0.49	0.61

	Argentaria Group			Banesto Group				
	1994	1993	1992	1992	1991	1990	1989	1988
Financial revenue	8.38	9.87	10.27	11.70	12.54	11.31	10.27	9.76
Financial costs	6.34	7.93	8.00	8.30	9.10	7.76	6.30	5.57
Financial margin	2.04	1.94	2.27	3.40	3.44	3.55	3.96	4.19
Fees	0.53	0.41	0.38	0.70	0.91	0.67	0.63	0.64
Gross margin	2.57	2.35	2.65	4.10	4.36	4.21	4.29	4.83
Operating expenses	1.50	1.52	1.60	2.60	2.75	2.86	2.72	2.86
Operating margin	1.07	0.83	1.05	1.60	1.60	1.36	1.87	1.97
Pretax income	0.84	1.02	0.98	0.40	1.10	1.60	1.29	1.54
Net income	0.65	0.74	0.71	0.10	0.88	0.51	0.79	1.19

* Including Banesto.

Source: Annual reports.

TABLE 1.4 *Spain: return on equity* (1989–1992) (%)

	Banks	Non-financial companies	Spread	Savings banks	Non-financial companies	Spread
1989	17.78	13.24	4.54	17.76	13.24	4.52
1990	16.80	9.67	7.13	15.58	9.67	5.91
1991	16.23	6.76	9.47	15.15	6.76	8.39
1992	11.43	2.38	9.05	14.68	2.38	12.30

Source: Gual (1994).

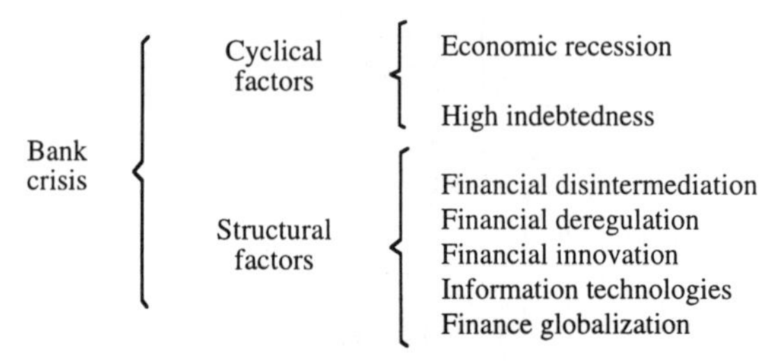

FIG. 1.1 *Reasons for the bank crisis*

the differences in favour of the banking industry are quite striking. In other words, the fall in the banks' profitability has been less acute than in other sectors of the economy.

In a preliminary analysis of this significant fall in the banking industry's profitability, we can draw a distinction between strictly cyclical reasons and other, structural, deeper-lying reasons (Figure 1.1). The most significant cyclical reasons are the following. First, the problems that arise after an extraordinarily intense period of economic expansion in some industrial countries in the second half of the 1980s (Torrero, 1993). Spain and Italy are particularly significant cases in point.

In years of strong economic growth, with the stock market spiralling endlessly upwards, some investment decisions that during periods of normal activity or recession would never be made, get the stamp of approval.

During those years of heady growth, some banks decided to invest in securities, other financial instruments, real estate, or industrial projects. Such investments generally have a higher risk than that of normal lending activities. The economic recession has shown once again not so much these investments' implicit risk—which may be greater or lesser, depending on the individual case—but the risk of decisions that are not always made in accordance with strict professional criteria.

Furthermore, the real estate crisis—one of the reasons for some financial firms' insolvency—has become general in many countries, after a spectacular growth of property prices during the 1980s. This crisis has severely hit

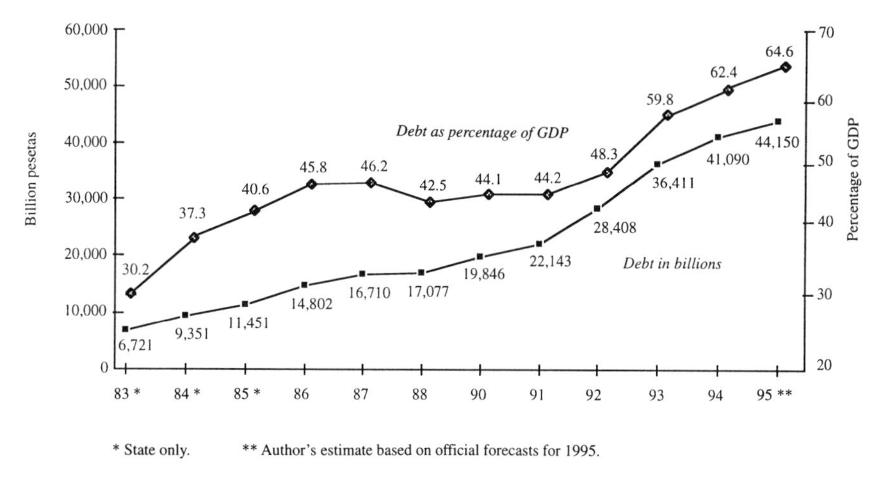

FIG. 1.2 *Spain: total public debt*

financial firms in countries such as Australia, Sweden, Canada, Great Britain, Norway, and the United States.

The stock market crisis has played a crucial role in the incubation and subsequent course of the bank crisis in Japan. The heavy investment by the Japanese banks in stock market securities and the peculiar accounting practices these banks were allowed to use—for example, posting capital gains in securities without performing any transaction—are some of the reasons for the extraordinarily fragile state of the Japanese financial industry in recent years.

A second cyclical reason related to a considerable degree to the previous reason is the increased level of public debt since the second half of the 1980s (Figure 1.2). One of the necessary prerequisites to enable companies to sustain debt is that the growth in turnover, for example, be, at least, sufficient to pay the interest and return the principal.

When growth is high, this prerequisite can be satisfied with relative ease. However, during periods of recession, with low economic growth and high interest rates, as was the case in 1992 and 1993, indebtedness becomes a rope around the economic agents' necks that can start to asphyxiate them at any time.

Non-financial companies are the first to suffer the consequences of these financial difficulties but, immediately afterwards, banks cease to receive their interest payments and see part of their debt turn into write-offs. When this situation becomes general, it threatens the bank's asset and liability management and, in some cases, places the bank in an untenable situation that opens the door, in the best of cases, to intervention by the monetary authorities.

These cyclical factors may cease to play a significant role as catalysts of the banking crisis when the economy enters a phase of sustained recovery, as has been the case since early 1995. However, there are a series of structural, non-

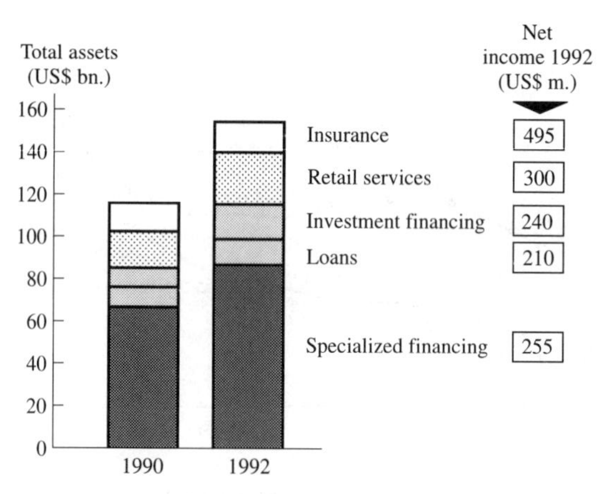

FIG. 1.3 *General Electric Capital*

cyclical factors that continue to operate in the banking industry, undermining the banks' traditional business.

1.2. The structural reasons for the banking crisis

The first of these factors is the emergence of new types of internal and external competition in the banking industry (Vives, 1991), resulting from three major developments: financial deregulation, financial innovations, and new information technologies. Let us take a closer look at each of these developments.

During the 1980s, the barriers separating the activities of commercial banks from the activities of other financial companies became increasingly thinner. Thus, banks faced new competition not only from foreign banks or savings banks operating in fields from which they were previously excluded, but also from various types of financial firms that competed with the traditional banks for different chunks of financial business. Universal banks seemed to prefer the integration of financial activities rather than its separation.

One of the paradigms of this type of financial organization is General Electric Capital, a company with more 150 billion dollars in assets in 1993, a triple A (AAA) rating in 1994 and one of the leading commercial paper issuers in the USA. Figure 1.3 shows General Electric Capital's business structure in 1990 and 1992.

General Electric Capital was created by General Electric to finance the purchase of some of the expensive and complex items of equipment sold by this company. With time, General Electric Capital continued to grow independently from the business of its parent company, which continues to be its main owner.

Since its creation, General Electric Capital has diversified into such varied businesses as leasing production facilities or flight equipment, financing major industrial or building projects, consumer credit through its own credit card, managing the credit cards of small and medium-sized retail establishments, insurance, and, finally, an investment fund including holdings in companies such as BBV and Avis. Also, until September 1994, it was a shareholder of Kidder Peabody, an investment bank that it bought in 1986 and which, after innumerable problems, was finally sold to Paine Webber.

The company's managers stress that its main advantage lies in having an exceptional team of specialized managers, the financial backing of a large company such as General Electric, and the necessary independence to respond quickly and accurately to its customers' needs.

One of the most surprising things about General Electric Capital is not so much its high level of diversification but, primarily, its high profitability and careful control of risk exposure. A number of financial industry analysts suggest that this performance is perhaps due in part to the dominant business culture in the parent company, which is highly geared towards the quality of management processes and the achievement of results. In 1994, this company accounted for roughly one-third of the General Electric Group's total earnings.

The emergence of new competitors in the banking industry (Gual, 1993; Vives, 1991) affects both assets and liabilities operations. Banks have historically played a role as financial intermediaries between savers—households or companies—or suppliers of funds and investors—primarily companies and households—and, more recently, governments. Banks took deposits which they turned into investments in securities, loans to companies and households, or public debt.

On the assets side, capital markets have attracted companies that previously relied on bank financing. Banks have lost customers to the stock market or the capital markets. Table 1.5 shows the changes in the corporate financing structure in the United States in the last 30 years. Table 1.6 shows the market share of different types of financial firms in the United States between 1900 and 1990. Particularly striking are the fall in market share of commercial banks, the stagnation of the savings banks, and the growth of the insurance companies and investment funds.[2] Figure 1.4 shows the changes in the weight of bank lending in Spain, which has fallen at a slower rate than in other industrial countries.

The banks have also lost customers in certain consumer credit operations, which had been fairly significant in some countries. The services nowadays offered by departments stores, distribution chains or car companies to finance the purchase of their products clearly compete with banks.

On the liabilities side, banks have suffered from a clear loss of customers. Many savers prefer to invest in public debt, the stock market or investment companies, instead of the traditional bank deposits. In order to counter this loss of liability customers, the banks have created new business units to retain those customers, either within the bank itself or as a legally separate organization—

[2] For a useful analysis of these dramatic changes, see Sirri and Tufano (1993), and Edwards (1993).

TABLE 1.5 *United States: non-financial companies' financial structure* (%)

Type of instrument	1965	1970	1980	1983	1984	1985	1986	1987	1988	1989
Bank loans										
US banks	57.3	16.8	48.7	32.1	28.9	22.6	24.4	3.2	16.5	16.5
Foreign banks	0.0	0.0	2.2	4.9	7.7	1.1	5.4	1.3	5.6	5.7
Commercial paper	1.7	6.2	6.9	1.5	12.8	11.0	4.6	1.6	5.9	10.6
Loans from finance companies	5.2	0.6	3.7	14.1	9.7	9.6	5.5	11.6	8.0	5.7
Bonds	25.6	69.4	66.6	46.5	39.3	72.8	54.7	68.0	57.8	57.7
Mortgages	11.7	3.1	–36.2	–8.0	–0.8	–13.5	13.9	10.7	7.1	2.3
Government bonds	1.9	3.9	8.1	11.9	2.4	3.6	0.6	3.6	0.9	1.5
TOTAL	100.0	100.0	100.0	100.0	100.0	100.0	100.0	100.0	100.0	100.0
Memorandum item:										
Total funds (in US$ trillion)	18.9	28.5	57.8	54.8	169.6	132.4	203.7	145.5	197.5	196.0

Source: Federal Reserve Board

TABLE 1.6 *United States: market share of intermediated funds* (%)

	1900	1912	1922	1929	1939	1949	1960	1970	1980	1990
Commercial banks	55.2	55.3	54.9	45.9	40.0	42.3	38.6	38.5	37.2	26.8
Savings and loans	16.0	12.7	10.9	12.0	10.6	9.9	20.1	20.8	23.3	16.0
Insurance companies	12.2	14.2	12.9	16.0	21.2	19.7	24.0	19.1	17.4	19.1
Pension funds	16.6	17.8	21.2	22.2	25.5	25.5	9.8	13.0	13.0	19.3
Investment funds	0.0	0.0	0.1	2.1	1.0	0.9	2.9	3.7	3.7	10.9

Source: *Federal Reserve Bulletin* (1990).

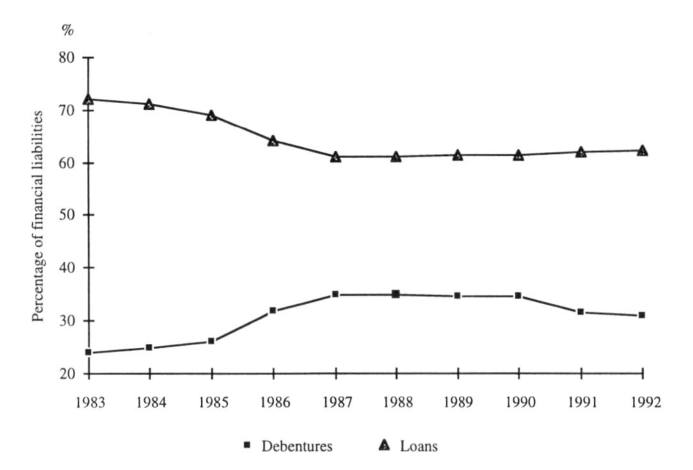

FIG. 1.4 *Financing of non-financial companies in the form of loans and debentures in Spain between 1983 and 1992*

as the various countries' regulations allow—and thus avoid losing liability customers. Figure 1.5 shows the strong growth of investment in the money market in the United States between 1950 and 1990. However, two important facts should be taken into account when interpreting these data. First, banks have developed a growing activity in off the balance sheet operations and which, by definition, do not show up in the figures normally used. The second consideration is that foreign banking has become increasingly important as a lender to North American companies. This activity does not show up in these figures either.

These developments clearly show that the traditional intermediation offered by banks has lost ground to other companies—financial or non-financial—thus giving rise to the phenomenon of financial disintermediation.

The financial disintermediation originating with the emergence of new competitors has a number of immediate causes. First, the financial deregulation process allowed by the financial authorities in many industrial countries. This deregulation process has led many non-bank financial firms to start to offer

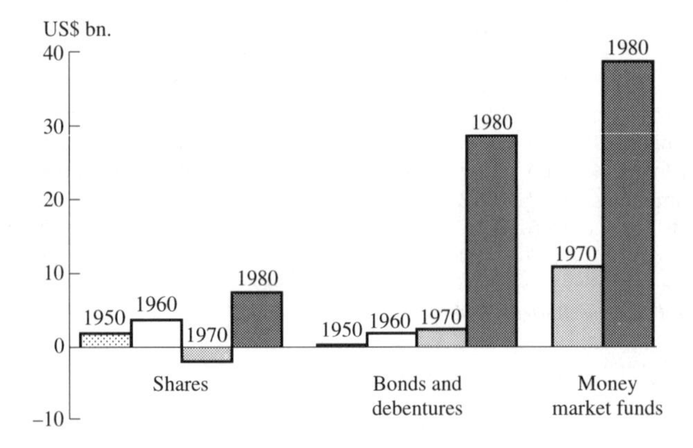

FIG. 1.5 *United States: other investment alternatives*

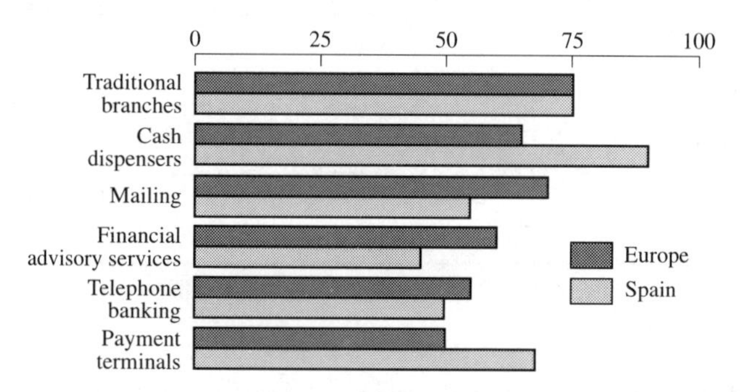

FIG. 1.6 *Distribution channels considered most important in the next few years (%)*

banking services. Deregulation has also affected the stock exchange market, whose liberalization has provided greater flexibility both to the companies that turn to it for financial resources and to the investors who desire to place resources.

Financial innovation is the second cause. By financial innovation we mean the set of new products or services that provide certain advantages over traditional financial products. Investment funds, futures, or the combination of several financial services into a single package are just a few examples of financial innovation.

Financial innovation affects not only the products offered by financial companies but also the way they are distributed and presented to customers. Enormous changes have taken place in the distribution of financial services. According to a Europe-wide survey carried out by Price Waterhouse, bank branches are losing relative weight to cash dispensers (see Figures 1.6 and 1.7) and telephone banking. Likewise, direct marketing is gaining ground quickly, in part thanks to the ever-expanding use of the telephone (see Figure 1.8). Finally, intelligent

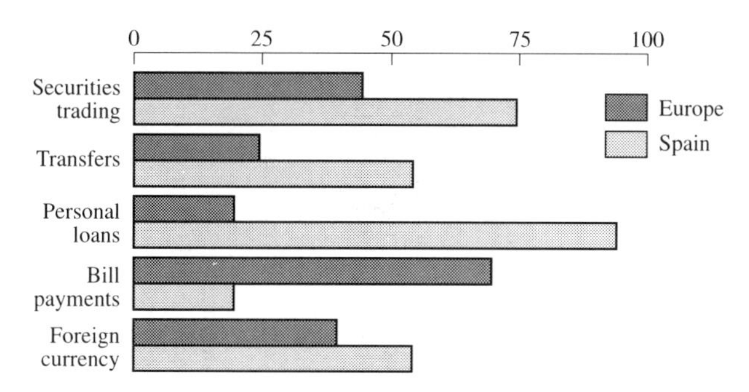

FIG. 1.7 *Services that can be arranged through cash dispensers (%)*

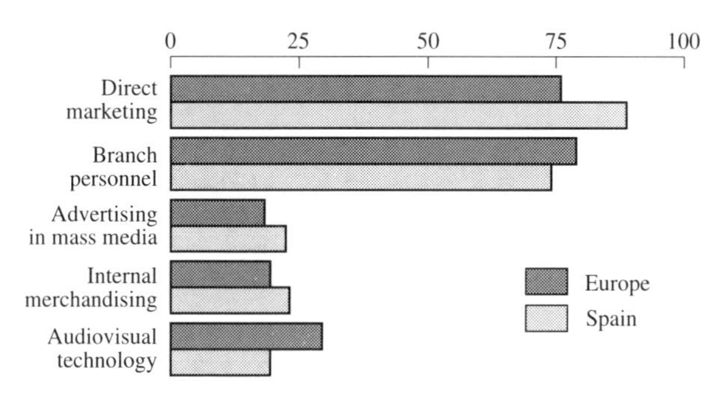

FIG. 1.8 *Sales promotion methods used in banks (%)*

cards are also eating away at part of the bank branches' traditional field of business (Table 1.7).

In spite of a number of early failures, such as that of Chemical (1980), telephone banking is gaining a firm foothold in the industry for the distribution of certain financial services. In Great Britain, First Direct, a subsidiary of Midland Bank, has achieved quite spectacular results. In Spain, Bankinter has been the bank that has been pushing the concept hardest, as we will see further on, since 1992, with the so-called Bktel service. This service allows current account holders to make enquiries or transfers or borrow with a single telephone call.

Bankinter's strategy has since been copied by other Spanish banks. Thus, Argentaria has formed a subsidiary, called Banco Directo, that operates as a separate division. BCH started to implement its 'Línea Central Hispano' in 1994, which will provide services to all of the bank's users. BBV also offers this service to large companies, using the so-called 'Sistema Siete', and to small and medium-sized companies through videotex. In April 1995, Banco Santander launched its Open Bank with a strong financial backing.

Telephone or electronic banking has been widely used by foreign banks to gain market penetration in other countries. Thus, Citibank has used this marketing tool to increase its presence in a traditionally difficult market, Germany.

TABLE 1.7 *Use of credit cards* (1993)

Bank	Cash dispensers	Branches	Transactions*		Cards issued	
			No.	%	Debit	Credit
La Caixa	3,046	2,630	54.0	n.d.	Caixa Oberta (Red 6000)	Visa classic and gold, Mastercard, Multivía, Multinén
Caja de Madrid	1,919	1,208	49.0	65	Red 6000	Visa classic and gold, Mastercard, Eurocard
BCH	1,300	2,750	28.0	n.d.	4B	Visa, Mastercard, Gasoleo bonificado, Eurocheque
Banesto	1,052	2,244	21.3	15	4B, 4B Europ Assistance	Visa, Business Card Classic, Mastercard, Affinity
Popular	848	1,779	n.d.	50	4B	Visa, Mastercard
BBV	840	1,937	28.7	50	Servired, Visa Electron	Visa, Eurocard, Servired Gasoleo
Argentaria	781	n.d.	n.d.	n.d.	Servired	Visa, Mastercard
Caja de Cataluña	752	658	27.5	n.d.	Red 6000	Visa classic and gold, Eurocard
Santander	627	1,328	12.5	n.d.	4B	Visa, Mastercard, American Express

* In million operations and percentage of total operations.

n.d. means no data.

Citibank bought KKB Bank, one of Germany's oldest commercial banks, in 1973. Over the next 20 years, Citibank's business grew at an extremely slow rate. However, in 1992, this bank introduced the round-the-clock, telephone banking concept, which enables users to carry out any type of operation with the bank, anywhere at any time.

This service was launched shortly after another revolutionary financial product in Germany: the 'Formula One', high interest-bearing current accounts. Both services have led to significant boosts in Citibank's business. In the course of just one year, the number of customers grew by 11 per cent, revenues by 13 per cent, and earnings by 55 per cent. Likewise, in 1993, productivity per employee in Citibank was 20 per cent above the German banking industry average.

This innovation process has mushroomed in the 1980s for two main reasons. First, the financial deregulation process blasted apart the traditional barriers that separated different types of financial organization, so that now all are competing on the same level. Hence, rivalry encourages innovation and financial deregulation enables these innovations to be marketable.

Second, the new information technologies have introduced, among other activities, a greater availability of data on the situation of financial markets all over the world, thus opening up new business opportunities. The new information technologies also provide a different way of distributing traditional financial products, such as current accounts or securities trading or, alternatively, serving the customers for traditional products better and more quickly (Figure 1.5). Finally, information technologies enable customer information to be handled in a consistent, systematic, and strategic fashion and have become an indispensable tool for modernizing the marketing function in the financial services industry. Without this powerful tool, neither financial innovation nor the emergence of new competitors would have achieved the power and scope they are currently showing in many countries.

The relentless growth of information technologies has also increased the cost of investments and their complexity. Consequently, some banks have chosen to subcontract the service offered by these technologies to specialized outside suppliers, such as EDS or Andersen Consulting.

The advantages obtained with such a decision are readily understood. It reduces the volume of resources that must be invested (see Figure 1.9) and obtains full benefit from the economies of scale and the experience of an expert supplier in the management of complex information systems. The main drawback is that information technologies are critical for the design and distribution of new financial products. Consequently, it may be economical to subcontract them in the short term but this may prevent a bank from developing a capability that will be vital for its future.

A second factor of structural change in the banking industry is the globalization of finance. In turn, this factor is related to two of the previously discussed forces driving change: new information technologies and the deregulation of financial activity.

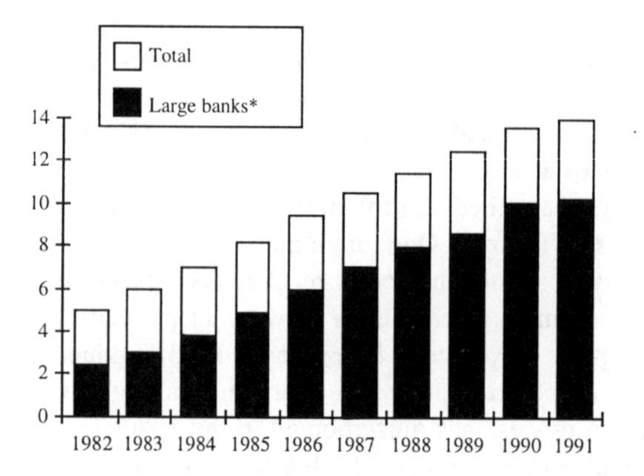

FIG. 1.9 *United States banks: investment in information technologies*

The globalization of the financial industry has not led to globalized banking. Indeed, there are several segments of traditional financial intermediation activity performed by banks that have a clear national bias, for example, attracting savers' deposits or granting loans to private consumers or to small and medium-sized companies. However, today's capital markets are distinctly global. Companies can raise funds in any part of the world, institutional investors buy and sell financial assets in any country, and the movements of share prices or interest rates in countries such as Germany, United States, or Japan have an immediate impact on other countries. On that level, this group of financial activities is global. By way of example, Table 1.8 shows the growth of the derivatives market.

Why has this financial globalization process been possible? This phenomenon is not only inexorable but also difficult for other industries, where globalization is more limited, to imitate. The reasons, as we have already said, are financial deregulation and the new information technologies.

The role played by financial deregulation and, in particular, the disappearance of the controls on capital movements, has been crucial. If capital could not flow freely, there would not be any possibility of globalization, in the same way that if cars made in an EU country could not be sold in another country, for example the United States, then we could not really talk of a world automobile industry. The liberalization of capital movements implemented by most industrial countries in the late 1970s and early 1980s has been a major factor in this dramatic process of financial globalization.

However, deregulation is a necessary factor but it is not sufficient by itself. It needs to be complemented by the information technologies, which have enabled the use of this greater freedom in capital movements to take advantage of opportunities in financial markets, offer new products and services, and, in short, satisfy the investment, financing, or risk coverage requirements of companies, governments, and institutional investors.

TABLE 1.8 *World derivatives market*

Instruments	Annual volume of contracts (US$ bn.)					Open positions (Dec. 1992)
	1988	1989	1990	1991	1992	
Interest rate futures	156.3	201.0	219.1	234.7	335.4	3,048.1
Short-term instruments, of which:	33.7	70.2	75.8	84.8	130.8	2,802.3
Eurodollar at 3 months	25.2	46.8	39.4	41.7	66.9	1,389.6
Euroyen at 3 months	0.0	4.7	15.2	16.2	17.4	431.8
Euro-DM at 3 months	0.0	1.6	3.1	4.8	12.2	229.2
Long-term instruments, of which:	122.6	130.8	143.3	149.9	204.6	245.9
US Treasury bills	73.8	72.8	78.2	69.9	71.7	31.3
France Treasury bills	12.4	15.0	16.0	21.1	31.1	21.0
Japan Treasury bills	18.8	19.1	16.4	12.9	12.1	105.9
Germany Treasury bills	0.3	5.3	9.6	12.4	18.9	27.8
Interest rate options and futures	30.5	39.5	52.0	50.8	64.8	1,385.4
Exchange rate futures	22.1	27.5	29.1	29.2	30.7	24.5
Exchange rate options	18.2	20.7	18.8	21.5	23.0	80.0
TOTAL, of which:	227.1	288.6	319.1	336.2	453.9	4,538.0
In US	165.3	198.1	205.7	199.7	238.7	2,538.2
In Europe	32.6	49.0	61.0	84.4	140.5	1,055.4
In Japan	18.8	23.7	33.6	30.0	28.7	537.6

Source: Futures Industry Association and Bank for International Settlements.

This set of structural and cyclical changes, as we have just discussed, raises two major types of challenge. The first is for banks. These have lost part of their traditional business—financial intermediation—to new competitors. This has given rise to a process of replacing products by other new ones—which affects the demand for financial services—and the appearance of new competitors in traditional financial services—affecting the supply of financial services. This process has had an enormous impact on the banks' financial performance (Figure 1.10).

If the market for some of the banks' classic financial services—for example, company lending—could be represented by a model of perfect competition, the situation could be shown in Figure 1.11, where the function D represents the demand for financial services by companies—for example, loans—while the function S represents the supply of financial services by banks that can satisfy that demand.

The increased supply of traditional bank loans (from S_0 to S_1), for example—due to the increased competition from savings banks or foreign banks—and the decreased demand for loans (from D_0 to D_1)—due, for example, to the appearance of alternative products such as the securities markets—give rise to a fall

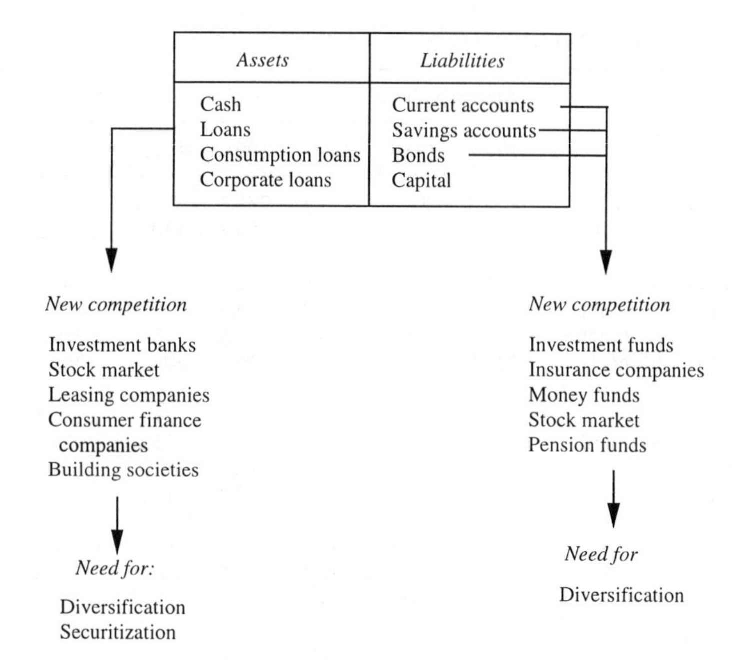

FIG. 1.10 *Changes in the balance sheets of commercial banks*

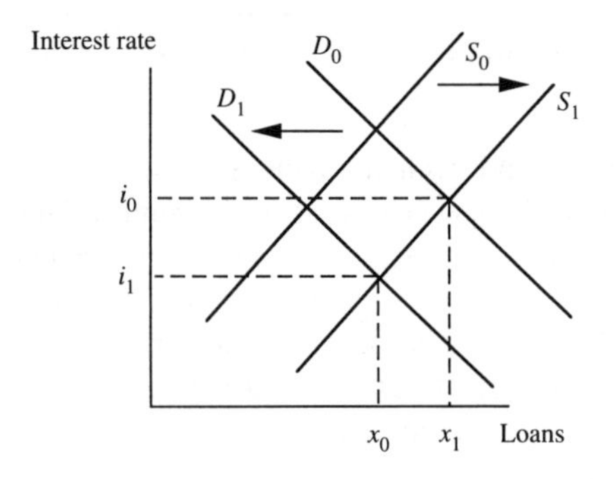

FIG. 1.11 *Corporate loans: supply and demand*

in the banks' interest rates (from i_0 to i_1), which has an immediate negative impact on bank performance.

This deterioration in bank profitability has led to a number of responses—sometimes desperate—by the banks. These responses include the purchase of other banks, the drive to internationalize financial activities, sometimes accompanied by purchases of banks abroad or alliances with other banks, diversification of activities, such as entering new financial businesses—for example, stock

TABLE 1.9 *International bank lending* (US$ bn.)

Year	Bank loans	Bonds	Euro-notes	Total	Bank loans as percentage of total
New issues					
1984	90.0	81.0	5.0	176.0	51.1
1986	195.0	160.3	13.0	368.3	53.0
1988	225.0	137.9	19.5	382.4	58.8
1989	330.0	171.6	6.9	508.5	64.9
Balance					
1984	1,330.0	401.0	5.0	1,736.0	76.6
1986	1,630.0	680.7	28.0	2,338.7	69.7
1988	2,390.0	1,085.4	72.0	3,547.4	67.4
1989	2,640.0	1,252.3	79.0	3,971.3	66.5
Growth (1984–9, %)	98.5	212.3	1,480		

Source: Bank for International Settlements.

TABLE 1.10 *Mergers and acquisitions in the European Union* (no. of transactions)

Sector	1984/5		1985/6		1986/7		1987/8		1988/9		1989/90	
	No.	%	No.	%	No.	%	No.	%	No.	%	No.	%
Banks	52	11	62	11	92	13	189	18	170	15	239	17
Insurance	24	5	16	3	41	6	87	8	78	7	101	8
Other financial organizations	76	16	78	14	133	19	276	27	248	22	340	25

Source: EU.

markets or foreign exchange markets—or direct involvement in other industrial projects.

Table 1.9 shows the importance of the internationalization of bank business, as measured by the number of international loans issued.[3] Table 1.10 shows the strong growth of bank mergers and takeovers in the last few years within the EU.

In contrast to this diversification of activities, other banks have chosen the opposite strategy: business or geographical specialization. According to the managers of this second group of banks, banks must respond not by becoming giant institutions with an enormous but slow-reacting internal organization but by specializing. This is the case of Banc One.

Banc One is the clearest example of the emerging power of the so-called

[3] Walter (1988) provides a good discussion of the globalization process of the financial industry and banks.

regional banks in the United States. With corporate headquarters in Columbus (Ohio), in 1993 this bank's capitalization was above that of Citicorp and it had become one of the strongest growing and most profitable banks in the United States in terms of return on assets (1.5 per cent in 1992). Between 1980 and 1992, its assets increased sixfold, thanks to a careful policy of buying regional banks, mainly in the Midwest. During that period, it bought 108 banks and it has up to 1400 branches.

Its product and business focus is very specific. In the 1980s, this bank avoided the craze for leveraged buy-outs (LBOs) and other emerging segments in the financial world and, instead, concentrated on managing commercial banking activities in a very professional manner. Indeed, its lending activities are conservative and concentrated on small and medium-sized companies. One of its features is that, by going against prevailing fashion, Banc One has been able effectively to capitalize and refocus the role of the bank branch.

Its policy of buying other regional banks is also worth mentioning. This policy, which lies at the root of the bank's extraordinary growth, is articulated around a few key principles. First, it has a highly decentralized decision-making structure. Control is tight but consists of sharing common management procedures and a strong corporate culture. The decentralization philosophy, on the other hand, helps the employees of the banks that have been taken over to trust their new owner. Second, the banks bought by Banc One must be at most one-third of the size of Banc One and never, if possible, very close competitors. Third, Banc One transfers to the acquired banks information technologies and new products developed at the corporate headquarters. At the same time, it shares information processing and back office operations with all banks, thus helping to reduce these banks' costs. Fourth, the reporting system required by the bank from the various branches is highly elaborate, enabling monthly monitoring of results by operations. This financial reporting system is considered to be one of the most sophisticated in the USA. Finally, the bank has successfully introduced a variable component in the compensation of banks' managers, seeking to link their compensation with the turnaround of the acquired bank.

Banc One's strategy has been imitated in other parts of the United States, with regional adaptations. An interesting example is First Wachovia, with its head office in Winston-Salem (North Carolina). During the 1980s, this bank also avoided loan operations in the real estate market or financing LBOs or high-risk operations.

Instead, First Wachovia focused on the traditional commercial banking business, particularly retail banking and lending to small and medium-sized companies. In recent years, First Wachovia has added a few products to attract large companies based in North Carolina. One of its most successful products has been cash management.

Another similar case is that of Wells Fargo, the Bank of America's main competitor in California. This bank is very strong in commercial banking and, in particular, in retail banking, like First Wachovia. Perhaps the most striking

TABLE 1.11 *United States banks: ranking by assets* (volume of loans)

1992	1993	Holding bank	Volume of loans (US$ bn.)
1	1	Chemical Banking	65.52
2	2	Citicorp	51.48
4	3	Nationsbank	44.95
6	4	Bank America	37.30
7	5	J. P. Morgan	35.95
3	6	Chase Manhattan	33.65

Source: *The New York Times*, 18 July 1993.

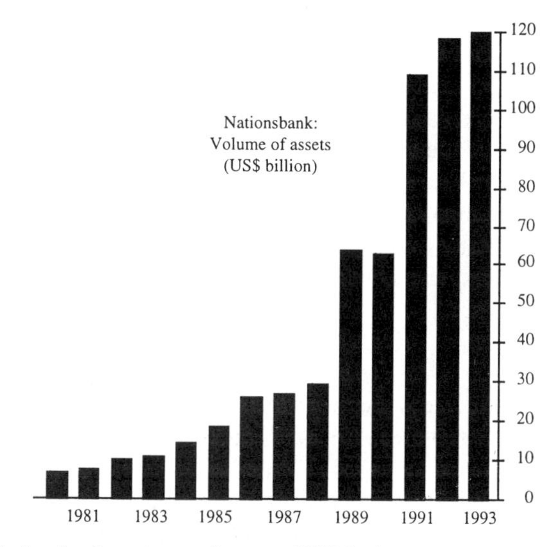

FIG. 1.12 *Nationsbank: volume of assets (US$ bn.)*

aspect of Wells Fargo's strategy in recent years was the merger with Crocker Bank in 1986. This merger was spectacular, not only because of the results achieved (the bank doubled its volume of assets over a short period of time) but also because of the success of the merger process, which is still considered even today a model to be followed in bank mergers.

A US bank that is particularly interesting because of its geographical specialization is Nationsbank, which ranked third in loans volume in 1993, after Chemical and Citicorp as Table 1.11 shows. The growth of this North Carolina bank between 1983 and 1993 has been quite spectacular, as Figure 1.12 shows.

This growth has been achieved through a highly aggressive acquisition policy in several states and a particular attention to the financial needs of companies. The wholesale banking division, together with the retail banking division, are the group's biggest profit-earners.

Some experts think that the future belongs to specialized financial firms able to offer financial products at a lower cost and a quality of service superior to that of the products offered by large financial groups. The dilemma between universal banks and specialized banks is one of the major choices that will face banks in the next few years and is keener than ever, although it may be possible that the answer will not be the same for all banks.

A second challenge raised by these dramatic changes in the banking industry directly affects central banks and the regulation of financial activity. The 1980s were a period of intense deregulation. The strength of the new competition and the explosion of new technologies made it unfeasible to continue with the constraints artificially imposed on banks. Deregulation has been a far-sweeping change in the financial industry.

However, deregulation—together with the previously described forces—has led to a less profitable banking system, with a greater degree of risk and, for the present, with some organizations in crisis or having required to be rescued by the central bank. The dilemma between regulation and deregulation or whether an excessive degree of freedom may lead to an increase in the overall risk of the banking system is back on the agenda.[4]

A large part of this book will deal with the options banks have open to them in the face of this drastic change. However, the dilemma between deregulation and freedom in the banking industry will be discussed specifically in Chapter 11.

2. INTERMEDIATION AND FINANCIAL SPECIALIZATION IN THE INTERNATIONAL FINANCIAL SYSTEM

The globalization of finance is one of the clear outcomes of the change currently operating in financial systems. Events taking place in any important financial market have an almost instantaneous impact on the others. Never before has it been so easy to obtain financing on markets outside one's own country. At the end of 1994, the money flows on the foreign exchange markets amounted to no less than one trillion dollars per day.

Furthermore, the deregulation processes implemented in the United States, Japan, and Europe in recent years have confirmed the trend followed by the various national financial systems towards internationalization. This development has affected not only fixed and variable income capital markets but also the very core of the financial intermediaries: banks and other financial organizations.

In fact, the liberalization of the capital markets (the so-called Big Bang recorded in most European stock markets) has also sparked off a greater liberalization

[4] This issue is currently under heated debate among both monetary authorities and academics. See the contributions to the symposium organized by the Federal Reserve Bank of Kansas City (1993).

of banking activities and those of other financial intermediaries. The reason for this chain of events is the growing competition between capital markets and bank-like intermediaries in channelling savings flows towards investment. An improvement in the competitive conditions of capital markets, for example, seems to be to the detriment of the competitive position of traditional bank intermediation.

The deregulation of financial activities has become particularly significant in the EU. Indeed, the financial services industry has been one of the most affected by the 1992 single market programme, as in the past that industry and its agents were hampered by numerous restrictions. The single market of 1992 has sent new winds of freedom blowing through the industry and, with this, increased competition.

However, in their construction of the single financial market, both the EU and the various national financial authorities have avoided any reference to a critical issue: what should be the respective roles of capital markets and bank intermediaries in the new European financial space? Or, to put it another way, should the markets—the capital markets—prevail over bank intermediation—the financial institutions?

Ultimately, this issue leads to an even deeper dilemma, namely, which system—capital markets or traditional bank intermediation—is more efficient in the long term in allocating financial resources. Will the flow of financial resources placed in productive investment be greater and cheaper in a system based on the capital market or in a system based on bank intermediation?

This is a decisive issue, not only to determine the financial system's configuration in the future, but also to ensure the growth rates of savings needed to finance a country's investments and sustainable growth.

The international evidence provides two basic financial models. Table 1.12 shows the main features of the two financial models. It presents the different forms of bank-based financial systems in industrial countries and compares these with market-based systems. Those features will be discussed later, in Chapters 2 to 5.

The market-based model shows a clear predominance of capital markets over bank intermediation. A large part of the growth of capital markets in these countries is due to the high level of initial involvement of the banks. Banks seem to have played a less important role in financing firms. Tables 1.13 and 1.14 provide information on the debt level in the balance sheet structure and the volume of bank financing over total debt, respectively.

At the other extreme, there is another model where financial intermediaries, mainly banks, still have a strong influence. This is the case of Germany, Spain, and Japan. All of these countries share a series of common circumstances. First, the weight of bank financing in industrial companies.[5] Second, the less developed state of the capital markets. Third, the significant presence of banks in

[5] Observe that the level of bank debt in France is significantly low.

TABLE 1.12 *Characteristics of financial models*

Model	Countries	Banks as financial intermediaries	Banks as lenders to companies	Banks as shareholders	Banks as strategic shareholders	Banks as managers
I. Bank-based model						
1. Specialized banks	United States Britain	Yes	No	No	No	No
2. Main bank	Germany Japan	Yes	Yes	No	No	No
3. Universal bank	Germany Spain France Italy	Yes	Yes	Yes	No	Yes
4. Conglomerate groups	Germany Japan Spain	Yes	Yes	Yes	Yes	Yes
II. Market-based models	United States Britain	Yes	No	No	No	No

TABLE 1.13 *Industrial companies: total debt over total liabilities (%)*

	1983	1984	1985	1986	1987	1988	1989	1990	1991	1992	1993
Spain	74.4	70.2	67.3	65.3	61.7	57.0	54.4	53.9	56.5	63.9	68.9
Germany	70.3	69.6	68.8	67.0	66.5	66.8	68.0	67.7	68.4	68.3	—
Belgium	68.2	62.8	60.0	58.0	57.4	58.4	58.2	58.1	59.1	63.9	63.4
France	82.0	84.2	79.6	76.8	72.4	69.0	66.3	66.1	65.0	63.9	63.9
Netherlands	55.8	49.2	49.4	47.7	47.1	47.4	48.2	49.4	40.5	54.4	51.7
Italy	73.2	73.8	72.4	70.6	71.2	72.6	72.8	73.5	72.8	74.8	—
Portugal	—	—	74.4	68.4	66.7	60.9	58.2	55.7	58.4	59.2	57.9
United Kingdom	51.2	48.6	48.8	50.6	50.7	50.9	54.0	60.1	—	—	—
United States	54.3	55.6	57.8	59.9	61.7	63.5	65.6	66.2	66.5	69.9	70.7
Japan	74.7	73.9	72.7	71.4	70.2	69.3	68.2	67.9	67.3	67.0	66.6

Source: BACH (European Commission: General Directorate II).

TABLE 1.14 *Industrial companies: bank financing over total debt (%)*

	1983	1984	1985	1986	1987	1988	1989	1990	1991	1992	1993	1994
Spain	52.9	49.6	47.9	42.4	38.7	31.9	31.7	34.7	35.6	36.1	33.1	28.5
Germany	29.9	29.4	29.0	29.8	29.1	29.3	30.1	30.4	30.4	30.7	—	—
Belgium	28.9	26.8	26.6	27.0	26.3	25.0	26.1	26.1	23.9	24.2	23.2	—
France	—	25.2	26.0	23.6	22.1	20.1	20.5	20.5	19.7	17.4	16.2	—
Netherlands	24.9	23.3	21.6	22.3	23.6	22.5	20.3	18.7	20.5	21.8	20.6	—
Italy	32.1	32.4	31.3	29.7	29.5	28.6	29.2	31.6	31.5	31.8	—	—
Portugal	—	—	46.1	45.2	43.4	42.6	41.1	36.3	37.9	39.1	35.3	—
United Kingdom	32.6	34.1	31.5	22.0	18.8	23.5	27.2	27.9	—	—	—	—
United States	14.0	15.2	14.3	15.8	16.2	18.0	18.0	18.3	16.9	15.8	14.5	—
Japan	41.9	40.2	41.2	43.1	41.0	38.9	36.3	35.8	37.1	40.1	42.5	—

Source: BACH (European Commission: General Directorate II).

capital markets themselves as an indirect means for controlling their growth and sharing in the results. Finally, a greater or lesser degree of control, depending on the situation, exercised by banks in the management of industrial companies, either through direct stock ownership or through membership of these companies' boards.

However, this initial classification requires further subdivision. Here are a few examples. In the category of bank-based systems, we would have to distinguish between at least two subgroups. The first would consist of countries whose governments have not traditionally played a significant role in configuring financial groups, such as Germany, Belgium, or Switzerland. The second group would include those countries where governments have historically played a major role, for various reasons, in the formation of financial groups, such as Spain, France, or Italy.

While it is a fact that relations between banks and industrial companies in Japan are very close,[6] it is also true that capital markets are by no means insignificant in Japan either. This situation leads to another factor that must be taken into account in these classifications: the level of industrial companies' bank debt as an indicator of the latter's dependence on banks (Table 1.14).

The existence of such divisions does not allay one serious doubt: namely, whether the financial systems' varying structure has any real bearing in terms of investment and income growth in a particular country. Indeed, given the diversity of financial models and the existence of a considerable historical experience, it seems reasonable to ask about each one's advantages and disadvantages, particularly during a period of profound change in the shape of the EU member countries' financial systems.

Unfortunately, this issue has not been raised explicitly in the course of creating a single market in Europe. Therefore, a unique opportunity has been lost to debate an issue which seems to be important for the member countries' economic development.

The absence of an explicit discussion of these issues has led, in practice, to a situation in which the various systems and models for organizing financial systems are in competition. For the moment, this competition is still low key but will no doubt step up in some countries over the next few years, mainly led by universal banks.

There are two main reasons for this growing competition. The first is related to the process of securitizing loans and financial assets held by banks. This process—which essentially consists of assigning to third parties loans that banks have granted to companies or individuals—has been driven by different forces, such as financial innovation or information systems, but leads to the same goal: the desirability of reducing the weight of loans in the banks' balance sheets.

Securitization offers clear advantages. By being able to sell their loans as

[6] We will discuss this complex issue in more detail in a subsequent chapter. The reader can also consult Aoki (1984), Aoki and Patrick (1994) and Kester (1991).

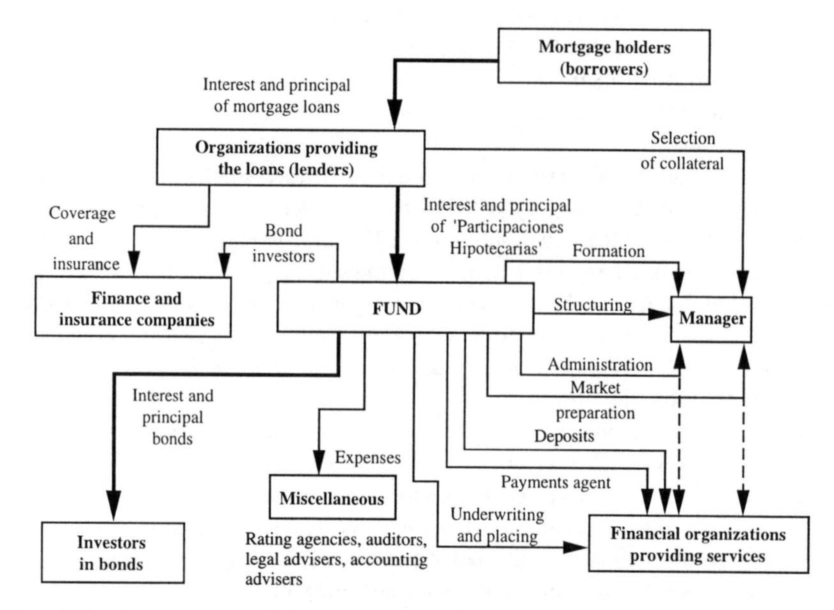

FIG. 1.13 *Mortgage securitization: payment flows*

financial assets to other investors, banks are able to reduce their equity requirements and reduce their processing costs, and, what is more, the revenues obtained from these new assets are not subject to statutory ratios.

The type of loans where securitization has become particularly popular are mortgage loans. Another advantage offered by mortgage securitization is the ability to reduce their cost for the borrower, thereby facilitating their growth.

The industrial countries' monetary authorities have trodden with considerable caution in this process. In Spain, for instance, the first steps were taken in this direction with Act 19/1992 of 7 July, which enabled mortgage loans to be converted into negotiable bonds. These are sold to a Securitization Fund which issues bonds that are sold to third parties (Figure 1.13).

However, the securitization process is a double-edged sword for banks. On the one hand, it enables them to reduce their credit risk and capital requirements. However, on the other hand, this process requires highly developed financial markets to ensure the new financial products' liquidity, and the natural arena for trading these instruments is not the banks but the capital markets.

Thus, the securitization of financial assets helps tip the balance in favour of capital markets and against banks in attracting savings to be channelled towards investments. This is one of the reasons why banks in European countries have taken such strong positions in capital market brokerage firms: it is a move designed to avoid losing customers and business.

Another force behind this increasing competition between banks and financial markets is the globalization of finance, which we have already mentioned.

While financial markets are already global, the banking industry is still local: each country has a group of national banks that dominate a large part of the market.

Furthermore, foreign banks play a limited role in such countries, even after the lowering of national barriers associated with the creation of a single financial market in Europe. The number of truly global financial organizations that could be identified in the retail banking industry is indeed very small: Citibank, Barclays, Deutsche Bank, and Crédit Lyonnais. Although the presence of the Japanese banks in Europe is growing, this is still very small.

On the basis of this overview, it can be inferred that capital markets enjoy the advantages of being global, and also the disadvantages, in this case, of increased rivalry, which enables them to offer at all times the best financial conditions for a particular financing or investment operation.

On the other hand, most banks are limited to their own country and their ability to identify opportunities world-wide is clearly less than that of the capital markets. Hence the interest of the banks in taking part, directly or indirectly, in capital markets.

Consequently, both securitization and globalization are taking business away from the banks in favour of the capital markets. Is this trend desirable? Is it wise?

In order to answer these questions, we first have to ask a number of basic questions: What is a financial system's function in a modern economy? What purpose should it pursue?

3. SOME ELEMENTS OF THE FINANCIAL INTERMEDIATION THEORY

The essential function of any financial intermediary is to transform one financial asset, in certain conditions, into another financial asset. Thus, for example, commercial banks usually convert savers' deposits into mortgage loans. In general, this function of converting one series of financial assets into another is carried out by the different financial intermediaries operating in the economy.

The study of financial intermediation is usually approached from two different viewpoints. The first is the institutional approach: financial intermediation is studied through the detailed analysis of the institutions that comprise the financial system. From a slightly more dynamic viewpoint, the institutional analysis could raise questions as to the ability of financial institutions to adapt in a context of dramatic change in the sector, the required level of regulation or the separation of activities within universal banks (Llewellyn, 1989).

The second is the functional approach. This approach asks what are or should be the functions that a society expects from the financial system and financial intermediaries. Institutions may react more or less promptly to change or they may oppose it but the functions that society expects from its financial intermediaries might be basically the same, although they may be carried out more efficiently as financial intermediaries improve or bring in new services.

Indeed, the improvements that can be expected from a financial system are related not so much to new functions that the financial system may or should perform but with the efficiency with which the financial intermediaries perform the functions expected of them and improve that efficiency over time.

Efficiency, as we will see later on, has a number of different aspects, although they are all related to some of the basic functions of a financial system, such as risk control, smooth transfer of resources from savings to investment, and reduction of transaction costs (the cost of carrying out the financial asset exchanges or the agency costs arising from situations of asymmetric information).

Some authors (Merton, 1993, 1995; Pierce, 1991) stress the desirability of adopting the second approach, the functional one, in order adequately to study financial intermediation and its changing nature.

What are the financial intermediaries' functions in an advanced economy? We can identify five primary tasks that should be carried out by an efficient financial system.[7] First, the financial system must enable and guarantee the operation of the payments system that facilitates the exchange of goods and services. Second, a financial system must facilitate the allocation and transfer of resources over time (savings and investment) between different sectors or between different geographical areas. Third, a financial system must offer a system of guarantees that reduces the uncertainty regarding the true value of money and which provides investors with a reasonable and sufficient control of the risk of the various financial instruments. Fourth, the financial system must make possible the issue of financial products—debt or capital—in order to finance real investment projects. These projects are different from financial investments undertaken by a private investor or by a financial institution.

Finally, the financial system must provide information on the price of financial assets—which, in some cases, may be related to the price of real assets—to the other sectors in a country. The functional approach to financial intermediation goes hand in hand with the complex issue of the financial innovation process. In fact, financial innovation represents an adaptation by financial intermediaries who are attempting to carry out their basic functions but in a setting that is different from that which existed in the past. The features of this new setting are those we have briefly discussed in previous sections of this chapter: deregulation of the financial sector, increased rivalry, emergence of new competitors, the growing importance of information technologies, and the relentless internationalization of financial activity.

In fact, the supply of new financial services by the intermediaries is not only a process deriving from financial innovation, but also a path leading financial

[7] Merton (1993) suggests six functions for a financial system, which refine or expand on some of the functions discussed here.

intermediaries towards a voluntary specialization. This hypothesis fully concurs with the reality of the financial systems in industrial countries.

Increased competition in the various segments of financial activity induces universal banks to sharpen the focus of their activities or specialize in a few businesses. As we will see later, there are increasingly fewer universal banks with a vocation to be exactly that and which, at the same time, are efficient. Therefore, the processes of institutional or strategic change take place in financial institutions not as a consequence of new functions that the intermediaries must carry out but of new ways of offering new financial services within the new regulatory and technological environment.

Therefore, the dramatic changes experienced by the international financial system and the various financial intermediaries and the hectic process of financial innovation are responses to this change in competitive conditions.

However, the changes in regulatory and legal conditions governing the financial sector and financial innovations that these changes have triggered do not stop here. As a result of the process of financial innovation, there are signs of rethinking not about the financial system's functions but about which institutions can carry out the functions described most efficiently.

Thus, the growth of international capital markets has reduced some non-financial companies' dependence on universal banks, which had traditionally acted as lenders to such companies. Capital markets provide banks with a new competitor that, in some cases, may act more efficiently.

However, there is not just new competition between financial firms and financial markets but also intense rivalry within the two segments. Thus, there is increasing rivalry between universal banks, savings banks, and insurance companies, for example, to attract savings. Or there is a considerable rivalry between national stock markets and international capital markets to attract corporate debt or equity issues.

These examples clearly show that the function carried out by these intermediaries is basically the same; the difference is that some intermediaries have been able to adapt more quickly and are more efficient than others in this dynamic game of innovation. In other words, financial firms and financial markets should not be viewed as two opposing, rival realities.

Obviously, firms—hierarchies—are different from markets (Williamson, 1975) and their functioning responds to different mechanisms. However, in the changing scenario of the financial industry, both financial companies and markets are complementary—and not necessarily mutually exclusive—ways of organizing a financial system.

In other words, both can coexist in the same country, even though each country's financial model may indicate a preference for one or other. From the viewpoint of society as a whole, this coexistence is desirable, not only because it encourages competition, but also because it reduces transaction costs within the financial system, increases its efficiency, and, ultimately, helps improve resource allocation within the economy.

A completely different matter is the desirability of a financial organization specializing either in activities that are traditionally associated more closely with banking or in activities that are slowly moving toward the capital markets. We will come back to this point in a subsequent chapter.

However, we will say at this point that a priori, no one choice is better than the other. The optimal strategy simply does not exist. In the best of cases, there will be a preferable strategy to specialize or become a universal bank. The merit of such a strategy will depend on many factors, including the various types of resources the organization has available to it, its history, its reputation among its customers, and its positioning in the various segments of the financial market in relation to competitors.

Consequently, the financial system's functions continue to be basically the same. What has changed is the regulatory and competitive framework within which financial organizations and markets carry out their activities. This change of framework has triggered two closely related processes: a process of intense financial innovation and a strategy of change and/or specialization of financial organizations within the new framework. It is not possible to generalize about the quality of the latter without a thorough knowledge of the history and resources available to each organization to deal with this change.

4. THE FINANCIAL SYSTEM FROM THE PERSPECTIVE OF THE THEORY OF THE FIRM

The present configuration of modern financial systems is the result of a large number of historical factors, such as the industrialization process, the role played by financial organizations in this process, the degree of government intervention in the creation of companies, or a country's savings patterns induced, for example, through the tax system.

With all the appropriate caveats, we can say that the various financial systems have been formed in accordance with the principle of efficiency in resource allocation. In other words, the decisive factor behind a certain financial system is the perception, maintained by the various actors in a country, that a certain framework, and no other one, was the best for articulating the financial system in order to guarantee the resources required for investment.

The financial system's efficiency in resource allocation involves at least four dimensions.

1. The intermediation as such, in so far as it ensures a flow of financial resources towards the real sector of the economy at competitive prices.
2. The control of the risk incurred by the savers or holders of the funds. In this aspect, the financial system must articulate mechanisms to measure, at any given time, the risk incurred with a view to controlling it or to limit or broaden the risk of a particular investor.

3. The financial system should provide suitable diversification of risk. It is not sufficient to control it, but it is necessary to enable savers to reduce as much as possible the variability of the various financial assets' price and yield.
4. The financial system must implement the necessary mechanisms to reduce the risk of a financial crisis—normally, in the form of supervision by the financial authorities—and mitigate, when necessary, the effects of a possible financial crisis.

Although the features defining the financial system's efficiency seem to be clear, criteria are needed to help make the above-stated outlines operational. The modern theory of the firm has a number of arguments that are helpful in this discussion.

The view of the firm offered by neo-classical economics is that of a production function that the entrepreneur seeks to maximize, with the constraint of certain costs deriving from the use of production factors. Or, alternatively, the problem could be stated as the minimization of costs for a minimum production volume.

This view of the firm has become consolidated and enriched in recent years thanks to the spectacular growth of the models based on game theory and, particularly, those based on the so-called strategic behaviour of firms.

Neo-classical economics has paid little attention to the institutional and organizational aspects of the firm. In fact, the contributions by Berle and Means (1932) on the separation between ownership and control in organizations, or that by Coase (1937) on the firm as an alternative organizational mechanism to the market did not make any serious dent in thinking about firms until the early 1980s.[8]

In the last few years, there have been successive attempts to reconcile the two views of the firm: the neo-classical maximization approach—and the internal efficiency of organizations—the institutional approach—(Holmstrom and Tirole (1989)). The gap between the two approaches has been narrowed but it has not disappeared completely.

The neo-classical view of the firm was reflected in the dominant approach to investment and finance until the 1970s. The main hypothesis of classical financial theory states that there is no conflict of interest between the financial investors lending funds to companies and the interests of the companies receiving the funds. Fisher (1931) states that, in a setting of perfect capital markets, a financial investor's decision about an investment project depends solely on the investment's expected return and the interest rate. Personal consumption decisions or other temporary considerations are not relevant for this decision.

[8] This matter has been the subject of recurrent debate in recent years. In general, the concept of corporate governance is a complex matter that has been made even more complicated by the enormous changes that have taken place in the financial industry. For further discussion, see the comparative work of Charkham (1994).

This is the so-called Fisher's separation theorem, as it states that the investor can separate the financial investment decision from the consumption decision over time.

This theorem was consistent with the Walrasian paradigm, according to which an economy's state of equilibrium does not need financial intermediaries to act as an interface between savings and real investment. The reason for this argument is that the Walrasian paradigm assumes the perfect functioning of anonymous markets. These markets configure an optimal institutional model which any other institutional model (for example, a financial system based on the existence of banks) will tend to resemble.

A few years later, Modigliani and Miller (1958) went a little further with their theorem, according to which a firm's financial structure does not have any effect on its capital cost or its value.[9] This theorem was subsequently reformulated by Stiglitz (1974).

Transposing this thesis to the area of financial intermediation makes clear the absolute irrelevance of the debate about whether banks are more efficient in providing financing to firms than capital markets. According to this view, the debate between one type of financing or another, or between one type of creditor or another, is irrelevant.

In other words, in real life, these authors say, there is a complete separation between investment decisions and financing decisions. Fama (1970) stresses this separation in a more graphic manner by stating that firms have a series of investment projects they intend to undertake and investors decide to provide the necessary financing (equity or debt) to those firms with the most interesting investment projects.

Logically, this conception of financial theory leads to a complete separation between investment decisions and financing decisions. According to this view, the financial system would confine itself to an absolutely neutral task of mere financial intermediation, governed by the price-formation mechanism for financial assets in near perfect markets. Such a financial system would ensure capital flows from savings to investment. At the same time, the market itself could gauge the risks incurred by investors, forcing a sensible risk diversification.

A financial system operating in accordance with these guidelines would doubtless induce proclamations about the superiority of the systems based on the capital markets—in which the financial agents decide where to invest their resources—to the systems based on bank financing. The contrast is particularly significant in the case of those financial systems where banks are shareholders of industrial companies.

Against this apparent superiority of capital market-based systems, certain recent contributions (Mayer, 1988; Porter, 1992) suggest that some financial systems have been more successful than others in steering financial resources

[9] For more discussion about this theorem, see the excellent comments by Miller (1988), Modigliani (1988), Ross (1988) and Stiglitz (1988).

towards investment.[10] This superior performance is confirmed particularly in industrial restructuring processes (Kester, 1991), as a result of the situation of crisis affecting certain sectors of the economy. In such circumstances, the bank system seems to be more efficient than the capital market in achieving prompt allocation of resources.

Subsequent contributions to modern financial theory also express certain reservations about the results obtained by Modigliani and Miller. First, the perfect financial markets hypothesis does not exist in the real world. In some cases, a high degree of efficiency is observed in financial markets but it is a long way from being perfect.

There are many reasons for these imperfections. Perhaps the most important are the following. First, the existence of asymmetric information problems between savers, financial intermediaries, and company managers. These problems prevent prices from reflecting the proper value of financial assets and, on occasions, may give rise to an excess or shortfall of resources for certain investment projects (Stiglitz and Weiss, 1981).

Second, the existence of asymmetric information leads to agency problems, in which the relationship between economic agents may become difficult not only because of bounded rationality but also because of the search for and exploitation of opportunities at the expense of the other agent—opportunism, to use the generally accepted terminology (Williamson, 1975).

Third, as Jensen and Meckling (1976) have pointed out, the combination of debt and equity is a way of structuring the governance of companies. This combination generates a series of incentives guiding the behaviour of the firm's managers, so that the capital structure influences the firm's performance through the behaviour of managers. Looking at it another way, a certain combination of debt and equity may be a better instrument for achieving a match between the managers' goals and the shareholders' goals. In other words, an ideal financial structure would enable a solution to be found for the asymmetric information and moral hazard problems arising between the investors in funds (lenders or shareholders) and managers.[11]

Fourth, financial intermediation carried out by banks when they lend money to firms leads financial companies to deploy monitoring and supervisory activities. In some cases, there may be significant economies of scale to be obtained in such tasks (Benston and Smith, 1977; Diamond, 1984). In so far as this is so, the cost of the resources provided by banks could perhaps include a lower cost and risk premium than that levied on the resources provided by capital markets, with less capacity for monitoring and supervision.

[10] However, this opinion is contested by other authors, who stress the efficiency of the capital markets. See, for example, Miller (1994).

[11] In an argument which we will discuss later, Mayer (1988) points out that the different financial systems have mechanisms for solving the asymmetric information and agency problems arising between a firm's lenders, shareholders, and managers.

As a result of this role of financial intermediaries, the transaction costs (deriving from asymmetric information between lenders and borrowers or possible opportunistic behaviour) will be less than those generated by transactions on capital markets. The outcome is that the cost of the financial intermediation would be lower.

In addition, a company's financial structure raises agency problems, which have become the subject of discussion on the distinction between ownership and control in the modern corporation, raised many years ago by Berle and Means (1932) and more recently by Jensen and Meckling (1976) and Grossman and Hart (1980).

The question that is asked in this intellectual debate is who controls whom and in return for what. Is it the managers who really influence the firm's decisions or the shareholders? Whether it is one or the other, who should it be to guarantee the greatest possible efficiency in the economic system, expressed in terms of a higher growth of productive investment? Does the concentration of ownership in the hands of a few shareholders favour firms' efficiency?

We do not intend to give any answers to these questions now, which are far beyond the scope of the present book. However, this debate amounts to saying that the traditional separation between investment and financing decisions does not exist in the real world. In one way or another, to a greater or lesser extent, a company's shareholders and creditors wish to take part in business decisions.

Recently, a study sponsored by the US Council of Competitiveness and run by M. Porter (1992) stressed the importance of a greater connection between the financial system and industrial companies to improve efficiency in the allocation of resources for investment. This study's authors argue that one of the causes of the decline of US companies' international competitiveness must be looked for in a financial system that favours short-term considerations over long-term real effects.

Considerations of the ownership and control of companies therefore have a deeper impact on a financial system's efficiency than would initially appear. It is not enough that it simply transmit the price of financial assets, depending on the sector and the company's risk within the sector. If the financial system unbalances relations between investors, intermediaries, and companies, sooner or later, the results will be catastrophic.

Although none of the arguments we have just made is enough to prove the opposite of Modigliani and Miller's thesis, they are enough to enable us to say that that thesis will only be valid under certain conditions. In other circumstances, the combination of debt and capital may have major consequences for a company's long-term growth.

To summarize, looked at from the viewpoint both of modern financial theory and of empirical experience, the conception of the financial system as a mere chain for transmitting the savers' decisions to the investors' decisions seems to be definitely inappropriate. To think that the financial system should confine itself to ensuring that this chain operates as efficiently as possible contradicts both recent experience and numerous academic contributions. The real world is more complex than certain sophisticated theoretical models suggest.

The features of the financial system that we have highlighted are also applicable to other sectors of the economy. To think that markets, through the mechanism of the invisible hand, always lead to optimal resource allocation again goes directly against empirical evidence.

Indeed, the successful development of the industrial company in the twentieth century, which replaces the exchange of products or services on the market by a hierarchy that organizes operations under the control and supervision of a team of managers, is one example of the market's limits. This reality leads Chandler (1977) to state that, in modern societies, Adam Smith's 'invisible hand' has been replaced by the visible hand of professional managers.

The ultimate reason for the success of the modern corporation and professional management is their greater efficiency compared with the market. In certain circumstances, the market's transaction costs are much higher than is stated by traditional price theory. These transaction costs—which do not include production costs as such—refer to the costs arising from writing, supervising, and enforcing compliance with the contracts that are to regulate the transactions that would be carried out on the market (Williamson, 1975). In short, the market and the organization of transactions within the company itself appear as two alternative mechanisms for organizing economic activity.

In the market mechanism, efficiency in resource allocation is highest when there are no transaction costs such as those described above. However, when these costs appear on the scene, the market's advantages are no longer so clear.

On the other hand, the organization of activities within the company is based on the reduction of transaction costs or, to put it another way, on reducing the cost of carrying out a particular activity. This decision will be the most efficient for the company. However, it may be that the same cannot be said for society as a whole, for example, due to an excessive accumulation of economic power in the hands of a few people or of a certain market power in some sectors.

These considerations about the organization of the economic activity can be applied to the financial system. The question is whether the market—capital markets—will be more efficient than the firm—banks—in providing the necessary flows of funds for the non-financial company.

A second question, directly related to the former, is whether banks should become active shareholders of industrial companies in order to narrow the gap between the investors in savings and the holders of savings. In this sense, the banks would carry out the role of stabilizing financial flows and putting long-term considerations before short-term priorities.

		High	Low
Financial system	Capital markets	United States	Great Britain
	Banks	Japan South Korea	Spain France

FIG. 1.14 *Financial models: degree of regulation*

Obviously, these two extremes—market and firms—are two cases which are not incompatible in real life. In fact, both resource allocation mechanisms co-exist in many countries' financial systems. The critical issue we wish to stress here is which of the two mechanisms is right in which circumstances and at what price.

In Figure 1.14, we show the relationship that exists in real life between alternative systems for organizing the financial model, taking into account the degree of regulation of the banking industry. The two extremes are dominance of capital markets and the strong presence of banks in the industrial sector. Other alternatives in between are also possible, which will be more or less efficient, depending on the size of the transaction costs.

5. SOME CONCLUSIONS

The dramatic changes that have taken place in the international financial system are leading to major innovations in the financial intermediation process.

In particular, the construction of the single market in Europe has opened up new opportunities for agents and financial intermediaries. However, these changes have not been used to debate in depth the advantages and disadvantages—theoretical and empirical—of the various financial models that exist in industrial countries.

On the one hand, we have described the model dominated by the capital markets, well established in the United States, where firms seek financing on organized capital markets. On the other hand, we have identified a second type of financial model dominated by bank financing. In the latter case, the financing provided by the banks may even consist of a share in the firm's equity capital.

Until a few years ago, financial theory argued that investment and financing decisions were separate in terms of the firm's market value. This is implicitly equivalent to considering the capital markets superior to bank financing. However, the empirical evidence available and a number of additional developments suggest that this superiority is doubtful because of, among other reasons, the transaction costs incurred on the market.

The doubts that have been raised with regard to the dominant thesis, arising both from empirical observations and new theoretical developments, lead us to ask the question once again of what is the best way of organizing an economy's financial system. In particular, in the EU member countries, this question leads one to ask which is the most suitable model for financial intermediaries to ensure a better resource allocation and, hence, a more sustainable economic growth.

2

Capital Markets versus Bank Intermediation

1. THE CONFIGURATION OF THE FINANCIAL SYSTEM: THE CAPITAL MARKET-BASED MODEL

In the previous chapter, we outlined the types of financial models that can be observed in the major industrial countries, without considering the specific details of their configuration or their effects on industrial companies, or the investment rate.

In this chapter, we will discuss some of these aspects in order to understand in which contexts a particular financial model can work better than others, and whether it is possible or advisable to force the organization of financial activities towards any of the existing models.

We will start with a few empirical observations that will indicate the levels of bank and non-bank financing in a number of OECD countries. Table 2.1 provides information on the total indebtedness of non-financial companies with respect to the country's GNP. Of note are the high rates in Germany, Japan, and France, with Great Britain and Canada lagging some distance behind. Corporate indebtedness in the United States is surprisingly low, in spite of the large number of debt-instrumented financial operations carried out during the 1980s. These figures also show a major change in tendency after 1988. One of the reasons for this change is the unique situation of capital markets and the increasing appeal of bank loans compared with security issues on the capital market as a result of the decrease in the interest rates.

Figures 2.1 and 2.2 provide further information on the type of debt according to maturity. It will be seen that in France corporate debt is mainly short term while in Japan it is long term. These remarks confirm the thesis that bank–company relationships in Japan have a unique long-term nature that does not exist in other countries, except Germany.

Tables 1.13 and 1.14 in Chapter 1 show, respectively, the debt/equity and non-bank debt/bank loan ratios in several OECD countries. Some of these data are particularly significant. First, there is the low debt/equity ratio in American companies. Furthermore, corporate debt in US firms is mainly non-bank, as can be seen in Table 1.14. The case of Britain is interesting, as it shows a low debt/loans ratio, contrary to the opinion that British firms raise financial resources primarily from capital markets and not from financial institutions. Second, we

TABLE 2.1 *Net debt in non-financial companies* (% GNP)

Country	1980	1981	1982	1983	1984	1985	1986	1987	1988	1989	1990	1991
United States	5.31	5.94	2.45	4.19	7.74	6.15	5.78	5.14	5.63	4.48	2.55	0.22
Japan	9.65	10.42	8.50	8.96	10.49	8.90	5.73	14.55	17.38	21.55	16.16	7.81
Germany	9.80	9.94	7.50	7.92	7.80	6.52	4.23	3.82	5.18	7.59	8.14	8.43
France	11.46	12.80	11.30	10.57	9.40	4.49	2.72	6.37	8.38	10.64	9.24	5.50
Italy	9.18	9.53	5.51	6.11	6.30	5.98	4.77	5.25	6.59	—	—	—
Great Britain	—	3.97	2.99	1.69	2.04	2.65	2.70	4.42	8.98	10.52	6.85	5.24
Canada	10.12	14.33	3.59	1.82	3.68	3.50	3.32	4.15	6.50	6.23	5.39	4.42

Source: OECD.

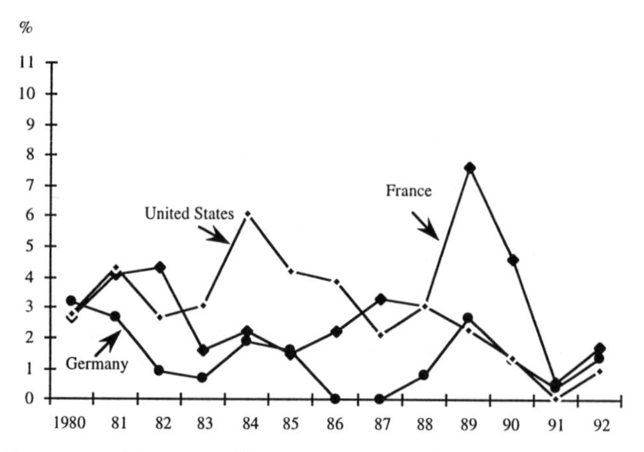

FIG. 2.1 *Short-term debt (% GNP)*

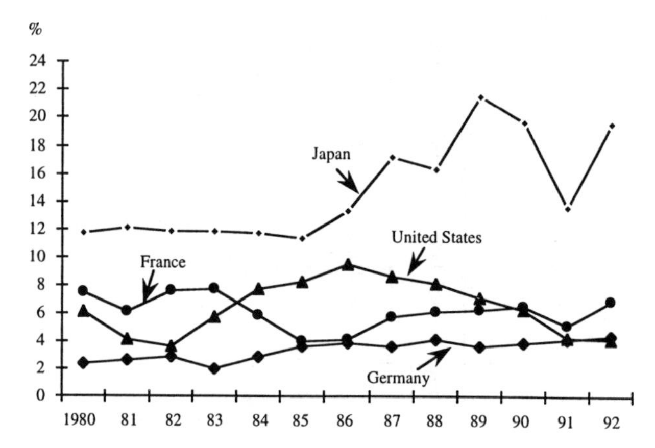

FIG. 2.2 *Long-term debt (% GNP)*

should note the high indebtedness of Japanese companies compared with their equity. This is bank debt, as Japanese companies very rarely resort to the capital markets. In Germany, the corporate debt/equity ratio is clearly below that of Japan. However, the figures of Table 1.14 confirm once again that this debt consists mainly of bank financing.

Let us now return to the discussion of financial models that, implicitly, underlie these figures for corporate indebtedness and financing in different industrial countries.

In the last chapter, we introduced the two main models of organization of the financial system: the capital market-based model and the bank intermediation-based model. We point out once again that both models are stylized cases of a more complex reality.

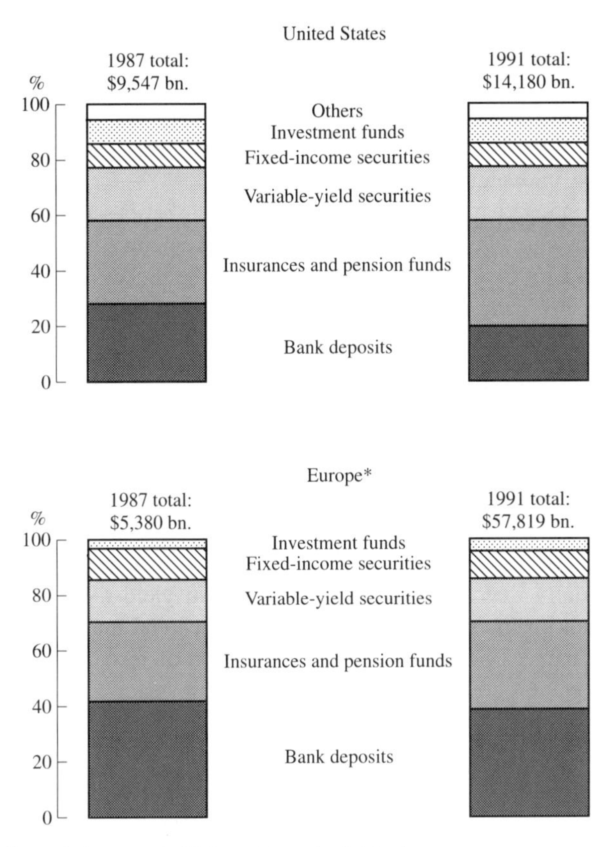

FIG. 2.3 *Financial assets held by private individuals*

The paradigms of financial systems based on capital markets intermediation are those of the United States and Britain. Figure 2.3 provides an overview of privately held financial assets in the United States and some European countries in 1987 and 1991. The differences are striking and reflect considerable discrepancies in the functioning of the respective financial systems. The American model basically follows the following patterns. First, companies mainly obtain their financing by fixed and variable yield security issues on the capital markets.

Second, financial innovation in these markets is permanently fostered, thereby enabling operations to be closely tailored to companies' real needs.

Third, there is a complete separation between investors acting on capital markets and non-financial companies. The former play no part in managing the non-financial company's daily tasks or in setting its long-term strategy. Their only influence arises from the assessment—which may be more or less accurate—made by capital markets of the company's business decisions and performance.

Finally, governments play absolutely no part in the process by which companies and capital markets freely agree the most suitable ways to finance business projects. The government's only involvement—occasionally—consists of the regulations it imposes on certain operations on capital markets. In particular, these restrictions are especially significant in the case of international operations, as a result of the more or less strict controls still existing on international capital movements.

As can be inferred from these observations, market-based financial systems provide a constant valuation of the various instruments through price mechanisms, which is of invaluable help in improving the process of allocating financial resources between alternative projects competing for the same financing.

Furthermore, capital markets provide a means of efficient risk diversification, performed by the investor of the funds. That investor is ultimately responsible for the decisions made in allocating the resources. Capital markets separate the risks of one financial asset from all the others, so that investors know at any given time where the risk is located and how much of it he is bearing, unlike the bank intermediation systems, where the bank takes on the entire risk *vis-à-vis* its asset customers. The securitization process implemented by the banks pursues precisely this aim: to break loans up into assets and distribute them among potentially interested investors in a certain yield-risk combination and release the bank from credit risks. Consequently, capital market-based systems, in principle, enable a more efficient diversification of resources; they also provide a much greater spread of the risk borne by investors.

Likewise, the scope of transactions on capital markets provides a high degree of liquidity to the holders of financial assets which always gives an excellent incentive for underwriting the placement of new issues in the future. The markets also enable an investor's assets portfolio to be adapted to new personal needs and to any changes that are observed on the market.

Alongside these advantages, the system based on capital markets also has a number of disadvantages which we will describe below. The first is the difficulty in monitoring and supervising companies due to the fragmentation of company ownership.

When there are no shareholders clearly involved in the company—due to the complete separation between capital markets and the company—the 'free rider' problem may arise: no one shareholder is large enough to be concerned about adequately supervising the quality of a company's management. In such situations, it is unlikely that the mistakes made by the company's managers will be detected in time by the shareholders.

It is true that financial intermediaries operating on capital markets try to provide ongoing information on what is happening in companies. However, this information may be incomplete, insufficient, or out of date, as these intermediaries do not always know what is really going on inside the companies concerned or else they have information that is different from that being handled by the companies' managers.

In addition to this problem, capital markets are also affected by the so-called agency problems, that is, delegation problems between shareholders or bond holders—principal—and the company's managers—or agents.[1] Agency problems occur in situations where asymmetric information arises, that is, in a context in which certain information is available to one of the parties but not to the other.

Agency problems can be partly solved by incentives that tend to correct inadequate behaviour in the use of this information, for example, by means of a management compensation scheme that reflects or takes into account certain variables, such as annual financial performance, performance over a period of years, or domestic or international market share. However, no matter how sophisticated the incentives are, it is obvious that any of the above-stated design variables has advantages and disadvantages and will never be sufficiently precisely targeted perfectly to induce certain types of behaviour (Milgrom and Roberts, 1992).

In the final analysis, one cannot forget that incentives are necessary but insufficient. Without a clear respect for ethics by managers in the performance of their professional tasks, even the best designed incentives schemes will eventually fail, as has been shown by the events of the second half of the 1980s in the United States.

Some authors (mainly Jensen, 1986, 1989) have pointed out that the best incentives that managers of listed companies have are capital markets and the possibility of their company, if its performance is poor, being bought by other investors who will change its management team. The phenomenon of LBOs (leveraged buyouts) is basically a manifestation of this rationale, in that it aligns the interests of owners and managers and, consequently, improves the managers' efficiency.

Although this argument may be right, it is only partly so. The reason is that LBOs generate a tremendous amount of uncertainty, not only for managers but also for the company's workers, customers, and suppliers. Furthermore, it is not clear either whether LBOs considerably improve the company's profitability subsequently (see, for example, Shleifer and Summers, 1989), and, consequently, their effectiveness is not universally proven.

A third major limitation of capital markets comes from the fact that there are no controlling shareholders in companies, except in cases where this is justified by historical reasons (for example, a company which has traditionally been family owned and has recently been admitted to the stock exchange). This lack may be serious because there are no shareholders who, at certain times, may act as counterweights to the power of the company's management. In other words, the shareholders' social responsibility is much more diluted. This leads to a situation in which, should it be advisable to carry out major surgery

[1] See Jensen and Meckling (1976) for an introduction to these problems.

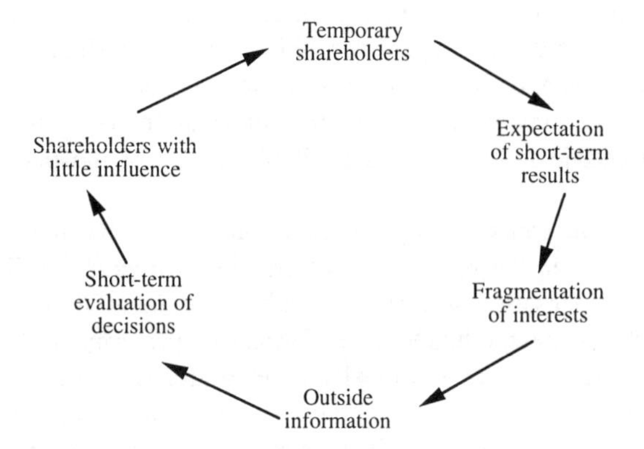

FIG. 2.4 *The fluid capital system: the Anglo-Saxon model*

—close production plants, reduce overhead, sell off some of the company's businesses—there is no guarantee that capital markets will properly evaluate those decisions.

This situation may sometimes lead to serious conflicts and only in societies such as the United States, where there is no strong union pressure, is it possible to carry out this type of action without too much attention from the media. These processes are more difficult to implement in European countries, where people are much more sensitive about closing companies and geographical flexibility is less.

Finally, one cannot ignore the exclusive emphasis of some shareholders on short-term performance generated in the capital market-based systems. The unique emphasis on performance and efficiency leads to situations in which shareholders look only at short-term results. The system generates a major shift in investors' outlook in this direction.

Some authors have accused the US capital markets of being the main cause of the declining competitiveness of American firms on the international markets and on the US domestic market (Jacobs, 1991; Porter, 1992). Other authors are not so sceptical about the real functioning of the US capital markets, pointing out that the emphasis on results is a guarantee of efficiency (Jensen, 1989).

Porter (1992) has expressed these doubts in a graphic and systematic manner. Referring to the capital market-based financial system, he speaks of fluid capital markets, thus underscoring one of the basic features of the market-based financial system. The fluid capital system is the opposite of what he calls the dedicated capital system, represented primarily by the German and Japanese systems. These systems are based on bank intermediation and a relative presence of banks in the financing of industrial companies.

Figures 2.4 and 2.5 give an overview of the virtuous (the system based on bank–company relationships) and vicious (the system based on capital markets)

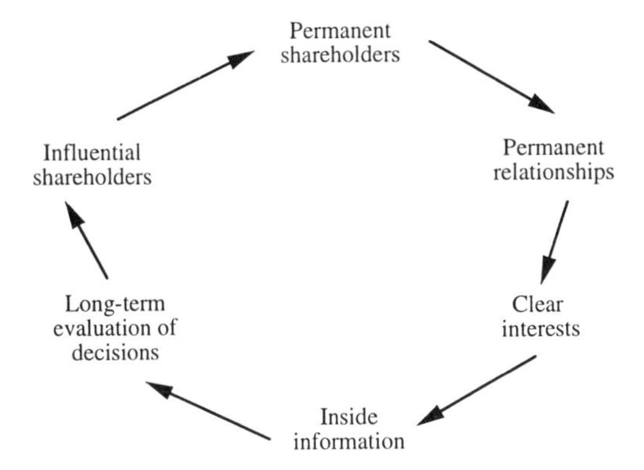

FIG. 2.5 *The committed capital system: the German model*

circles that can be created in each case. These figures underline the idea that the capital market-based system can offer higher economic performance for the investors, but not necessarily for the company or for society as a whole. Indeed, the system enables opportunities to be identified immediately and offers great mobility in the investment of funds and a smooth functioning of the information available on the companies.

Some critics point out that the capital market-based system may lead to a lower level of investment, particularly in assets where the return appears in the long term, such as technology or intangibles (for example, brand image). Also, it is a system that favours investment in mature industries but not in emerging high-technology industries. A case in point are the biotechnology companies which are heavy loss-makers during their first years of life and only start to pay after a fair number of years have passed. These statements require some qualification. Thus, if we look at the geographical location of these emerging industries, we see that they are concentrated in the United States, where the financial system is primarily based on capital markets. It could perhaps be that the disadvantages of the market-based financial model are outweighed by its relative advantages (Allen, 1994), or by the greater entrepreneurial influences in the United States. However, these are hypotheses that have not been proven empirically and should therefore be handled with caution.

Finally, the main incentive in the market-based system is hostile take-overs, a procedure that does not always guarantee the company's stability or success in the medium and long term, as we have already discussed.

These considerations lead Porter (1992) to state that far-reaching reforms of the US financial system are needed if the investment rate in US industry is to continue to grow and not lag behind that of other industrial countries with financial systems based on a strong bank presence.

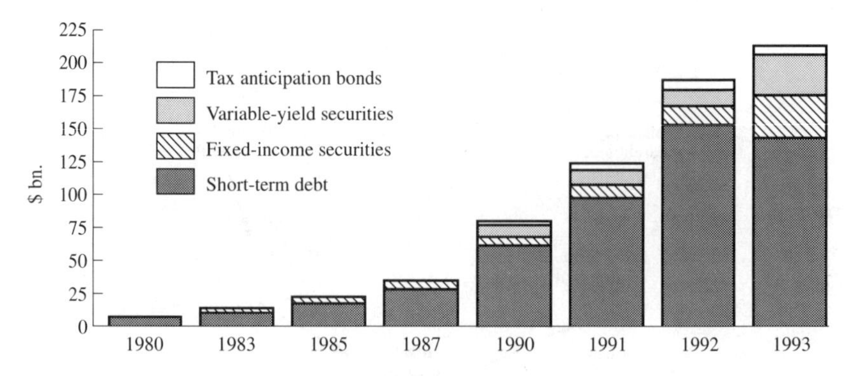

FIG. 2.6 *United States: assets of investment funds controlled by banks*

2. BANKS IN A MARKET-BASED FINANCIAL SYSTEM

The growing importance of financial markets and the emergence of new financial instruments seem to predict a decreased weight of banks in the financial system of industrial countries as a whole. Are banks in the process of disappearing? When we look at the banking industry in industrial countries, we see that some banks have reacted to this trend by becoming active agents on the financial markets. Figure 2.6 shows, for example, the spectacular growth of the investment funds handled by banks in recent years. This growth shows their great ability to adapt to the new environment of increasing dominance of the capital markets.[2]

Bertero (1994) analyses the reasons why the liberalization of financial markets in France has given rise to two apparently contradictory phenomena. On the one hand, companies have reduced bank debt, particularly short-term debt. On the other hand, the universal French banks have become the capital markets' main agents and consequently their weight in the financial system as a whole has increased. A similar situation seems to be developing in Germany, Spain, and Italy.

This bank diversification is not without its hazards; for example, revenue volatility in activities such as stock market trading is high. Table 2.2 shows changes in revenues obtained from this activity by some North American banks between 1985 and 1994. As can be seen, changes are very marked and the volatility is high.

We will now provide a brief description of the strategic change implemented by a North American bank, Bankers Trust, as an example of a possible reaction by a bank in the face of the increasing weight of the capital markets in the financial system. In 1994 and 1995, Bankers Trust seems to have suffered

[2] See, for example, the exhaustive study by Bertero (1994) on France.

TABLE 2.2 *United States banks: income from stock market trading* (% capital)

	1985	1993	1994
J. P. Morgan	6.0	22.0	11.2
Citicorp	8.7	19.2	5.4
Bankers Trust	5.2	38.1	10.8
Lehman Brothers	6.6	127.0	36.5
Salomon	28.7	39.7	–15.9
Paine Webber	76.8	65.2	35.9
Morgan Stanley	80.5	43.0	32.4
Merrill Lynch	38.3	55.2	42.4
Bear Steams	88.9	76.3	62.4

Source: IBCA.

from non-ethical behaviour in trading and selling complex products which will have a negative impact on its outstanding reaction to changes in the financial system. This bank, which was founded in 1903 in the United States as a commercial bankers' bank to act as lender and agent in the payments system, speedily turned into a universal bank after 1914. The main reason for this change was the birth in that same year of the Federal Reserve in which was assigned by law the tasks that Bankers Trust had started to develop as a bankers' bank.[3]

Alongside the change to commercial banking activities, this bank embarked upon a major diversification into foreign markets in the 1920s, with operations in Paris and London, and a diversification into the investment banking business.

By the early 1960s, Bankers Trust had become a major universal bank, operating both in the classic commercial banking business and in the investment banking business. The bank's financial performance, during those years, was excellent: its return on assets was one of the highest in the industry in the United States.

However, during the late 1960s and early 1970s, the bank experienced a series of major failures, particularly in its lending activities on the real estate market. However, Bankers Trust suffered a particularly hard blow when Citibank started to invest heavily in its commercial banking division.

In 1975, Citibank announced a plan to invest more than $US100 million in cash dispensers to modernize its retail banking network. Bankers Trust's management was completely shocked: this amount was equivalent to the bank's net annual income. If Citibank were to step up its investment pace, Bankers Trust would be squeezed out of the commercial banking business within a few years.

Faced with this situation, in 1976, Bankers Trust's senior management started to explore different possibilities. The first was to try to attract capital so that it too could invest large amounts in automating the commercial banking network.

[3] See Rogers (1993) for a brief history of this bank.

The second possibility was to withdraw from this segment of financial business. The third possibility was to close some of its branches and maintain its share in commercial banking in the most profitable urban areas.

Finally, in 1978, the bank decided to withdraw completely from the commercial banking business, precisely at a time when both Chase Manhattan and Citibank were investing heavily in this business. It was a risky decision and was widely criticized within the American financial community. However, Bankers Trust's managers had done their sums: the conclusions of a study performed on both the commercial banking and the investment banking divisions showed that the latter offered a clearly superior return to Bankers Trust.

Coinciding with this exit from the commercial banking business, Bankers Trust also sold its credit card division, which it had never managed to turn into a profitable business. This by itself is a curious fact. At a time when many banks were pointing to credit cards as a business with a brilliant future ahead of it, Bankers Trust, a bank renowned for its good management, was pulling out.

This apparent paradox has a simple explanation. Bankers Trust was in many different businesses and could not manage each one with equal effectiveness. Faced with the dilemma of continuing to be a universal bank with management problems due to lack of focus, Bankers Trust decided to turn itself into a new type of bank.

In 1979, Bankers Trust presented a new organization of its activities, which were grouped around four units: capital markets, investment banking (particularly, financial consulting and mergers and take-overs), corporate banking (lending to companies), and portfolio management (including funds safekeeping). The reorganization task faced by the bank was simply enormous: not only did it have to define its new business areas but it also had to break the structures that had traditionally separated the various units and co-ordinate them in line with the new strategy.

In contrast with the difficulties experienced by other universal banks in refocusing their business to bring them into line with the changes taking place in the financial services industry, Bankers Trust was able to detect these changes in time and readied itself to assimilate them with a strong internal leadership, even though this meant selling the commercial banking business which, until then, had been one of its bastions from the viewpoints of image and revenues. Neither the prompt recognition of the approaching change nor the willingness to face it head-on were virtues shown by other universal banks in the 1980s.

This change of business focus was made possible by the flexibility shown by the bank's senior management and key executives in the various businesses and the existence of a streamlined organizational structure that allowed for a high degree of horizontal and vertical mobility.

A key person in this turnaround was Charles Sanford. Head of Bankers Trust's trading division for many years, he was appointed President in 1983 and CEO in 1987. Sanford personally experienced for many years what the investment banking and trading business consisted of. In fact, this division was physically separated from the rest of the bank and occupied offices alongside other investment and trading firms.

Sanford's experience was crucial, not only to give shape to the vision of Bankers Trust's business in coming years, but also to implement new management, control, and incentive systems. These systems were a complete departure from those of a classic commercial or universal bank, as Bankers Trust had been until 1978. However, they were the right ones for a competitive investment bank in the 1980s. The underlying idea behind these changes was that each unit within the bank had to develop its vision of its own business, procure the necessary resources for it, obtain results in line with the resources used, and perform in these businesses with the flexibility and professionalism of the best specialists.

As a result of these drastic changes, Bankers Trust's strategy in recent years has been innovative. In fact, Bankers Trust has managed to face the problem of financial disintermediation and the growing dominance of the capital markets, particularly in the United States and Western Europe, presenting itself as an ally for companies and investors wishing to operate on these capital markets.

A recent operation by Bankers Trust in Europe provides a good illustration of the nature of this change.[4] Within the context of the major privatization programme initiated by Edouard Balladur's government in France in 1993, Bankers Trust offered a tremendously attractive privatization formula that was implemented in the privatization of the French Rhône-Poulenc group.

The details of this operation were as follows. With the privatization of that and other French state-owned companies, the French government wished to create a broad base of small shareholders, thereby spreading ownership of those companies among more citizens and avoiding possible concentrations of voting power in a few large shareholders. The problem faced by the French government and its advisers was how to persuade small private investors—perhaps employees of the companies being privatized—to buy shares.

In contrast to the proposal by some investment banks to sell the companies' shares to its workers at a discount or financing with a special loan from some public bank, Bankers Trust designed a very innovative procedure consisting of assuring the future shareholders that they would not lose money if the shares' price fell after a certain period of time. In return, if the shares rose and shareholders decided to sell them, part of the capital gains would go to Bankers Trust.

The operation designed by Bankers Trust was the following. This bank managed to obtain the co-operation of French banks to grant a personal loan to each investor wishing to buy one share with his or her savings, using the loan to buy another nine shares. After five years, the minimum time during which the buyer had to hold the shares, if the shares' price was below the original

[4] For a more detailed description of this operation, see *The Economist*, 30 April 1994.

purchase price, Bankers Trust would pay the investor the difference. If at the end of those five years, the market price was above the purchase price, the investor could sell: two-thirds of the gain would be for him or her and one-third would be for Bankers Trust.

The French banks were not taking on an excessive risk: the personal loans were guaranteed by the shares. In turn, the shares' value had a minimum ceiling which was guaranteed by Bankers Trust. The operation also appealed strongly to the prospective investors: they could buy shares without too much risk and pay for them with a low-interest loan. The result of this combination is that both the French banks and the small investors showed an unusual interest in the operation, which proved to be a resounding success.

For Bankers Trust, the operation had two parts. The first consisted of the consultancy fees charged to the French government. The second part included the possible capital gains to be obtained from an increase in the shares' price. However, there was one catch: what would happen if the shares' price fell below the purchase price?

To cover this possible contingency, Bankers Trust adopted a risk hedging strategy, which consisted of following the classic 50:50 rule. Bankers Trust had no way of knowing if the share price would be above or below the initial selling price. Therefore, the most logical option was to hold half of the shares offered in its portfolio and sell the other half. Depending on how the share price evolved over the next few months, Bankers Trust would adapt its portfolio accordingly.

The problem is that the shares would not be held by Bankers Trust but by the investors. So what Bankers Trust did was to contact investment funds interested in purchasing these shares but unable to do so and sell them a financial derivative. The financial derivative consisted of a financial instrument whose value was derived from another financial asset, in this case, the Rhône-Poulenc shares.

The financial derivatives sold to these investment funds by Bankers Trust simulated the dividends and actual course of the price of that company's shares on the market and the bank bought or sold these products as the shares' value dictated. In view of the success of this operation, the French government commissioned a second privatization to the bank with a similar structure: that of the oil company Elf Aquitane.

These operations confirm Bankers Trust's strategy to move away from traditional financial intermediation and become a financial consultant to companies and private investors who wish to gain access to financial services provided through the capital markets. Thus, Bankers Trust's strategic reaction in the face of financial disintermediation has been radical.

However, a price has been paid for this change in management systems, incentives, and culture. Some of the bank's managers have been unable to keep up with the pace of change and the bank has a reputation for burning out young professionals (Rogers, 1993). Perhaps Sanford's vision and thrust have been right but too intense. In 1994 and 1995, this bank was accused by two client companies of not explaining in detail the risk they were taking on when they invested in complex financial by-products. Although this is an ethical problem more than a financial problem, opportunism and the breaking of basic ethical rules might hinder this strategic revolution.

Those are important factors that may affect Bankers Trust's future: without consistency between mission, strategy, and organization, the best professionals may not be attracted to an institution such as Bankers Trust. This possible outcome is serious for an organization that depends heavily on its professionals' talent.

To summarize, in a financial system in which the financial markets play a dominant role, banks are not doomed to disappear. On the contrary, some of them, such as Bankers Trust, have undergone an internal revolution to become highly active agents on the financial markets.

3. THE CONFIGURATION OF THE FINANCIAL SYSTEM: THE BANK INTERMEDIATION-BASED MODEL

This financial model rests largely on the intermediation carried out by banks. This process is the main mechanism for allocating financial resources obtained from family savings by channelling them towards financing corporate investments. The role played by financial markets, in this case, is less important.

In Chapter 1, we explained that this second model of the organization of the financial system is not unique but allows for a large number of variants. For the moment, we will discuss only two. The first is that of those systems in which banking plays a major role in the industrial sector, as is the case of Germany, France, and Spain.[5] The second type consists of those countries in which the share of banks in total corporate financing is high, but mainly consists of short- or long-term financing in the form of loans or credits, but not of large holdings in companies' equity. The prototype of this model is Japan.

However, this division into two types is subject to many qualifications. The first and most important is that the accounting figures usually do not provide all the information. In Japan, the accounting figures suggest that banks' involvement in the industrial sector's total capital is less than in other countries. However, the functioning of the Japanese industrial groups ('keiretsu') around a major bank leading the group renders the accounting figures meaningless.

A similar finding is obtained—going back to the case of Japan—when one considers its economic history. In fact, relations between banks and industry have been very close in that country since the second half of the nineteenth century, at the time of the Meiji restoration, which was when the country started

[5] We will discuss the German system, which has a number of interesting features, in more detail in a later chapter.

to enter the modern era. These historic factors are as important as (or more so, in this case) anything that the accounting figures might suggest.

In this section, unless we specify otherwise, we will be referring to the extreme case in which the banks play a major role in financing industrial activity, either as a lender or as holder of part of industrial companies' equity.

The differences between financial systems reflect highly varied historical contexts. Thus, Great Britain (and later on, the United States) experienced an unparalleled surge in technological innovation in the second half of the eighteenth century. The new opportunities were exploited by numerous entrepreneurs who marketed the new innovations, particularly in the textile and steel industries.

The fact that, at that time, Great Britain dominated a large number of international markets provided many British companies with a monopoly position that, among other advantages, enabled them to accumulate reserves that would be used later to finance new investments.

On the other hand, families' savings were channelled towards investment banks and capital markets, which started to specialize in issuing financial securities. This gave rise to a parallel development of the internal financing of companies and capital markets, while banks' involvement in industrial projects was clearly less.

In countries such as Germany, Spain, or Japan—each one with very important differential aspects—the lag in the industrialization process, a traditional presence of the state in economic life, and the absence of private capital led governments and banks to take part in this process.[6] The combination of the government-bank interaction was crucial in this process: the government encouraged banks to become involved in certain companies, either through long-term loans or by acquiring an interest in their share capital.

The paths subsequently followed by these systems have been very different. In Germany, government involvement in industry has been very low. In Spain, involvement has been greater, although banks have been mainly controlled by private shareholders. On the other hand, in Japan, the connection—through informal links—between government, banks, and industrial companies has been unquestionable down to modern times.

Strangely enough, however, there are certain similarities. Thus, even though they are two different systems, both Germany and Japan have the concept of the main bank leading one or several industrial companies—the 'hausbank' in German.[7] This bank may or may not have a major interest in the industrial companies' equity. However, it plays a critical role in the relationships between companies and financial intermediaries, shareholders, or domestic and international capital markets.

A study of the role of banks in financing companies raises a number of basic

[6] Gerschenkron (1962) studies these issues from a broad historical view and points out that bank involvement in financing economic growth is a sign of economic backwardness.

[7] Kester (1991) and Harm (1992a) discuss the importance of the 'hausbank' in both countries.

questions. What are the advantages that are offered by banks compared with the markets? Is it not enough to have a series of well-developed financial markets to provide financing for companies?

The classic explanation of the function of financial intermediaries is that these obtain financial resources from savers by issuing deposits or other financial instruments and channel these resources towards companies that need them to finance their investments. In the final analysis, financial intermediaries act as a bridge between savings and real investment. In addition, this function enables the savers' risk to be diversified.

However, this classic view of financial intermediation seems to have been overtaken by events. Indeed, the growing sophistication of financial instruments and markets in recent years has enabled the markets' efficiency to be improved, thereby enabling a better diversification of the risk. It therefore appears that the classic argument is insufficient to account for the rationale and role of financial intermediaries.

In recent decades, a new approach has developed that accounts for the existence of banks in terms of the asymmetric information and moral risk problems that arise between savers and companies that receive funds from them. Savers usually have incomplete information on the companies' situation, which could make it more difficult for the latter to obtain the financing they need.

Thus, bank intermediation may offer significant advantages for companies as it mitigates the above-mentioned agency problems.[8] In fact, when the cost of acquiring information on companies by the providers of financial resources is high, the process of financing companies may be done more efficiently if the prospective investors delegate the obtaining of this information to a specialized organization (Diamond, 1984). Therefore, financial intermediation can be justified on the grounds of the information collection and company-monitoring functions performed by the banks.

The delegation of this function to banks offers significant advantages due to the economies of scale involved: this activity is associated with substantial fixed costs that can be absorbed by a greater volume of operations. Thus, banks may have a loans portfolio whose respective returns do not correlate with each other at any time. Its only condition is the existence of true competition between the various financial institutions, so that the cost of the financing does not include monopoly income. Therefore, the presence of financial intermediaries provides significant incentives that enable a major part of the above-mentioned agency problems to be solved.

This argument is useful but it cannot be taken to extremes. If it were universally valid, companies would operate with only one financial organization, which does not happen in real life (Hellwig, 1991). Therefore, an important aspect of financial intermediation is that banks may enjoy significant economies of scale in information collection and processing.

[8] See, particularly, Jensen and Meckling (1976), Diamond (1984), and Tirole (1993).

Second, banks may be better situated to solve asymmetric information problems and thus reduce the transaction costs resulting from the behaviour of small shareholders who are not interested in spending the effort or resources required to monitor a company's progress. We will come back to the issue of the effects of the concentration of ownership in companies at a later point.

A third aspect, related to the previous point, is that financial intermediation may solve better than capital markets the problem of the small investors who wish to invest but lack the information to do so efficiently. The function performed by banks in turning deposits into investments provides an alternative to directly placing the savings of small investors on the capital markets.

Another important aspect is that financial intermediation enables long-lasting relationships to be established, something that capital markets cannot develop. These relationships take the form of implicit, long-term contracts that the company considers beneficial. Mayer (1988) and Porter (1992) propose the concept of capital committed to companies. In fact, a basic problem of the relationship between investors and companies, the establishment of complete contracts, is solved by the supervisory role played by the banks. This function would enable an alternative solution to the long-term contracts between savers and companies. This argument is elegant but, as we will see further on, even in systems where bank intermediation plays a crucial role, the average maturity of bank loans tends to remain fairly short.

In a series of more general discussions, Allen (1993, 1994) has shown that the supposed advantages of financial intermediation over financial markets will depend on the type of industries concerned and, in particular, on their maturity and degree of technological innovation.

In mature markets, with a low level of innovation and, therefore, with less uncertainty, financial intermediaries offer clear advantages over capital markets. When there exists an agreement as to what can and cannot be done to compete in such an industry, banks have advantages over capital markets. This argument is related to that of Diamond (1984): provided that the uncertainty is low, the banks can diversify the risk among a number of companies, so that these companies' respective yields is relatively uncorrelated.

On the other hand, in emerging industries, with significant financial and technological risks, knowledge about the industry is much more imprecise. In this case, a financial intermediary's opinion will be less reliable. The high volume of information exchanged in the financial markets may, however, help to achieve a better allocation of financial resources.

In other words, banks may be the best agents for financing companies' investment or growth projects in consolidated or even mature industries. But the stock markets may obtain better information in emerging industries, where technological, financial, and commercial uncertainty is usually greater.

This explanation is fairly consistent with what happens in the real world, although it may not be the only explanation of why it happens. The United

States is the country with the greatest rate of product innovation and, in recent years, new industries have been born in the United States, where financial markets have greater weight than financial intermediaries. On the other hand, in countries where the degree of technological innovation is lower, such as France or Japan, banks play a more important role as the relative efficiency of their activity is greater.

Another advantage of the bank intermediation-based financial systems is the existence of a major shareholder—the bank itself—which, as owner of the company, is interested in its performance (Jensen, 1989; Berglof, 1990). This shareholder may influence the company's development, for example by appointing its senior managers. This relationship with the management team also enables it to mitigate the asymmetric information problems previously mentioned in our discussion of the capital market-based system.

In general, banks are able to exercise control over companies at a lower cost for the reasons we have stated above. Consequently, in a context of asymmetric information and incomplete contracts, banks may exercise control over a company more efficiently than financial markets could do.

Observe that this argument goes beyond that of Jensen and Meckling (1976). These authors point out that debt and capital are two different mechanisms for governing companies and discuss how control is exercised with each mechanism. Here, we have advanced this argument a little further and one wonders why a country, its banks, and companies choose one system or the other.

The answers to this question have been provided indirectly elsewhere (Diamond, 1984; Mayer, 1988; Hellwig, 1991). However, there are two institutional aspects that must not be forgotten in this context (Roe, 1994). First, in the United States, the bank legislation passed in the 1930s has prevented banks from playing a more active role in company financing. However, it is also true that we do not know what would have happened if that legislation had not been passed.

The second aspect is the specific concentration of the ownership of banks and companies in each country. The presence of a major shareholder—or, at least, of a major creditor—may ensure the establishment of relationships between banks and companies that are geared towards the long term, less exposed to passing circumstances, and generate the emergence of capital committed to the long-term financing of companies. This argument was developed by Demsetz (1983), who points out that controlling shareholders take on a greater risk in the company and consequently the benefits to be obtained from monitoring the company exceed the costs.

Generally speaking, there seems to exist a positive correlation between concentrated ownership (or, failing that, controlling interests) and efficiency. The reason is that when members of a board of directors (for example, banks who are shareholders or creditors) who play a major role in the company also have an interest in it (as shareholders or creditors), the company's and investors' incentives are more consistent and agency problems tend to disappear (Jensen and Meckling, 1976; Shleifer and Vishny, 1986).[9]

These long-term relationships provide a financial structure for industrial companies which contains a greater proportion of external debt with a lower cost. This structure may give a slightly lower capital cost. A financial structure such as that described here is less easy to sustain in a system based on financial markets, due to the agency problems described above and which would lead to a higher capital cost. Hoshi, Kashyap, and Scharfstein (1991) provide interesting indirect evidence on this point: Japanese companies with bank shareholders invest, on average, more than those that do not have bank shareholders.

The concentration of ownership may enable conflicts between a company's shareholders to be resolved more quickly, as there is one shareholder—a bank—that is genuinely interested in the company's future. This system also allows for less traumatic solutions to be applied in situations of crisis; on many occasions, bankruptcy is avoided and the restructuring process is less harsh, thereby reducing the intensity of the resulting social conflicts. This is an important argument that is used when describing the advantages of the Japanese financial system (Aoki, 1988; Kester, 1991). Thus, Hoshi, Kashyap and Scharfstein (1991) show that the cost of company restructurings in Japan is lower.

On the other hand, as we have already mentioned, in the capital market-based systems, bankruptcy is usually the mechanism used to solve a feasibility problem. Obviously, this system involves a greater degree of social conflict.

Together with these undoubted advantages, the model based on financial intermediation also has its problems and limitations. The first and most important is the excessive risk accumulated by the banks through their loans and shareholdings. These holdings have been the cause of many bank crises, such as the US crisis in the 1930s, or the Spanish crisis in the 1970s and 1980s. The recent cases of Crédit Lyonnais and Banesto are illustrative examples.

A second limitation of the financial intermediation-based model is that control mechanisms are no longer based on the prices set by the market for certain financial assets but on the bank's ability to supervise the companies with which it has commercial and financial relations. Obviously, this second situation requires a much greater effort on the part of the main shareholder or, in the case of the bank, the main shareholder and/or creditor.

Third, the lack of stricter disciplinary mechanisms, such as the one provided by capital markets, may lead some companies to be overcomplacent. This is particularly true in those cases where the products offered by the company are not subject to market discipline. However, if there is a high degree of rivalry in the industry in which the company is operating, this risk is lower.

[9] Demsetz and Lehn (1985) cannot confirm this hypothesis empirically although other authors have confirmed it in other contexts. See Shleifer and Vishny (1986), Hill and Shell (1988) and Pound (1992), among others. Lowestein (1991) offers another argument against this thesis, according to which many controlling shareholders do not spend time on supervisory tasks.

A fourth limitation of the bank intermediation-based model is the tendency to overinvest and, therefore, create excess production capacity in those industries where companies operate with bank financing (Hoshi, Kashyap and Scharfstein, 1991). The reason is that the assumption of continued support of a bank may lead to situations of complacency within the company and prolong indefinitely a situation of mediocre management.

In spite of these limitations, the model based on bank intermediation has achieved good results in countries such as Japan and Germany, both in terms of highest productive investment and in terms of a greater social stability. We will discuss these aspects in another section.

In some cases, these superior results have led some authors (Kester, 1992, Porter, 1992)[10] to argue the desirability of capital market-based systems progressively including features of the bank intermediation-based system, as a means of maintaining high investment rates and increasing corporate competitiveness.

The recent crises of Crédit Lyonnais and Banesto show the operational difficulties encountered in efficiently managing universal banks' corporate holdings. These cases will be discussed in the following sections.

3.1. Crédit Lyonnais

Crédit Lyonnais undertook the most ambitious bank growth experiment in the 1980s and early 1990s in Europe. When one talks of global European banks, two names immediately come to mind: Deutsche Bank and Crédit Lyonnais. Both shared the same banking philosophy: they assumed the concept of the universal banking model, with banks playing a significant role in financing and controlling industrial companies, and they believed in the need to be present in the various European countries, either through internal growth or by buying local organizations.

The course of Crédit Lyonnais' business is highly eloquent. Its capital increased from 37 billion francs in 1988 to nearly 80 billion francs in 1993. Its lending activities increased 2.5-fold during the same period and its results went from a profit of 3.7 billion francs in 1990 to losses amounting to more than 7 billion francs in 1993. At the same time, this strategy led it to the pinnacle of glory in 1993 as the largest bank in the world in assets terms, after the Japanese banks. Its assets at the end of 1993 amounted to 2.3 trillion French francs. As a headline in one business magazine report said, Crédit Lyonnais was the bank 'that couldn't say no'.[11] Table 2.3 shows the bank's recent performance. The increased losses were mainly due to the increased provision for bad debts and the capital losses generated by its industrial holdings. The book value of these holdings grew from about 11 billion francs in 1988 to about 50 billion francs

[10] However, the arguments are hotly countered by other authors, who maintain that the capital markets are an efficient mechanism for governing companies. See Allen (1994) and Miller (1994).

[11] *The Economist*, 9 April 1994.

TABLE 2.3 *Crédit Lyonnais: economic performance* (French franc trillion)

	1991	1992	1993	1994
Financial margin	1.10	1.20	1.40	1.30
Net operating result	0.40	0.37	0.34	0.24
Provisions	0.25	0.37	0.46	0.44
Net profits	+0.08	−0.05	−0.20	−0.30
Consolidated net worth	1.30	1.6	1.50	1.20

Source: Crédit Lyonnais.

TABLE 2.4 *Corporate holdings of Crédit Lyonnais* (1993)

Business	Industry	% capital
MGM	Leisure	100.0
FNAC	Distribution	66.0
Arnault	Luxury goods	29.5
Usinor Sacilor	Steel	20.0
Adidas	Sport	19.9
Aerospatiale	Aerospace	18.0
Bouygues	Construction	10.0
Rhône-Poulenc	Chemicals	6.0
Lagardere	Publishing and defence	3.0

Source: Crédit Lyonnais.

in 1993. Another important factor behind Crédit Lyonnais' performance were its high operational costs which, in 1993, accounted for more than 70 per cent of the bank's total revenues. In a well-managed bank, this percentage is usually about 60 per cent.

Table 2.4 shows some of Crédit Lyonnais' industrial holdings. For example, the initial interest in Usinor Sacilor was 10 per cent, for which Crédit Lyonnais paid about 22 billion francs. Subsequently, it carried out a share swap with the French government by which the latter received a parcel of Crédit Lyonnais shares in return for a parcel of Usinor Sacilor shares. This example is indicative of the bank's presence as a shareholder in a wide range of industries, some of them high risk, such as film-making or oil.

These problems have forced the French government to step in to rescue the bank on two occasions: the first in early 1994 and the second in April 1995. Figure 2.7 shows the outline of the second plan.

Crédit Lyonnais, with the problems caused by what was probably a low-quality management and lack of rigour in granting loans to its related companies, was a further example of the failure of the universal bank model with large business holdings. Circumstances that work against effective management of such businesses include the complexity of managing these groups and the

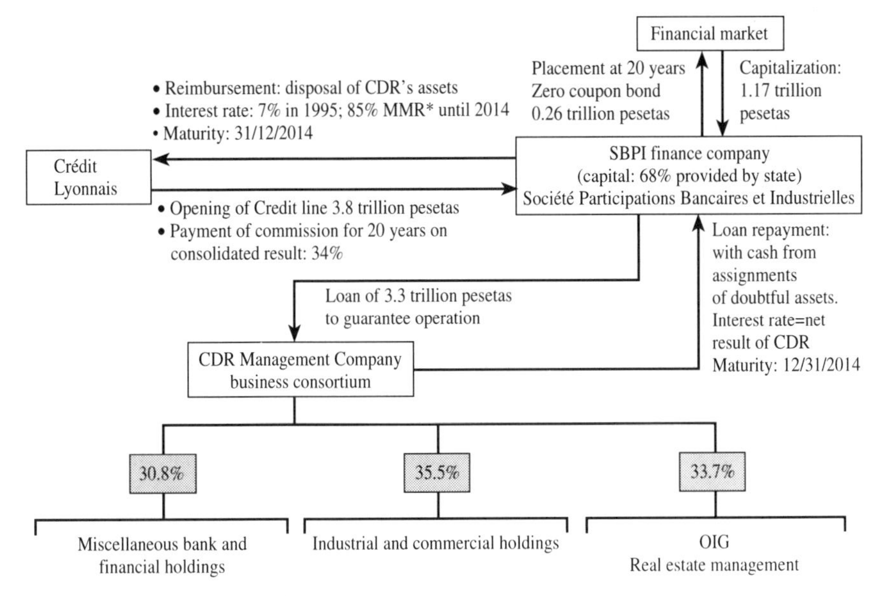

FIG. 2.7 *Crédit Lyonnais' turnaround plan*

bank's slowness to pull out in time when a company reaches a point of no return. If we also take into account the difficulty of managing a universal bank in the 1990s, failure seems almost inevitable.

3.2. Banesto

Banesto (Banco Español de Crédito) was the largest Spanish commercial bank in volume of assets until the first half of the 1980s. The increase in bad debts as a result of the economic recession in Spain and problems regarding the future of the management team led to a loss of direction in the bank. Within this context, in November 1987, Banco de Bilbao launched a take-over bid for Banesto with a view to subsequently merging the two banks.

Take-over bids as a mechanism for acquiring control of a company were growing continuously in the United States during the 1980s, but their introduction in Europe was much slower. Strong political pressures and a belief within the industry that concentration was good for Spanish banks and for the industry as a whole led Banco de Bilbao to make this move.

The take-over bid was turned down by Banesto's board of directors and subsequently Banco de Bilbao had to withdraw it as there were defects of form that were not adequately provided for in Spanish legislation. However, the take-over bid triggered major changes in Banesto, which appointed a new president and a new management team with the declared purpose of relaunching itself.

Banesto's strategy from 1988 until the intervention of the Bank of Spain in December 1993 can be summarized under three headings.

(a) a new image of a modern universal bank;
(b) a growth in turnover, which picked up speed particularly after the price war broke out to capture deposits;
(c) the consolidation of its holdings in major industrial companies by means of the creation of the Corporación Industrial Banesto in 1990.

While other Spanish and foreign banks adopted a strategy of strengthening and matching their banking activities to the recent changes in the finance industry, Banesto focused two competing centres: the banking business and the non-banking business, represented by the industrial companies belonging to the Corporación Industrial. Table 2.5 shows the development of Banesto's holdings in a number of companies between 1990 and 1993.

However, any bank that needed revitalizing to the extent that Banesto did could hardly afford to disperse its attention over so many different fronts. The result is that Banesto started to grow in volume of assets and deposits, mainly thanks to a very aggressive pricing policy and lax risk-management and loan-client-selection policies. Banesto's assets increased twofold between 1987 and 1992 but the bank's profitability fell dramatically, in part because of the squeezed financial margins and in part due to the significant increase in bad debts.

Indeed, between 1988 and 1991, Banesto's loans investments increased by 109 per cent while those of the other large banks only grew by 56 per cent. In addition, the mean cost of creditors was 7.8 per cent by the end of 1991, compared with 7 per cent for the other large banks.

According to the Bank of Spain's Certificate of Inspection issued after the intervention in December 1993, the doubtful debts amounted to more than 120,000 million pesetas by the end of 1992 and about 340,000 million pesetas by the end of 1993. The provisions required to cover these possible losses amounted to about 150,000 million pesetas in 1993, three times more than the bank's pre-tax profit.

When the Bank of Spain audited Banesto in December 1993, Banesto's financial 'hole' was estimated at more than 560,000 million pesetas, which was approximately distributed as follows: 280,000 million pesetas for doubtful debts not provided for, 100,000 million pesetas for unposted capital losses in its corporate holdings portfolio, about 60,000 million pesetas for the bank's holdings of its own stock, and about 120,000 million pesetas for endowments not made to the bank's pension fund and other uncovered contingencies.

In addition to poor management quality in the areas of industrial holdings, stock management, and lending policies, a business-oriented reading of these figures could reveal the difficulty of developing simultaneously an industrial business requiring a considerable amount of operating attention—beyond mere buying and selling transactions—and a bank business facing fierce competition and in a state of uncontrolled growth.

TABLE 2.5 *Banesto: selected business holdings*

Company	Sector	Per cent capital			Gross profits*	Net profits*		Capital*
		1990	1991	1992	1990	1991	1992	
AGF Seguros	Insurance	—	—	—	—	133	—	1,877
Acerinox	Mining	26.07	26.89	33.61	6,799	5,750	3,064	9,667
Agroman	Construction	38.92	42.12	48.23	2,308	2,508	454	12,639
Asturiana de Zinc	Mining	42.35	44.63	100	6,502	–5,861	–10,795	15,400
Celulosas Del Nervion	Paper	19.31	—	21.37	–33	—	–2,138	4,042
Cementos Portland Iberica	Construction	38.72	—	—	10,413	—	—	3,600
Grupo Inmobiliario de la Corp. Banesto	Real Estate	—	76.66	84.01	—	–284	3,087	8,732
Inmobiliaria Urbis	Real Estate	18.28	25.14	28.19	1,582	2,557	2,220	13,921
Petroleos del Mediterraneo	Chemicals	28.61	—	—	4,651	—	—	10,051
Promocion del Deporte	Services	38.72	—	42.01	106	—	1,534	4,000
Quash	Chemicals	77.44	76.66	83.99	–2,142	–1,626	–418	30,372
Sdad. Española de Carburos Metalicos	Chemicals	17.28	23.45	24.02	1,722	1,854	1,883	13,012
Sdad. Nac. Indus. Aplic. de Celulosa España	Chemicals	24.00	20.05	—	594	–4,124	—	19,526

* In million pesetas.

Source: Banesto, Memorias Anuales.

The turnaround process followed prior to the sale of Banesto was as follows: a reduction in the bank's share capital of about 300,000 million pesetas—the aim was to retain a symbolic value for the shares in order not to frighten off foreign investors, even though their real value was almost zero—and a contribution by the Bank of Spain and the private banks to cover the rest.

On 25 April 1994, the Bank of Spain auctioned Banesto. The three bidding banks were Banco Santander, BBV, and Argentaria. Their bids were 762 pesetas, 667 pesetas, and 566 pesetas per share, respectively. Thus, Banco Santander became the new owner of Banesto for the sum of 312,700 million pesetas. After an initial placement of shares among the old shareholders, the final cost of the operation for Banco Santander was 280,000 million pesetas.

With this purchase, the Santander Group rose to the head of the list in volume of assets, with about 18.5 billion pesetas: 10.4 from Banco Santander and 8.1 from Banesto.

Having started its turnaround, and with the new management team proposed by Banco Santander, Banesto started the process of selling off its holdings in the non-bank companies. The goal, according to the bank's new managers, was to move away from the idea of an industrial bank or an industrial group around a bank to become a modern commercial bank particularly focused on private individuals and small and medium-sized companies.

One can also argue the opposite case, in that the ultimate reason for these crises is to be found not so much in bank holdings in industry as in the fact that the loans and equity holdings did not follow professional criteria but other, more suspect criteria. However, as soon as one allows bank involvement in industry, the risk appears and, on occasions, it becomes quite significant.

4. THE ORGANIZATION OF INDUSTRIAL COMPANIES AND THE SPECIALIZATION OF FINANCIAL SYSTEMS

In the previous sections, we have discussed the main features of the two extreme models of organization of financial activity that can be observed in industrial countries. One of our conclusions is that the historical context of these countries' industrialization process is important in explaining the particular configuration of their financial systems.

However, this explanation on its own is not enough. It is reasonable to think that certain features of the industrialization process—for example, the role played by governments and banks in encouraging the process—have weighed heavily in the subsequent evolution of the financial system. However, we would also have to add to this explanation those institutional aspects of each country that, in practice, have enabled this evolution to take place. The most important of these institutional aspects is how companies are organized and managed (Williamson, 1975; Chandler, 1977).

Companies—whether they be industrial or services companies—operate in a context of different types of relationships with customers, suppliers, competing companies, or financial organizations. A critical decision for the company as a whole is the degree of vertical or horizontal integration that it wishes to attain in order to achieve greater efficiency in its operations. This degree of integration will affect the investment decisions that the company will make and, in particular, those investments in highly company-specific assets whose value outside the company is consequently very low (Williamson, 1985).

These investments in specific assets bear a high risk. Thus, if the investment ceases to be profitable as a result of sudden changes in the demand for the final products or in raw material prices, the investment's value will fall sharply. This volatility in the rate of return of certain investments is an adverse factor when deciding on their viability.

Consequently, for investments in specific assets, the existence of a long-term relationship between the capital market and the company takes on particular importance. As we have already discussed, the financial models based on capital markets tend more to capital fluidity and short-term mobility, whereas the models based on bank intermediation may look more to the long term, as a result of the intrinsic nature of the bank business. If this is so, then the financial models with strong bank involvement would show higher investment rates (Mayer, 1988) or, at least, a higher percentage of outside financing for new investment projects. On the other hand, in the financial models based on the capital markets, non-financial companies would show a lower percentage of long-term outside financing.

We will discuss later some empirical observations on the outside financing of non-financial companies in a number of countries. For the present, in this section, we will describe a few basic features of the nature of this relationship between non-financial companies and the financial system in some countries (from the viewpoint of the non-financial firms), developing the discussion in Chapters 6, 7, and 8.

4.1. Relationships between non-financial companies and the financial system in Japan

At first sight, the organizational structure of the Japanese company is special, at least if we look at it from the Western viewpoint. However, as some authors have pointed out (Aoki, 1984; Kester, 1991), the Japanese model of business organization has a coherent, homogenous internal structure, which accounts for—at least, in part—the successful penetration of international markets by Japanese companies in the 1970s and 1980s.

The first feature of Japanese companies is their membership, in many cases, of a broader industrial group, composed of a number of large industrial corporations and one or more banks: this is the famous 'keiretsu'. The best-known 'keiretsu' are those that have been formed around the large automobile companies, such as Nissan or Toyota, and around the large consumer electronics and computer companies such as NEC or Matsushita.

The companies belonging to a group comprise an individual economic system, like a microsystem within the Japanese economy. These companies have a high degree of production specialization, through which they serve both the companies in the group and other outside companies.

The Japanese firms belonging to a 'keiretsu' are also extremely stable. Indeed, the close relationships formed between them encourage situations in which, when one of the member companies experiences periods of financial difficulties, the other members tend to lighten this financial burden. At the core of these decisions, there is usually one of the large Japanese banks leading these operations.

Obviously, membership of a group and the requirement of loyalty and solidarity *vis-à-vis* the group's companies give rise to a tremendous degree of flexibility and adaptability to a changing environment. Think, for example, of the just-in-time system implemented by Toyota to manage the supply of components for its automobiles. Without this close relationship between the Toyota Group's companies, extended to its suppliers, this system is extremely vulnerable. In terms of efficiency and flexibility this system is successful. However, the system places an additional burden on the group's companies when one of them starts to falter or is not able to offer the products that other companies need with the same quality-cost combination as other companies outside the group. In this case, relations between companies become strained and, more likely than not, the profits of some of the companies may take a dip.

Consequently, the system is flexible and favours long-term relationships but the rates of return may, on average, be lower. This is what is observed in international comparisons of the return on equity between US, European, and Japanese companies. The latter are usually grouped at the bottom of the list.

The factors defining the relationships between the companies belonging to the 'keiretsu' can be synthesized as follows.[12] First, there exists an explicitly declared business relationship between two or more companies. These agreements usually are not of a legally binding nature: fulfilment rests not on the force of the law but on the trust between the companies concerned.

A second feature of the Japanese system is the exchange of senior managers between companies belonging to the same group. The existence of a group is sometimes due to a shareholder holding shares in more than one of the companies of the group. Thus, it is not uncommon to see that the president of a Toyota supplier is, for example, an ex-Toyota manager; or that a top executive of one of the large Japanese banks sits on Nissan's board of directors.

Such practices have a twofold purpose. First, they familiarize managers with the functioning of different types of company. However, these exchanges also enable managers to get to know each other and build personal relationships

[12] See Kester (1991) for a detailed study.

which, generally speaking, (Suzuki, 1980), help professional relations run more smoothly.

As a result of these personal relationships explicitly encouraged by the member companies of the 'keiretsu', these companies' managers are more open to sharing information on the status of their own companies, the industry, or other aspects that are useful for the group's progress. Thus, this sharing of information between the group's members enables the situation of a company to be monitored in much greater depth than could be possible for a financial intermediary in the capital market (Gilson and Roe, 1992). Likewise, these continual flows of information provide a powerful incentive to make sure that a company's performance does not lag behind others, either within the same group or competitors not belonging to the group. In this sense, it should be stressed that the information and the indicators that can be examined in this case are much richer than the simple indicators of financial return used in capital markets. For example, they can include aspects such as the number of new products recently introduced, the reaction time in responding to customers' needs, the degree of customer loyalty, or the quality levels in the supplies to other companies in the group. As can be seen, the wealth of information that is shared can be overwhelming.

The third feature of Japanese industrial groups is the existence of cross-holdings between companies. Thus, at the end of 1990, holdings by companies belonging to different 'keiretsu' of the capital of the other companies in the group were as follows: in Mitsubishi, 25.3 per cent; in Fuyo, 18.2 per cent; in Sumitomo, 24.5 per cent; in Mitsui, 18 per cent; in DKB, 14.6 per cent; finally, in Sanwa, 10.9 per cent. Clearly, these holdings are not particularly high and by no means provide an absolute majority. However, they provide a means for controlling the other companies and create a closely knit structure on which to base relationships between the group's companies. In the case of shareholdings by banks in industrial or services companies, a very interesting situation arises. Bank holdings in such companies are not very high. However, in practice, these banks are also these companies' main lenders.

Indeed, in practice, the distinction between debt and capital in these companies becomes less well defined as, in both cases, the financial resources usually remain for prolonged periods in the company that has received them. This stability in the sources of financing may cause problems for some banks when the companies are insolvent but, on the other hand, it provides an incentive for the companies to consider investments that have a longer payback period than is normal.

There is one final feature that is unique to the Japanese industrial groups, namely, the so-called selective intervention in some companies by other companies in the group and, above all, by the group's leading bank. This selective intervention takes place when major problems appear in the affected company's management and, particularly, in situations of persistent deterioration of the company's profitability or of its levels of financial solvency.

In many industrial countries, serious financial troubles might lead to bankruptcy. In Japan, on the other hand, such an outcome is avoided by all means possible. The explanation is to be found in the Japanese culture: above all other considerations, the group's companies wish the group's survival and the preservation of jobs. Logically, this context guarantees a tremendous social stability.

In such cases, the group's leading bank—which, in addition, is usually the troubled company's shareholder and lender—takes on a prominent role. Normally, it takes on the debts of the other creditor banks and becomes the main creditor. As leading bank, it is perfectly aware of the company's internal situation and designs plans for recovering the loans tailored to the company's possibilities. Access to information also provides a decisive advantage to the banks, compared with the situation in the capital markets, where access to information on the company is more limited.

Japanese commercial banks cannot hold more than 5 per cent of the equity capital of industrial corporations. However, by virtue of their membership of a 'keiretsu', in practice, their influence is usually much greater. Thus, in a sample of large Japanese companies, the largest shareholder was a Japanese commercial bank in 72 per cent of these companies (Sheard, 1989). There is also a close link between bank holdings of equity capital and volume of credit granted. Indeed, in one study performed by Prowse (1990), in about 60 per cent of the companies surveyed, the largest shareholder was a bank which was also these companies' main lender.

In recent years, however, these bank practices have started to show signs of strain. The reason is the erosion of the Japanese banks' profitability, which has limited their ability to raise capital in international markets. This circumstance has made banks increasingly sensitive to the return on equity, which has already led them to abandon some companies in their groups for fear of damaging their solvency.

Consequently, the Japanese model has functioned in an unusual manner in recent decades, with a very close relationship between banks and industrial companies. These relationships are not going to disappear, at least in the short term. However, the Japanese banks may become increasingly less inclined to rescue group companies whose financial viability is not clear, particularly during times of recession, as has been seen in the recent economic downturn. If this trend is confirmed, it will mark a major shift in the relationships between Japanese banks and industrial companies.

4.2. Non-financial companies and banks in Germany

On many occasions, the German and Japanese financial systems are grouped together, with the argument that the strong presence of the banks and the lesser importance of the capital markets are factors common to both countries.

Indeed, the way banks work in the two countries has a number of similar features. One example is the presence of a leading bank in some medium-sized and large companies in Germany (the so-called 'hausbank'), which behaves in a similar manner to the leading banks in Japanese industrial groups.

This presence also includes shareholdings in many cases. The large banks are shareholders of large companies in Germany. Thus, at the end of 1990, German banks were shareholders of 9 per cent of all listed German companies. Furthermore, they held more than 25 per cent of the equity capital of the 33 largest German companies (Harm, 1992a). Likewise, the insurance companies held 11 per cent of the equity of these 33 companies.

These figures reflect a significant bank involvement in the share capital of German industrial companies. However, one very important distinction must be made. The presence of banks as shareholders of industrial companies is confined to large companies. In other words, German banks hold no interests in the equity of small and medium-sized industrial companies, unlike the leading banks in the Japanese 'keiretsu', which do have holdings in the small and medium-sized companies that form part of the industrial conglomerate. In Chapter 6 we will offer a wider discussion of those points.

This distinction is important because one must not forget that the core of Germany's industrial might is not its large companies but the vast fabric of highly innovative small and medium-sized companies with their strong international vocation.

In any case, the presence of German banks in industrial firms is not confined to shareholdings in large groups. The German banks also act as main depositaries of the shares traded on the Stock Exchange. At the end of 1990, the German banks held on deposit about 40 per cent of the market value of the shares of listed companies. If to this we add the 9 per cent directly held by the banks, we find that banks control directly or indirectly about 50 per cent of the equity capital of listed companies.

It is true that having shares on deposit does not guarantee, *per se*, the ability to influence shareholders' decisions. However, in Germany, a mechanism known as 'Vollmachtstimmrecht' operates by which, under certain conditions, the banks act as proxies for those shareholders who have deposited their shares in the bank.

For many years, this proxy was almost automatic (Harm, 1992a) and did not require any special conditions imposed by the shareholder. Nowadays, the situation is somewhat different. The bank must ask for instructions from the shareholders. Furthermore, each proxy is valid for 15 months, after which it must be renewed.

Public listed companies (AG) are legally required to have two types of board: the 'Vorstand', which is a management committee that takes on the company's executive responsibilities, and the 'Aufsichstrat' or supervisory board. The members of the 'Vorstand' are appointed by this supervisory board.

The specific channel for influencing shareholders of listed companies is the supervisory board or 'Aufsichtsrat'. By virtue of a regulation passed in 1976, half of this board's members are elected from among the workers' representatives.

The other half are representatives of the shareholders. These boards have been considered as being one of the pillars of Germany's social stability in recent years.

As in Japan, the shareholders' representatives may be managers of other companies and, particularly, of the banks that are shareholders or depositaries of shares in the company. Hence the relative importance of the banks' presence in German industry, at least in listed industrial companies.

There are clear similarities between the German and Japanese cases. However, there are also significant differences. The first is that in Germany—with a few exceptions such as the Daimler-Benz group—there are no industrial groups like the Japanese 'keiretsu'. Relations between companies and banks are more direct. One of the consequences of this reality is that relations between industrial companies and their suppliers are more often governed by transactions on the products markets and not by agreements deriving from the existence of cross-holdings in these companies' equity.

There is also a clear difference between bank presence in industry in Japan and that in Germany. Thus, while in Japan direct shareholdings by banks in large industrial companies exceed 20 per cent, in Germany, as we have already indicated, they amount to about 9 per cent. In any case, these two figures are not comparable, because the Japanese figure includes unlisted companies while the German figure only includes listed companies.

However, both the German and Japanese cases show that the relations between banks and industrial companies, shaped by a very specific historical context, help account for the specialization of financial systems. A combination of historical circumstances and government decisions has led to direct or indirect involvement of banks in industry being greater in some countries than in others.

A subject of major debate is the degree to which one can force a change in the financial model in a country that has operated for many years with a particular model. A number of highly individual experiences have been observed in some developing countries (such as South Korea and Mexico).

However, the situation is very different in an industrial country. The incentives to change are, as a result of existing vested interests, less powerful, although some experts maintain that change is highly desirable.[13]

In any case, what does seem to be beyond doubt is that in countries such as Germany or Japan, banks have played a major role in financing the industrial sector, although this has not been without costs and inefficiencies. The one big doubt is whether these systems—intimately associated with certain financial practices that revolve around a leading bank—will be profoundly changed as a result of the securitization and financial globalization processes we have discussed in the last chapter.

Our opinion is that this dramatic change is not likely to occur, at least in the foreseeable future. What is growing is the importance of capital markets in

[13] See particularly the persuasive arguments of Porter (1992) and Bhide (1994).

corporate financing in these countries, as an inevitable result of development and financial innovation.

There are also serious reform attempts taking place in the United States, a country with a market-based financial model, aimed, among other things, at allowing a greater degree of competition between banks and other financial intermediaries. These reform attempts include the possibility of commercial banks acquiring shareholdings in industrial companies, within certain limits (Bryan, 1991).

To summarize, the financial models of the United States, Germany, and Japan are evolving towards a convergence which, while not absolute, is opening each model to the advantages of the other models. We can predict that, in the next few years, industrial countries will witness a combination of universal banks, playing a major role in the financing of industry, and increasingly sophisticated capital markets, with heavy involvement of bank groups in the long-term financing of companies.

With the strengthening of the universal banks, it will be necessary to re-examine advantages and disadvantages of each of them and introduce the necessary changes in specific organizational strategies in order to ensure that the bank group is managed efficiently. These two issues are the subject of Chapter 4.

5. EMPIRICAL EVIDENCE ON THE EFFECTIVENESS OF MODELS OF THE FINANCIAL SYSTEM: AN OVERVIEW

In this section, we propose to ask whether there exists any empirical evidence that supports the supposed advantages and disadvantages of the models of organization of the financial system we have described above, without prejudice to a more comprehensive study of this issue in Chapters 6, 7, and 8.

Within the empirical studies that have been performed, we would like to single out the following. Cable (1985) puts forward a number of hypotheses on the relationship between the degree of integration between banks and industrial companies in Germany and the latter's profitability. The first hypothesis is the supposed existence of market power on the part of the companies controlled by the banks due, for example, to possible collusive agreements between these companies. This situation would generate profits above market levels.

The second hypothesis refers to the transfer of management skills from the banks to the companies, which may have a positive impact on the companies receiving them. Note that this hypothesis assumes both that banks have a higher level of professional management skills than industrial companies and that it is more efficient for companies to attain this level of professionalism through the bank than by contracting these services on the market.

These two early hypotheses, although interesting, suffer from a certain lack of realism in practice. The third hypothesis postulated by Cable is much more appealing: the formation of an internal capital market—obtained from the integration between banks and industrial companies—offers significant advantages for industrial companies.

Indeed, the presence of banks on boards of directors or supervisory boards may lessen the asymmetric information problems between banks and companies and, consequently, the transaction and monitoring costs of the lending relationship. Also, as we will see later in the Japanese case, these relationships mitigate the effect of sudden lending restrictions. Finally, the consistency between control, ownership, and management offers major, long-term advantages for industrial companies, which must focus their competitiveness efforts on the final products markets.

Cable concludes that, for the sample of German companies observed, companies that have a bank as one of the shareholders are more profitable overall than the companies that do not. However, these findings do not indicate any direct causal relationship and must be treated with caution.

This author also states that the source of this superior performance is to be found mainly in the existence of an internal capital market within the bank-industrial companies group, enabling more stable sources of financing over time to be assured.

The important point that Cable's study does not consider is whether or not bank holdings in industrial companies' equity capital have a positive effect on the banks' economic performance and stock market appraisal.

There are virtually no studies that attempt to answer this question explicitly. An interesting study referring to the case of Spain is that of Bergés and Sánchez del Villar (1991). These authors ask in their study whether there are any differences in the stock market appraisal of banks when they have interests in industrial companies. They also ask a similar question for companies that include banks among their shareholders. The conclusions drawn by those authors are not unequivocal. On the one hand, they observe that the banks with industrial holdings show asymmetric behaviours. Thus, at one extreme, there would be Banesto, whose stock market value is highly sensitive to the stock market value of the companies it has holdings in. At the other extreme, there would be banks like Santander and BBV (the former bank having less significance in this study because of the lower volume of assets placed in industrial company shares) where the banks' value is relatively independent of the stock market value of the companies they have holdings in. On the other hand, the companies which have banks as shareholders are not significantly more profitable than other listed companies. However, their share prices are slightly less volatile, which is consistent with the hypothesis that the presence of banks provides a greater stability for the industrial company in the medium term.

Harm (1992a, b) also discusses the presence of banks in German industrial companies, although his contribution is more qualitative than quantitative. After carefully observing the means by which this presence is materialized, Harm draws, among others, two interesting conclusions. First, the presence of banks in Germany industry is not a generalized phenomenon. To be more exact, it should be stated the banks have a major presence—less than 10 per cent of total shareholders' equity—only in large listed German companies.

The second conclusion is that the presence of banks in these large companies has two types of effect, which are observed in some individual cases. The first is the greater stability of the sources of financing that may lead to a higher long-term investment rate, compared with the companies that do not have this close relationship with banks. The second effect is that the presence of banks in industry provides the company, at times of crisis, with a less painful restructuring and adjustment process—in terms of labour disputes. This is an interesting finding, which we will also discuss for the case of Japan. However, in order to have a complete view of this phenomenon, we also need to know whether being a shareholder of these industrial companies in difficulties has any medium-term effects on the profitability and share price of the banks concerned.

Another group of studies deals with the relationships between banks and industrial companies in Japan (Aoki and Patrick, 1994; Corbett, 1987; Kester, 1991).

Aoki and Patrick (1994) survey some interesting findings. First, companies with bank shareholders have a lower dividend distribution rate than the companies without bank shareholders. This observation is consistent with the fact that companies with bank shareholders compensate their shareholders in the form of stability. The thesis of stability is also confirmed directly in this study by reference to the share prices. In Japan too, these prices are less volatile when a company has a bank among its shareholders. Moreover, the presence of banks in industrial companies does not affect these companies' profitability when long time periods are considered. However, they may have a short-term impact. Again, this result would be consistent with a previous statement, namely, the presence of banks in the equity capital of industry companies ensures their medium-term stability, which leads to reduced volatility in their share prices.

These results referring to Japan concur in part with two qualitative studies on the functioning of relationships between banks and business in that country. The first of these studies, in chronological order, is that of Corbett (1987). The study describes the practical functioning of the operations carried out by banks with industrial companies, from the initial activities of obtaining information on the company concerned to the types of loan, interest rates, and repayment times.

Corbett reaches a series of conclusions, of which we would like to mention the following. First, implicit contracts, not recorded in any document, between banks and industrial companies in Japan, guarantee continuity in the sources of finance for the company; in return, the company pays relatively higher interest rates compared with the capital market. Industrial companies are willing to accept these conditions in consideration of the greater stability of the sources of finance. The result is that Japanese industrial companies have higher interest expenses than if the financing was agreed at market prices, and this in turn affects these companies' profitability and capital cost.

The final conclusion is that banks have a greater variability in their profitability. At times of high economic growth, when companies do not have any serious financial problems, banks obtain a higher return on assets, in relative terms, than other banks in industrial countries. On the other hand, during periods of slower economic growth, with a greater number of companies in difficulties, the banks' return on assets drops considerably.

Kester (1991) reaches similar conclusions, although his study does not measure the direct effects on the companies' or banks' profitability. The key point of Kester's argument is that long-term relationships between banks and industrial companies are basically stable, and that these provide for higher business investment rates and also a significantly lower number of business failures.

The problem raised in Japan, as we will discuss later, is that the higher interest rates that banks charge their borrowers is and will continue to be increasingly less accepted by companies. The phenomenon of financial disintermediation is also pointing in this direction. Kester discusses the nature of the tension that is already appearing between banks and companies as a result of the higher interest rates that the latter have to bear.

This tension does not mean that relationships between banks and industrial companies are going to disappear in the short term. What it does mean is that the capital markets will start to play a larger role in firm financing in coming years in those countries where, so far, bank intermediation has played the dominant role. It is also to be expected, as is already happening in some countries such as Spain, Germany, or France, that banks will take on a more active role in the functioning of capital markets. Obviously, none of the studies discussed here offers unequivocal or universal conclusions. In later chapters, we will have the opportunity to look at these results more closely in the course of a more detailed study of bank–company relationships in certain countries.

6. SOME CONCLUSIONS

In this chapter, we have identified two major models of organization of the financial system. The first is the model based on capital markets as the primary nexus for the flows between savings and investment. The second model described is based on the essential role played in it by banks and other financial organizations. Unlike the first model, in the model organized around banks, the financial markets play a much less important role in financing real investment. These two models, deeply rooted in different countries, are not static but are in a process of continual change or mutation. This process seems to be tending to bring the models closer together rather than to pull them further apart.

Thus, on the one hand, in countries such as Japan and Germany—countries where banks play a crucial role—capital markets are becoming increasingly important. This is due, in part, to the growing volume of banking activity on the capital markets. On the other hand, in the United States—a paradigmatic country for the financial market-based model—there are growing pressures for banks to play a greater role in corporate finance. Something seems to be moving on the international financial stage. And these movements seem to be going in one direction: an eclectic model in which both banks and financial markets will play an important role in corporate finance.

3

The Separation between Commercial and Investment Banking in the United States

1. INTRODUCTION

The banking crisis that shook the United States in the 1930s meant the end of the universal banking system that, until then, had shaped that and many other financial systems. In fact, the American bank crisis was and still is the main historical experience customarily used as reference point when establishing the limits of bank involvement in activities other than pure and simple financial intermediation.

Such was the importance of those events that a discussion of the reasons for the banking crisis in the United States and the relationship between the cause of the crisis and the universal banking system prevailing at that time warrants a deeper discussion. We will also ask whether we can infer from those events any conclusions that can be used to determine with greater accuracy under what conditions a universal banking system can operate and under what conditions such a system creates too high a risk for financial firms as a whole.[1]

Between 1930 and 1933, the number of banks in the United States fell by 11,000, from 25,000 to 14,000 (Benston, 1990). This decrease in the number of banks was due both to the winding up of many of them and to smaller banks being bought by larger banks.

The US Congress, the Federal Reserve, and the Roosevelt administration were concerned about some of the courses being taken by the banking industry. The first was that banks were investing in equity and bonds issued by non-financial companies. These investments, at a time of significant drops in the prices of these assets, were causing potential or real capital losses which, in some cases, were quite substantial.

The second concern, caused by some isolated, flagrant cases, was that some investment banks were forcing their customers to invest in certain assets that banks themselves were offering them as a specific means of reducing risk or possible capital losses.

The third concern was in response to a practice applied by certain banks.

[1] The excellent studies by Benston (1990), Wheelock (1995), and White (1986), among others, raise these issues in a highly critical tone compared with the more conventional view of the 1930s crisis.

This consisted of holding the price of certain financial assets by means of loans to third parties who used them to buy shares, thus feeding a buying run on those securities.

In response to this crisis, the Roosevelt administration initiated a large-scale reform of the financial system. The so-called 1933 Banking Act represented a new approach to the problem of financial regulation which, for the first time, followed two distinct lines.

On the one hand there was the separation between financial intermediation or commercial banking activities and investment activities in financial assets or non-financial companies, which was promoted by Senator Carter Glass. On the other hand there was the institution of a deposit insurance to guarantee that deposit holders would receive a certain minimum sum in the event that their bank should fail. This provision was promoted by Senator Henry Steagall.

Thus came into being the Act known as the Glass–Steagall Act which, with certain exceptions, remains in force today in the United States and which was the model of financial regulation followed later by other industrialized countries. In fact, any introduction to the issue of the regulation of financial organizations, both in the United States and in other countries, comes to this Act at some point in the discussion.

The provisions of this Act that are directly related to the separation of commercial banking activities from investment banking activities are the following. First, Section 16 prohibits banks belonging to the Federal Reserve from buying financial assets on their own behalf, although this prohibition did not affect national banks, which could buy financial assets up to 10 per cent of their capital.

Second, Sections 16 and 21 also prohibit commercial banks (banks that basically receive deposits from their customers) from issuing, selling, or distributing any type of financial security, such as bonds, debentures, or shares, with the exception of debt instruments issued by federal or state administrations. It is important to point out, in this context, that the 1933 Banking Act does not prohibit American banks from carrying out such activities outside the United States.

A considerable controversy has been built up around these two sections, particularly when some banks started to offer investment funds to their customers in the 1970s. Is this an investment by the bank in financial assets or is it an investment on behalf of its customers? If it is the former, it is prohibited by the Act. If it is the latter, the situation is rather ambiguous. In 1987, the US monetary authorities agreed that banks could offer these products through the creation of subsidiaries that took on the risk associated with any possible losses.

Third, Section 20 of the Act prohibits commercial banks from associating with other financial companies to issue or distribute financial assets. However, this provision was subrogated by a directive of the Federal Reserve by which commercial banks could undertake such activities provided that the assets were commercial paper, municipal bonds, and other financial assets backed by mortgages or other sureties.

Finally, as regards the separation of activities between commercial banking and investment banking, Section 32 is also important. This section prohibits a commercial bank from sitting on the boards of finance companies that operate on the capital or money markets or including in its board officers of such companies, even if neither organization holds equity of the other.

To summarize, the legal provisions contained in the 1933 Banking Act establish a distinct separation between commercial banking and investment banking and make it legally impossible for the same financial organization to combine both types of activity. At the time, this separation of activities was viewed as being the best solution to the most serious financial crisis in the history of the United States prior to 1930.

2. THE RISKS OF A UNIVERSAL BANKING SYSTEM

As we have discussed above, in the 1930s US banking crisis, the regulators acted with a clearly conceived intention of separating the typical activities of commercial banking (taking deposits and investing in commercial and mortgage loans) from the activity of investing in financial assets. However, some authors (Benston, 1990; Roe, 1994; White, 1983, 1986) think that the 1933 Banking Act was an overreaction to a series of real but distorted problems which only affected a relatively small number of banks.

In fact, according to these authors, the 1930s bank crisis is to be accounted for not only on the basis of the high risk of the investments made by some banks but also by the combination of a highly recessive business cycle and excessively high interest rates. In the following pages, we will briefly recapitulate the empirical evidence available in the US case with a view to assessing more accurately the objective reasons underlying these measures.

The first question that should be raised is whether there existed or it is possible to detect during those years any major differences in the results of those financial organizations that actively traded in financial assets and those of other organizations that did not.

The most comprehensive study carried out on this issue is that of White (1986). For the period 1930–3, White estimates that of all the banks that declared bankruptcy during those four years (in total, 26.3 per cent of all banks), the failures affected only 4 out of a total of 62 banks that had subsidiaries specializing in the trading of financial assets and 11 out of 145 banks that operated directly on the stock market. Therefore, only 15 banks of a total of 207 national banks engaging in the trading of financial securities failed.

The second significant finding made by this study is that financial asset trading did not seem to be the primary or the most important cause of these banks' failure. The reason for this is that investments in financial assets accounted for only a small part of these banks' total assets. Thus, in the case of the First National Bank of Detroit, which was the most catastrophic bank crash, only 10.5 per cent of its total assets were invested in fixed and variable-income securities. Furthermore, the 15 banks that failed and which operated on the stock market accounted for a relatively small share of the total American banking system.

Another generally voiced criticism of the banks that engaged in transactions on capital markets is that these assets' price volatility posed a hazard to these banks' results and, in the final analysis, to their solvency.

White proceeds to analyse this statement statistically, using the information gained from the income statements of 18 banks operating in financial assets between 1925 and 1932. The result he arrives at leaves no room for doubt: banks operating with financial assets had a higher return, although this return's variance was also higher.

However, White obtains a second result that significantly qualifies the first one. The falls in bank return do not match the falls in the return on financial asset trading. If we combine the two results, we can conclude that operating in financial markets did not decrease these banks' risk but did increase their return.

This conclusion should be treated with considerable caution: the sample of banks used is small as these were the only banks that filed complete financial statements for the entire period under consideration. Therefore, the results obtained cannot be extrapolated immediately to banks as a whole.

Finally, White tries to verify the rationale of another view widely held during that period: that the banks operating in financial assets had a proportionately lower net worth than the other banks, were more dependent on third party resources, and, therefore, their risk of insolvency was greater.

The evidence presented by White does not concur with this general statement. Indeed, after performing different regressions with six different variables, he concludes that this statement is not correct, as the banks operating in financial assets were not less capitalized than other banks that did not engage in such operations. In any case, whether or not a bank traded in financial assets was not a decisive factor in accounting for the bank's equity capital.

It cannot be concluded from the results we have just presented that the cause of the 1930s banking crisis in the United States was the stock market activities carried out by some banks. Some results even seem to indicate that the losses could have been higher if the banks had not been able to count on the gains from the operations in financial assets.

These results are important because they situate the American regulatory effort of the 1930s within a rationale that was not strictly economic or financial. One should not forget that there were other concerns shared by regulators behind the 1933 Banking Act. We discuss these in the next section.

3. OTHER REASONS FOR THE GLASS–STEAGALL ACT

In the previous section, we discussed the evidence available on the first of the arguments used by US regulators to separate commercial banking and investment banking activities: the supposedly higher risk of investment banking activities, with the increased risk this implied not only for the commercial banks' shareholders but also for their depositors.

However, there were other reasons behind this legislation, without which it is not possible to understand the historical origin of the separation of commercial and investment banking activities.

3.1. The deposit insurance system and the financial system's safety net

The legislators' major concern was to protect depositors should another bank crisis as severe as that which took place in the United States in the 1930s ever happen again. Therefore, Congress approved a body of provisions, incorporated in this Act, which form the so-called safety net for financial organizations and, through them, for depositors.

This protective legislation for the banking system included the following items. First, a Deposit Guarantee Fund was created, which guaranteed a series of minimum balances to the depositors of failed banks. Second, the Federal Reserve was empowered to step in and provide immediate liquidity to banks experiencing difficulties in cashing deposit withdrawals.

An important issue related to the deposit guarantee in the event of failure of a bank is whether there exists the problem of moral risk, that is, whether banks, having the ultimate guarantee that their deposits are assured, incur risks exceeding those they would assume if this guarantee did not exist. Opinions on this matter are divided: while some experts maintain that the deposit guarantee fund induces banks to take on more risks than is advisable, others point out that risk-taking is related to factors other than the existence of deposit insurance.

Perhaps this issue is more important now than in 1933 when this scheme was introduced in the United States and, from there, was extended to many more countries. This is why it is important to consider it here since it is one of the most hotly debated elements of the possible reform of the Banking Act in the United States and, hence, in other industrialized countries.

The issue, within the context of the current public debate, is not whether there should or should not be insurance for depositors—something that seems to be accepted by many experts, although there is no absolute unanimity due to the problem of moral risk—but whether the insurance should be extended to activities performed by banks that are not directly related to traditional banking activity, as would be the case of stock market operations.

The critical question for settling this point is whether the combination of commercial and investment banking activities increases or decreases the bank's risk and, therefore, the risk of failure. The empirical studies are not conclusive. While some authors show that the correlation between the revenues generated by the two activities is low or negative (Heggestad, 1975; Litan 1987), which would suggest that the combination of the two activities would reduce the bank's risk, other studies show a positive correlation and, therefore, conclude exactly the opposite (Brewer, Fortier, and Pavel, 1988).

So there is no final answer to this question. Prudence in bank supervision seems to advise that deposit insurance should only cover those activities that are strictly related to traditional commercial banking and that it should not be extended to other financial operations that banks might engage in.

In fact, two recent events seem to underscore the validity of this statement. The first is the heavy losses that some banks have suffered with financial derivatives and public debt trading in 1993 and 1994; both activities are clearly outside the scope of traditional commercial banking.

The second event is the difficulties of some universal banks with major industrial and real estate operations, such as Banesto or Crédit Lyonnais. Aside from any consideration of whether these cases are or are not a good example of the moral risk problem, it seems reasonable to argue that these two banks' depositors had a right to know that they were depositing savings in institutions that were deliberately taking on a greater risk than other organizations.

3.2. Potential abuses in the use of information and financial resources

A second type of argument used to support the 1933 Banking Act was related to a conception of the banking business according to which traditional financial intermediation and activities related to financial asset transactions inevitably lead to situations of conflicts of interest and abuses.

Within this category of arguments, it is necessary to make a distinction between several situations: abuses in the use of information, application of one activity's resources to another activity, and conflicts of interest. Let us start with the first.

The supposed abuses in the use of financial resources or information gave rise to an argument that was used in the debates prior to approval of the Glass–Steagall Act. During the debates, some senators referred to allegedly harmful speculative activities carried out by some banks to alter artificially the price of certain shares (Benston, 1990).

Two observations must be made that considerably reduce the possible impact of this phenomenon. The first is that the stock market crash in the United States was not caused by the activities undertaken by commercial banks, as their weight in the financial markets was not particularly significant. In fact, the Glass–Steagall Act fell considerably short of fulfilling the expectations that had been generated before the Act was approved as regards helping to solve the stock market crisis.

The second consideration is that, in spite of the opinions expressed by some senators, the Glass–Steagall Act did not prohibit commercial banks from lending money to securities traders. Indeed, although it is desirable to look for some kind of relationship between the two variables, one must proceed with caution before formulating unequivocal conclusions.

In fact, as we have already discussed, the results of those banks that, before 1933, combined bank intermediation activities with financial assets transactions were significantly better than those of the banks that confined themselves to financial intermediation.

3.3. Conflicts of interest

Another argument related to the combination of activities within a bank concerns the possible conflict of interests and, therefore, the possible illicit behaviour of certain banks that could misuse the information available to them in favour of shareholders and against depositors or investors.

Benston (1990) has carried out an important piece of historical research in compiling, ordering, and interpreting the transcriptions of the addresses made by senators and members of Congress on this issue during the debate on the Banking Act. After carefully examining the arguments used in some of the cases most often quoted as examples of this conflict of interests in the 1930s, such as the National City Bank, the Chase National Bank, and the Bankers Trust, that author concluded that the information handled was specific to particular occasions and, in some cases, anecdotal, and it cannot reasonably be concluded that the alleged conflicts of interest could harm the interests of depositors or investors.

3.4. The argument of the concentration of financial power in the hands of the universal banks

A fourth type of argument used during the debate on the 1933 Banking Act was the supposed concentration of power in the hands of commercial banks, were they to be allowed to act as intermediaries and invest in the stock markets.

This argument is related, in turn, to a genuine occurrence: the stiffening competition in the investment banking industry in the early 1930s. In addition to the traditional competition between banks and specialized intermediaries, the 1930s economic slump and, particularly, the stock market crash turned the customary rivalry between investment banks into a war to survive.

Within this context, it could be considered that prohibiting commercial banks from entering the investment banking business was a forced agreement to protect the investment banks and limit rivalry within the industry (Roe, 1994).

Another argument that was heard fairly often during that period was the supposed superiority of the universal banks over the investment banks. The reasons for this superiority were varied but can be summarized basically as follows. First, the banks had an initially low risk and, therefore, could obtain funds at a lower cost. In fact, this argument became even stronger when the deposit insurance scheme was approved.

The second reason was that the universal banks had an almost captive market of customers—due to their role as service providers for the system of payments—while the investment banks did not. Finally, the banks' network of branches, in some cases fairly extensive, gave them an edge in reaching new customers or distributing certain financial assets—bought beforehand by the bank—among their customers.

On the basis of these arguments, a number of experts of the time pointed out that commercial banks could end up dominating all segments of the finance industry, thus giving rise to a significant concentration of power. However, the truth is that business concentration in the 1930s was greater in the investment banking industry than in the commercial banking industry.

In order to offset any possible abuses of power, it could be wise not so much to limit commercial banks' activities in securities trading or issues, but rather, to encourage their involvement in such activities so that the increased rivalry would tend to push prices downwards.

Roe (1994) has used these and other arguments to formulate a complementary theory of the US financial crisis in the 1930s. He says that financial legislation in the United States since the second half of the nineteenth century prevented the creation of universal banks. The reasons for this orientation are to be looked for in three facts:

(a) the weight of US public opinion against the concentration of economic power;
(b) the restrictions on commercial banks imposed by certain lobbies;
(c) the United States federal system gave great power to the interests of each state. The states' representatives generally defended the interests of the financial institutions in their constituency, avoiding the competition of the national banks, and at the same time prevented the formation of financial groups around the large New York banks.

These restrictions help explain the high concentration of risks in certain market segments and in certain geographical areas that was borne by the US banks. The impossibility of diversifying businesses or territories only served to sharpen the effects of the crisis (Wheelock, 1995).

4. SOME CONCLUSIONS

In this chapter, we have briefly reviewed the main arguments used in the United States in the early 1930s in favour of separating commercial banking from investment banking. The ultimate reason for this separation, enshrined in the 1933 Glass–Steagall Act, was the supposed relationship between the securities trading activities carried out by some commercial banks and the catastrophic bank crash which led to the disappearance of about 11,000 banks in the early years of the decade.

However, the arguments used—often based on incomplete data—are not unequivocal. In fact, banks that combined commercial banking with investment banking were generally less sensitive to the bank crisis than the banks that confined themselves to pure commercial banking. Therefore, in terms of profitability, the number of banks that failed, or bank solvency, the arguments are not in favour of separating activities.

A plausible historical interpretation of the genesis of this Act combines two types of factor. First, there is the initial impression that, given a major stock market crash combined with a very deep economic recession, bank failures were related to the involvement of some banks in stock market activities.

The second factor underlines the specific features of interest groups in any democratic country and, particularly, in the United States. Using the argument we have just mentioned, investment banks tried to limit competition in their own business, shutting the door on the commercial banks. Thus, the ultimate reason for the separation was not a technical one—although technical arguments were brandished in favour of it—but a political one: the defence of private interests.

In this chapter, we have very briefly reviewed the conclusions of a fair number of studies of the 1930s banking crisis. The reason for this review is that the separation of commercial and investment banking activities in industrialized countries is a direct consequence of this historical, institutional, political, and economic background. In essence, the aversion to universal banking systems in the United States can only truly be understood in the light of this historical context.

However, the possible return of the United States to the universal banking system should not cause any panic. The combination of different activities within the same banking organization does not necessarily imply a greater risk or conflict of interests. The precautions to be taken, such as limiting deposit insurance to traditional commercial banking operations, seem to be perfectly reasonable.

The primary difficulty facing universal banks in the 1990s does not lie only in the possibly increased risk of their operations and, consequently, of their solvency. The chief problem is the tremendous complexity that universal banks must deal with when operating in businesses which, while sharing as common denominator the provision of financial services, differ considerably in their internal dynamics and distinctive features. Basically, the most important challenge a commercial bank must face in the 1990s is that of increasing management complexity, a challenge that is heightened by the competition from banks specializing in certain businesses.Î

4

Universal Banks versus Specialized Banks

1. INTRODUCTION

The dramatic changes that have taken place in the banking systems of industrial countries in recent years with the advent of new information technologies, financial disintermediation, deregulation, and increased rivalry have forced banks to reconsider their positioning in a changing industry facing an uncertain future. An idea of just how drastic these changes have been can be obtained from Tables 4.1 and 4.2, which show the dramatic variations that have taken place in the relative positions of the banks ranked as the largest in the USA and the world.

One of the critical issues banks must face is the choice between specialization of activities and the provision of universal financial services, that is, whether they are specialized banks or universal banks.[1] Each of these categories contains a number of models that share features of the other category. For example, within the category of universal banks, there are those that offer a very broad range of services and those that, in addition, invest directly in the equity of non-financial companies.

In Chapters 1 and 2, we discussed the advantages and disadvantages of the models of organization used to carry out financial activities: capital market-based systems and financial intermediaries-based systems. This chapter will discuss in detail the second model, that based on bank intermediation, and especially, the advantages and disadvantages of universal banking as opposed to specialized banking.

This chapter is structured around two main themes. The first, which we will cover in Sections 2 to 7, is a discussion of the advantages and disadvantages of universal and specialized banks from the perspective of the financial organizations themselves. The second theme (Section 8) is the analysis of the advantages and disadvantages of both models for a country as a whole.

Before that, however, one preliminary point must be made: in our discussion of the advantages of universal banks, we have deliberately left the analysis of the advantages and disadvantages of bank involvement in industry and industrial groups to Chapter 5. In this chapter, we will talk about the advisability or

[1] On the nature and advantages of universal banks, the literature is diverse. Among others, see Baums and Gruson (1993), Benston (1994), Llewellyn (1995), and Saunders and Walter (1994).

TABLE 4.1 *Top world banks* (by capital, US$ trillion)

1980		1994	
Bank	Capital	Bank	Capital
1. Crédit Agricole	6.2	Sanwa	22.6
2. National Westminster	5.1	Dai-Ichi Kangyo	22.4
3. Barclays	4.8	Fuji	22.2
4. Bank of America	3.9	Sumitomo	22.0
5. Citicorp	3.9	Sakura Bank	21.4
6. Banco do Brasil	3.6	Mitsubishi	19.8
7. Lloyds	3.3	HSBC	18.0
8. Midland	3.2	Crédit Agricole	17.3
9. Paribas	3.0	Citicorp	17.2
10. Algemene Spaar-en Lijfrenteras	3.0	Union Bank of Switzerland	16.2

Source: *The Banker.*

TABLE 4.2 *United States banks: ranking by capital and assets* (US$ m.)

1994			1983		
Bank	Capital	Assets	Bank	Capital	Assets
1. Citicorp	17,216	250,489	Citicorp	4,815	120,680
2. Bank of America	13,865	215,475	Bank of America	4,577	115,242
3. Chemical Banking	10,002	171,423	Chase Man.	3,286	77,050
4. Nationsbank	9,761	169,604	J. P. Morgan	2,710	54,695
5. J. P. Morgan	8,863	154,917	Manufacturers Han.	2,474	60,113
6. Chase Manhattan	8,162	114,028	Chemical	1,945	45,530
7. Bank One	7,152	88,738	First Interstate	1,789	39,330
8. First Union	4,514	77,314	Continental III	1,710	42,209
9. First Chicago	4,452	65,900	Bankers Trust	1,556	37,805
10. Bank of New York	4,025	48,879	First Chicago	1,491	34,410

Source: *The Banker.*

not of a bank deciding either to offer a very wide range of financial services, some of which have their own unique competitive dynamics, or to specialize.

2. THE SCOPE OF BANK ACTIVITIES

Increasing rivalry in the various segments of the financial industry have forced banks to reconsider their strategy both as regards the product-customer mix and the geographical range of their operations.

In this section, we will analyse the strategic refocusing undertaken by some banks in recent years. Their experience will help us to understand better not

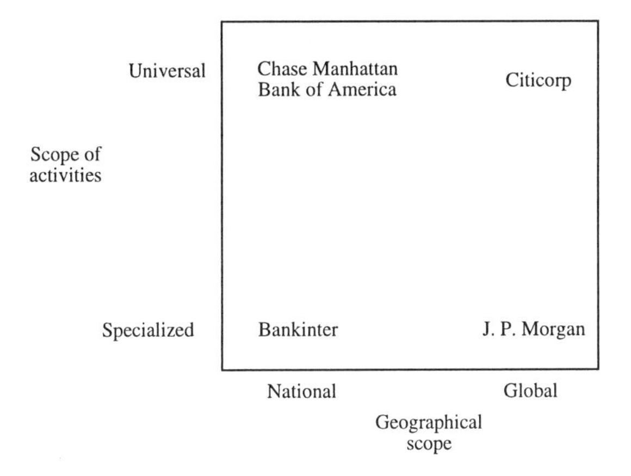

FIG. 4.1 *Universal banks: strategic focus*

only the reasons for this change but also the internal consistency of the decisions made and their fit in the outside environment. Figure 4.1 shows the positioning of the banks chosen as regards the type of business carried out and their geographical coverage.

2.1. Chase Manhattan Bank: the reorganization of a universal bank

Chase Manhattan Bank,[2] founded in 1877 in New York, is one of the large money centre banks and, right from the very start, has followed a universal banking strategy, seeking to cover all segments of financial intermediation: commercial banking, wholesale banking, money markets, capital markets, and foreign exchange markets. Its traditional rival has been Citicorp, another of the New York-based money centre banks. A major part of Chase Manhattan's business is concentrated in lending to large corporations and governments, both in the United States and abroad.

After a decade of meteoric growth during the 1960s, Chase Manhattan's performance started to fall off in the 1970s for external and internal reasons.

One of the external reasons was the ground lost in the North American bond market in the face of the strong advance by other specialized banks, such as Salomon Brothers or Citicorp. Furthermore, the collapse of the real estate market in the 1970s was a particularly hard blow for the bank, as it had invested significant resources both in financing real estate projects and in a mortgage company (the Chase Manhattan Mortgage and Realty Trust) which, at that time, was a real innovation.

One of the main internal reasons was the lack of a consistent strategic vision

[2] Chase Manhattan and Chemical Banking announced their intention to merge on 28 August 1995.

in the bank, whose efforts were divided into different businesses which neither utilized the possible synergies that could be obtained nor had the operational decentralization that would enable them effectively to compete in each of their respective businesses.

These circumstances alarmed the bank's shareholders and the financial community. In fact, as a result of that combination of factors and the increasing competition, Chase's return on assets fell below 0.5 per cent in the first half of the 1970s. This figure was considered a kind of minimum threshold below which there were clear inefficiencies.

This situation persisted into the following decade, to the point that the bank's poor performance fed occasional speculations about the possibilities of a hostile take-over bid by another bank to obtain control of Chase Manhattan and restructure it, selling off those businesses that were no longer profitable.

In a way, the situation of Chase Manhattan reflects the consequences of the dramatic changes that took place in the financial system during the 1970s—particularly intense in the United States—and the considerable difficulties experienced at that time by the universal banks (which they continue to experience) to adapt to the new situation. Some experts suggest that Chase went from being a bank that adapted slowly to change but protected its competitive advantages in the 1970s to being an absolutely passive bank, merely reacting to the changes in the environment and competitive situation, in the 1980s.[3]

The year 1982 was a particularly bad one for Chase. The reason was the occurrence of three financial fiascos within a very short period: two loans operations to brokerage companies on the North American public debt market ($117 million and $42 million, respectively) and investment in a bank that failed as a result of the energy crisis ($161 million).

The fact that these three fiascos happened in a climate of extreme anxiety about the Latin American countries' external debt crisis, which broke in August 1982, precipitated the adoption of a conservative stance by Chase's management. Now, the emphasis was on avoiding excessive risk. However, this changed outlook concealed a certain passiveness in reacting to the major changes that were taking place in the US financial industry. Thus, while Bankers Trust was transforming itself into a financial engineering company and Citibank was pushing hard for overseas growth, Chase seemed to be sunk in a certain degree of lethargy.

The perception of the urgent need for a change led Chase's senior management to implement a new action plan in 1985. The purpose of this plan was to strengthen its presence in commercial and wholesale banking in the United States, leaving the international market somewhat to one side. To this end, the bank's executive committee took a series of steps, two of which we consider particularly important.

[3] Wilson (1986) provides an interesting account of the progress of Chase Manhattan. Rogers (1993) also offers an interpretation of Chase's performance over the last 20 years and the underlying causes of its behaviour.

First was the purchase of a bank, First Lincoln Corporation of Rochester, New York, with 172 branches, and the purchase of six savings and loans associations which Chase immediately turned into commercial banks. The purpose of these actions was to increase market share in the commercial banking and medium-sized company loans segments.

The second measure was to reorganize the bank into three main areas: retail banking, investment banking, and institutional banking (including relations with financial institutions, cash management, portfolio management, and leasing). At the same time as this redistribution of businesses, with a vice-president at the head of each area, the bank's executive committee started to work on a project aimed at developing a new corporate vision for Chase, specific procedures for co-ordinating and utilizing the synergies obtained from the three major business units, and the possible development of a common culture for the various businesses.

However, these efforts failed to achieve the hoped-for results. In 1990, the bank's pretax income was so low that Chase's share price on the New York Stock Exchange fell to an all-time low.

There were two reasons for this poor performance. First were the difficulties in implementing the bank's new three-pronged strategy. The bank's managers were not used to this new way of working and their reaction was slow. Second were the difficulties experienced by the American economy at the end of the 1980s, with industries heavily damaged by the economic slowdown, strong overseas competition, and high interest rates causing major headaches to the corporate loans division.

Rumours of a hostile take-over bid or the advisability of a merger with Chemical or Manufacturers Hanover were rife in 1990. However, with the change of executive management in 1991, the bank started to climb out of its trough.

This new period opened with three major decisions. The first was the alienation of those business units that were clearly unprofitable or in which Chase had no particular expertise. These measures included the discontinuation of commercial banking operations in Europe, which Chase had found to be unprofitable and fiercely competitive; the dismantling of certain retail financial services operations such as credit cards or mortgages in Britain, where local competition was also exceptionally fierce; finally, the withdrawal from the leasing and pension fund businesses.

The second decision was to consolidate several business areas that were important for Chase: the retail banking division, which accounted for 50 per cent of the bank's total revenues in 1989, and cash management, portfolio management, and safekeeping services. Other businesses, such as operations on the capital, money, or exchange markets slipped significantly lower in the bank's priorities.

The third decision, which was closely related to the other two, was the reorganization of its businesses into three units, from which all of the bank's businesses were co-ordinated:

(a) a commercial and retail banking unit concentrated on the East Coast, seeking to operate with private households and small and medium-sized companies;
(b) a retail financial products unit for the entire United States, including credit cards, investment products, mortgages, and financing consumer durables such as automobiles;
(c) a general financial services unit, mainly targeting North American companies and Chase customers. This unit was concerned with risk management, portfolio management and international corporate banking.

Chase's senior management continued its efforts to improve the focus of the businesses it still competes in. Its results for 1993 and 1994 have shown a considerable improvement, thanks in part to the recovery of the American economy during this period and in part to the restructuring of the bank's businesses and its own internal reorganization.

However, at least two doubts still remain unresolved. First is the advisability of continuing to strive to increase business with industrial companies, particularly loan operations. Lending is invariably associated with a significant element of risk and, during periods of capital shortage, with high minimum ratios under the requirements of the Bank for International Settlements in Basle. However, investment in debt or involvement in corporate debt issues has a lower risk and does not tie up capital. Which is the right investment option for Chase?

The second doubt is that in certain businesses—for example, in international financial services—other banks are much more competitive than Chase. In fact, Chase's greatest strength is currently domestic banking. Chase's situation reflects the dilemma that many universal banks presently find themselves in: is it possible to be competitive in all segments of financial business? A few years ago, it was thought that a global universal bank could be successful. The fruitless efforts of giants such as Citibank or Deutsche Bank have shown that, for the moment, this goal is very difficult to achieve. Another unanswered question related to this is whether a universal bank not wishing to be a global bank can be competitive in countries where rivalry is intense in the various segments of banking, such as the United States or other European countries. Chase's dilemma is an accurate reflection of this situation.

Chase's merger with Chemical Banking will allow the new bank to cut down on costs and gain market share in some businesses, but will not give a clear answer to those questions.

2.2. Bank of America: geographical specialization

Bank of America was Citicorp's number one rival in the United States during the 1960s and 1970s. After two disastrous years between 1984 and 1986, when the bank lost more than 2 billion dollars in loan write-offs, Bank of America made an impressive corporate comeback, to the point that today it is one of the healthiest universal banks in the United States.

The cause of Bank of America's desperate plight in the mid-1980s was the one that most besets universal banks: strong growth in lending, increased investment in real estate and energy projects (both tremendously cyclical), and a hectic, disorganized expansion overseas that brought the bank more headaches than profits.

Bank of America's restructuring after 1987 followed three main lines of action. The first was to strengthen the retail and commercial banking unit, which had been Bank of America's home ground until the 1970s and where the bank was impressively strong thanks to its extensive distribution network. The second was to alienate lending units that had caused the bank serious problems. The third was to cut back on international activities and operate in other countries using criteria of common sense rather than the desire to be present in many locations. Thus, while the commercial banking unit is strongest in the United States, this activity has a very low profile in Western Europe. Instead, in some European countries like United Kingdom or Spain, the bank acts as an investment bank, advising companies and syndicating loans.

The results could not be more telling when compared with Citicorp. Bank of America's return on assets was 1 per cent in 1993, compared with Citicorp's 0.2 per cent. Bank of America's total net income was double that of Citicorp. Finally, its return on equity was 20 per cent, approximately four times that of Citicorp.

Bank of America's economic recovery has enabled it to make two important acquisitions, which confirm its strategy to become the leading commercial bank in the United States. The first was the purchase of Security Pacific in 1991, another large Californian bank with a strong presence in retail banking, and second was the purchase of Continental Bank in 1994, which is particularly strong in corporate business in the Chicago area.

Bank of America has chosen a strategy that departs significantly from that of Bankers Trust or Citibank. It differs from the former in its choice of future business: Bank of America continues to concentrate on retail banking and prefers not to enter the risky and uncertain business of being an active agent in financial markets. It differs from the latter in its pragmatic approach. After the 1980s crunch, Bank of America decided to concentrate its efforts on a few areas of business, mainly in the United States. Citicorp, on the other hand, is present in many areas of business and in 92 foreign countries. If a company's ability to define its strategic approach well is important, Bank of America seems to have found its particular formula for successfully competing in the global financial services market.

2.3. Bankinter: specialization in financial services

At the end of 1994, Bankinter was considered to be one of the most innovative banks in the Spanish financial system. In the space of a few years, it had succeeded in increasing the volume of deposits and its net income. Its return on assets was 1.38 per cent in 1993, after many years with returns exceeding 1.5 per cent. Its return on equity was 18.4 per cent in 1993.

Bankinter was founded in 1965, within the Banco Santander group, as an industrial bank. Since 1962, the Bank of Spain had been encouraging a certain degree of bank specialization in medium and long-term financing. These banks were called industrial banks. Thus, for many years, its main activity was to obtain funds by issuing cash warrants to finance long-term investments.

The formal end of bank specialization in 1974 and the changes that were looming on the horizon of the Spanish financial system during those years forced Bankinter to change direction. The bank therefore started to discontinue its industrial activities and operate more and more like a commercial bank.

However, the really big changes in Bankinter started to happen in 1985, when the bank decided to refocus its business completely and become a leader in the provision of financial services to medium and large-sized companies, households, and individuals above a certain income level.

However, the first signs of a significant change in Bankinter's operations came in 1987, shortly after the Bank of Spain liberalized interest rates on deposits. Bankinter launched two products at the same time: a current account paying 8 per cent interest, which was an unusually high rate at the time; and the special deposit, a short-term deposit, invested in Treasury debt, that paid its holder market rates.

Both financial products had enormous commercial success and launched the bank on its subsequent growth path. However, the bank's focus started to change again when Banco Santander launched its superaccount in September 1989 and, shortly after, a major battle broke out between Spanish commercial banks and savings banks to attract deposits.

In order to be able to maintain its position in the Spanish banking system, Bankinter restructured its businesses in 1990, creating four separate business units: private banking, retail banking, small and medium-sized company banking, and corporate banking.

In addition to restructuring its businesses, however, the most important step taken by Bankinter was the change in its use of information systems. The bank's managers sensed that the role of the traditional bank branch had changed: it seemed necessary to seek a more efficient segmentation of customers and look for the best distribution channels for each group. On the other hand, it was very expensive to maintain an extensive network of branches and, in times of increasing competition, a streamlined cost structure could provide a significant advantage. Thus, in January 1992, Bankinter started to operate in the field of phone banking with its Bktel service. This service enabled current account holders to make enquiries about their account status, open new accounts, or make transfers with a single telephone call. The service was a success: by 1994, this service already had more than 100,000 customers.

The introduction of electronic banking in a commercial bank's deposit

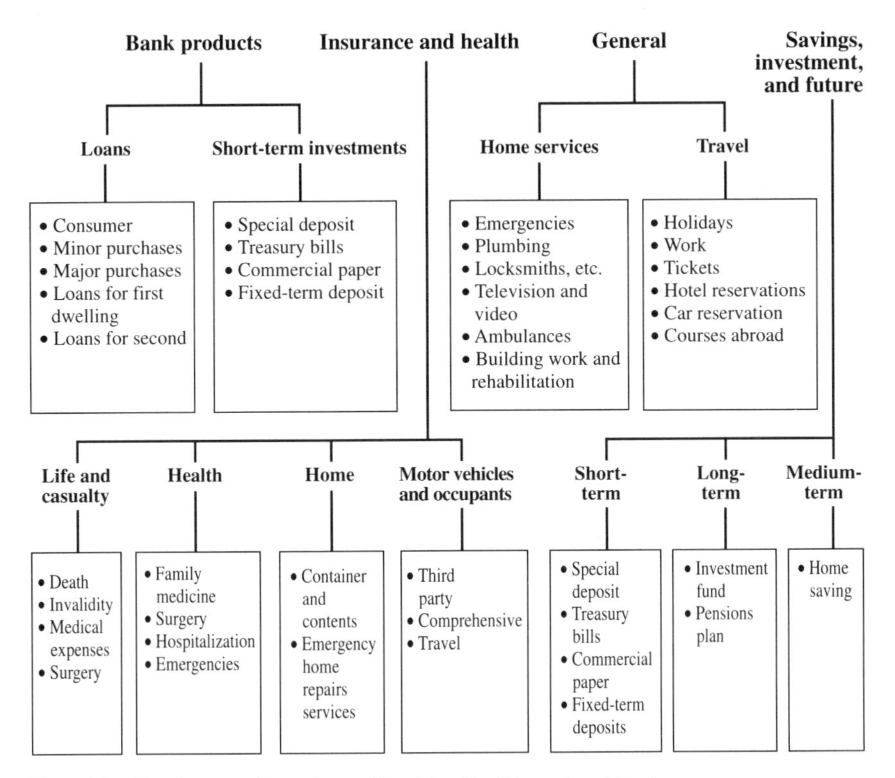

FIG. 4.2 *Products and services offered by Bankinter Servitiendas*

operations required a heavy initial capital outlay in computer equipment, but enabled the bank to achieve an extraordinary efficiency. Against a processing expenses/total revenues ratio of 0.6–0.7 per cent in many Spanish banks, the new service could be operated with a ratio of only 0.3 per cent. Productivity per employee was also increased, as the service enabled a larger number of customers to be served.

The second major innovation implemented by Bankinter was the electronic banking concept. Although this service was started in 1986, in 1991 it became a division in its own right within Bankinter, with the name of Nexo. This division provided services to companies by making it easier for them to obtain information on account balances, current account movements, payments to suppliers, domiciliations, and information on the financial markets.

The third innovation is related to the creation of a network for distributing financial products to private individuals and services to companies outside the traditional bank branches. For individuals, Bankinter started operating shops called Servitiendas. These shops mainly distribute savings instruments, such as Treasury bills, bonds, promissory notes, or mortgages. (See Figure 4.2.)

Bankinter is a clear example of reinventing banking in an environment of marked financial disintermediation. The way it regenerates the business does not consist of operating on the capital markets as a broker or a corporate consultant, as banks such as Bankers Trust or J. P. Morgan have been doing. Instead, it has chosen to segment the financial market, perform specific sales activities targeting each segment, and add value and reduce costs in the financial services that medium-sized companies and private individuals continue to demand from financial institutions. In order to achieve these goals, it has made major investments in computer equipment, which have been crucial to achieving this superior quality service at a lower cost.

2.4. Citicorp: a global universal bank

If asked to name the global universal bank *par excellence*, it is likely that financial experts will be able to agree on one name: Citicorp. First National City Corporation, Citicorp, is the name of the holding company of a group of financial institutions operating in various segments of the financial industry. This bank was formed in 1812 and its original name was City Bank of New York. In 1955, it merged with First National Bank of New York, thus marking the birth of Citicorp.[4]

By the close of the nineteenth century, it was already the largest bank in the United States, with a tradition of innovation and service acknowledged by corporate customers and rival banks alike. Before the Great Depression of the 1930s, Citibank had started on a major diversification of businesses, entering the capital market, investment banking, and international banking businesses. However, this diversification process came to a stop when Congress approved the Glass–Steagall Act.

After the Second World War, innovation in Citicorp, as in the other large American banks, dropped off considerably. The main reason for this was that the package of regulatory measures approved in the early 1930s considerably limited the bank's penetration into new businesses.

In fact, this restriction was one of the reasons that Citicorp started to promote its international banking business in the early 1960s, under the influence of its CEO, George Moore. Moore's vision consisted of two clear principles. First, give the best possible service to the American companies that were starting to expand abroad, particularly in Europe. The aim was to make Citicorp the natural choice for those American companies with business abroad. The second principle was to recruit young professionals with significant entrepreneurial and innovative potential as a key to developing the financial services that the large companies might need.

As a result of this expansion in its financial businesses, the bank started to redefine its mission: from being a mere financial intermediary, the bank wished

[4] Cleveland and Huertas (1985) describe the history of Citicorp and its successive transformations.

to become an organization that offered all the financial services that another, non-financial organization could possibly need. This vision of banking would probably be shared nowadays by all banks with a vocation in universal banking. However, in the early 1960s, this vision was far from common.

The expansion of Citicorp in the United States and the rest of the world during the 1970s and 1980s was based on a series of critical actions. First was the creation of a holding company in 1967 to guarantee that each of the bank's businesses had the decentralization and initiative it needed. Second was the consolidation of a strong retail banking sales network in the United States and the rest of the world, aimed at providing all types of financial services to households and private individuals. Third was the penetration of financial markets, particularly the exchange market, with all manner of financial instruments, in some of which Citicorp is still market leader. Fourth were major investments in information technologies. The measures described above show a vision of the financial business that goes beyond mere financial intermediation to the provision of financial services in an increasingly uncertain world. In this new world, information management was becoming a critical factor for the bank's future.

George Moore stepped down in 1967 and was succeeded by Walter Wriston, who was CEO until 1984. Wriston consolidated this strategy under the general formulation, the five I's: institutional banking, individual banking, investment banking, information technology, and, finally, insurance. During his mandate in Citicorp, the bank's business increased both in volume and in degree of diversification and complexity. However, in the early 1980s, particularly with the economic recession in the United States and the North American foreign debt crisis, Citicorp started to suffer increasing difficulties in managing the giant conglomerate with its unprecedented business diversification and geographical expansion.

Wriston was succeeded by John Reed in 1984. Until then, Reed had been chairman of the retail banking unit. The first years of Reed's management were marked by a series of external events. First were the large provisions for write-offs as a result of the Latin American foreign debt crisis. In 1987, Citicorp decided to set aside an extraordinary provision of 3 billion dollars against future losses. Second, the stock market crisis in October 1987 meant heavy losses for Citicorp. As a result of this crisis and the depression into which the stock market subsequently fell, Reed decided to cut back on the scope of activities of the investment banking division, an action which created hostility among some of the bank's senior managers.

Together with these two decisions, based in part on reasons unrelated to the bank, Citicorp made two new and interrelated decisions. First, Reed decided to enlarge the retail banking unit, in which he had worked previously, and which was profitable and less risky for Citicorp. This action also included growth abroad. Although this division's performance had been poor during the last few years of Reed's tenure there, in 1990 it generated 60 per cent of the bank's total revenues and the tendency was for this proportion to increase. Meanwhile, the lending business—particularly loans in developing countries, loans to companies, and financing large-scale projects—was experiencing major difficulties. Second, there was strong investment in information technologies, in part to strengthen the retail banking service by introducing new services such as telephone banking.

However, the economic recession in the USA at the end of the 1980s once again severely dented Citicorp's results. The downturn in company profits and the fall or stagnation of family incomes meant increased payment arrears and falling profits for the bank. Citicorp's poor performance at the end of the 1980s made it more difficult for the bank to place long-term debt issues or capital increases to finance its growing investment requirements.

This situation was paralleled by a growing complexity of the financial services industry due to the intense global rivalry in the various segments of financial activity in which Citicorp was engaged. In this respect, Citicorp seemed to be one of the sick organizations that were suffering the consequences of being universal banks and having to compete with a large number of financial institutions that were more specialized and focused in their respective businesses then the banks were.

Indeed, in the early 1990s, Citicorp was the US universal bank that offered the most financial services. Thus, the retail banking unit was very strong in a number of financial services, particularly credit cards and mortgage loans. In credit cards, Citicorp was the top US bank and the second largest financial institution, after American Express. Finally, the retail banking unit has powered Citicorp's international expansion in recent years.

On the other hand, the institutional banking unit suffered major setbacks due to the circumstances discussed above. Consequently, the bank decided to reduce significantly its involvement in pure lending activities, and also the number of professionals and volume of assets committed to these activities.

Certain products in this division have been—and still are, in some cases—important for Citicorp, such as the operations in the exchange market, risk management, transactions processing, asset securitization, and loan syndicating. However, there is still a lot of deadweight of traditional lending business.

Another major headache for Citicorp has been the investment banking division, which started to operate separately from other divisions in 1982. This unit was spun off from the other businesses to give it a greater entrepreneurial thrust. However, Citicorp came up against a problem that Bankers Trust also had to face when it decided to follow the same path: the need to pay very high compensation to the professionals it wanted to attract, in line with what other similar organizations were paying. Citicorp's main problem was that its commercial banking unit was much bigger and more profitable than this new division. Therefore, to discriminate in favour of professionals just because of the division they were working in, when it had not even proven itself, created very thorny problems in a highly competitive organization like Citicorp. In 1987, the investment banking division was merged with the institutional banking area in order to help alleviate some of the cultural problems and try to improve supervision of its operations. However, this decision and a slight dip in take-over and merger operations after October 1987 have meant that the investment banking unit now has less weight within Citicorp.

The bank also had to pay a high price for its strong global expansion. By the end of 1992, the bank operated in 92 different countries and had about 88,000 employees. It is well known that financial patterns vary from country to country and therefore a considerable amount of local adaptation is required of staff.

So, although Citicorp initially tried to operate as uniformly as possible in all countries, exporting its particular skills developed in the United States, it has had to modify this policy in view of the poor results obtained. A striking case of this organizational crisis is the bank's division in Europe, which underwent a number of major changes in focus in just five years, bewildering employees and customers alike.

Citicorp's clout in the financial services world is undeniable. The question that still remains to be answered is whether a global universal bank like Citicorp can adequately manage its different businesses in so many geographical markets with the same efficiency as a local specialist. Again, the dilemma between size and flexibility appears critical for Citicorp.

2.5. J. P. Morgan: a reconverted bank

J. P. Morgan enjoys one of the highest reputations among the US banks. Indeed, of all the major US banks, it is the only one that has managed to maintain an AAA Standard and Poor's rating for its debt in recent years.

In June 1991, the market/book value ratio was 193 per cent. The values obtained by Bankers Trust, Chase, and Citicorp on this ratio were 176 per cent, 66 per cent and 64 per cent, respectively. Its average return on assets during the 1980s was 0.93 per cent, compared with 0.76 per cent for Bankers Trust, 0.55 per cent for Citicorp, and 0.51 per cent for Chase. Its asset write-off rate was 1.2 per cent between 1970 and 1980, the lowest of the industry in the United States. These data reflect the excellent financial performance of this unique bank.

J. P. Morgan was founded as a merchant bank in 1838 in London. It started to operate in New York in 1860. In 1876, it started operations as an investment bank in the United States. When some analysts say that J. P. Morgan's reconversion has been similar to that of Bankers Trust, Morgan's managers are always quick to point out one important fact: its involvement in investment banking dates back to 1876, while that of Bankers Trust started in 1976, exactly one century later.

In fact, J. P. Morgan operated as an investment bank until the Glass–Steagall Act passed by the US Congress in 1933 mandated the separation of commercial and investment banking.

The second difference between J. P. Morgan and Bankers Trust or any other large North American bank is the combination of professional excellence and a delicate balance between innovation and tradition. This combination is what has prevented J. P. Morgan from diving head first into the junk bond or the LBO business, together with the emphasis on promotion from within instead of bringing in professionals from outside the bank who would perhaps not understand its culture, and, finally, its compensation policies which, while generous, do not seek to compete with the salaries or performance bonuses offered by other investment banks or security firms.

These facts reflect a strong corporate culture in Morgan, whose most interesting traits are the following.[5]

1. An emphasis on relationship banking and on providing a high quality service to the customer. If a customer's real financial needs are not satisfied, the bank receives nothing in return except a tarnished reputation.
2. The importance of teamwork, collegiateness, consensus, and, in contrast, the rejection of prima donnas who do not fit into the organization.
3. A series of recruitment and career design practices for young managers that include horizontal promotions, an intense socialization process with the company's values and, in many cases, a prospect of life-time employment.
4. Extreme professionalism in all of the bank's relations with its customers and between colleagues.

From the vantage point of these deeply ingrained cultural values within J. P. Morgan, this bank saw at the end of the 1970s what other US banks were also perceiving at that time: the intense financial disintermediation process and, through this, the loss of relative importance that interest and commissions on bank loans would have in the future. Until the late 1970s, J. P. Morgan's most important source of business was its wholesale banking activities, as it barely operated in commercial banking and lacked an abundant and stable source of bank deposits.

A few figures will make clear the magnitude of this change. In 1980, before refocusing its business, non-interest income—fees—accounted for only 15 per cent of J. P. Morgan's total revenues. By 1988, the share of this non-interest income had already increased to 47 per cent of total revenues and, in 1990, it was generating more revenue than the interest income from traditional lending operations.

A breakdown of the sources of non-interest income also raises a number of interesting observations. The most important activity is the financial markets business: the foreign exchange market, the public debt market, the public and private securities market, and, around these markets, the corresponding risk management instruments, including futures and options. Thus, J. P. Morgan is

[5] For a longer description, see Rogers (1993).

a world leader in interest and exchange-rate swaps. These activities accounted for about 30 per cent of total revenues in 1993.

The second business area is investment banking, particularly advising companies in sale, merger, and take-over operations. The third business area is investment and pension fund management. The fourth major business area is assets custodianship and fund transfers.

Another remarkable point is that J. P. Morgan's activities are undergoing a process of considerable geographical diversification, particularly in Europe, where this bank obtains about 40 per cent of its gross income.

There are two important factors in this strategic repositioning process. First, the change has been quite considerable, particularly when one compares the situation in 1980 with that 15 years later. However, the change has been much less traumatic than that suffered by other large bank institutions. In fact, for some analysts, J. P. Morgan has returned to its roots as an investment bank from which it was separated by the Glass–Steagall Act.

Second, this strategic change has meant, on the one hand, a reaffirmation of the bank's traditional culture (described above). In this respect, little has changed. However, the change of bank business undertaken by Morgan has required adaptation to new circumstances in certain respects: a flatter organization structure, introduction of performance-linked compensation mechanisms, emphasis on decentralization, cost control, and results by business area, and, finally, a strong commitment to information technologies, whose efficient use has become a distinctive hallmark of Morgan's new strategy.

Obviously, none of these changes guarantees that everything will go well in the future. In fact, some industry analysts have argued that J. P. Morgan's unsuccessful entry into Banesto's capital was just one indication of this bank's loss of its sense of mission within the framework of a new financial system. Perhaps this judgement is too harsh. The financial industry has changed dramatically and enormous uncertainty surrounds many decisions. Nobody, not even the best of banks, is immune from mistakenly conceived or executed decisions. In fact, the decentralized decision-making implemented by J. P. Morgan allows this sort of decision to happen without the bank's executive committee being able to monitor them efficiently a priori.

In any case, the professional experience and prestige that have been built up over many years are recommendations for a new J. P. Morgan which, in the process of its modernization, has gone back to its roots, namely, to become an investment bank that utilizes the financial disintermediation process to help its customers find the best solutions for their financing or investment decisions.

3. FINANCIAL INTERMEDIARIES' AREAS OF SPECIALIZATION: A CONCEPTUAL FRAMEWORK

Financial intermediaries specialize in response to three major decisions: those concerning the type of products they offer, those concerning the customers they

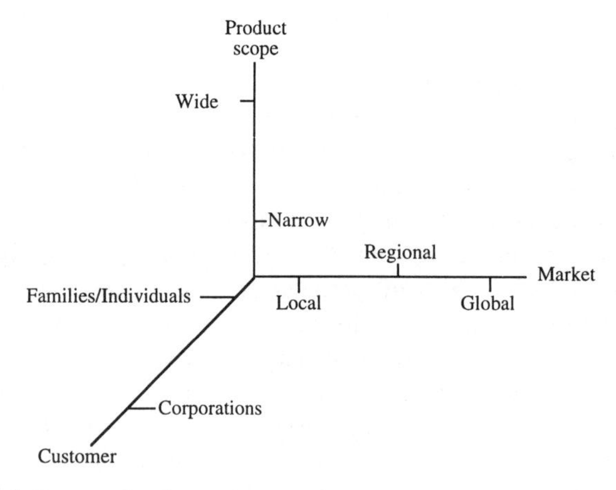

FIG. 4.3 *Banks' strategic alternatives*

target, and those concerning their geographical field of operations.These decisions shape financial organizations' strategy *vis-à-vis* their market. Figure 4.3 shows these three generic options.

When comparing universal banks with specialized banks, we refer to the type of products offered, the type of customers, and the geographical markets in which it operates. In the final analysis, products and customers are, by definition, closely related. Universal banks are those banks that offer a full range of products to a vast number of customers. Specialized banks concentrate their business in certain products for certain customers.

In this chapter, we will leave to one side the question of the geographical dimension of banking, which we will discuss in Chapter 9, and we will centre our analysis on the selection of products and customers. This will be the core theme of this section.[6]

An important feature of the financial services industry is that different financial products create markets with unique features. Consequently, when studying segmentation by products, we will refer to the particular markets in which they are offered.

A number of criteria can be used to segment financial markets. Here, we will follow one of the most widely used criteria, which is based on the main spheres of banking business: the corporate financing market, the retail financing market, the money market, and the capital markets. There follows a brief analysis of each.

[6] For a more detailed discussion of these issues, see Canals (1993). Llewellyn (1989) suggests another way of carrying out the business segmentation process.

3.1. The credit market

One of the features of the credit market is that the two parties involved in it—banks and borrowers—negotiate the conditions under which the loans are granted. Within the credit market, three main areas of activity can be identified: wholesale credit, retail credit, and mortgages.

An important development in industrial countries is the decrease in bank lending to companies, which has helped fuel the so-called financial disintermediation process by which companies have turned less and less to the classic bank loan as a means of financing. The causes for this are clear. One of the most important is the development of capital markets, which has enabled companies to go directly to them to obtain funds at a lower cost.

One of the reactions to this disintermediation process has been the emergence in the United States and Britain of the phenomenon known as securitization. By means of this process, the loans held by banks are divided into parts which, in turn, are placed with investors. The banks thus pass on the solvency risk, mobilize the credit, increase liquidity, and also obtain certain additional revenues.

The traditional bank loan is losing importance for many banks as a result of this growing rivalry. The banks that, by tradition or vocation, continue to provide this type of service to companies must also consider the possibility of placing out their loans portfolio in order to mobilize resources and reduce capital requirements.

3.2. The consumer finance market

The second category of the credit market is the consumer loan, the basic purpose of which is to finance private consumption. The most popular form of consumer credit is that instrumentalized by the credit cards although, in recent years, loans financing the purchase of consumer durables (cars, furniture, or domestic appliances) have increased enormously in companies like Spain or France. The development of this credit instrument has provided banks with the possibility of offering a new service to their customers—and thereby increasing their revenues—at the same time as it has brought them into contact with potential customers such as retail sale establishments. Hence there has been a sharp increase in competition in this market segment.

Consumers' higher standard of living and growing financial literacy hint at a significant growth in the volume of credit cards in circulation and in their use and sophistication (for example, as an intelligent card). This service will become a major source of revenues for those banks able to adapt their services continually to the increasingly stringent demands of their customers.

Although in this area banks had a good start, it would be unwise to dismiss the growing competition that will enter—and is already entering—this field of business from other areas: non-financial institutions such as Sears in the United

States, Marks and Spencer in Great Britain, or El Corte Inglés in Spain. The business is interesting but only those institutions that closely follow market developments, commit resources, and understand their customers' financial needs will be able to obtain maximum benefit from it.

Consumer credit has also increased in recent years as a result of the higher standard of living of families, their greater financial sophistication, and a more favourable attitude towards borrowing. In the atmosphere of economic growth in the late 1980s, the demand for credit from families grew considerably in almost all industrial countries and showed a low sensitivity to interest rates. Thus, the banks that have served this market segment have enjoyed substantial growth opportunities.

Mortgages are another important credit product for families. This instrument is very attractive for several reasons, although, obviously, to a varying degree—depending on the country and the magnitude of the variables that we will mention below. The first reason is the growth of the housing construction industry in recent years. The second reason is that the legal treatment of mortgages has recently been changed in many countries to enable the issue of securities backed by mortgages (mortgage shares).

The future of this business depends on the creation of an organized secondary market where shares in mortgage loans can be readily bought and sold. Obviously, this is not the only way of mobilizing mortgage credit; there are also securities backed by mortgages. However, the former has the advantage for the issuing banks that the risks are normally not computable when calculating maximum risk as a proportion of share capital. Furthermore, the shares have the advantage that investors can recover their investment as the mortgage is repaid, without having to wait for final maturity of the loan.

This feature makes these securities particularly attractive. However, their development requires a sufficiently broad secondary market. For the moment, with the exception of United Kingdom which is more advanced, the respective financial systems still have a long way to go, which is what makes it a particularly attractive business. A number of factors seem to suggest that progress will be made in this area. The first is the governments' interest in creating a large market for financing operations within the real estate industry. The second is the growing supply of products which the banks wish to offer to finance consumption and to draw new customers whom they can retain with greater ease.

3.3. The savings market

Attracting savings is one of the traditional forms of bank activity. In recent years, three events have taken place that affect this segment of activity. The first is the fall in the household savings rate with respect to the GDP in many countries. During periods of recession, the fall in savings was just one more of its consequences: disposable income was not growing and, in some cases, was shrinking, while consumption was increasing. In the second half of the 1980s, the increase in economic growth in Europe drove an overproportionate growth in consumption and a decrease in savings.

Second, the growing financial culture of savers has led them to demand increasing returns on savings deposited in banks. Obviously, this has had negative consequences for net interest income which, as we have already seen, has shrunk in many countries.

Finally, new competitors seeking to attract household savings have particularly affected the deposits received by banks. Within this area, we can distinguish three categories of competitor:

(a) the public sector, which has had to issue public debt—sometimes with a clearly favourable tax treatment—to finance its public deficit, thus attracting direct savings from the public;
(b) non-financial companies, which have replaced the classic bank loan with commercial paper, attracting a certain volume of private savings to this instrument;
(c) insurance companies, money funds, and pension funds have also contributed to this process by offering very attractive ways of placing savings, with the additional interest in some cases of offering solutions to the economic problem of retirement.

Faced with this process, banks have tried to react in recent years by offering new products—such as the high interest-bearing current accounts—or offering investment or retirement funds through subsidiaries. However, these products create significant problems for the traditional commercial banks: they increase the volume of off-balance-sheet operations, they do not allow increases in lending activity, and, furthermore, they introduce an additional risk in the bank's interest-rate management.

3.4. Money markets and capital markets

Money markets consist of a series of agents (primarily, the public sector, financial companies, and banks) that trade securities having in common a high liquidity, a well-developed secondary market, and a short maturity.

The first money market is the interbank market, used by some banks to place temporally inactive liquid funds. Other banks use the interbank market to cover maladjustments in the ratios required by the monetary authorities. In recent years, there have been new entrants in the money market, particularly the public sector and non-financial companies, with their commercial paper issues. All of these changes have provided banks with a series of liquid financial instruments having a relatively high return.

However, what may be an advantage for banks in improving their asset management may become a serious threat in attracting deposits, as we saw in the previous section. On the one hand, the securities issued by the public sector, sometimes accompanied by a package of significant tax advantages, have attracted considerable volumes of private savings. This phenomenon has not only affected deposit-taking but also the placing of any other type of instruments on these markets. On the other hand, commercial paper has taken on an increasingly important role in recent years. This instrument has had a twofold harmful effect on banks. First, it has diminished their relationship with companies, in so far as an increasing number of companies have taken to using this instrument. Second, this instrument is competing with banks as an attractive way of placing savings.

Some banks have perceived this development as a threat, while others have interpreted it as an opportunity and have chosen to offer their services as agents in placing commercial paper issues. Thus, some banks may obtain additional revenues via commissions by acting as leader in a commercial paper issue. This instrument also offers new business opportunities both with traditional customers and with prospective customers whom they can approach to offer them a new service. By entering this activity, some banks are starting to develop operations more like those of an investment bank.

The growth in capitalization volumes observed in recent years in the major international financial centres is without doubt one of the most prominent features of the new global economy. This growth has also been preceded or accompanied—depending on the individual case—by reforms of the legal framework governing the stock markets, in order to provide them with greater flexibility in their operations, heighten competition between operators, and increase monitoring by the financial authorities.

In any case, it can be said that the capital markets present an advantage and a potential risk for banks. The advantage obviously arises from the assumption that, with a rising stock market and a more open operating framework, there are greater possibilities for diversifying businesses and operating in that market with a satisfactory degree of success. However, this involvement also presents a potential risk, which in many cases has had dire consequences for certain organizations.

4. UNIVERSAL BANKS VERSUS SPECIALIZED BANKS: THE VIEWPOINT OF BANKS

From the viewpoint of banks, the arguments for or against universal and specialized banks can be articulated around the following points. First is the presumed advantages for universal banks arising from economies of scale and scope. Second is the ability to attract or retain customers on the basis of offering a broad range of financial products (the advantage of a universal bank) or a reputation for professional excellence in certain financial services (the advantage of a specialized bank). The second point also raises the possible advantages for competing more effectively in different markets or with different products, or of making cross-selling of products to the same customers. Third, there is the risk of substitution of banks by other companies. We will discuss each of these arguments to see if they shed any light on the debate between specialized banks and universal banks.

4.1. Economies of scale and economies of scope

Universal banks may offer two major types of cost advantage. There are the advantages arising from possible economies of scale: the larger the volume of operations in a certain activity for a given level of overhead or investment, the greater the organization's effectiveness. There are also the advantages arising from sharing costs between different business units, so that the total cost of offering these activities by different units is greater than cost incurred when they are offered together: these are the so-called economies of scope. Specialized banks primarily offer the advantage of greater experience in certain products or services and enjoying a reputation or image for excellence in certain segments of the banking business.

Which of the two arguments is the stronger: that of the universal bank's economies of scale or scope or that of certain specialized banks with the presumed economies of experience and benefits arising from a strong image of excellence in certain services?

There is no single answer. Ultimately, this question can only be answered by looking at the empirical evidence. There are two types of empirical evidence: statistics and case studies. Let us start with the first.

The aggregate empirical studies performed to observe the existence of economies of scale in universal banks do not give any categorical results. From a methodological viewpoint, in universal banks one should distinguish among scale economies for each one of their activities or business units. For instance, a universal bank might enjoy scale economies in its investment banking and securities units, but not in traditional commercial banking. Most of the empirical literature on scale economies in banking focuses on commercial banking. Many studies seem to confirm that the economies of scale in commercial banking are exhausted at very low deposit levels (less than 100 million dollars in deposits) (Benston, Berger, Hanweck, and Humphrey, 1983; Clark, 1988). Noulas, Ray, and Miller (1990), in a study of North American banks in which very small local banks are not included, find certain economies of scale for assets exceeding 600 million dollars. However, the evidence on the existence of economies of scale is very limited. Some studies even show diseconomies, as is the case of Mester (1992), and Saunders and Walter (1994).

However, these studies suffer from marked limitations. Studies of individual countries, such as those analysed by Clark (1988), include a small number of truly universal banks. On the other hand, the studies carried out in the United States are not significant in this context as the concept of universal bank still does not have the meaning it has in Europe, because of the regulatory limitations within which banks in the former country operate.

Furthermore, against the advantages of concreteness provided by their figures, the empirical studies have the disadvantage that they do not reveal or discuss the nature of the sources of the economies of scale or scope in universal banks, many of which may be very subtle and difficult to measure, such as the brand image of the group as a whole.

So we can see that the information provided by the empirical evidence available is not unequivocal, but rather conveys a certain amount of scepticism regarding the supposed size of the economies of scale and leaves the door open to possible advantages arising from economies of scope. The problem is that the empirical evidence of scope economies is not clear, either. The studies that suggest that they emerge with the joint use of infomation technologies (e.g., Gilligan, Smirlock, and Marshall, 1984) admit that they are small.

The basic problem faced by universal banks in realizing economies of scale is that the process of amalgamating under a single umbrella, managing and co-ordinating different businesses, is becoming increasingly complex. In other words, the economies of scope are not always found immediately because the management of universal banks has become extremely complex.

Some universal banks in Europe have improved their performance considerably as they have expanded their business lines, moving more resolutely towards the universal bank model. In Spain, we could quote Banco Santander, in Britain, Midland or Barclays. However, it is true that this improvement in performance may not be due solely to the transition towards a clearer model of universal banking but to other factors.

However, the increased revenue obtained from new business units has contributed significantly to improving performance (Canals, 1993). Consequently, the hypothesis that there exist major economies of scope cannot be dismissed.

Discussion of these concepts should be accompanied by a comparison with what happens in real life. In many banking systems, we see that there are successful universal banks and disastrous specalized banks, and vice versa. Among the successful universal banks, we could mention Banco Santander, Deutsche Bank, or the ABN–Amro Bank. Among the successful specialized banks, we could mention Banco Popular, Bankinter, or Bankers Trust.

If the advantages of one direction or the other were clear and unequivocal, then banks would tend to focus on one of the two alternatives, so that there would either be a majority of specialized banks or a majority of universal banks. When, in real life, we see better or worse managed banks in both categories, the conclusion is that, in the end, the result depends more on the quality of the bank's management than on the specialization or diversification of activities.

Consequently, the assumed cost advantages associated with universal banks as compared with specialized banks cannot be generalized. In some cases, the former will work better than the latter, as in the Spanish financial system, with banks like Santander, BBV, or Caja de Madrid. However, we also find universal banks with serious problems such as Crédit Lyonnais or Banesto. On the other hand, there are also a large number of successful specialized banks, such as J. P. Morgan, Popular, or Caixa de Catalunya, the latter two focused on the traditional financial intermediation business.

In the banking industry, it is not difficult to follow the course of universal banks that have ended up as business disasters. However, we can also identify some specialized banks, offering a narrow range of products and services, which have been forced by the industry's internal competitive dynamics to withdraw from the industry or to be taken over by or to merge with other banks. Some regional banks in France and Spain provide good examples of this type of situation.

Therefore, the experience with universal banks and specialized banks shows that it is not possible to extrapolate general experiences. There are successful specialized banks and universal banks with problems, and vice versa.

However, it is not sufficient to stop the discussion at this point. So, we will add a couple of further points. First, the question of specialization or diversification of activities must be placed in the context of an organization's experience, resources, and capabilities. When a financial organization has the resources and capabilities to carry out certain activities, the question of specialization becomes less important.

The second factor to be mentioned is that a specialized organization runs a greater substitution risk than a universal bank, for the simple reason that its business base is more limited and, therefore, more vulnerable to drastic changes in the financial services industry. On the other hand, a universal bank offering several, more or less interrelated products and services is able to rebalance its various businesses depending on internal resources and the dynamics of competition in each financial product. In other words, to use a concept taken from modern finance theory, a universal bank has an option to penetrate the more quickly emerging segments within the financial services industry. We will address this point analytically in Section 4.3.

4.2. The advantages of being a one-stop supplier for various financial services

One of the arguments used by the universal banks is that they are organizations that can offer a wide range of financial products and services to their customers, so that they do not need to depend on different financial firms. Or, to put it another way, universal banks may hold a greater appeal for the customer than the specialized banks, due to the comprehensive service they can offer. If a universal bank did not offer the more innovative products or services of a specialized bank, it might find it difficult to gain new customers or retain old ones.

This latter case is illustrated by some recent events in the German and Spanish financial systems. The explosion of investment funds as an alternative to traditional bank accounts for placing savings has forced the universal banks to enter this segment of financial business, which goes beyond the mere taking of deposits, in order to offset the slower growth or fall in the balance of current and savings accounts. Therefore, for some financial organizations, the universal banks are the model to follow if they do not wish to lose operations, customers, or both.

At this point, it should be pointed out that, in real life, companies usually work with several banks at the same time, which is an indication that the concept of the one-stop supplier of financial services perhaps does not match business reality. However, when a universal bank has a company as a customer, it has a greater chance of satisfying a greater number of its financial needs.

We would like to stress that in this section we are not talking about costs, economies of scale, or economies of scope. We are only referring to a universal bank's ability as compared with that of a specialized bank to attract and retain customers.

A variant on this argument is that universal banks are usually larger than specialized banks. A larger size is usually interpreted by the customer as meaning greater solvency. Size acts as a signal to investors (Milgrom and Roberts, 1992). This credibility or reputation factor may be particularly useful when gaining new customers or retaining old ones.

On the other hand, a specialized bank usually has an image for experience or excellence in certain financial operations; for example, in private banking, securities management, portfolio management, or financing operations for large corporations. In each of these fields, and in others, there are specialist banks with an exceptional reputation that can be used to attract any possible customer interested in these services. Names such as Goldman Sachs, Bankers Trust, or S. G. Warburg enjoy a tradition and a large pool of excellence in their respective activities.

In so far as specialized banks are able to anticipate changes in the demand for the services they offer and manage the change towards future increase in demand for those services, their possible disadvantage disappears. However, when this is not so, their vulnerability is greater than that of universal banks.

Note that this condition is also related to an aspect we have already mentioned: the resources, capabilities, and management quality of a specialized or universal financial organization. When an organization has this ability to adapt, it is less important whether it is specialized or universal. It will find it more or less difficult, depending on the case, but it will be capable of making actions in the right direction.[7]

With respect to this latter point, in organizational theory, it is usually assumed that large organizations are harder to change, or the management of the change is more complex, than in small organizations. This may be valid in some cases

[7] In section 4.3, we will formalize somewhat more this relationship between innovation, replacement risk, and adaptability.

but it is not a universal truth. It is true that smaller organizations may be more responsive in the face of change but let us not forget that it is people, not organizations, who manage and promote change. So, rather than compare universal banks and specialized banks in terms of the requirement to adapt to new competitive conditions, it would be more correct to talk of well-managed banks with the right resources and worse managed banks without the necessary resources for change.

Finally, from the revenues viewpoint, the universal banks may have an advantage—or disadvantage, depending on the circumstances, as we will see later—over the specialized banks, namely, the correlation between the revenues obtained by a universal bank's different business units. When the correlation is high—that is, the various units' revenues follow the same course—the risk to a universal bank is higher as, in the event of revenues falling in one of the units, the situation may deteriorate, simultaneously or not, in all of the business units. Therefore, economic performance is less stable.

4.3. Universal banks, specialized banks, innovation, and substitution

In Section 4.1, we pointed out the substitution risk that specialized banks run when facing a drastic change in the demand for financial services. In this section, we would like to say a little more about this phenomenon and its impact on financial innovation and the diversification of universal banks' activities.

The phenomenon of the substitution of mature financial products (for example, bank loans) by new financial services (for example, investment funds) can be analysed from two complementary conceptual approaches. The first is that of the diversification of activities within a company that is already operating in one or several different businesses. The second is that of research and product innovation. While the first approach has been amply discussed in the literature on strategic management,[8] it has barely been used to understand the nature of universal banks and, therefore, the entry of universal banks in new businesses.

A similar situation exists with respect to the product innovation approach. Although it has been developed considerably in modern industrial organization theory,[9] its conclusions have been rarely used to understand the replacement of mature products by other emerging products within the financial system.

Looking at the situation from the viewpoint of product innovation, let us consider the case of a universal bank that is studying the possibility of entering a new emerging business. This could be the case of pension funds or multiuse credit cards.

Faced with the possibility of entering one of these emerging businesses,

[8] See, for example, Chandler (1962).

[9] See Reinganum (1982, 1989) and Dasgupta and Stiglitz (1980), among others. They offer an excellent overview of these developments.

the bank should consider the following questions: How much of a threat is there that other banks will take the initiative and lead these businesses? Are there clear advantages in being the first[10] to develop and market a financial innovation? How many customers will be lost in the traditional business if we enter this new business? Does the bank have the necessary skills to compete in this new business?

One of the most intensely debated issues in the literature on innovation and R&D is which companies have the greatest incentive to innovate:[11] The industry leaders or the followers? The large companies or companies that are smaller but have a higher growth rate? The main reason for these questions is that, in the short term, innovation has a clear cost and, therefore, the company undertaking any such innovation expects that it will be able to recoup this cost in the future. On a first analysis, an industry leader[12] has less incentive to innovate because, as a result of the innovation, it may accelerate its entry into maturity or the decline of its traditional businesses. In the literature on these subjects, this is known as the replacement on substitution effect. However, if the leader is threatened by the potential entry of a competitor who may jump in ahead of it in introducing the innovation, the former will be forced to spend to innovate and thus avoid losing customers.

In fact, under certain conditions, the newcomer or the smaller financial firm may have a greater incentive to enter. Scherer and Ross (1990) offer an argument that we will modify and apply to our case. Let us suppose that both banks can launch the product almost at the same time, which is fairly common in the banking industry, where product imitation does not pose any significant complexity. Let us consider that bank A, on the basis of its market share in deposits, can capture 70 per cent of the new product, while bank B can capture the other 30 per cent.

Figure 4.4 shows the revenue split obtained by both banks introducing the product on the same day. However, let us suppose that if one of the banks introduces the product two months, say, before the other, it can capture an additional 25 per cent of the other bank's revenue. In this case, it is obvious that bank B has a better chance of capturing a larger volume of business if it gets in ahead of bank A. However, we should not forget that the latter, due to its specific situation, has an equivalent cost in the event that it does not innovate. The final result depends on the two banks' reaction and possible collusion.

Until now, we have only considered the economic incentives that a bank, in particular, has to innovate in financial products. However, in a broader and more dynamic framework, the decision a bank will make will depend on two factors: the additional revenues it expects to obtain by distributing the new

[10] See the review by Lieberman and Montgomery (1988).

[11] Dasgupta and Stiglitz (1980), among others, formalize this issue.

[12] In the literature, one usually talks of 'races' between two companies to win first place in the technological dispute. See, for example, Harris and Vickers (1985) and Reinganum (1982).

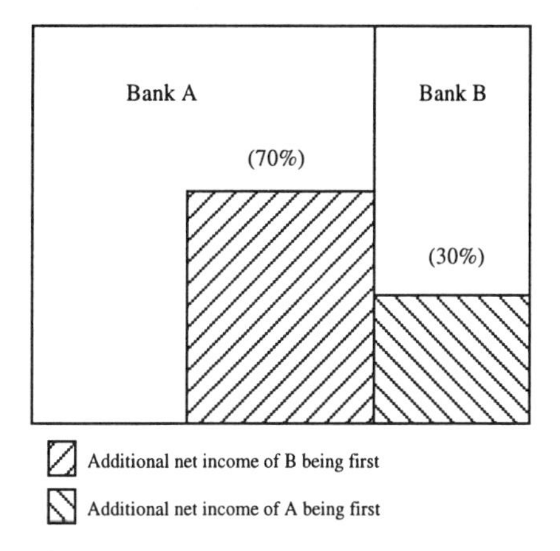

FIG. 4.4 *Net income distribution bewtween two banks*

financial service—in part, already discussed—and the cost of developing the innovation and offering the financial service. Within the costs, we should also include the loss of net income (income less direct expenses) arising from a possible cannibalizaton of the bank's products which would be partly replaced by the new products.

In particular, in any period t_i, the results arising from an innovation for the bank will be:

$$c_i \alpha D_o - MF_i D_0 - G_i - R_i, \tag{1}$$

where c_i is the commission charged for selling the new financial service generated by a business, D_0 is the volume of resources in old products cannibalized by the innovation, α is the percentage of D_0 that the bank is able to retain, MF_i is the financial margin on the funds D_0 that the bank would have if there was no innovation in new services—that is, if there were no cannibalization, G_i are the marginal expenses for managing the new financial service and R_i is the imputation of the expenses incurred in developing the new financial service to the period i.

In principle, the bank will be interested in innovating in new financial services provided that:

$$c_i \alpha D_o - MF_i D_0 - G_i - R_i > MF_i D_0, \tag{2}$$

that is, that the results after the innovation exceed those before the innovation, after discounting the replacement effect. Observe that the coefficient α already includes the cannibalization of funds, both by the bank's own actions and by the rival bank's actions.

Therefore, bank A will innovate provided that:

$$c_i \alpha D_o > G_i + R_i. \tag{3}$$

In principle, the larger are α and c_i, the greater is the expectation that the bank will obtain positive results with the innovation. The problem for some banks is that the percentage α of deposits that it has managed to retain in new products has not been very high and the intense rivalry has reduced the value of the commission c_i.

The formalization of the innovation process we have outlined in this section gives limited results. However, our purpose has been to underscore two points. First, the process of replacing a series of financial products by others can be analysed under the prism of R&D models. Second, on the basis of this prism, a bank's entry into new financial businesses may be interpreted as a competition to get a head start in launching the product on the market and thus capitalize on the advantages of being the first, or to prevent other banks taking away its customers.

In this case, the advantages of being the first to launch the product may consist of gaining new customers (to whom, furthermore, the bank may be able to sell other products), raising the customer's switching costs to other banks, attracting a greater volume of funds, enabling it to achieve economies of scale, or developing a special corporate image (that of leader, for example). Obviously, on the cost side, there are those arising from the cannibalization of present revenues (equation (2)) and uncertainty about the evolution of the demand for the new product.[13]

5. UNIVERSAL BANKS AND SYNERGIES: A CONCEPTUAL MODEL

5.1. The model's general framework

In this section, we will sketch a model that will enable us to understand better the rationale of a universal bank compared with a specialist bank from the viewpoint of synergies. We will discuss the critical variables influencing a universal bank's choice of corporate strategy and, therefore, what should be the ideal field for its businesse. We will first introduce a general case, which we will expand in the next section.

Let us consider a universal bank with two business units: unit A could be a commercial banking unit while unit B could be a corporate banking unit. The bank's total profit, BT, is equal to:

$$BT = BT_A + BT_B - C, \tag{4}$$

where BT_A and BT_B are the total profit of A and B, respectively, and C is the cost of the bank's corporate centre that sets and co-ordinates the bank's cor-

[13] Lieberman and Montgomery (1988) offer an excellent review of the advantages and costs of companies who act first.

porate strategy. In this case, C could be interpreted as the total of the bank group's co-ordination, contract design, and monitoring costs.

Let us assume that there may be the following relationship or synergy between divisions A and B. Unit B obtains a profit B_B with a probability of 1 in a baseline situation. Unit B may spend C_B to obtain an additional profit which is added to the ordinary profit B_B which B would obtain in any case. The probability of its obtaining this additional profit with the cost C_B is P_2. This expenditure could be, for example, the bank's generic advertising. The probability of this additional profit not being obtained is $1 - P_2$. Let us suppose that there are no intermediate results: either the additional profit is achieved or it is not achieved. On the other hand, we formulate the hypothesis that $\beta > C_B$ as, otherwise, B's managers would never incur the expense. Therefore, B's total profit, BT_B, will be:

$$BT_B \begin{cases} B_B & \text{with probability 1 (irrespective of the corporate strategy)} \\ B_B - C_B & \text{with probability } (1 - P_2) \\ BT_B = B_B - C_B + \beta & \text{with probability } P_2. \end{cases} \tag{5}$$

Unit A obtains a profit B_A with a probability of 1 irrespective of B. However, if unit B spends C_B and obtains an additional profit β, unit A may benefit from the expenditure by B (to continue with the example, in the bank's generic advertising) by the amount α, with a probability P_c. Therefore, A's total profit, BT_A, will be:

$$BT_A \begin{cases} B_A & \text{with probability 1 (irrespective of the corporate strategy)} \\ B_A & \text{with probability } (1 - P_2P_c) \\ B_A + \alpha & \text{with probability } P_2P_c. \end{cases} \tag{6}$$

From the viewpoint of the bank's management, the bank would come out best if it invested and managed both units corporately provided that:

$$BT = BT_A + BT_B - C > B_A + B_B, \tag{7}$$

that is:

$$\begin{aligned} BT = {} & B_A(1 - P_2P_c) + (B_A + \alpha)P_2P_c + (B_B - C_B)(1 - P_2) \\ & + (B_B - C_B + \beta)P_2 - C > B_A + B_B. \end{aligned} \tag{8}$$

Otherwise, the best option would be for each unit to operate with autonomy, without any corporate strategy.

Grouping terms,

$$\begin{aligned} BT &= B_A\{(1 - P_2P_c) + (P_2P_c)\} + \alpha P_2P_c + B_B\{(1 - P_2) + P_2\} \\ &\quad - C_B(1 - P_2) + (-C_B + \beta)P_2 - C \\ &= B_A + \alpha P_2P_c + B_B - C_B + \beta P_2 - \text{C}. \end{aligned} \tag{9}$$

In the light of this result, we can say that the bank would do best to adopt a corporate strategy[14] if the following condition is met:

$$B_A + \alpha P_2 P_c + B_B - C_B + \beta P_2 - C > B_A + B_B. \tag{10}$$

Grouping terms,

$$\alpha P_2 P_c - C_B + \beta P_2 - C > 0, \tag{11}$$

that is,

$$\alpha P_2 P_c + \beta P_2 > C + C_B. \tag{12}$$

The interpretation of this result is immediate. A universal bank makes sense when the expected profits obtained from joint actions exceed the specific costs of such actions plus the overheads of the group's corporate management.

This model differs from that elaborated by Rotemberg and Saloner (1994) in several respects. The model presented here indicates the possible sources of synergy between A and B in a context consistent with the hypothesis of the economies of scope or synergies, while those authors' model centres on the agency problems and the incentives of the two units' managers to innovate. We consider that the first critical decision that a universal bank should tackle is what advantages a universal bank has over a specialist bank. Or, to put it another way, are corporate strategy's benefits greater than its costs? If it passes this test, it will be followed by the incentives issue.

In the next section, we will develop a somewhat more general model that partly includes this aspect. One important difference is that Rotemberg and Saloner discuss a multiple-period model, drawn on the behaviour structure modelled by Hart and Moore (1988), while the model discussed here has only one period. This is an interesting extension which we do not consider here.[15]

5.2. *An extension of the general model*

In this section, we will consider a universal bank with a centralized corporate management that diversifies its activities into two divisions: division A and division B (Canals, 1995b). These divisions may correspond, as in the previous case, to the commercial banking division and the corporate banking division.

The expected profit of division A is B_A. This profit may be larger, $B_A + \alpha$, if division A is prepared to invest, for example, the quantity I_A in information systems. The probability of α is P_1.

For its part, division B has an expected profit equal to B_b. However, if this

[14] We assume that, in this case, the corporate strategy consists not only of managing and co-ordinating the two units A and B but of looking for synergies from expenses (or investments) like C_B.

[15] Faulí-Oller and Giralt (1995) approach this issue from another viewpoint by developing a model of a diversified company with several divisions which offers several reasons for co-operation or rivalry between divisions.

division spends the quantity I_B in information systems, its profit may increase to $B_B + \beta$ with a probability of P_2.

Also, as a result of the interrelationships between divisions A and B, this increased investment by B in information systems (or any other expenditure or investment that can be shared by both divisions) may give rise to an increase α_c in A's profits, with a probability of P_c.

However, division A is more interested in investing in its own information system than obtaining a marginal utilization of the system developed by B. Let us suppose that this relationship is asymmetrical: if A invests in its own information system, the value for B is nil. One possible reason is that it may be very difficult or useless to adapt for B the information that is useful for A. We will assume that A and B amortize the investments I_A and I_B in n years.

If division B carries out its investment project and it has a positive impact α_c for A with a probability of P_c, in this case, A's profit will be $B_A + \alpha_c$. We assume that division A prefers to carry out its own investment I_A, although for the universal bank, it may be interesting to forget about division A's investment if the investment in B is satisfactory.

For the corporation or universal bank as a whole, the total profit will be the sum of both business units' profits, less the management and co-ordination cost C. In particular, the value for the universal bank of division B's decisions in any period i is the following:

$$B_B - \frac{I_B}{n} + \beta P_2 + \alpha_c P_c P_2, \tag{13}$$

if B's decision has a positive effect on division A, and:

$$B_B - \frac{I_B}{n} + \beta(1 - P_2), \tag{14}$$

if B's decision does not have an effect on division A.

For their part, the value of A's decisions for the bank will be:

$$B_A - \frac{I_A}{n} + \alpha P_1 - \alpha_c P_1 P_2 P_c, \tag{15}$$

and:

$$B_A - \frac{I_A}{n} + \alpha P_1(1 - P_2). \tag{16}$$

Equation (15) shows A's contribution to the company's value when both A and B's decisions are positive. Equation (16) shows the value of A for the bank when A's investment decision gives positive results while B's decision does not.

The value of both decisions for the company will depend on whether division B obtains satisfactory results that benefit A or not, as this factor has implications in division A.

In the event that division B does not obtain satisfactory results for A, the corporate group's profits will be:

$$B = BT_A + BT_B - C$$
$$= B_A - \frac{I_A}{n} + \alpha P_1(1 - P_2) + B_B - \frac{I_B}{n} + \beta P_2 - C. \tag{17}$$

Therefore, the corporate group will be interested in managing both divisions provided that:

$$\alpha P_1(1 - P_2) + \beta P_2 > C. \tag{18}$$

For values $\alpha + \beta < C$, the corporate strategy is always meaningless. If $\alpha + \beta > C$, the final outcome will depend on the values of the respective probabilities. In principle, the lower P_2 and the higher P_1, that greater the likelihood that (18) will be met.

On the other hand, when company B obtains satisfactory results for A, the group's profits will be:

$$B = BT_A + BT_B - C = B_A - \frac{I_A}{n} + \alpha P_1 - \alpha_c P_1 P_2 P_c$$
$$+ B_B - \frac{I_B}{n} + \beta P_2 + \alpha_c P_c P_2 - C. \tag{19}$$

Therefore, the corporate group will be interested in grouping and managing both divisions in a co-ordinated fashion provided that:

$$\alpha P_1 - \alpha_c P_1 P_2 P_c + \beta P_2 + \alpha_c P_c P_2 > C. \tag{20}$$

Grouping terms,

$$\alpha P_1 + \beta P_2 + \alpha_c P_c P_2 > C + \alpha_c P_1 P_2 P_c. \tag{21}$$

The results obtained enable us to discuss (only tentatively) in what conditions a universal bank may have clear advantages over a specialist bank. In particular, the result expected in (21) suggests that the universal bank will be interested in increasing its operations' complexity and managing them in a co-ordinated fashion provided that the profit from both divisions implementing their projects plus the profits from the presumed synergies, $\alpha_c P_2 P_c(1 - P_1)$, exceed the co-ordination costs plus the costs of incurring in an additional expense $\alpha_c P_1 P_2 P_c$ when both units implement both projects.

6. UNIVERSAL BANKS AND SPECIALIZED BANKS FROM THE VIEWPOINT OF ORGANIZATIONAL ECONOMICS

In order to understand and formalize better the critical issues concerning the organizational problems of universal banks, in this section we will briefly review these issues using a strictly formal approach: the contributions made by what is today called Organizational Economics (Milgrom and Roberts, 1992).

From the viewpoint of Organizational Economics, a universal bank, following a terminology developed by Alchian and Demsetz (1972) can be considered as a nexus of contracts with two basic types of link. First, the links between the bank's workers and the various organizations—if there is more than one—in which they perform their professional services. Second, the links, legal or purely organizational, between the universal bank's different business units.

In particular, when a universal bank is structured as a holding company, these links are what relate each business unit with the holding company and the additional organizational or legal links that bind together the different business units. An example of the latter type would be the relationships between the commercial banking division and the corporate banking division within a universal bank.

Of the two types of link, in this section we will consider those that concern the relationships between the various business units under a single parent company. The parent company acts as the corporate headquarters. We will therefore not consider the contractual relationships between the employees and the various companies with which this universal bank operates.

Let us start with a very general question. What is the *raison d'être* of universal banks? In principle, a specialized bank exists because the cost of organizing financial intermediation activities through a company is lower than if these activities are organized and carried out in open markets.[16] The existence of a universal bank, on the other hand, cannot be justified by the same reasons. Indeed, a universal bank only has meaning in so far as the management of its various business units is more effective if conducted within the universal bank than if each one were operated separately, as if they were specialized banks.

Among the possible advantages of a universal bank over a specialized bank, there is the possible existence of economies of range between the various businesses, the creation of an internal capital market, and the supposed diversification of risks within the banking group itself.

We will not discuss these arguments here. Let us suppose that a banking group has decided to operate as a universal bank, with different business units under the same corporate umbrella. We propose to discuss now the main dilemmas and organizational problems that are specifically posed by a universal bank.

The first specific problem of universal banks is the agency problems[17] that are generated between the managers of the corporate headquarters and the managers of each of the business units. In general, agency problems appear as soon as there is a separation between the owner and the manager or employee who

[16] See Coase (1937) and Arrow (1974) on the concept of organization as an alternative to the market.

[17] On agency theory and agency costs, see, among many other authors, Jensen and Meckling (1976), Holmstrom (1979) and Ricart (1987).

must carry out the plans drawn up by the owner or the top manager.[18] The principal offers the agent a contract so that the latter may carry out a certain activity. In turn, the agent may have information that the principal does not have. There can be two types of asymmetric information problems. The first is that the agent has private information, which leads to adverse selection problems. The second is that the principal cannot control the agent's actions, which generates the problem known as moral hazard.

These agency problems are different from those that occur within a specialized bank with a simpler organization structure. In the latter, the agency problem is that the incentives of the managers of each of the universal bank's business units may or may not be compatible with the corporate headquarter's general objectives.

The agency costs in a universal bank consist of the costs of designing the explicit contracts between the corporate headquarters and the business units, the cost of supervising them, and the cost of ensuring fulfilment of the commitments that have been taken on. Normally such contracts do not have any legal force—with the exception of those which the corporate headquarters so establishes—but rather are involved with the creation of goals and policy systems, performance appraisal methods, and remuneration systems which the corporate headquarters decides to apply to the corresponding business unit.

A second problem concerning universal banks, and related to the fact that the various agents involved have asymmetric information,[19] is the moral hazard problem. As we have already indicated, this problem arises when those who have important information within the organization have interests that are different from those of the people responsible for making a decision with that information. This situation opens the door to possible opportunistic behaviour, by which those who have the information may manipulate it so that they benefit by the decision the individual must make.

The moral hazard[20] is a classic problem in an insurance company or a commercial bank that accepts deposits: the existence of a deposit guarantee fund, that guarantees depositors the full amount or part of the deposits if the bank should fail, may induce certain banks to adopt excessively risky investment policies. The bank's managers know that if the bank fails, there will be no financial panic as the guarantee fund covers the amount of the deposits.

In a universal bank, moral hazard may arise between the business units and the corporate headquarters. For example, in financial operations requiring fast

[18] In turn these may concur or not with the objectives of the bank's shareholders. However, for the moment we are not discussing this type of agency problem but that which occurs between a bank's business units and its corporate headquarters.

[19] The more general asymmetric information problem is also found in the above-mentioned agency problems. In general, a distinction can be made between precontractual asymmetric information problems and post-contractual asymmetric information problems. Moral hazard problems are post-contractual problems.

[20] See, for example, Arrow (1974) and Pauly (1968).

decisions—such as operations in the foreign exchange markets, in the secondary product markets, or in the money markets—a great deal of decentralization is required, with funds being allocated to the various units to handle autonomously. This case raises two different aspects of the moral hazard problem.

The first dimension is the nature of the information that flows from the business unit to the corporate headquarters. The problem is that this information is usually conveyed a posteriori, that is, after the operations have already been carried out. Therefore, once the operations have been executed, whether they are good or bad for the bank, the decisions are already irreversible and can only be offset, if they have been negative, by better operations in the future.

In addition, in such operations, the business unit's agent or agents usually earns an additional bonus linked with the profits gained from his operations, while he does not lose part of his fixed salary if the operations lose money. In other words, his income structure is asymmetrical and benefits from making high-yield decisions, which are those that bear most risk. However, the consequences of negative results in high-risk operations are borne not by the agent or the unit in which the agent operates but the universal bank as a whole.

We are therefore faced with a clear case of moral hazard in a universal bank. Observe that this problem may also exist in a specialized finance company between the company's agents and owners. However, the existence of universal banks raises additional problems such as those we have just described.

A third organizational problem faced by universal banks is that of the costs of co-ordinating the various business units. In general, co-ordination problems come about as a result of the specialization of the work performed by different people or different units within an organization.[21]

Each person or unit usually has partial or incomplete information about the rest of the organization. Consequently, it is vital to find formulas that enable this information to be shared and achieve efficient actions. One of the specific goals of this co-ordination in a universal bank is to use the supposed synergies that exist between the different business units to achieve concrete results such as a lower general cost level or increased revenues.

Again, the co-ordination problem, which is a classic problem of any organization (Williamson, 1975), has particular aspects in universal banks that make it different from the co-ordination problem within a specialized bank.

There are several types of solution to co-ordination problems:

(a) an organizational design that takes into account the different information requirements of each of the agents involved in the process;
(b) correctly allocating each agent's responsibilities;
(c) creating formal communications channels between the various agents involved;
(d) setting up control and compensation mechanisms.

[21] For a general formulation of the problems of resource allocation and co-ordination, see Cooper and John (1988).

A fourth organizational problem is related, in a way, to the co-ordination problem. This is the so-called organizational problem with design attributes (Bolton and Farrell, 1990; Milgrom and Roberts, 1990). Business problems with design attributes are those that occur in any organization when the information available to make reasonably good decisions[22] is very abundant and, furthermore, when the cost of not making the right decision, or of not achieving the right degree of co-ordination between the various individuals taking part in it,[23] can be very high.

In such cases, highly decentralized solutions do not work well—an extreme solution would be to organize these transactions on an open market: in this case, the price mechanism is not an efficient mechanism. Centralizing the decision usually gives more efficient results.[24]

At the business level, problems with design attributes arise when economies of scale, economies of range or scope, or complementary qualities are obtained between the products offered by the same company (Bulow, Geanakoplos, and Klemperer, 1985). When any of these circumstances exists, the best solution usually consists of centralizing activities in an organization.

A fifth key organizational problem in a universal bank is the motivation problem, which occurs on two organizational levels. The first is between employees in the same division. This is a common problem in any specialized bank and so we will not discuss it here.

The second is the problem of the compensation systems and career patterns followed by managers with the same ability and basic training in different units, for example the commercial banking unit and the investment banking unit. These businesses have different competitive features and different skill demands. It is therefore logical that the motivation systems be different. However, these differences could generate a certain amount of distrust between managers in different divisions, which could destroy any possibilities of co-operation between different businesses.

Universal banks have a sixth problem, related to motivation: how to design reward and compensation systems within the bank to avoid opportunistic or self-interested behaviour by decision-makers that is not in the interests of the bank as a whole. In general, this is also a problem that any organization faces.[25]

[22] Economists who have worked on these issues would talk of optimal solutions. However, we know that optimal solutions to organizational problems in the world of real-life organizations do not exist: at the very most, there will be ideal solutions according to certain contingent variables which, as soon as they change, will also modify the organizational solution (Lawrence and Lorsch, 1967).

[23] These problems arise in those decisions in which it is essential to synchronize the various decisions. One example of these synchronization problems occurs in task forces within a car manufacturing or assembly plant or between production and sales departments in a company that works to order and with significant production capacity limitations.

[24] Macho-Stadler and Pérez-Castrillo (1992) offer an excellent introduction to the decentralization problem. Vickers (1985) proposes pioneering models of the delegation problem.

[25] Again, some refinements are necessary. In general, the concept of Pareto efficiency, defined as that state that cannot be improved without harming one or other of the agents involved in it, is

Finally, there is an additional problem that occurs in universal banks that is typical of all complex organizations. This is the so-called influence cost.[26] Influence costs belong to the more general problem of rent-seeking activities, that is, those activities that are not productive and which seek to modify income distribution between different groups of individuals. The defence of protectionist interests for certain sectors of the economy is a clear example of an income-seeking activity (Tullock, 1967).

In complex organizations such as universal banks, influence costs arise in those activities or decisions that seek to transfer costs or income from one set of business units to another. For influence costs to be incurred in an organization, there must be decisions that establish ways of distributing costs and profits within the organization as a whole. It is obvious that such decisions exist in a universal bank (in general, in any diversified company) and they are the subject of frequent discussion between managers.

If influence costs are inevitable, the question that is raised is whether they can be controlled or their impact minimized. There are some general criteria for achieving this objective: decentralize the resource-allocation and decision-making process as much as possible; try to limit the negative consequences of possible income redistributions, for example, by setting similar remuneration structures in all of the corporate group's units; or establish, or agree, a priori the policies affecting resource distribution with the commitment not to revise the decision. The very nature of these general criteria indicates that the likelihood of such criteria working in practice is very limited. In fact, on occasions they may create unnecessary rigidities and, in some cases, greater rigidities than those they seek to solve.

In order to solve these complex organizational decision problems facing universal banks, it is necessary to combine two indispensable elements. The first consists of using those organizational forms that minimize, a priori, the costs deriving from the inefficiencies described above. One concrete way of doing this is through a holding organization structure in which each business becomes a unit with a high degree of autonomy but with certain performance measurement systems and reward and internal promotion mechanisms that facilitate co-operation between business units; in other words, the aim is to design systems that truly enable benefits to be gained from the possible synergies that may exist within a universal bank.

The second element required is the eradication of these inefficiencies, such as those deriving from asymmetric information, moral hazard, and influence costs. The only way to achieve this goal—or to steer the organization towards its achievement—is for the organization's top management to create the

useful from a conceptual viewpoint, but not very practical in decision-making. One incentives system would be more efficient than another under a certain set of circumstances. If these change, the system will lose this greater efficiency it had.

[26] See, for example, Milgrom (1988) and Milgrom and Roberts (1988).

conditions, in both the formal and informal systems, so that the universal bank has opportunities not only to earn money but also to learn and work in an atmosphere of trust.[27] All three dimensions are necessary. None of them by themselves guarantee that the problems will be eliminated. Neither does an adequate combination of all three guarantee this, although it could be said that, when this combination is obtained, the possibilities of minimizing conflicts and their consequences are better than ever.

This final point is important. Companies are dynamic. The more complex they are, the more dynamic they become. This means that supposedly optimal solutions obtained in certain economic models are valid under certain very limited conditions and, normally, in a static context. However, the functioning of real-life organizations shows the opposite features: it is not possible to establish certain conditions because of the extremely varied nature of reality and the occasionally hectic pace of the organization's dynamics.

In spite of these caveats, the economic models have often contributed interesting concepts that have helped obtain a better definition of the problems of complex problems and propose solutions that, without being optimal, may be less inefficient than those currently available.

7. UNIVERSAL BANKS AND SCALE: SOME REASONS BEHIND BANK MERGERS

Increasing competition in the financial services sector has generated a race to consolidate the industry and achieve a greater scale as a necessary prerequisite for improving efficiency. Table 4.3. shows the main bank mergers between January 1992 and June 1995. Behind strategies to increase market share is an implicit hypothesis that a greater market share is always equivalent to greater profitability. However, experience shows that this relationship is not always so clear. Some medium-sized banks are more profitable than many large banks. On the other hand, there are large banks that are extraordinarily profitable, such as J. P. Morgan, Banc One, or Banco Santander.

However, the scale argument does not end here. There are banks that have thought that the best way of increasing size by a relatively quick route is merging with another bank. In the banking industry, alliances cannot be used to achieve economies of scale and internal growth is a very slow process. Thus, the least bad path is often mergers or take-overs.[28]

The Spanish banking industry, within the EU as a whole, is one of those that has undergone most consolidation since 1988 through mergers and take-overs.

[27] These dimensions have been taken from Pérez-López's conceptual model of organizational design (1993). In his study, these dimensions are called effectiveness, efficiency, and consistency.

[28] In this section, we do not aim to discuss at length the reasons for and the empirical evidence on mergers and acquisitions. Among others, see Manne (1965), Jensen (1986), Roll (1986), Fama (1980), Shleifer and Vishny (1986) and Williamson (1985).

TABLE 4.3 *Major mergers among the largest banks*

	1992–1993				1994				1995				
	Ranking	Capital ($m.)	Assets ($m.)	Ratio %	Ranking	Capital ($m.)	Assets ($m.)	Ratio %	Ranking	Capital ($m.)	Assets ($m.)	Ratio %	Capital %
Mitsubishi	5	15,928	424,348	3.77	6	17,651	458,906	3.85					
Nippon Trust	296	801	10,986	7.29	281	909	12,982	7.01	6	19,832	547,737	3.62	3.2
Bank of Tokyo	22	8,977	220,956	4.06	18	10,570	242,445	4.36	14	12,495	271,214	4.61	7.3
Swiss Bank Corp.	23	8,847	137,981	6.41	28	9,139	139,891	6.53	19	11,607	161,807	7.17	7.6
S. G. Warburg	190	1,396	29,114	4.97	179	1,567	33,472	4.68	183	1,679	31,050	5.41	4.0
ING	24	8,598	178,461	4.82	15	11,068	174,888	6.33	62	5,202	125,343	4.15	16.4
Barings	505	384	6,789	5.65	489	432	8,796	4.91	545	432	8,796	4.91	37.9
Bank of America	25	8,580	179,371	4.78	13	12,058	186,933	6.45					
Continental Bank	199	1,299	22,315	5.82	147	1,923	22,601	8.51	12	13,865	215,475	6.43	28.7
CS Holding	32	7,384	171,259	4.31									
Swiss Volksbank	174	1,516	31,649	4.79	26	9,337	234,190	3.99					
Neue Aargauer Bank	567	320	6,565	4.88	607	320	6,565	4.88	17	12,055	298,359	4.04	12.0
Banca di Roma	36	6,847	77,774	7.00	45	6,035	89,586	6.74	63	5,139	93,373	5.50	1.1
Banca Nazionale Dell'Agricoltura	362	599	27,613	2.17	243	1,061	33,452	3.17	342	790	26.407	2.99	−47.3
Dresdner Bank	40	6,254	204,178	3.06	37	7,077	220,562	3.21	35	8,856	253,818	3.49	13.2
Kleinwort Benson	357	609	15,582	3.91	349	684	18,574	3.68	359	750	14,232	5.27	20.6
San Paolo Bank	48	5,082	161,937	3.14	46	5,921	147,072	4.03	47	6,215	153,115	4.06	6.3
Banca Nazionale delle Comunicazione	451	450	3,028	14.87	481	450	3,028	14.87	594	389	3,415	11.40	2.1

TABLE 4.3 (*cont.*)

	1992–1993				1994				1995				
	Ranking	Capital ($m.)	Assets ($m.)	Ratio %	Ranking	Capital ($m.)	Assets ($m.)	Ratio %	Ranking	Capital ($m.)	Assets ($m.)	Ratio %	Capital %
National Australia Bank	55	4,670	64,960	7.19	59	4,599	66,603	6.90	49	6,034	81,215	7.43	34.9
Michigan National Bank	305	772	10,690	7.21	303	802	10,252	7.82	340	794	8,727	9.09	15.5
Banco Santander	73	3,719	61,527	6.04	80	3,640	73,430	4.96					
Banesto	80	3,416	60,747	5.62	110	2,517	38,652	6.51	66	4,990	114,174	4.37	27.7
Credito Italiano	89	2,989	74,544	4.01	120	2,370	70,093	3.38	104	3,084	74,823	4.12	3.4
Credito Romagnolo	227	1,061	33,452	3.17	362	599	27,613	2.17	278	1,010	22,382	4.51	11.2
First Union	92	2,925	51,174	5.71	62	4,363	70,787	6.16	74	4,514	77,314	5.84	31.9
First Fidelity	176	1,501	30,066	4.99	121	2,324	33,786	6.88	149	2,240	36,214	6.19	29.3
Fleet Financial	101	2,729	47,115	5.79	82	3,496	47,914	7.30	95	3,615	48,727	7.42	28.8
Shawmut National	213	1,192	25,315	4.71	168	1,698	27,430	6.19	157	2,097	32,652	6.42	19.5
Bank Austria	121	2,200	48,009	4.58	127	2,260	48,209	4.69	128	2,590	58,738	4.41	5.6
GiroCredit	253	936	28,567	3.28	258	992	27,234	3.64	260	1,088	29,368	3.70	1.6
Landesbank Berlin	129	2,056	50,246	4.09	134	2,103	72,959	2.88					
Berliner Bank	187	1,427	38,523	3.71	201	1,389	40,962	3.39	61	5,209	157,197	3.31	9.0
Berliner Hypo	556	328	12,985	2.53	603	326	14,234	2.29					
Unitas Group	156	1,706	28,433	6.00	188	1,451	26,508	5.47	200	1,497	31,987	4.68	–15.4
Kansallis-Osake-Pankki	183	1,442	32,971	4.37	224	1,164	31,790	3.66	197	1,527	33,695	4.53	–26.6
STS Bank	590	305	3,913	7.79									
Society Corp.	161	1,647	24,999	6.59	158	1,856	27,040	6.86					
Keycorp	203	1,280	25,449	5.03	137	2,045	32,648	6.26	80	4,255	66,798	6.37	42.0
Nordbanken	167	1,591	48,175	3.30									
Gota Bank	332	664	12,752	5.21	173	1,617	49,875	3.24	160	2,068	46,342	4.46	24.9

Source: *The Banker* (1995).

Indeed, after the merger of Banco de Bilbao and Banco de Vizcaya, there followed the announcement—although it later fell through—of the merger between Banesto and Banco Central, the merger between Caixa de Pensions and Caja de Barcelona, the merger between Banco Central and Banco Hispano Americano, the merger under the corporate umbrella of Argentaria of all of the publicly owned banks in Spain, and, in April 1994, the purchase of Banesto by Banco Santander, to quote only the largest operations.

The Spanish banking industry therefore offers quite a few lessons on the advantages of concentrating the industry through mergers. The political and financial authorities have wholeheartedly encouraged this consolidation process, an example that was followed later by Italy.

Corporate mergers are complex processes from both the strategic and the cultural viewpoints. The problems that exist in the banking industry probably make them even more complex. In fact, bank mergers are not good or bad in abstract terms: they are good or bad on the basis of at least two criteria. First is the natural compatibility of the two merging organizations, both from an external, market viewpoint and from an internal, organizational design viewpoint (planning systems, control, and incentives). Second is the clarity in planning the merger process and the effectiveness of the merger implementation process, which, to a great extent, depend on the personal empathy between the key people involved and the compatibility of the two institutions' cultures.

Mergers that are strategically well focused may encounter numerous obstacles when the implementation process is not managed adequately. The unsuccessful merger between Banesto and Central in 1990 or the failed attempt—this time, between two investment banks—between S. G. Warburg and Morgan Stanley are good examples of the importance of planning and adequately carrying out the merger and consolidation process. In the following pages, we will briefly discuss a number of mergers that have been successful in practice.

In July 1991, the presidents of Chemical Bank and Manufacturers Hanover announced the merger of the two banks. The new bank would have total assets amounting to about 136 billion dollars, which would make it the second largest North American bank in volume of assets.

The advantages of the merger resulted from the likely cost reduction obtained from sharing (mainly) information systems, corporate headquarters, and bank branches. The operating cost savings were estimated at 15 per cent, in addition to foreseen future savings from sharing investments in information systems and the extraordinary proceeds to be obtained from the sale of certain assets.

By 1994 it could be said that the merger had been a business success. The two banks' strategic compatibility—Chemical Bank was very strong in traditional commercial banking while Manufacturers had a network of large companies—was complemented by the good personal relationship between the banks' top managers and, particularly, between the two presidents. The consolidation process was clear and consistently executed. Furthermore, the American economy started to recover in the second half of the 1992, which meant that provisions for write-offs also started to drop. All of the ingredients necessary to make the merger work were there. Later on, in August 1995, the Presidents of Chemical and Chase announced their intention to merge their banks, in an attempt to consolidate their branch network and share some assets.

A second interesting case is the purchase of Midland in 1992 by the Hongkong and Shanghai Banking Corporation (HSBC), after a fight with Lloyds, which was also interested in buying Midland. The history of the rivalry between Lloyds and HSBC is interesting in its own right. The former was interested in buying Midland's retail network, because the banking industry in Great Britain had excess capacity. Therefore, a merger between two banks could ease the path towards reducing costs and capacity. Furthermore, if the buying bank had good management skills, as was the case of Lloyds, the final result could be excellent.

HSBC's intentions were slightly different. This bank, which had held a 15 per cent interest in Midland's equity since 1987, was extraordinarily strong in South-East Asia but its presence in Europe was virtually nil. The purchase of Midland would enable it to establish itself in Great Britain and, from there, expand to the rest of the EU.

Therefore, while Lloyds hoped that the advantages of the take-over would come from cost reductions, HSBC hoped that the profits would come from the possibility of offering a full service to customers operating in both Asia and Europe. These possibilities seem to exist for investment banks, as Morgan Stanley or Goldman Sachs have shown with the passing of time. However, HSBC and Midland are mainly commercial banks, and commercial banks are national rather than international or global businesses, due to the importance of a strong distribution network.

However, two years after the take-over, the results have been very positive. By the end of the second year from the announcement of the takeover on 10 July 1992, HSBC's share price had almost doubled. The group's results between 1989 and 1993 are shown in the graphs included in Figure 4.5.

However, the logic of a global commercial bank is not proven. The big question is whether the results will continue to be as positive when the British economy's growth cycle comes to an end and enters a recessive phase again.

In the United States, other highly public mergers and acquisitions in the banking industry in the last 10 years have been the merger of Crocker Bank with Wells Fargo in 1986, and the acquisitions of Security Pacific (1992) and Continental (1994) by Bank of America, and that of First Fidelity by First Union (1995).

The first take-over (Crocker Bank) had a clear purpose: the bank urgently needed financial resources and a better management, and Wells Fargo could provide both. The merger was a success.

The take-overs by Bank of America have followed a different rationale. Security Pacific was bought to strengthen Bank of America's traditional commercial banking business in California. The purchase of Continental seeks to

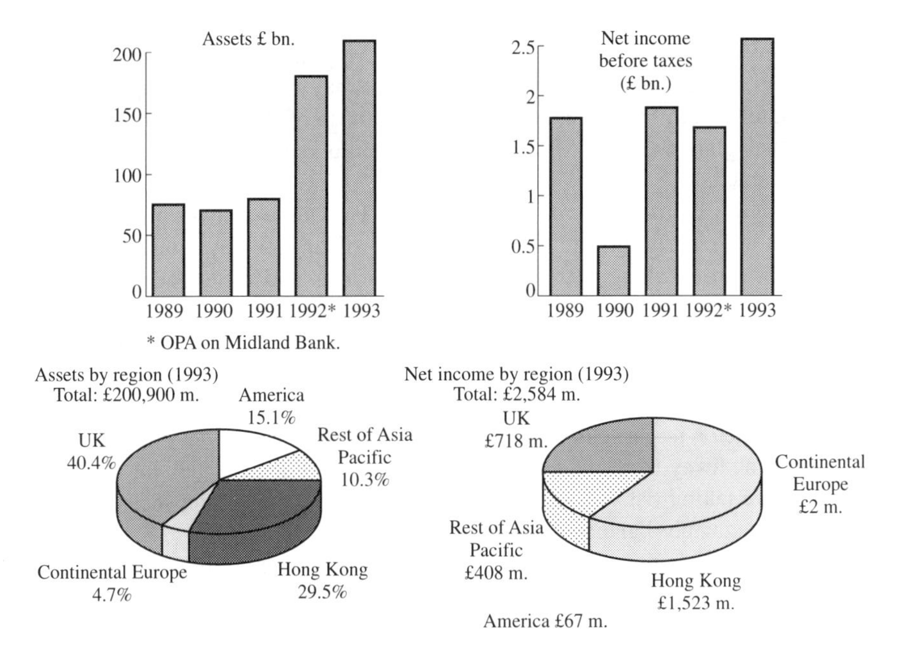

FIG. 4.5 *HSBC Holdings*

provide Bank of America with a business relationship with large corporations in the Chicago area.

Another bank that has repeatedly used mergers as a procedure for achieving growth is Banc One, which, in recent years, has been acknowledged several times as the most profitable bank in the United States and it is the eighth largest in terms of assets. One of the formulas used by Banc One has been to buy banks having a volume of assets at least one-third of the size of Banc One, with a compatible corporate culture and an efficient management. Banc One provides product innovation, excellent information systems, and effective day-to-day management of its asset and liability customers.

The merger between Mitsubishi and the Bank of Tokyo, announced in March 1995, meant the creation of the largest financial group in the world in asset terms, way above the second largest bank, Fuji, which is also Japanese. The capital ratio required by the BIS was 9.5 per cent. This merger caused a considerable stir in the financial world, particularly in Japan. Initially, it is apparent that the two banks have certain complementary features, both because of the type of business and because of their geographical location. However, the critical success factor in this merger is the necessary management skills to enable the new group to operate with improved efficiency, as efficiency is still low in the Japanese banking world.

Finally, we will mention a merger that was announced but never implemented by two investment banks: S. G. Warburg and Morgan Stanley. On 8 December 1994, both banks' management announced that they were negotiating a merger. Immediately, both banks' shares, particularly those of Warburg, started to rise. The initial plan was that Morgan Stanley would own two-thirds of the new bank's capital.

The logic of this merger is quite simple. Trading and investment banking activities are clearly global. The globalization of financial systems and capital flows has carried along with it the capital markets and the organizations that operate in them. The international expansion of these activities has two important additional aspects. The first is geographical diversification, which enables more balanced investment portfolios to be built, as regards stock price levels and interest rates, which are both critical variables in this business. The diversification factor is particularly important at this time as the investment banks are breaking away from the traditional securities trading activities for third parties and are taking risks on their own account. Hence, the greater incentive they have to adequately balance their investments.

Second, there is the possibility of gaining access to emerging markets where there are more opportunities than in consolidated markets such as Europe or the United States. Therefore, investment banks having a global presence seem to possess significant advantages.

However, although Warburg expected to gain from the merger, as its international presence was lower than that of Morgan Stanley, the latter bank did not seem to have so much to gain as it already had a strong presence in Europe. Perhaps Morgan Stanley's primary incentive was the possibility of combining its asset management division with that of Warburg, Mercury Asset Management—of which Warburg holds 75 per cent—which is the leading investment fund in Great Britain.

However, one week later, on 15 December, both banks announced the end of the merger talks. The reason was the request by Mercury Asset Management's managers for a special premium in the price offered for the merger and the guarantee that they would retain their operating independence. Upon learning of this reaction, Morgan Stanley's managers announced that, effectively, consolidating the two banks' investment management firms was the main reason for promoting the merger. The banks never reached an agreement. Finally, in May 1995, Swiss Bank Corporation bought S. G. Warburg's investment banking division.

Irrespective of the final result of that frustrated merger, the episode, together with the purchase of Midland by HSBC, indicates that in certain segments of the financial business, there are clear advantages for a larger-sized organization having a diversified geographical presence, as in investment banking. However, in commercial banking, the arguments in favour of a merger are more difficult to justify, unless one resorts to possible cost reductions, as Chemical Bank and Manufacturers Hanover did.

8. UNIVERSAL BANKS AND SPECIALIZED BANKS: THE PUBLIC POLICY VIEWPOINT

In the previous section, we discussed a series of advantages and disadvantages of universal banks *vis-à-vis* specialized banks, considered from the viewpoint of the banks themselves. In this section, we adopt a different viewpoint, and examine whether universal banks have advantages over specialized banks from the viewpoint of society as a whole. We will therefore use a series of criteria which will help us appraise, in each case, the advantages and disadvantages of each of the models we are presently considering.

8.1. Financial stability

Bank specialization seems to promote the greatest efficiency possible in the provision of financial services, while at the same time it limits the financial risk of the various banking organizations. On the other hand, universal banks may be less efficient than those specializing in the provision of certain financial services and, furthermore, have a higher risk level. This greater risk, so the argument goes, follows from the fact that part of universal banks' business consists of lending money to non-financial companies or in purchasing a direct interest in their equity capital. This argument has been used extensively in the debate on universal and specialist banks.

This argument needs to be broken down into several parts. First, more or less efficiency in the provision of financial services has not so much to do with a financial organization's degree of specialization as with its resources and capabilities, as we have discussed above.

Second, the greater risk that universal banks may have depends on two factors. First is the degree of correlation between the revenues from different types of business unit in the universal bank. The greater the correlation, the greater the risk. Second is the quality of the loans granted and the investments in non-financial companies. In principle, lending always has a risk, although it has been and continues to be one of the mainstays of universal banks' results. Therefore, this activity's risk lies not so much in the activity itself as in the quality of the loans and investments in non-financial companies.

This argument can turn against specialized banks, which may have a greater risk because their revenues are not diversified. When their main activity goes into temporary or permanent recession, the possibilities of survival are less than those of a universal bank with an adequately diversified revenue structure. Therefore, from this viewpoint, specialized banks would have a greater risk.

What does seem certain is that specialized banks are usually smaller than universal banks. Therefore, the financial and social problems posed to the financial authorities by their possible failure are on a smaller scale than those posed by the failure of a larger universal bank, with a larger number of depositors and shareholders. However, this aspect is related more to size than to specialization.

In fact, universal banks usually have a strong commercial banking business and depend particularly heavily on a high volume of deposits. When deposit insurance exists, the cost of rescuing a universal bank with a significant volume of deposits, through a deposit guarantee fund, is much more expensive than saving or liquidating a specialized bank with a smaller volume of deposits, or, because that is not its main activity, no deposits at all.

Historical experience offers contradictory examples. Thus, in the United States during the banking crisis of the 1930s, universal banks that offered commercial and investment banking services had a lower rate of failures than the specialized banks, as we pointed out in Chapter 3. This was because the securities trading business provided a significant diversification of revenues (White, 1986; Benston, 1990).

A major factor explaining the Savings & Loans (S&L) crisis in the second half of the 1980s in the United States was the inadequate distribution of loan and deposit maturities. In particular, these organizations specialized in granting fixed-interest, long-term mortgage loans, obtaining their funds from short-term deposits which, in addition, bore variable interest rates that fluctuated with the variations in money market conditions. When interest rates started to rise in the United States in the 1980s, the S&L associations had to increase the remuneration of their deposits in order to not lose customers. Their financial margins plummeted.

The study of the German situation by Franke and Hudson (1984) gives a slightly different view. These authors analysed the three most serious bank crises recorded in Germany in the twentieth century and their bearing on the universal bank system prevailing in that country. Their main conclusion is that it does not seem possible to establish a close relationship between universal banks and financial crisis, although it can be said that the hyperinflation of the 1920s seriously weakened the German banks' solvency.

A third area of historical experience is the crises suffered by banks in several European countries during the recession of the second half of the 1970s and the recession of the early 1990s. Spain is a classic example. The banks that suffered most from the consequences of these recessions—and which ended up going bankrupt or being bought by other banks—were the medium and large-sized universal banks and, in particular, banks that had major stakes in the industrial sector (Cuervo, 1988). The list is very long but includes banks such as Banca Catalana, Bankunión, the Rumasa Group, Urquijo, Hispano Americano, and, more recently, Banesto.

So, it does not appear that specialized banks imply a lower general risk for the financial system as a whole nor that the universal banks imply a greater risk. This will depend, again, on each organization's business units and the quality of its management, resources, and skills. As we have already said, we could find factors for and against each type of financial organization.

8.2. *Universal banks, specialized banks, and concentration of power*

The image of universal banks with a variety of business units and a major presence in the financing of industrial companies—and even equity holdings in these companies—may lead one to think of the possibilities of a concentration of power and even of monopoly practices in the financial industry. This issue could be of greater concern if the universal banks were to misuse their relationships with customers of some of their business units to sell, in an improper manner, other financial services. This is the phemonenon known as tie-in.

We will state at this point that tie-in is objectionable when a company that is highly indebted to a bank or a large share of whose capital is held by a bank has no choice but to acquire other financial services and products from this bank. However, on occasions, the bank itself will have a keen interest in ensuring that such a company has access to and operates with other financial organizations.

We will discuss this issue again in Chapters 6, 7 and 8. It is true that in some countries with universal banking models such as Germany, France, or Spain, the image of financial groups such as Deutsche Bank or Crédit Lyonnais may be one of a high concentration of economic and financial power.

This observation has two different sides to it. First is the degree of power accumulated by a universal bank. In principle, this is not a question of absolute volume but of relative volume in relation to other business groups in the country in question, and the real, practical influence that the group may have on the country's political, economic, and social life. Although these financial groups are usually large, one cannot generalize about the degree of concentration of power as, in advanced industrial societies, such centres of power are usually numerous and widely spread and there does not necessarily exist any co-ordination between them that would enable misuse of such power.

The second issue is the degree of monopoly power that these organizations bring to bear on the banking system. In principle, in a situation of regulated oligopoly such as that of the banking systems existing in the EU countries before the advent of the single market, rivalry between banks was not very strong—among other reasons, because it was not possible to compete on price—and, therefore, in an oligopoly *de facto*, the larger organizations tended to set the trend in prices.

However, financial deregulation and freedom of foreign investment and capital movements between the EU member countries have placed considerable limitations on any possibilities of abusive practices by the large financial groups. In fact, in countries such as Spain, Britain, or Germany, where there are large financial groups, bank rivalry is very strong. One proof of this is the dramatic fall in financial and operating margins suffered by these organizations as a result of the increased competition.

8.3. The existence of potential conflicts of interest in universal banks

Universal banks have different divisions or business units with different goals that, on occasion, may come into conflict (Edwards and Fischer, 1994; Saunders and Walters, 1994).

The situations of potential conflict of interest are extremely varied. They include the granting of loans to customers to buy shares in the bank itself (a situation that occurred in Banesto before the Bank of Spain intervened in December 1993); the insider information that a bank's large companies department may have on a particular customer and which may flow to its competitors through another department in the same bank; the granting of loans to companies in difficulties whose issues on the capital markets are led by the bank's own corporate finance department; finally, insider information on a particular company that may be received by the securities department from the bank's companies department and which may lead it to buy or sell, as circumstances dictate.

However, these situations, or other similar situations, may also arise in specialized organizations, mainly in investment banks that combine operations on the capital markets with financial consulting. Therefore, it is only in pure commercial banks and specialized banks with a single business that conflicts of interest would not exist.

The recent crises of Banesto and Crédit Lyonnais have shown that such conflicts of interest exist and may lead to malpractices in the financial industry by the large universal banks. However, they have also been found in more specialized organizations such as Salomon Brothers or Drexel. Therefore, it seems that the root of the problem is to be found not so much in whether banks are universal or not but in the ethical behaviour of their managers and employees. It is true that a universal bank seems to offer, a priori, more opportunities for dishonest behaviour than a specialized bank but the experience of recent years seems to indicate that such behaviour is not to be found only in the employees of commercial banks.

Consequently, conflicts of interest are not a conclusive argument in favour of or against universal banks. However, they do seem to suggest that both universal banks and specialized banks should have supervisory procedures that minimize this risk.

However, it must be pointed out that no regulatory standard, no matter how perfect, is complete proof against the inventiveness of dishonest behaviour. It is difficult to make sure that these conflicts of interest do not turn into abuses if the financial organizations' managers and employees do not follow basic standards of professional morality. It is not easy when, in a society as a whole, these standards have been pushed into the background and corrupt behaviour in some sectors seems to be an accepted—or at least exonerated—norm.

8.4. Universal banks and economic growth

Some economic historians have credited universal banks with the economic growth in some countries, particularly Germany and Japan (Gerschenkron, 1969). In particular, universal banks in such countries seem to have played a significant role in financing industrial companies, either through loans or directly by acquiring an interest in its share capital.

On the contrary, in those countries where bank specialization has prevailed, such as in Britain, it seems that the banking system's impact on the country's economic growth has been less. In the next few paragraphs, we will discuss some of these points.

First, it is important not to concentrate on specific cases that may offer a distorted view of the issue. Counter-arguments can be offered, such as the slower economic growth experienced by a country with universal banking such as Spain or the incredibly fast econonic growth of the United States, a country with a more specialized banking system.

Second, it is important to clarify the relationship between the financial system and economic growth. Recent studies of economic growth have shown the major role played by the financial system in this process, particularly in the financing of industrial companies. However, the nature of this relationship is not unequivocal and, therefore, is subject to different interpretations (King and Levine, 1994).

Third, in Germany—a country often quoted as an example of such a situation—direct financing by banks of large listed companies is less than certain superficial comments may suggest (Edwards and Fischer, 1994). Therefore, it is necessary to clarify the terms of this relationship, a task we will tackle in Chapter 6, where we analyse the involvement of the German banks in financing the country's industry. To anticipate some of the conclusions that we will discuss in greater detail in that chapter, we will say that the phenomenon of economic growth is one of the least understood in the academic world. It is a complex process, containing different components whose interrelations are not always unequivocal. The role played by institutions and cultural traditions is also decisive (Lodge and Vogel, 1987).

The only indubitable conclusion that can be made about the relationship between the financial model and economic growth is that high savings rates facilitate low real interest rates, enabling investment projects to be financed at a lower cost. This statement is pure economics but, unfortunately, any discussion of the relative advantages or disadvantages of universal banks versus specialized banks in promoting economic growth would be partial and fragmentary and, probably, would leave out other factors that would be equally, or more, important, such as the role of education in countries' economic and social development.

9. SOME CONCLUSIONS

In this chapter, we have presented some key arguments to evaluate the advantages and disadvantages of universal banks compared with specialized banks, both from the viewpoint of the banks themselves, their solvency, and their profitability, and from the viewpoint of society as a whole.

The arguments we have analysed—some of them widely used in debates on the financial system or on public policy regarding universal banks—are not totally conclusive in establishing the superiority of one type of bank over the other.

Perhaps we could condense this discussion into two points. First, the choice of a particular system based on universal banks or specialized banks by the financial authorities is extremely dangerous, as there is no guarantee that they will choose the right one. Also, as happened in the United States with the Glass–Steagall Act of 1933, lobbies may tilt the balance towards their particular interests. Therefore, it is necessary to regulate both types of organization carefully but it is dangerous to exclude activities beyond what is clearly necessary. The approach taken by the European Commission in the Second Banking Directive seems to be heading in the right direction.

The second conclusion is that from the viewpoint of banks, it cannot be stated, in a vacuum, that universal banks are superior to specialized banks, or vice versa. It all depends on the banks' people, resources, skills, and management quality. We can find successful universal banks and specialized banks, as well as universal and specialized banks that have been resounding business failures.

5

Universal Banks and Corporate Diversification

1. UNIVERSAL BANKS IN A GLOBAL FINANCIAL SYSTEM

The choice between universal banks and specialized banks was presented in Chapter 4, with a consideration of the benefits and costs of each type of bank. In this chapter we will move forward and discuss the topic of banks' diversification into other business. We will use the concept of corporate strategy to broach the issue. Consequently, after discussing the basic elements of corporate strategy, we will present a conceptual model that will help us outline more clearly its benefits and costs and will discuss some cases of universal banks with a high level of diversification that seek to obtain certain benefits from corporate strategy.

In Chapter 2 we presented two models of the organization of the financial activity in industrial countries, the first based on financial markets and the second upon financial intermediaries.

Within this second model, we can distinguish between several categories. One of them corresponds to the presence of public sector interests in the banks' equity. The French or Spanish models would be included within this group. Another category refers to the presence of banks as shareholders of industrial or non-financial services companies. In Chapter 2, we discussed the lines this presence takes in countries such as Germany, Spain, and Japan.

Irrespective of the presence of banks as shareholders of industrial companies, we observe two opposing forces in the second model. The first consists of the disintermediation process: savers and investors go directly to the capital markets, skipping financial intermediaries. The advantages of this trend—which explain its rapid growth in recent years—are to be found in the flexibility of the specific formulas chosen and the lower cost of capital for companies.

The second trend is that universal banks, assisted in the EU by favourable legislation, tend to widen their field of operations, going from being simply commercial banks to banks with a full range of sophisticated financial services for companies of all sizes. These new financial services also include those that result from the growing presence of banks in the capital markets, caused by, among other reasons, the intent not to lose market share in the corporate financing business.

The latter phenomenon has been common in the 1980s in many European countries, such as France, Spain, and Great Britain, where the subsidiaries of commercial banks, specializing in stock market trading, have acquired an increasing market share and, in countries such as Spain or France, have even come to dominate the market.

In Chapter 2 we outlined a possible future scenario in which these two opposing forces—financial disintermediation and universal banks—tend to trade off their effects in an eclectic mixture that takes the least bad from both worlds.

Thus, traditional commercial banks wish to be a witness to the present-day transformation of markets as a result of disintermediation and, at the same time, to be involved directly in company financing. The creation of financial consultancy services by some banks is one more sign of this phenomenon.

Consequently, we can state that in many industrial countries, financial systems are moving towards an eclectic model of universal banking and sophisticated financial markets. This scenario is compatible with the existence of specialized financial firms, such as investment banks and commercial or savings banks with services that specifically target private households. However, the large financial institutions are moving in the eclectic direction we have described above.

This trend is also confirmed by changes in the regulatory system in the EU and the United States. Within the EU, the Second Banking Directive approved by the European Commission consolidates the principle of universal banking which accepts, among other things, a bank's involvement in financing industry, either through loans or by a direct stake in companies' equity.

This Directive proposes certain precautionary measures. Thus, in the area of risk concentration, the EU establishes a ceiling for risk concentration in a single customer equivalent to 10 per cent of the total loans granted by a particular bank. With regard to holdings in non-financial companies, the ceiling is 5 per cent of such companies' equity capital. The bank cannot concentrate holdings of a single company above 15 per cent of its own capital. Total holdings in industrial companies may reach up to 60 per cent of the bank's total resources. Higher holdings are possible but, in this case, the holding must be covered by the bank up to 100 per cent of the share capital.

These precautionary measures may seem very restrictive but, in practice, they allow for a considerable degree of flexibility. In fact, even with holding less than 5 per cent of a company's equity capital, a bank can still be the largest shareholder. Also, if to the holdings in equity capital we add the financing provided to the company in the form of loans, a bank can easily control this company's future course.

In the United States, the starting point is very different from that of Europe. While in Europe, the principle of universal banking was more or less recognized in all banking systems, in the United States, the Glass–Steagall Act of 1933 imposed a strict separation of functions between the commercial banks—specializing in retail banking for private households—and the investment banks—mainly specializing in wholesale banking and operations on the capital markets. In fact, the existence of such regulatory measures is the main reason why

North American banks play a much smaller role in corporate finance (Berglof, 1990).

This situation began to be questioned in the early 1980s when the US financial system started to enter a deep crisis as a result of the heavy indebtedness of Latin American countries and the collapse of the real estate market in the United States.

Some experts (Bryan, 1991; Pierce, 1991) have proposed an alternative model by which the US administration would allow the traditional commercial banks to lend directly to companies, thus imitating the European model. It was also thought that only with such measures would it be possible to develop a financial system able to compete with the large European and Japanese banks.

The political vicissitudes that the United States has suffered have meant that, in November 1995, this reform has still not been passed by Congress. However, it appears that this movement has acquired sufficient momentum and it will not be easy to stop it. Thus, it is possible that we may witness in the United States the gradual transformation of commercial banking into universal banking, more geared towards financing non-financial companies. In any case, we do not think that this evolutionary process will substantially change the key role played by the stock and bond markets in the US financial system.

2. CORPORATE STRATEGY AND DIVERSIFICATION OF BANK ACTIVITIES

The diversification of bank activities and, in particular, the strategic option of being and acting as a universal bank, may have political causes. Thus, for example, a universal bank may exert a greater influence on a country's financial system if it is large and has a strong presence in all segments of the financial markets.

In other cases, the diversification of financial activities within a bank group may be for purely historical reasons. In the large North American banks, the different business units under the corporate umbrella of companies such as Citicorp or Chemical owe their existence to the reaction made by these financial groups in order to penetrate other emerging sectors of the financial business. The regulatory separation of businesses imposed in the 1930s prevented this expansion of activities from taking place within the commercial bank itself. Therefore, the solution chosen was to create new companies which, with due legal independence and a greater or lesser degree of management autonomy, would be able to penetrate these new businesses.

In Spain, we can see a similar process in the case of the so-called industrial banks, which appeared in the 1960s and 1970s and which sought, among other goals, a certain degree of specialization of financial organizations. The ultimate goal was to provide new types of long-term finance to Spanish companies. Many commercial banks created their own industrial bank. In time, it was seen that this enforced specialization was not leading to particularly favourable results. The end result was that many banks found themselves saddled with industrial banks whose existence was no longer justifiable in the new regulatory and competitive environment within which the banking industry was operating in the 1980s.

As a result of these and other similar events, many universal banks in Europe provide permanent financing to companies or even take a stake in their capital, thus forming a group of companies.

It is therefore important to discuss in some detail the problems of these business groups in which a number of universal banks have decided to play a dominant role. Only by so doing is it possible to discuss in depth the advantages and disadvantages of this model of bank organization.

Perhaps it would be useful to start with a practical definition of a group of companies or an industrial corporation. Generally speaking, by group of companies we understand a collection of companies in which one of them holds shares in the others—which does not exclude cross-holdings between companies in the group—and exercises a function of co-ordination and control in these companies. Normally, the group of companies has a strategy, called a corporate strategy, which is distinct from the business strategy of each of the individual member companies.

This definition follows functional and not legal criteria. Thus, in Spain, Act 24/1988 on the stock market defines the group of companies as a collection of firms in which there exists unity of decision as a consequence of the control that one of the companies exerts over all the others. This ability to control may come about as a result of holding not only most of the shares but also an interest which, while not controlling in terms of number of shares, leads effectively to *de facto* control of the group's decisions.

The main difference between a group of companies and an industrial corporation—although both revolve around a universal bank—is one of emphasis. The industrial corporation usually plays a very active role in the strategic processes of the companies in which it has invested. A group of companies normally has a parent company at the centre, which could be a universal bank.

In general, the appearance of industrial groups or corporations is very closely related to the birth and development of the large company in the twentieth century. The growth and development of the modern company has been the subject of excellent studies by Chandler (1962, 1977, 1990). This author distinguishes between three distinct stages in the evolution of a company. First is the birth of a company which concentrates on a particular market with particular products.

In the second stage, the company decides to integrate vertically (Figure 5.1) or expand to other markets (for example, by internationalization) in order to consolidate and promote the growth of the company's basic business. This business, therefore, would continue to be the same one that brought the company into being.

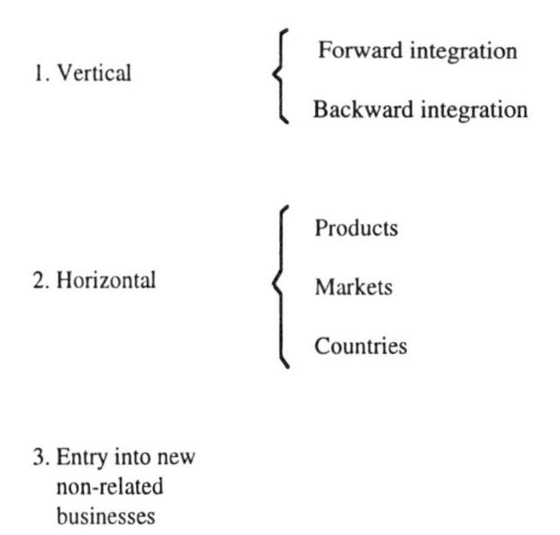

FIG. 5.1 *Generic growth diversification strategies*

The third stage consists of the diversification of the company into other businesses. Thus, new business units appear, each one with certain products in particular markets. These business units may be legally separate from the parent company or they may form a more or less independent unit within that company.

In addition to these historical or political developments, the diversification of bank activities is a particular case of the business diversification that many companies—financial or non-financial—undertake at some time in their lives. This diversification has economic or organizational causes. Such decisions are common, and have been carefully studied in the literature on business strategy (Rumelt, 1974).

The diversification undertaken by a company may be either related diversification or unrelated diversification. In the former, the new businesses are related in some way to the initial businesses, either because they usually share some of the activities of the latter or because their products are sold on the same markets or to the same customers. A classic related diversification in a traditional commercial bank is its entry into corporate banking.

The second type of diversification targets companies or businesses with little or no common ground with the existing businesses in the corporate group. An unrelated diversification which became popular among commercial banks during the 1980s was the acquisition of interests in companies providing data processing services.

Information technologies are crucial for bank management in the 1990s. However, the fact that they are crucial does not mean that commercial banking organizations and information technology companies need the same type of resources or skills or that their respective industries are governed by the same competitive dynamics.

In principle, any diversification decision is made because it is hoped that the decision will create value added. If this were not so, then these decisions would probably never—or almost never—be implemented. However, alongside this principle of common sense, there is one objective fact: the number of diversification decisions that end up as failures is simply enormous (Porter, 1987).

One possible reason for these failures (which seems to go against what some managers argue) is that in all diversification decisions one tends to rate very favourably the benefits of diversification, while tending to forget the possible costs.

We turn now to some of the benefits and costs of diversification decisions. Obviously, the first benefit expected is the growth of the company's value added and/or of its value.

In more detail, among the benefits that will contribute in the future to increasing value added are the possibility of sharing resources or activities between the old businesses and the new business, the possibility of transferring resources or skills from the old businesses to the new one, the management skills of the corporate group (which could be superior to those of the purchased company), and the formation of an internal capital market within the group that would enable more informed investment or divestment decisions to be made than would be made by an external capital market.

Among the possible costs of diversification decisions are the complexity of managing a corporate group with business units in different industries, the co-ordination and control problems involved in obtaining some of the above-mentioned benefits (such as the transfer of resources or the efficient functioning of the internal capital market), and, finally, the sheer size of the group, which may create a bureaucracy that eliminates innovation, entrepreneurship, and the ability to make decisions quickly in each of the businesses.

Logically, each of these possible benefits and costs of a diversification decision plays a unique role depending on the nature, resources, and structure of the corporate group, of the newly bought company, and of the industry it belongs to. On the other hand, the importance of these factors also varies depending on whether the decision concerns a related diversification or an unrelated diversification.

Before discussing in more detail the arguments in favour of diversifying businesses in a group of companies and, in particular, in a bank group, we will briefly synthesize the evolution of the corporate strategy concept in the theory and practice of company management.

By corporate strategy we refer to the strategy of a group of companies that contains within it more than one business unit, each one having a degree of economic or legal independence that varies depending on the individual case. The primary feature of this definition is the existence of more than one business unit. A business unit is a division of a company that competes in a particular industry, seeking to serve prospective customers with a series of products in a certain number of markets. Business units therefore share the identifying feature of having a certain combination of products, customers, and markets.

This concept has been developed from the work of Chandler (1962) and

Andrews (1971). The basic elements of the corporate strategy are the following: definition of a mission for the group of companies, selection of the businesses in which the group will operate, creation of a unique differential expertise in each business, and co-ordination between different business units.

These ideas about corporate strategy, elegantly expressed by those authors, were widely accepted by large and medium-sized companies in the United States and Europe during the 1960s. The climate of economic growth favoured expansion and investment in businesses other than that of the initial company, with the result that companies progressively added new businesses to those already existing.

The oil crisis and its impact on the level of economic activity and company investment forced the business community to reconsider the meaning of corporate strategy. In the mid-1970s, with industrial economies in a state of semi-paralysis as a result of the economic crisis, investment requirements within each business unit started to grow. These units, therefore, started to compete with each other in order to obtain the resources they needed for their projects.

The existence of business units with different competitive dynamics marks the starting point of the concept of the business portfolio popularized by the Boston Consulting Group. This consultancy firm developed the concept of business matrix with two determinant variables: the industry growth rate and the firm's market share. Among the practical conclusions suggested, there is the recommendation to manage a group with a balanced portfolio of business units so that they could share the financial resources of the entire group, which can therefore act as an internal capital market.

A first empirical study on this issue was undertaken by Rumelt (1974). He classified business diversification strategies into two groups: related diversification decisions—that is, those in which the new business shares assets in common with the initial businesses of the group of companies—and unrelated diversification decisions. Rumelt shows, with a wealth of empirical evidence, that the economic performance of the former is clearly superior to that of the latter.

These results were an early signal of the likely outcome of diversification decisions: there are some decisions that are better than others. After this first warning, Rumelt himself (1982) and other authors (for example, Montgomery, 1985) adopted a more cautious attitude: in several empirical studies, it was found that related diversification decisions did not lead systematically to a superior economic outcome either.

In studying the evidence on take-overs, mergers, and acquisitions, Porter (1987), Kaplan and Weisbach (1992), Berger and Ofek (1995), and Comment and Jarrell (1995), among others, show that, after a few years, a significant percentage of acquisitions—many of them unrelated diversification decisions—have been disastrous for the buying company. It is interesting to note that these empirical results are presented in a precise context: the second half of the 1980s, when there was a veritable explosion of mergers and take-overs in Europe and the United States which, in many cases, were unrelated diversification decisions.

During the same period, the traditional public company belonging to many shareholders and, in particular, diversified companies that were not creating value for the shareholder came under ferocious attack. This was also the heyday of the LBOs.

Jensen (1986, 1989) is the main advocate of these new organization forms. He points out that public companies, where management and ownership are separate, give managers too much freedom of manœuvre and, sometimes, when the company is profitable, it places in their hands an excessive amount of financial resources which, instead of being returned to the shareholders, are invested in unprofitable projects. In other words, the separation between the ownership and control of companies that is typical of industrial countries was challenged with one simple argument: it is desirable to align the incentives of managers with those of shareholders. As writing complete contracts is complex (Jensen and Murphy, 1990; Milgrom and Roberts, 1992), an alternative solution is to turn the managers into shareholders, thus departing from the tradition of separating the two distinctive functions of modern companies.

This is the argument proposed by the free-cash-flow theory (Jensen, 1987). LBOs can be more efficient than diversified public companies for several reasons:

1. They bring together the interests of managers and shareholders.
2. Financing the LBO with debt imposes a financial discipline on the company deriving from the commitment to return the loans and pay the interest on them, so that managers are much more careful when choosing investment projects.
3. Normally LBOs proceed to break up diversified companies into individual business units, so that the group ceases to exist. As the management of each business unit is more focused, this may help increase management effectiveness.

These explanations challenge three of the basic hypotheses on which the traditional concept of corporate strategy rests. First is the existence of possible synergies between different businesses, which would lead to cost-sharing or generating a greater volume of revenues for a particular level of investment or expenditure.

Second, there is the value of the contribution of the corporate group's management. Indeed, under this new approach, there is the view that in many diversified companies, the corporate management's contribution to each of the business units does not warrant these units belonging to a corporate group. If each unit acts independently of the corporate core, it may generate as much economic value as it would if it were within a group (or perhaps even were).

Third, it is difficult to show how corporate strategy creates economic value. It is obvious that it derives from all of the business units within the group competing in their respective industries and markets and creating economic value for all the parts of the company (Porter, 1985).

The criticisms of business groups have given rise to the need to refocus the concept of the group of companies. This refocusing can be applied, as we will see below, to the financial groups grouped around a universal bank.

The new conception of corporate strategy raises three basic issues. First, what are the advantages and disadvantages of a business unit belonging to a group of companies? Second, how is it best to organize and run a group of companies and, at the same time, create value in the process? Third, what are the limits and scope of a group of companies or, in other words, what is the limit to a group of companies' growth?

Goold and Campbell (1987), Collis (1991), and Montgomery (1994) have tried to provide some answers to these questions. These authors have based themselves primarily on recent contributions to the field of business strategy known as the resource-based theory of the firm. However, these explanations are not conclusive and the failures of diversified companies and, particularly, of universal banks during the 1980s and early 1990s raise once again the issue of whether groups of companies make sense from the efficiency viewpoint.

What are the advantages and disadvantages of a business unit belonging to a group of companies? The answer these authors give leaves no doubts: the critical resources that the corporate management provides to each business unit. These strategic resources must be scarce resources with a clear economic value for the individual business units.

In other words, these resources must be ones that are scarce, difficult for other competitors to imitate, difficult to substitute with other resources, and, as a result, cannot be bought on a market (Barney, 1991; Collis, 1991). If it were possible to buy them, these resources would cease to have a special economic value for the group of companies and it would be very easy to replace or imitate them. There are two types of strategic resources: material, tangible assets or intangible assets.

Tangible assets include the capacity for innovation or technological development, or the creation of an internal capital market enabling access to financial resources at lower cost. This latter resource is tremendously important in explaining the growth of diversified groups of companies.

An internal capital market in a corporate group may work, in practice, by means of three types of complementary action:

1. An ongoing management of the business portfolio, buying or selling business units in order to maintain the portfolio's balance.
2. Setting financial goals for each of the business units and intervening when these goals are not reached.
3. Allocating the necessary financial resources to each business unit in the diversified group so that it can attain the planned individual goals.

Faced with this series of possible functions of an internal capital market, the next question that comes to mind is the following: What advantages does an internal capital market have over external capital markets, for example, the stock market? There are two main advantages:

1. The possibility of monitoring and controlling each business unit more closely than would be possible for the capital market, simply because the management has information that capital markets do not have.
2. The fact that the internal capital market can act with greater speed when an opportunity to buy or enter new businesses appears.

To summarize, an internal capital market is a major asset for a corporate group, although if the group is not well managed, it may become a millstone around the group's neck. The reason is that the immediate availability of investment resources may increase the number of high-risk operations, something that does not happen with the same frequency in the open capital markets.

Intangible assets include:

1. the corporate group's brand image or its reputation among its customers, suppliers, or lending institutions, in other words, what is known as its professional reputation;
2. a resource that is unique to the group: the ability to manage, co-ordinate, and control each of the business units from the group's head offices (Goold and Campbell, 1987). This type of resource is more difficult to create and maintain and, therefore, to justify.

It is obvious that certain business groups have this second type of asset and use it satisfactorily, for example, General Electric, ABB, or, in the banking industry, BBV or Deutsche Bank. However, successful corporate groups are thinner on the ground than the failures and this is particularly true in the banking industry, where attempts to discover and exploit synergies have gone beyond what is reasonable.

The resources related to the group's management sometimes manifest themselves in the form of two very specific types of management skill. The first is that of restructuring or turning a company around. Corporate groups such as Hanson Trust are specialists in discovering potential take-overs whose market value is below their real value and then turning them around with a restructuring plan. Normally, restructuring processes have a number of common features: redundancies (particularly of personnel in staff functions), changing the management team, flattening the organization structure, changing the employees' compensation schemes, refocusing the business on certain products and eliminating other less interesting products, and selling assets or businesses that are not vital for the bought company's core business.

The second skill consists of transferring management capabilities from the corporate centre to the business units or from one business unit to another. The capabilities transferred in the real world are extremely varied. In industrial companies, a significant resource is technological know-how. Think, for example, of the diversification strategy of Honda, where the various companies comprising the group share some of the group's basic technologies.

However, in a world of fast technological change, transferring certain technologies from one business unit to another does not always give effective results, either because expectations are too high or because the world is changing at a faster rate than the technology transfer process. Think, for example, of the purchase of Hughes Aircraft by General Motors. Realizing the growing importance of electronics components in the automobile industry, General Motors' managers thought that Hughes Aircraft, whose basic expertise was the application of electronics to industrial products and processes, could make a significant contribution to the automobile group. Shortly afterwards, it became clear that the synergies or technology transfers perceived a priori were not matched by reality.

In other cases, the transfer of resources consists of certain marketing or distribution capabilities. This is a typical strategy of large consumer product or food companies, such as Unilever, Nestlé, General Foods, or Philip Morris. Such companies buy other businesses in the food industry either to increase market share in a particular country or to revamp the bought company by implementing the parent company's superior skills in the marketing and distribution of food and consumer products.

The second critical question concerning business groups that the new approach to corporate strategy seeks to answer is how to design the organization structure so that the business units can operate with the required autonomy and, at the same time, benefit from belonging to the corporate group.

In general, organizational design is a complex issue that is dependent on factors that are specific to the company's business, the sector it operates in, the managers that work in it, the company's history, and co-ordination requirements (Milgrom and Roberts, 1992). Consequently, it is difficult to generalize on these issues. What is valid for one company in one industry is not valid for another company within the same industry. The reason is that the corporate culture or management profile is different and the number of features they share in common is severely limited.

Another reason that complicates any generalization in organizational design is the degree of relationship between the group of companies' different businesses. Think, for example, of a group in which the primary contribution of the group's management to each of the companies is its ability to improve decisions thanks to the superior quality of the information it holds. The type of information and control systems that a group having these advantages should implement will be different if the group's companies belong to a similar type of industry (for example, mature industries, highly technology-intensive industries, or global industries) or if, on the other hand, they belong to completely different industries. In each of these cases, the specific design of management, planning, and control systems may have to take into account very different requirements.

The third critical question for management under this new approach is what should be the optimal size of a group of companies. In other words, what is the limit to the corporate group's growth? The answer to this question has two sides to it. First, there is the ability to transfer resources from the corporate group to new businesses. The resources that the corporate group provides to

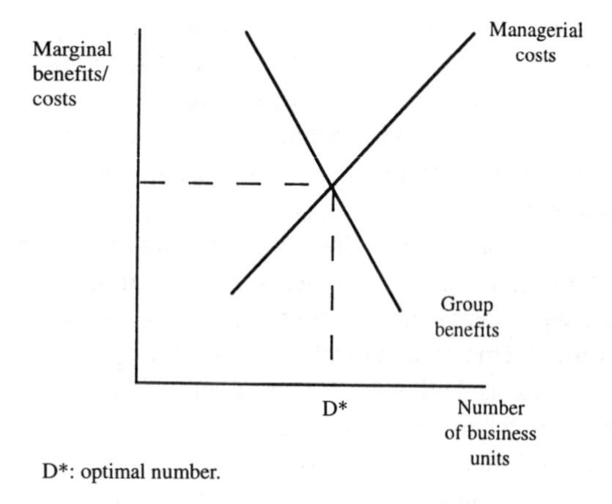

FIG. 5.2 *Marginal benefits and costs of a conglomerate*

the business units may or may not disappear when extended and applied to many businesses. In an internal capital market, it is obvious that the more businesses there are, the smaller the contribution that the group can make to each one. On the other hand, if corporate reputation is high, the possibility of this reputation becoming diluted—at least, at first sight—is less.

When evaluating the optimal size of a group of companies, according to the new approach to corporate strategy, one must also take into account the costs of being oversized. Management of a diversified group is complex and becomes more complex as the number of companies in the group grows. Furthermore, complexity combines with the effects of the group managers' limited supervision, control, and leadership capacity. Also, complexity tends to increase agency and co-ordination costs within the group.

Consequently, we are seeing two effects that evolve in opposite directions as the group grows. On the one hand, the benefits of belonging to the group tend to decrease as the number of companies belonging to the group increases. On the other hand, the group's management costs tend to increase as the number of companies in the group increases.

Figure 5.2 shows the evolution of benefits and costs depending on the number of companies in the group. Obviously, the break-even point determines the optimal size of the group. However, although the solution is obvious from a conceptual viewpoint, giving this solution concrete form in the management of a group is an exceedingly complex task, as daily experience never tires of showing.

The answer to these three critical questions concerning groups of companies also helps define what must be the main tasks of the management of groups of companies. We will define three types of functions or tasks that must be performed by a group's corporate management.

The first is identifying, promoting, applying, and renewing (to use the terminology coined by Hamel and Prahalad, 1994) the critical resources or skills of the group of companies that clearly add value to each of the group's businesses. This is a fundamental task in a business group. If the group justifies its existence to employees and shareholders by the value added it creates and this value added is influenced by the contribution made by the corporate management through certain resources, management of these resources—in the ways listed above—is critically important. The day these resources disappear or cease to have value for the different business units, it is in the shareholders' and employees' best interests that the group disappear.

The corporate management's second task is to articulate an organizational design, accompanied by a series of management, planning, and control systems that help maximize the contribution made by the unique resources held by the corporate group. In other words, the aim is to design a structure that minimizes internal conflicts and discrepancies in the various parties' incentives and reduces the possibility of the resources not being efficiently applied in each of the business units.

The third critical function of the corporate group's management refers to the study of possible decisions to take the group into new businesses. Such decisions can be broken down into at least three parts. The first is to analyse the intrinsic appeal of a new business, both the generic appeal of the industry as such and the specific appeal of the company that will be started up or bought.

The second part of a decision to enter a new business is to study how the resources that have been the prime mover behind the corporate group's success in the past can be deployed in the new business. This is a critical issue: sometimes, entry of a group of companies into a new business can be justified simply on the grounds of an exceptional real or expected return.

However, it will not be possible to apply some of the group's unique resources to this new business. In this case, the decision to enter a new business can be interesting from a financial viewpoint, but the basic question that the corporate management must ask is what the group brings to this business and what this business brings to the group. If the answer is not clear, it may still be interesting to enter the new business but perhaps it would be best done by the group's shareholders in a personal capacity; or that it be done by the group itself but keeping the new company at a wise distance, with a certain amount of autonomy with regard to the group's normal functioning.

The third issue related to the entry to new businesses refers to the way this is done. Specifically, it is necessary for the group to choose between entering on its own (either starting up a new company or buying an existing company) or entering in co-operation with other companies, that is, establishing an alliance. Which of these forms is finally chosen depends on criteria that are difficult to generalize. In the final analysis, they depend on the financial and other resources that the new business may need, the availability of such resources within the group, the group's familiarity with the new business, and the presence of more or less serious competitors in the new business.

These three core aspects of the task of a group of companies are absolutely critical issues in the management of universal banks where different financial service-related businesses are combined and which sometimes includes holdings in the equity capital of non-financial companies. Although managing the financial group in accordance with these criteria does not eliminate the risk or complexity of this task, it does help it to operate according to more professional criteria and not just historical or political criteria, or mere expedience.

3. UNIVERSAL BANKS AND CORPORATE DIVERSIFICATION FROM THE TRANSACTION COSTS VIEWPOINT

Chandler (1962) proposes a model of business diversification according to which a company's strategy determines its form of organization and the two combined determine its financial performance.

On the other hand, Rumelt (1974) underlines in his empirical research the fact that companies that diversify into related activities perform better than those that diversify into unrelated activities. This latter finding has stirred up a considerable degree of academic controversy.[1] One of the reasons for this controversy is that Rumelt's findings did not adequately control for the effects of the industry on the profitability of the companies analysed.

Furthermore, these findings contradicted a fact that is readily verified in business reality: the high number of companies that diversified into unrelated activities, especially between the late 1970s and the late 1980s, both in the United States and in Europe. However, this phenomenon becomes particularly interesting in the case of the universal banks. These banks comprise a special form of diversified company, with several, more or less related business units. Whether by means of an explicit corporate strategy or not, the universal bank's corporate office decides which businesses the bank will compete in, allocates resources to each business, monitors their performance, and delegates to a greater or lesser degree the responsibility for defining and implementing each business unit's strategy.

To help understand the problem of choosing a universal bank's strategy and, particularly, its diversification strategy—related or unrelated—we will present a model based on the transaction costs approach.[2]

In accordance with this approach, the choice of a strategy and the subsequent organization form by which to implement it, depend on two types of factors. On the one hand are the costs arising from designing the strategy, defining the corresponding contracts between the different agents, outlining the organization structure, and running a more or less complex businesses.

[1] See, for example, Christensen and Montgomery (1981) and Bettis (1981).

[2] This model follows the arguments of Williamson (1975), Teece (1982), and Jones and Hill (1988).

These costs, which we will call organizational, have different dimensions. We will concentrate on three. First, there are the agency costs arising from the delegation of authority from the corporate office to each of the business units. Second, there is the problem of bounded rationality which, in this case, applies not only to the difficulty of designing complete contracts but also to the difficulty of adequately managing a growing number of business units.

The third dimension concerns the advantages that specialist companies may have in each of the corporate group's businesses. These advantages may be associated with the fact that they bear lower costs, either because they do not have the costs of the corporate office or because specialization in certain activities provides certain economies of scale or experience. Also, while on the subject of the advantages enjoyed by specialists, it is worth mentioning that specialization, in principle, allows a company to remain closer to the market and the customers, thereby streamlining the decision-making process.

Consequently, the organizational costs related to the organization and execution of certain transactions within a group instead of on open markets place an additional deadweight on the corporate group.

However, organizational costs are not the only factor to be analysed when making this choice. The second factor we must consider concerns the benefits to be obtained from choosing the strategy and the corresponding form of organization. The best-known benefit obtained from a diversification strategy is usually the possibility of achieving synergies between two or more different business units. These synergies basically consist of the possibility of obtaining economies of scope between those business units as a result of sharing fixed assets or overheads that are not fully utilized and which cannot be sold on an organized market.[3] Generally speaking, there are scope economies in the production or distribution of two goods X_1 and X_2 if $C(X_1, X_2) < C(X_1, 0) + C(0, X_2)$; that is, the costs of the joint production (or distribution) of two goods are less than the sum of the costs of the separate production (or distribution) of these goods (Willig, 1979).

Another potential advantage of these synergies is that grouping the units under a single corporate management may enable them to obtain additional revenues. This would be the case of advertising expenditure on a common corporate brand name for two or more business units, the possibility of sharing information on common customers, or, finally, joint access to distribution channels.

However, synergies are not the only possible benefit. There are at least three additional benefits that may be obtained from diversification strategies. The first is the creation of an internal capital market, which we have already referred to in a previous section. The main advantage of internal capital markets is that they enable the problems arising from asymmetric information suffered by investors to be partly overcome.

[3] This is the case described by Willig (1979) and Baumol, Panzar, and Willig (1982).

This is one of the consequences of the separation between ownership, control, and management in modern corporations. A critical aspect of this advantage is that, when a corporation tries to make use of it, the expenses associated with its implementation tend to increase considerably. The reason is that the cost of monitoring and controlling the company, otherwise borne by the capital markets, is internalized by the group of companies, thus increasing their organizational costs.

Therefore, the benefit of better monitoring must exceed the correlative costs of the design and implementation of this monitoring. If it does not, it would be preferable for the corporate group's shareholders to externalize these monitoring and control functions.

Another possible benefit from an unrelated diversification strategy is derived from the possibility of achieving lower total costs or higher total profits, thanks to the integration of two consecutive business units in the value added chain. This is the benefit obtained by vertical integration.

A third benefit of an unrelated strategy is that it limits the risk of the products of one division being replaced by new products whose future growth is uncertain. If the company—or bank—decides to offer these new products or services, the problem of replacing the present products or services by new ones diminishes. It therefore mitigates the problem of decline of the division affected by the replacement.

In order to formalize the relationships between the costs and benefits arising from diversification, we will introduce the following relationships. We will distinguish between three possible situations from the company's viewpoint. The first situation is that in which each of the businesses is owned by its shareholders and each business is fully independent—legally and financially—of the other.

This is the case of specialized companies where there are no benefits obtained from diversification nor organizational costs associated with it. In the event that the company has surplus resources (Jensen, 1986), its shareholders may choose to reduce capital or pay higher dividends. The shareholders alone decide whether to increase the diversification of their financial investments.

The second situation is that of a corporate group with several, interrelated business units, in other words, a related diversification. The costs associated with the diversification can be expressed by means of the following equation:

$$C(d) = f(D, L, S, M), \tag{1}$$

where $C(d)$ is the specific cost associated with the diversification of businesses, D is the number of business units already existing in the corporation, L is the number and intensity of relationships between the various business units, S is the group's total sales turnover, and M is the differential cost associated with monitoring the various units from the corporate office.

The variable D provides an initial approximation of the problems of managing a diversified group in line with the hypothesis that the larger the number of business units—irrespective of whether or not they are related—the higher the organizational costs associated with the group. The variable L reflects the number of relationships between the various units. In general, the more there are, the more complex they will be. The variable S is another indicator of the group's complexity, expressed in terms of the group's size, which we measure by sales turnover or, in the case of certain companies, by its total value added. Therefore, the first partial derivative of the function $C(d)$ with respect to all four variables is negative.

For its part, the benefits function of a diversified organization can be expressed by:

$$B(d) = g(D, G, S_c), \tag{2}$$

where the variable D indicates the number of divisions in the group. The variable G expresses the reduction in the group's costs obtained from the possibility of sharing investments or overheads. S_c is an indicator of the possible increase in the various business units' sales as a consequence of the decision to diversify.

The sign of the relationships of the benefits function is as follows: the benefits increase when the number of divisions D decreases when G or S_c increase. The inverse relationship between $B(d)$ and D means the following: the marginal benefits of diversifying decrease as the degree of diversification increases. The economic rationale behind this hypothesis is that the possibilities of realizing synergies among divisions decreases when the number of divisions increases: each time, it will be increasingly difficult to find related businesses with which it is possible to realize synergies.

A simple approximation to the equilibrium is that the marginal benefit $B'(d)$ must be equal to the marginal cost $C'(d)$ of the diversification. If we consider that L, S, G, and S_c are short-term constants, equilibrium will be reached when $\delta C(d)/\delta D = \delta B(d)/\delta D$. In graph form, this equilibrium is expressed as shown in Figure 5.2. Logically, this equilibrium is purely intuitive. The reason is that the number of divisions is, by definition, discrete. This problem can be solved, for example, by assigning a coefficient that weights each division on the basis of its sales turnover.

The short-term equilibrium is indicated by the optimal number of divisions D^*. This number of divisions can undergo variations due to changes in the variables that appear in the above cost and benefit functions and which, to simplify the discussion, we have considered fixed, such as the monitoring costs, the total sales turnover, and the possibility of sharing higher cost volumes.

Let us now consider the case of the unrelated diversification. In this, the advantages associated with the diversification are those arising from the internal capital market that the corporation is trying to set up. The corporate management thus becomes a substitute for the capital market by allocating resources to the different divisions on the basis of the opportunities that it detects in each of the company's businesses.

In this case, the diversification costs function will be:

$$C(d) = k(RM - RG, S, M), \tag{3}$$

where $RM - RG$ is the difference between the mean profitability of the competing companies in each business that the corporate group operates in and the profitability of the corporate group. This variable constitutes an approximation of the possible opportunity cost associated with the supposedly better resource allocation by the capital market. The variables S and M are the same as in the previous case. The diversification costs vary with the same sign when the independent variables being considered vary. Therefore, the function $C(d)$ in the case of unrelated diversification excludes the variables D (which appears indirectly, in this case, under the variable S) and L (relationships between business units, which in this case do not exist) and includes the opportunity cost of the capital being handled on the internal capital market.

Thus, the benefit function of the unrelated diversification will be:

$$B(d) = q(C_c, O, S), \tag{4}$$

where C_c represents the capital cost differential between the cost of financial resources on an organized market and the cost of resources for the corporation. Assuming that the difference between the two costs is positive, the benefits of the diversification will increase when C_c increases. For its part, O represents the speed of response in investing or disinvesting in businesses when the corporate management detects opportunities that the markets do not perceive with the same speed. Therefore, the relationship between $B(d)$ and O will also be positive. Finally, as before, S is the group's total revenues. We assume that the relationship between sales and profits is positive up to a certain sales turnover S_o, after which the benefits of diversifying start to diminish. The explanation is that the corporate centre may find it increasingly difficult to find new business opportunities having an equal or greater return than the previous opportunities.

We assume that $RM - RG$ is a function of the capital cost differential C_c. In this case, we can replace $RM - RG$ in the cost equation by $RM - RG = m(C_c)$. In turn, we assume that the variable O depends on the degree of monitoring of the various business units by the corporate management, in accordance with the function $O = n(M)$.

By means of these hypotheses, we can find a first order optimum between the costs and benefits of diversification. Assuming that $RM - RG$, M, C_c, and O are constant in the short term, the optimal degree of diversification will be achieved when $\delta B(d)/\delta S = \delta C(d)/\delta S$. In this case, there will be two optimal solutions, depending on whether $S \geq S_o$, or $S \leq S_o$. The benefits of the more efficient monitoring will increase up to a sales turnover S_o, after which they will start to diminish. For their part, the diversification costs will increase in the same proportion. Figure 5.3 shows a new equilibrium S^* attained under the conditions described above.

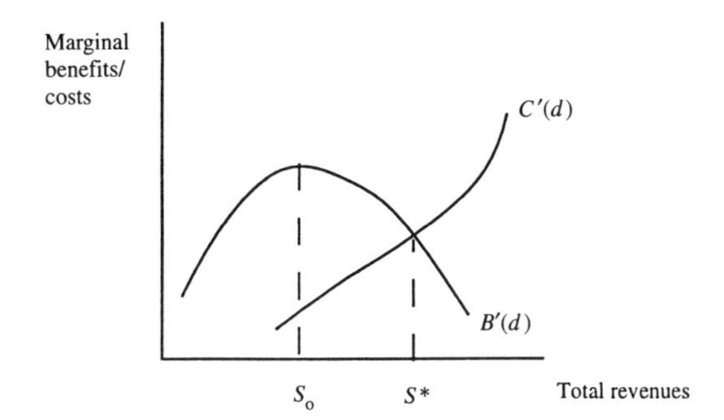

FIG. 5.3 *Marginal benefits and costs of unrelated diversification*

In this model, we have presented some of the main arguments that a universal bank has in choosing a diversification strategy. The related diversification strategy of a universal bank will consist of entering into certain financial activities that have a degree of connection between them. A specific case is, for example, that of a universal bank with a commercial banking unit, a wholesale banking unit, and a capital market unit.

The unrelated investment strategy of a bank could consist of adding investments in non-financial companies. This is the case of the so-called financial corporations with a main bank. The main difference here in financing a non-financial company either with loans or by acquiring a stake in its capital is that, in the latter case, the bank acquires the residual rights deriving from ownership, while, as a lender, it confines itself to financial intermediation and risk monitoring.

Where the bank invests as a shareholder in a non-financial company it hopes to gain benefit from certain economies arising from risk monitoring and the internal use of the capital market. Therefore, the results and conclusions on costs and benefits for the model we have described in this section can be generalized to all universal banks, both those that do not invest as shareholders in non-financial companies (related diversification) and those that do (unrelated diversification).

4. THE NATURE OF DIVERSIFIED FINANCIAL GROUPS

The diversification of activities in the banking industry has led to the entry of banks and other financial organizations into new segments of the financial services industry. Three different cases stand out in particular:

(a) the creation of diversified financial groups that turn into financial supermarkets;
(b) the alliance between banks and insurance companies;
(c) alliances between industrial firms and banks.

We will discuss each of these phenomena below, referring to a number of real-life cases.

4.1. Diversified financial groups

The main relationships between commercial banks and investment banks that warrant integration in the same bank group are the following. First, investment banks are financing a growing volume of assets and do not always have the right capital base. The support provided by a commercial bank's capital base can be very substantial.

Second, a commercial bank's branch network offers greater opportunities for the distribution of financial services—especially financial assets (shares and debentures)—which are a major part of the investment banks' business.

Third, commercial banks may provide customers to the investment banks in certain specialized financial services such as capital or debt issues, or in mergers and take-overs.

Fourth, a growing proportion of corporate debt, especially in large companies, no longer consists of bank credit but of bonds and commercial paper. Issues and transactions involving these financial instruments are typical investment banking operations.

In short, while the growing importance of financial markets in advanced economies does not completely exclude commercial banks, it does encourage them to increase their presence in these emerging markets. And the most logical step is to do so through investment banks, as the skills required in the two businesses vary.

In spite of the relationships between commercial banks and investment banks we have discussed above, there are also significant differences—particularly cultural differences—between the two. These differences are to be found in a number of areas. First, the attitude to risk: commercial banks avoid risk while the investment banks specialize in risk management.

Second, the investment banks' business requires a continual search for new, normally one-off operations with new customers. It could be said that investment banks start each year from scratch. On the other hand, commercial banks try to maintain a more or less stable customer base and grow from that.

Third, the role of managers in the results obtained by investment banks is usually more apparent—although not necessarily more direct—than in commercial banks. This difference gives rise to the demand for different types of compensation and incentives schemes. In the following pages, we will briefly describe some real-life cases of financial groups with a high level of diversification within the broad span of financial services. These cases will help us better understand the opportunities and challenges faced by financial groups.

American Express

American Express is a good example. This is a financial services company that, during the 1980s, competed with varying success in different segments of the financial market, although its results were not as exceptional as those of General Electric Capital.

American Express was the first company to market (in 1890) the concept of travellers' cheques. After the Second World War, the company started to expand abroad and, in 1950, introduced its credit card. From that time onwards, American Express embarked on a diversification that was consolidated in three business units until the end of the 1970s:

- the Travel Related Services Division, which included travellers' cheques, credit cards, and a travel agency;
- the American Express Banking Corporation, which carried out banking activities outside the United States, mainly in developing countries;
- the real estate division.

In April 1981, American Express's situation changed drastically when it decided to merge with Shearson Loeb Rhoades, one of Wall Street's most active investment firms. The main reason for this merger was the supposed synergies that could be realized by combining the two companies. Consequently, it was established that the new organization would act as a holding company that would supervise each of the group's divisions.

The main problem that the new financial group came up against was not only cultural but consisted of the fact that the very nature of the two companies' businesses was extremely different and the important transactions had to be approved at different management levels. This apparently harmless control mechanism had lethal effects for Shearson's securities trading business, which required—and continues to require—decisions virtually on the spot.

Shearson continued to grow, buying other investment banks when the opportunity arose. Thus, it bought Lehman Brothers Kuhn Loeb in 1984 and L. Messel (London) in 1986.

However, the growing competition faced by the group's various business units during the final years of the association exacerbated management problems to the point that the profitability of both American Express's units and Shearson's business took a severe plunge. Finally, in 1993, as part of a large-scale restructuring plan in American Express, this company decided to sell its investment banking business.

Prudential–Bache

Another major failure in the race to form financial groups is Prudential–Bache, which was born from the purchase of Bache Halsey Stuart Shields by Prudential in March 1981. Prudential was the largest insurance group in North America and Bache was a securities broker operating on the North American stock market.

Prudential's main reason for making this move was its belief that the concept of financial supermarket made sense, in the early 1980s, because of the large number of synergies that were perceived between the different businesses. It seemed that if both organizations sold a number of financial services to the same customers, they could save significant sums in information collection and processing costs and distribution costs.

In particular, Prudential hoped that Bache would enable it to offer new financial services to its insurance customers and that it would also be able to attract to its insurance business Bache's high-income customers.

However, Bache's internal problems prevented these advantages from materializing during the first few years. Then, three years later, Prudential considered that the trend in capital market trading was tending towards the investment banking business, that is, one step beyond the mere purchase and sale of shares and debt instruments.

This was the path that was already being followed by other organizations with more experience than Prudential, such as Citibank or J. P. Morgan. Stiffening competition and the stock market crashes in 1987 and 1989 played havoc with Prudential–Bache's results to the point that the group went into the red in 1989 and 1990.

Dresdner Bank and Kleinwort Benson

In June 1995 Dresdner Bank bought Kleinwort Benson, one of the leading British investment banks. This was the second acquisition of a major British investment bank in 1995, following Swiss Bank Corporation's bid for S. G. Warburg.

The premium Dresdner paid for Kleinwort Benson's shares was very high. It reflected, according to Dresdner's board, the highly attractive positioning of the British bank in the global market for mergers and acquisitions and privatizations as of state-owned companies.

For Dresdner, there was another reason for the acquisition: the opportunity to diversify its efforts into investment and international banking through one of the leading firms. It is very difficult to figure out how a universal bank, with very limited experience in investment banking, can enter the industry without a link of that type.

Dresdner now faces two new dilemmas. The first is how to integrate the investment bank into its old structure, without alienating too many people. The second is, what value Dresdner management will contribute to Kleinwort Benson in order to sustain its advantages in a very competitive segment of the financial services industry.

Some final ideas

The main risks that experience has shown in this type of merger, geared towards creating diversified financial groups, are the following. First, it is common for the businesses being merged to have very different competitive dynamics. For example, the insurance business is one in which risk must be carefully assessed on an ongoing basis. In principle, insurance companies do not want high-risk operations. On the other hand, investment companies or companies that operate on the stock market have precisely the opposite mentality.

Second, just as the businesses are very different, so too are the two organizations' cultures: this applies to their control systems, their entrepreneurial skills, and their management compensation and incentives schemes.

Third, there is a tendency to underestimate the specific experience required to operate with a minimum degree of success in new segments of the financial market. Diversification decisions require not only good analytical work to be successful but also a series of skills that make it possible for the diversification to achieve the results that are expected from it. And in businesses such as the investment banking business, these skills tend to be underestimated by newcomer companies.

These cases also clearly show that the problem of the complexity of managing financial groups is a problem affecting not only universal banks but all financial companies (such as American Express or Prudential–Bache) having different business units, where the synergies are seen a priori but are never fully realized a posteriori.

This is the main reason why a large proportion of the financial companies created under the umbrella of a non-financial company (such as Sears or Xerox) during the last few decades, originally intended to finance their parent companies' sales operations, have ended up being failures.

The severe recession of the early 1990s and the restructuring processes undertaken by large companies have led them to alienate businesses that are not essential for their future. Thus, Xerox sold its financial services unit in 1993; Westinghouse sold its credit unit; Weyerhauser sold its pension fund unit; Kodak sold its leasing unit; and Sears sold its financial services business.

The spectacular increase in competition in the various segments of financial business is not the only reason for their failure: the growth of these financial services units was accompanied by growing capital requirements. Thus, the financial services unit competes with the rest of the company in the allocation of resources to the various investment projects. When the parent companies analysed whether the financial business was critical or not for the group's future, they ended up concluding, at least in the above cases, that they were not. As a result, they decided to sell off these units and thus free up financial resources for businesses offering better prospects.

4.2. Alliances between banks and insurance companies

One of the diversification paths widely used by banks in recent years has been the penetration of the insurance industry, either directly or—most often—through an alliance with an insurance company. This phenomenon is known as 'Allfinanz' or 'Bancassurance'.

Among the banks that have used the former procedure are Deutsche Bank, Crédit Agricole, and TSB, who have started up their own insurance company in recent years. In Spain, this activity has been going on for longer and many of the large banks own a major insurance company or group, such as La Estrella

(BCH), La Unión y El Fénix (Banesto, until it was sold to AGF), and Aurora (BBV).

Other banks have chosen to buy insurance companies. For example, SE-Banken (Sweden) bought a 28 per cent interest in the largest Swedish insurance group in October 1990. Lloyds Bank became the largest shareholder of Abbey Life in 1988. In 1989, the Compagnie Financière de Suez bought Groupe Victoire (France) and Colonia (Germany).

A third group of banks have chosen to swap shares with insurance companies. Thus, UAP swapped 10 per cent of its equity with BNP. Sometimes these agreements have led to the creation of an alliance and the formation of a third comapny, as is the case of La Caixa (Spain) and the Fortis Group (Holland).

The merger between a Dutch bank, NBB (Portbank Group, the third largest Dutch bank) and Nationale Nederlander (the leading Dutch insurance group) in 1991 led to the creation of the International Nederlander Group, ING, which, by the end of 1994, was the second largest Dutch bank. This merger has been a success, both from the strategic and the organizational viewpoints.

Finally, it is interesting to note the way insurance companies have acquired stakes in some banks. Those shareholdings can be seen as an investment, as a way of diversifying from the insurance business, or, finally, as a procedure for promoting the distribution of insurance products through bank branches. This is the case of Generali in BCH or AGF in AMB (Germany). Other insurance companies have preferred to sign distribution agreements with banks, for example, Wintertur with Crédit Lyonnais, and the Norwich Union Group with Deutsche Bank.

In many cases these alliances between banks and insurance companies have sought to combine the commercial banks' distribution power with the insurance companies' ability to generate new financial products.

As usually happens with alliances, the agreements between banks and insurance companies have not been easy to manage. In fact, some banks have sought to improve their poor performance through these alliances. In general, few have succeeded and the improvement has sometimes meant cannibalizing their own banking products. Furthermore, the two organizations' business philosophy or culture is very different so integration is not easy.

However, the complementary features are also quite clear and insurance companies are particularly experienced in designing certain complex financial products. For this reason, it will not be surprising if we continue to see new alliances of this type in the future.

4.3. Industrial corporations around banking groups: advantages and disadvantages

After this discussion of the advantages and disadvantages of the diversification of financial activities (related diversification), we plan to connect this issue with the formation of industrial companies having several business units around a bank (unrelated diversification). We would warn the reader at this point that some of the advantages and disadvantages of groups formed by banks and companies are shared, in general, by the universal banks and have already been discussed in this chapter. However, in the case of groups composed of banks and companies, these arguments take on a special meaning, and new arguments are also raised.

The first significant reason for the formation of bank-company groups is the gathering of information (Diamond, 1984: Steinherr and Huveneers, 1989) and sharing customers (Canals, 1993). The obtaining of information on prospective customers for a bank is related to the essential nature of financial intermediation.

In principle, there is an asymmetric information problem between banks and industrial companies, as we discussed in Chapter 2. The obtaining of correct information by a bank is a laborious task, requiring time, experience, and effort.

However, if a long-term relationship is created between a bank and an industrial company, such as the relationship typically established by universal banks, there is a greater chance of the bank obtaining information at a lower cost. At the same time, the bank may have access to information that is not available to other banks that do not have a close business relationship with these companies.

On this point, there are no empirical studies confirming that bank-industry groups obtain better results—or have lower insolvency levels—than specialized banks. However, the argument holds certain advantages for some banks.

Nevertheless, we must point out two arguments against bank-industry groups that are related to the obtaining of information on present or potential customers. The first argument is that it is possible for loans to be overconcentrated in a few companies. Were they to become insolvent, this overconcentration could cause more serious problems for the bank than those that would arise if the risks were more widely spread.

The second disadvantage has to do with customers. When a bank concentrates a high degree of risk in a single company, the markets react favourably. The argument is that the bank knows the company better than anyone and that, if it increases its investments in the company, then the latter must be doing well. The problem arises when the company suffers temporary or permanent difficulties. In this case, if the bank significantly cuts its risks in the company, other banks or financial intermediaries—or the capital markets themselves—are being warned that the company is having problems and they may possibly follow suit, thus making the company's situation even worse. This is a general remark that would have to be adapted to each individual case. However, this phenomenon is not the result of a mere assumption—as is shown, for example, by the industrial and banking crisis in Spain in the late 1970s and early 1980s—and, therefore, cannot be dismissed as an argument against the universal bank.

Another interesting angle from which to study the reasons for bank/non-financial company groups is that related to diversification decisions. Normally, diversification decisions appear and are implemented when the company—normally, the bank—has a surplus of financial and technological resources, which lead it to study possible alternatives for investment and growth. The question that is raised at this point is why the initial company's shareholders do not invest these resources wherever they might wish, instead of letting the company itself make these investments. This is an issue that has been extensively discussed and settled in finance theory: in principle, it is better that risk diversification be carried out by the shareholder than by the company on behalf of the shareholder.

However, in practice, it is thought a priori that the bank enjoys a large number of advantages in investing these resources. All of these assumed advantages are related to the bank's chances of creating value by entering a new business.

The first possible advantage to be gained by the entry of a bank in the equity of another company or group of industrial companies is the transfer of excess resources from one group of business units to another: financial resources, technology, brand image, or managers who are experts in certain areas.

The transfer of resources means, in practice, that the group may benefit from certain economies of scope, thus reducing or holding costs for higher volumes of business. The economies of scope argument has already been discussed in Chapter 4.

Another important advantage of bank-company groups lies in the creation of an internal capital market formed by all the group's business units. This internal capital market may facilitate a smooth entry into new businesses that may help increase the group's value. The attempts made by several European bank groups to enter the burgeoning telecommunications business are a good illustration of this situation. These units are headed by a corporate management team belonging to the group—normally the bank—which is responsible for deciding on the acquisition of new business units or the sale of existing units.

This management team fulfils a twofold purpose. First, it formulates the investment strategy in each of the business units or in new companies it plans to buy. It also supervises and controls, either directly or through other managers, the various business units' goals, budgets, and programmes (Goold and Campbell, 1987).

Furthermore, this form of organizing business activity also enables a certain degree of risk diversification between different activities. To all effects and purposes, the company's corporate management becomes a mechanism for allocating scarce financial resources.

In short, the group's corporate management—with the bank in the forefront—replaces the external capital market in attracting funds and allocating investments in different companies. This mechanism is activated and controlled by the bank itself, instead of relying on the stock markets.

The advantages offered by this form of business organization are very clear. Through its more detailed knowledge of the situation of the companies it is involved in, the bank's corporate management is better equipped to weigh up the decisions it must make. By this means, it eliminates some of the asymmetric information problems that occur in the capital markets.

At the same time, the bank is able to detect, before the capital markets, any symptoms of crisis in any of the business units. And, if necessary, it can implement restructuring plans that are perhaps less dramatic or costly than the discipline that would be imposed by the capital market through hostile take-over bids (Aoki, 1988; Kester, 1991).

The disadvantages of this form of business organization are also well known, although they are sometimes forgotten. The first is that the close relationship between bank and companies means that the latter are protected from the watchful eye of the capital markets. The advocates of bank-company groups argue that the final product markets in which each business unit competes provide sufficient constraints to motivate the group to perform well, although it may not have the stimulus provided by the capital markets. We have already discussed this matter in Chapter 4.

Furthermore, the bank-industry group's own internal capital market raises some additional problems. Generally speaking, these are related to the problem of bounded rationality and to the capacity for managing complex organizations, which is usually limited. Indeed, the experience gained with bank-company groups and conglomerates has not always been positive and many conglomerates in different geographical settings have ended in failure (Berger and Ofek, 1995) and subsequent dismembering of its component units (Porter, 1987).

The possibility of carrying out a 'soft' restructuring of a company in difficulties, thanks to the internal capital market created in a conglomerate, is another reason that could justify, from the outlook of a country as a whole, the formation of bank-company corporations.

Why do bank-industry groups not always work in the real world, as the recent cases of Crédit Lyonnais and Banesto show? We have already suggested a generic cause: the increased complexity involved in an oversized organization.

Indeed, excessive spread of activities and the high number of different businesses lead to a situation in which the corporate management is no longer able to closely follow the course of each of the businesses and their competitive dynamics, with the result that the positive aspects of company groups—an internal capital market that is sometimes more efficient than the external capital market—disappears. This lack of information may lead to wrong decisions, particularly where corporate management is responsible for carrying out a large number of functions.

The second reason for the failures of those groups is that intangible or technological resources are not transferred smoothly from one company, as a result of communication, trust, or co-ordination problems.

As we have already pointed out, co-ordination and agency problems play a considerable role in resource transfer and prevent the advantages associated with the operation of a conglomerate or group of companies from being fully realized. This is a factor that helps explain why industrial groups and, in general, non-diversified acquisitions end up turning into a disinvestment after a few years, with the subsequent sale of the companies that were bought.

On the other hand, when organized as multidivision companies, universal banks do not always design efficient decentralization criteria or control and compensation mechanisms, for the reasons we have already given. However, even when this design is efficient and helps each division to operate properly, it may happen that the corporate office allocates or uses corporate resources inefficiently, for example, in the form of unrelated diversifications in activities in which the bank has no experience.[4]

5. SOME CONCLUSIONS

The discussion in this chapter has revolved around two arguments. The first is the diversification of universal banks' activities into other financial services (related diversification).

Among the advantages of a diversification strategy, we have mentioned the possible economies of scope between different financial services activities and the possibility of obtaining more accurate information on a company's situation, thus overcoming the objective difficulties that are found in the capital markets.

Among the disadvantages, we have underlined those arising from an excessive concentration of risks in certain companies, which brings an additional element of risk into the bank, both for the depositors and for the shareholders.

The second diversification decision analysed is that of banks' diversification into unrelated businesses. We have discussed a special case of universal banking: that in which the bank not only helps companies in their financing needs but also acquires a share in their capital. This is a situation in which the bank sits at the core of a group of industrial or service companies.

Here, the circumstances faced by that bank are slightly different from those of an ordinary universal bank. The bank is directly involved in these companies' management and the bank's market value is influenced not only by the present value of the companies it is involved in but by these companies' future prospects. Banesto and Crédit Lyonnais are examples of such banks.

Alliances of industrial corporations with banks may be useful in helping to create a country's industrial backbone or to ensure adequate financing for certain large-scale business projects. However, the difficulties faced by such projects are considerable, as empirical experience has shown. Normally, these difficulties are not related to the strategic approach of the companies the bank has invested in but to three types of problem: internal management and control problems of diversified, complex organizations; bounded rationality and asymmetric information problems; and problems arising from the management of companies competing in different industries and with their own competitive dynamics.

[4] Hoskisson and Turk (1990) develop and extend this argument to diversified companies. Silk and Berndt (1994) offer a somewhat different argument to account for the high degree of diversification in the advertising agency industry: the problem of the joint sale of services—something that also happens in the banking industry—and the impossibility of working with two customers in the same industry.

6

Germany: The Relationship between Banks and Non-Financial Companies

1. THE INVOLVEMENT OF BANKS IN NON-FINANCIAL COMPANIES

In the previous chapter, we discussed the main arguments that have justified, in certain cases, the creation of a financial conglomerate around a bank. In this chapter, we will analyse this situation from the viewpoint of a particular case: the bank-company groups in Germany.

One of the most widely held views on the German economy is that universal banks control a large part of the ownership and management of German companies. This situation, some authors argue (Porter, 1992), enables the emergence of capital committed to companies and makes it easier for them to adopt long-term strategies, and to undertake investment projects that are less appealing as regards short-term results. In addition, the link with a bank provides a source of resources for financing long-term projects.

Empirical evidence shows that the German companies' time frame is usually long term and that a large number of bank financing instruments are available for such investment projects. What is not so obvious, as we will discuss below, is that German banks control German industry.

German regulations regarding industrial holdings are as follows.[1] Purchase by a bank of an interest in a company exceeding 10 per cent of that company's equity must be reported to the Bundesbank. When a bank's interest in a non-financial company exceeds 10 per cent of the latter's equity, this holding must be secured by an equivalent volume of bank equity. This cautionary measure is also applicable whenever a bank purchases shares in another bank, whatever the size of the package bought. Finally, a bank's total investment in a company, both in shares and in loans, cannot exceed 50 per cent of the bank's share capital.

What is the true influence of German banks in German companies? An initial answer to this question is obtained by observing the historical role of banking in Germany's industrial development, particularly in the nineteenth century.[2]

[1] For a general overview of these issues, see Baums and Gruson (1993), Baums (1994), Edwards and Fischer (1994b), and Tilly (1986).

[2] See Baums and Gruson (1993), Franke and Hudson (1984), Gerschenkron (1962), and Tilly (1986).

TABLE 6.1 *Germany: banks' shareholdings* (1993)

	% of total capital
Deutsche Bank	
Daimler-Benz (Automobiles, aeronautics, electrotechnical)	24.4
Philip Holzmann (Construction)	25.9
Karstadt (Distribution)	10.0
Horten (Distribution)	25.0
Klöckner-Humboldt-Deutz (Machinery)	38.0
Linde (Machinery)	10.0
Südzucker (Foods)	12.8
Hapag-Lloyd (Tourism)	10.0
Continental (Tyres)	10.5
Metallgesellschaft (Metal)	10.6
Allianz (Insurance)	10.0
Münchener Rück (Insurance)	10.0
Dresdner Bank	
Bilfinger + Berger (Public works)	25.0
Brau & Brunnen (Restaurants)	25.6
Frankfurter Gesellschaft für Chemieworte (Chemical group)	20.0
Heidelberg Zement (Cement)	24.0
Hapag-Lloyd (Tourism)	10.0
Metallgesellschaft (Metals)	12.6
Allianz (Insurance)	10.0
AMB (Insurance)	13.7
Münchener Rück (Insurance)	10.1
Commerzbank	
Karstadt (Distribution)	10.0
Linde (Machinery)	10.3
Hochtief (Public works)	2.5
Thyssen (Steel)	5.0
DSD Dillinger (Steel)	30.0
MAN (Machinery)	6.3
Heidelberg Druckmaschinen (Machinery)	13.8
Linotype-Hell (Machinery)	6.7
Salamander (Footwear)	10.9

Source: Annual Reports.

The birth of heavy industry in Germany (coal, iron, steel, railways, etc.) is historically associated with the strong business thrust from the banks. This is probably one of the most distinctive features of the industrialization process on the European continent and what sets it apart from the economic history of the United States or Great Britain.

The existence of this historical precedent is perhaps one of the reasons why some authors point to the close relationship between banking and industry in Germany. However, this relationship is now very different.

Table 6.1 shows the main shareholdings of the three largest German banks in non-bank companies in 1993. Tables 6.2 and 6.3 show the changes in the composition of the shareholders and the true size of their respective holdings in the 50 largest German industrial corporations in 1978 and 1988. This information was prepared by the Monopolkommission, whose purpose was to determine the true impact of the bank's presence in industry in terms of potential monopoly power.

These tables show that banks do not hold an overwhelming controlling interest in the industrial sector. As we will see below, instead of saying that German banks control German industry, as is sometimes suggested, it would be more correct to say that the three largest German banks (Deutsche Bank, Dresdner Bank, and Commerzbank) possess significant holdings in some of the largest German companies (Harm, 1992a; Kester, 1992).

It should also be pointed out that there are no significant cross-holdings between companies with bank shareholders and other companies among the 50 largest corporations. In other words, cross-holdings between companies and banks within a group are small. If such cross-holdings were to exist, they would obviously increase the banks' true influencing power in industry (Immenga, 1978).

In order to help us understand the relationship between banks and companies, it may be useful to explain briefly the structure and functioning of boards of directors in Germany. The listed companies, 'Aktiengesellschaft' (AG), are in many ways similar to the Spanish 'Sociedad Anónima' or the British 'Public Limited Company'. These companies have two boards. The mission of the first of these, called the 'Aufsichtsrat', is more supervisory than executive. It meets approximately once every quarter and approves the company's most important investment and financing decisions. Its members are not company officials but professionals working in other fields or for other companies.

The second board is the 'Vorstand'. This is a true management committee with executive functions, whose members are company officials. In practice, this board has between five and fifteen members, it controls the company's day-to-day operations, and its activities are monitored by the 'Aufsichtsrat'.

The second type of legal structure used by many German companies is the 'Gesellschaft mit beschränkter Haftung' (GmbH), which is a limited liability company. In this type of company, there is a management committee and, if the company has more than 500 employees, it must also have a supervisory board.

The first reason why bank involvement is not, in fact, so pervasive is that most shares in industrial companies held by German banks are held in AG companies, some of which are listed companies. The turnover of this group of companies comprises only about 20 per cent of the total turnover of German companies (Harm, 1992a).

In terms of capital—not just turnover—it is more difficult to estimate the weight of the GmbHs. Tables 6.4 and 6.5 provide a comparison of sales turnover and capital of AGs and GmbHs. Obviously, the number of GmbHs is considerably greater than the number of AGs and the total capital of the GmbHs is

TABLE 6.2 *Germany: ownership structure of the 50 largest companies* (1978)

Name	Ranking	Owners (%)						
		Public sector	Banks and insurance	100 largest companies	Families	Foreign owners	Other investors	Small investors
Volkswagenwerk AG	1	20.00						60.00
Siemens AG	2							80.00
Daimler-Benz AG	3		>50.00	10.00		14.00		
Thyssen AG	4				>25.00			65.00
VEBA AG	5	44.00						56.00
BASF AG	6							>80.00
AEG-Telefunken	7							>50.00
Hoechst AG	8							>80.00
Ruhrkohle AG	9			27.20		13.02		
Bayer AG	10							>80.00
RWE AG	11	>50.00						
Friedrich Krupp GmbH	13				74.99	25.01		
ESSO AG	14							
Gutehoffnungshuette Aktienverein	15		30.00		–20.00			
Flick Industrieverwaltung KGaA	17				100.00			
Deutsche Shell AG	18							
Mannesmann AG	19							>80.00
Bosch GmbH	22							
Metallgesellschaft AG	23		>50.00	>25.00		16.46		
Reemtsma Cigarettenfabriken GmbH	24				65.00			

Gelsenberg AG	26			96.10				
Salzgitter AG	28	100.00						
Karstadt AG	30		>50.00					
ARAL AG	31			<84.00				
Deutsche BP AG	32							
Kaufhod AG	33		>50.00					
Gustav Schickedanz KG	40				100.00			
Oetker-Gruppe	41				100.00			
Henkel KGaA	43				100.00			
Kloeckner Humboldt Deutz AG	44			<50.00				>50.00
Deutsche Lufthansa AG	45	>75.00						
C&A Brenninkmeyer	47				100.00			
Bayerische Motorenwerke AG	49				>70.00			
CO OP Zentrale AG	50					22.40	77.60	

Source: Monopolkommission.

TABLE 6.3 *Germany: ownership structure of the 50 largest companies* (1988)

Name	Ranking 1972	Ranking 1988	Owners (%)						
			100 largest companies	Banks and insurance	Foreign owners	Public sector	Families	Small investors	Other investors
Daimler-Benz AG	3	1	2.00	34.90	14.00			44.60	4.50
Siemens AG	2	2					10.00	90.00	
Volkswagenwerk AG	1	3				17.60		82.40	
BASF AG	6	4						100.00	
Bayer AG	10	5						100.00	
Bosch GmbH	22	6					100.00		
Hoechst AG	8	7			>24.00			<76.00	
Ruhrkohle AG	9	8	90.50						9.50
VEBA AG	5	9						100.00	
Thyssen AG	4	10		9.90			25.60	64.50	
RWE AG	11	11	2.10		30.60			67.30	
Deutsche Bank AG	/	12						100.00	
Mannesmann AG	19	13					100.00		
Bayerische Motorenwerke AG	49	14	0.80	5.00			50.01	44.19	
Ford-Werke AG	/	15			99.80				0.20
Deutsche Lufthansa AG	45	16		5.00		71.45		23.55	
Adam Opel AG	/	17			100.00				
IBM Deutschland GmbH	/	18			100.00				
Dresdner Bank AG	/	19						100.00	
Friedrich Krupp GmbH	13	20			25.01		74.99		
MAN AG	/	21		21.20				78.80	
Allianz Holding AG	/	22						75.00	25.00
Messerschmidt-Boelkow-Blohm GmbH	82	23	13.7	14.60	10.70	52.30	8.70		
Commerzbank AG	/	24						100.00	
Karstadt AG	30	25		>50.00				<50.00	

Salzgitter AG	28	26				100.00			
Hoesch AG	/	27						100.00	
Allg. Deutsche Phillips Industrie GmbH	/	28			100.00				
Asea Brown Boveri AG	/	29			76.00			24.00	
Feldmühle Nobel AG	/	30						100.00	
REWE Handelsges. Leibbrand OHG	/	31					50.00		50.00
Deutsche Unilever GmbH	/	32			100.00				
Zahnradfabrik Friedrichshafen	/	33					100.00		
Standard Elektrik Lorenz AG	51	34			85.90			14.10	
Kaufhof AG	33	35						<50.00	>50.00
Gustav Schickedanz KG	40	36					100.00		
Bayerische Vereinsbank AG	/	37						86.00	14.00
Degussa	57	38	17.00	12.50				63.00	7.50
Saarbergwerke AG	56	39				100.00			
VEW AG	66	40	13.40	>15.9		>50.00		<20.70	
Bayer, Hypo. und Wechselbank AG	/	41		24.20				75.80	
Metallgesellschaft AG	23	42	8.68	42.50	35.00			13.82	
ITT Ges. für Beteiligungen mbH	/	43			100.00				
Carl-Zeiss-Stiftung	/	44							100.00
Bertelsmann AG	/	45					100.00		
Preussag AG	59	46		48.80			5.00	46.20	
Henkel KGaA	43	47					70.00	21.50	8.50
Nixdorf Computer AG	/	48					50.00	50.00	
BATIG Ges. für Beteiligungen mbH	/	49			100.00				
Continental Gummi-Werke AG	75	50						100.00	

Source: Monopolkommission.

TABLE 6.4 *Germany: Turnover by type of company (%)*

Type of company	1950	1972	1986
AG	16.5	19.1	21.1
GmbH	15.4	17.1	25.5
OHG	18.6	32.1	6.8
KG			24.0
Individual entrepreneur	36.9	23.8	15.4
Others	12.6	7.9	7.2
TOTAL	100.0	100.0	100.0

Source: Harm (1992a).

TABLE 6.5 *Germany AG companies: number and capital*

Year	AG companies		Listed AG companies	
	Number	Equity (DM bn.)	Number	Equity (DM bn.)
1954	2,530	20.2	677	10.6
1962	2,560	37.6	643	19.0
1970	2,304	55.6	550	29.7
1980	2,141	91.1	459	45.6
1989	2,508	132.0	486	65.6

Source: Edwards and Fischer (1994b).

almost three times that of the AGs. These figures highlight the limited scope of the supposed bank control of German non-financial companies.

Therefore, relatively few companies are listed companies. This implies that the number of listed companies in which the banks have major holdings cannot be too high. One reason for this is the general unwillingness of German entrepreneurs to list their company, due, in part, to cultural and family reasons.

The fact that many companies in Germany are family businesses is particularly interesting as, in direct contrast to popular belief, small and medium-sized companies comprise the overwhelming majority, as can be seen in Table 6.6. About 96 per cent of German companies in 1992 billed less than 5 million marks per year.

The existence of a main bank ('hausbank') in German companies is another important phenomenon. In companies where banks play a significant role, the relationship between banks and companies is not purely one of an equity holding. A company can have several banks among its shareholders but one bank is the 'hausbank', that is, a bank that acts as shareholder and leads a large part of the companies' financial operations. Generally, this relationship is longstanding, which means that the two parties tend to know each other very well. In this sense, the German 'hausbanks' perform a function similar to that of the

TABLE 6.6 *Distribution of German companies by turnover* (1985)

Turnover (DM '000)	No. of companies	Cumulative no. of companies (%)	Total sales (DM m.)	Cumulative sales (%)
< 50	299,541	14.8	10,357	0.2
< 100	336,304	31.4	24,551	0.8
< 500	821,656	72.1	196,846	5.4
< 1,000	238,193	83.9	167,885	9.3
< 5,000	248,384	96.2	512,984	21.4
< 25,000	60,940	99.2	627,452	36.1
<100,000	12,805	99.8	585,425	49.9
>100,000	4,011	100.0	2,129,802	100.0
TOTAL	2,021,824		4,255,302	

Source: Statistiches Bundesamt Annual Reports.

large Japanese banks that are at the core of the 'keiretsu', as we will see in Chapter 7.

A classic example of the relationship between a 'hausbank' and a company is that of Deutsche Bank and Daimler-Benz. Deutsche Bank has been Daimler-Benz's 'hausbank' and guided the merger process between the companies Mercedes and Benz. One of the consequences of this operation was that, until 1994, the president of this major industrial corporation was a senior Deutsche Bank official. This relationship has not prevented Daimler-Benz from having other banks as shareholders. Other classic examples of bank-industry close relationships in Germany are those of Volkswagen with Deutsche Bank and BMW with Dresdner Bank.

Finally, the sources of finance used by industrial companies provide interesting information on the relationship between banks and companies in Germany. Table 6.7 shows the changes that have taken place in the structure of German industrial companies' sources of finance between 1983 and 1991. The most important observations that can be made from this table are the following. First, the weight of equity capital is not very high (23.9 per cent in 1991) and barely varies during this period. Second, long-term debt is reduced by more than three points while short-term debt barely changes. Third, short-term bank debt remains virtually constant while long-term bank debt decreases by almost two points.

An important fact is the significant weight of long-term bank financing in total bank financing, which was 50 per cent in 1991. This means that, although bank debt has relatively little weight in companies' financial structure, more than half of this debt is long term. Another significant source of finance is the self-generated funds.[3]

[3] These facts seem to confirm Williamson's hypothesis—among others—according to which internal capital markets protect companies from asymmetric information and incentives problems of external capital markets.

TABLE 6.7 *Germany: financial structure of industrial companies*

	1983	1984	1985	1986	1987	1988	1989	1990	1991
Shareholders' equity	23.5	23.6	24.1	25.3	25.2	24.9	24.2	24.4	23.9
Long-term debt	16.5	15.6	15.3	15.1	14.1	14.0	13.6	13.1	13.1
Of this, with credit institutions	9.4	8.7	8.7	8.8	8.1	8.1	8.0	7.6	7.7
Short-term debt	38.4	37.9	37.1	35.5	34.9	35.2	36.6	37.0	37.8
Of this, with credit institutions	7.1	7.0	6.5	6.2	6.2	6.3	7.2	7.6	7.7
Provisions	21.6	22.9	23.6	24.2	25.7	25.9	25.6	25.5	25.3

Source: BACH (European Commission: General Directorate II) Annual Reports.

TABLE 6.8 *Liability structure of non-financial companies, Germany and the United States* (%)

	Germany		United States		
	1971	1991	1971	1991	1992
Shareholders' equity	25.8	23.9	47.0	—	36.8
Debt	63.1	50.9	46.0	50.4	63.1
Short-term	35.1	37.8	29.0	24.0	33.1
Long-term	28.0	13.1	7.0	12.4	30.1
Of this, debentures	2.8	3.3	10.0	23.1	—
Provisions	11.1	25.2	—	—	—

Source: Federal Reserve, Bundesbank, and BACH Annual Reports.

The financial structure of non-financial companies also has a number of important features. As can be seen in Table 6.8, German companies' level of indebtedness is similar to that of US companies. At the end of 1991, shareholders' equity accounted for only 24 per cent of German companies' financial resources, while in the United States, the percentage was 36.8 per cent. However, if we add provisions to German companies' shareholders' equity, the total amounts to 49.1 per cent. This figure indicates a lower level of indebtedness in German companies than in US companies. However, almost half of the debt of non-financial companies in the United States is long term, while, in Germany, only a quarter of non-financial companies' total debt is long term.

Thus, there are major differences between the behaviour of US and German banks when it comes to financing companies. However, it should be remembered that this behaviour depends not only on what banks want to do but also on the industry's regulatory context and the financing alternatives available to companies, particularly the development of financial markets.

Finally, Table 6.9 shows the sources of finance for investment used by non-financial companies in Germany (1970–89) and Britain (1970–87).

TABLE 6.9 *Origin of funds to finance investment: Germany and Britain (%)*

Germany (1970–1989)		Britain (1970–1987)	
Self-generated funds	58.8	Self-generated funds	59.9
Provisions	3.6		
Transfers	6.6	Transfers	5.7
Bank loans	18.0	Bank loans	27.2
Other loans	1.0	Fixed-income securities	2.4
Fixed-income securities	0.9	Variable-income securities	6.5
Variable-income securities	2.3	Commercial credit	1.2
Commercial credit	1.8	Adjustment	−2.9
Others	7.0		
TOTAL	100.0	TOTAL	100.0

Source: Edwards and Fischer (1994b).

We can see that in Britain the weight of self-generated funds is also quite significant. The differences between Britain and Germany are the following. First, British companies resort more to loans from financial firms (27.2 per cent versus 18 per cent in Germany). Second, British companies use equity capital (capital increases) to a significantly greater extent, generating three times as many funds by this means as German companies. Third, the volume of debt issued on the capital markets by British companies is almost three times that of German companies.

These figures show not only some features of German companies' financial structure but also that there are significant differences in the system of government and control, whose consequences we will discuss in the following sections.

2. BANKS AS SHARE DEPOSITORIES

If the analysis of bank shareholdings in industry does not confirm the banks' influence in industrial companies, are there other alternative procedures for measuring this apparent influence?

In Germany, there are indicators that can shed additional light. The first of these is the exercise of voting rights belonging to the shares deposited in German banks where administration of these shares has been delegated by their holders to the corresponding bank. Immenga (1988) points out that, in the late 1970s, German banks were custodians of 50–55 per cent of all listed shares.

One question that occurs immediately is the following: although the weight of capital is not very high in total corporate financing, who are the owners of these shares? If the answer were to be that the owners are mostly financial firms, it could be inferred that these organizations effectively control non-financial companies with a low percentage of total financial resources.

TABLE 6.10 *Germany: ownership of non-financial companies (%)*

	1960	1970	1988
Private individuals	28.1	29.8	21.1
Non-financial companies	35.7	36.9	43.0
Banks	7.0	7.6	10.4
Insurance companies	3.6	4.0	8.8
Government	13.6	9.3	4.6
Foreigners	12.0	12.4	12.1
TOTAL	100.0	100.0	100.0

Source: Deutsche Bundesbank Annual Report (1990).

TABLE 6.11 *Germany: ownership of AG companies*

	1984	1988
Private individuals	18.8	19.7
Non-financial companies	36.1	39.1
Banks	7.6	8.1
Investment funds	2.7	3.5
Insurance companies	3.1	2.7
Government	10.2	7.0
Foreigners	21.4	20.0
TOTAL	99.9	100.1

Source: Deutsche Bundesbank Annual Report (1990).

Table 6.10 provides some information on this. Thus, although the weight of banks in non-financial companies' share capital increased from 7 per cent in 1960 to 10.4 per cent in 1988, this percentage continues to be low.

Table 6.11 provides information on the ownership of the shares issued by German AG companies in 1984 and 1988. We can see that the percentage of such shares held by banks ranges between 7.6 per cent (1984) and 8.1 per cent (1988) of the capital.

Finally, Table 6.12 provides information on the AG companies with a controlling shareholder (more than 50 per cent of the voting shares) and the value of the holding. We can see that of the total number of companies with a controlling shareholder, banks were controlling shareholders in only 8 per cent of these in 1983. The market value of these companies out of the total value of AG companies amounted to only 3.3 per cent of total capitalization. Therefore, the weight of banks in controlling companies' market value is low.

A more recent study by the Deutsche Bundesbank (1989 Annual Report) pointed out that, at the end of 1988, shares worth 411,000 million Deutschmarks—approximately 40 per cent of the market value of all of the shares traded on the stock market—were deposited in German banks.

TABLE 6.12 *Germany: AG companies with a controlling shareholder* (1963–1983)

Type of shareholder	No.			Par value			Market value		
	1963	1973	1983	1963	1973	1983	1963	1973	1983
Families	26.7	23.8	22.6	15.0	8.9	6.9	10.2	7.6	6.4
Non-financial companies	6.9	11.1	11.3	5.5	7.9	7.1	3.0	7.2	5.3
Government	8.0	8.5	9.3	10.3	11.3	12.9	11.4	8.7	8.9
Foreigners	7.7	9.7	11.3	6.6	7.5	7.5	9.1	14.5	9.2
Banks	4.3	8.5	8.0	1.6	2.3	2.5	1.2	4.5	3.3
Insurance companies	1.6	0.9	1.7	0.3	0.2	0.5	0.4	0.3	1.1
Others	0.5	0.9	1.3	0.3	0.5	0.6	0.5	0.8	0.6
TOTAL	55.7	63.4	65.5	39.6	38.6	38.0	35.8	43.6	34.8

Source: Edwards and Fischer (1994b).

Obviously, the shares deposited in banks can be withdrawn at any time by their holders but the likelihood of hundreds of investors doing this at the same time is very low. This situation gives a certain degree of power a priori to the banks in their incursions in the boards of German industry.

A more thorough analysis of the situation brings additional information to light. Harm (1992a) points out that three-fifths of the value of the shares of listed companies is concentrated in ten companies, of which only eight seem to be under bank control, due to the extreme dispersal of share ownership. Again, with these figures, the supposed influence of banks shrinks considerably.

However, the custodianship of such a high volume of shares by the banks enables them to implement a process of monitoring these companies' strategy, results, and—generally—their strategy at all levels. Thus, German banks have access to abundant and, in many senses, unique information, which makes for a very special relationship with companies.

3. THE PRESENCE OF BANKS ON SUPERVISORY BOARDS

An alternative mechanism by which German banks could influence other companies is through the presence of bank-appointed directors on their boards. This presence could be the result of three situations: share ownership by banks; share custodianship by banks on behalf of others, as we have explained above; and, finally, lending capital or leading a public offering by a non-financial company. This combination of circumstances explains why many companies appoint bank representatives as directors of their respective supervisory boards.

In both AGs and GmbHs, bank representatives are on the supervisory board, composed, as we have already indicated, of people not employed by the companies themselves. They are not on the management committee, which is composed solely of professional managers.

In addition to approving the companies' ordinary, investment, and financing budgets, supervisory boards play a very important role in achieving accepted solutions to the problems that the company must face, particularly in situations of crisis and in the area of industrial relations. It is therefore understood that supervisory boards perform an important function in designing the company's long-term strategy and in solving possible temporary or permanent insolvency problems. In the latter case, the role of the banks represented on the supervisory board may be critical in refocusing the company's businesses and ensuring their continuity.

The evidence obtained from some German companies shows that the existence of these boards mitigates many potential conflicts within the company, enables longer-term time frames and, should it be necessary to restructure the firm, permits the pursuit of solutions that are acceptable to all parties. At the same time, supervisory boards may make it easier to obtain the necessary financial resources to overcome the crisis.

It is interesting to point out that one of the supervisory board's most important tasks is the appointment and dismissal of the company's senior managers. Thus, although the supervisory board does not take part in the dynamics of the company's day-to-day decisions, it does take part in them indirectly, through the selection and recruitment of senior managers.

Table 6.13 identifies the banks on the boards of some industrial companies, and vice versa. In an exhaustive analysis, the Monopolkommission (1989 Annual Report) carried out a survey of the presence of bank representatives on certain companies' boards of directors, not only AGs but also GmbHs. Of 84 companies with a supervisory board, 59 had at least one representative from the large banks on their board. The bank with the largest number of representatives was Deutsche Bank.

This presence of bank-appointed directors in industrial companies not only has the effect provided for by law and described above, but also creates the channels for the flow of information and communication between industrial companies and banks that is crucial for the formers' long-term survival. Furthermore, these information flows lead to a certain convergence of interests between banks and companies.

As a result of banks' presence, other financial institutions receive a clear signal when one of the large banks is involved in the company's management and long-term future, even though its direct involvement in financing is limited.

However, we would stress once more that the evidence is not conclusive. First, companies having a supervisory board represent a minority of industrial companies in Germany (about 30 per cent of the total number of industrial companies, which accounted for about 50 per cent of the industrial GDP in 1994).

Second, the number of bank representatives on the companies' supervisory boards is limited. In any case, the experience available does not seem to confirm

TABLE 6.13 *Boards of directors: some relationships between banks and industrial companies*

Company	No. of shareholders on board	Companies on board
BMW	11	Dresdner Bank
Daimler-Benz	11	Deutsche Bank
		Dresdner Bank
		Commerzbank
		Bayerische Landesbank Girozentrale
Porsche	6	Landesgirokasse öffentliche Bank und Landessparkasse
Volkswagen	10	Deutsche Bank
		Dresdner Bank
		Allianz AG Holding
Bank		**Companies on board**
Commerzbank	11	Bayer AG
		Hoechst AG
		MBB Messerschmitt-Bölkow-Blohm GmbH
		RWE AG
		SMS Schloemann-Siemag AG
		Volkswagen AG
Deutsche Bank	12	Beiersdorf AG
		Robert Bosch GmbH
		Siemens AG
Dresdner Bank	11	Altana Industrie-Aktien und Anlagen AG
		Hoechst AG
		Maschinenfabrik Goebel GmbH
		Thyssen AG

Source: Annual Reports.

the existence of a close relationship between the number of bank representatives on a supervisory board and the number of delegated votes (proxy votes) held by a bank in a particular company (Baums and Gruson, 1993; Edwards and Fischer, 1994b).

Third, on average, these companies have a lower percentage of debt than other industrial companies; in other words, bank debt has a significantly lower weight than in other companies. Furthermore, these companies obtain finance from all types of banks, including the three top banks.

4. BANK INVOLVEMENT IN CORPORATE RESTRUCTURING

It is generally believed that, in the past, the presence of representatives of the major German banks has been helpful in solving industrial companies' crises.

This argument has two sides to it. First, the presence of bank representatives makes it easier for banks to monitor the companies' operations more closely, thus avoiding hasty decisions or decisions that are excessively risky.

The second line of reasoning is that the presence of a bank on the board of a company in difficulties provides a powerful stimulus to find a less traumatic solution to the problem, as it is in the bank's interest—for a number of reasons (from the collection of possible debts to its reputation)—to arrive at an acceptable solution.

However, these arguments are not so black and white in real life. First, in recent years, there has only been one clear case of co-ordinated bank involvement in a major industrial crisis: the crisis of AEG. There are no other known cases of major business crises in which the bank system has intervened in a co-ordinated fashion. Metallgesellschaft's crisis in 1994—a company with close links with Deutsche Bank—required a different type of bank intervention.

Second, the ability of a director on the supervisory board to detect the company's problems in time to forestall them is limited. At times of sweeping technological change, global competition, and acceleration of the processes by which certain products are replaced by others, the directors' capacity to detect problems is not as great as might be imagined a priori, as they can only follow the company's performance in a partial and limited manner.

Finally, the directors' ability to detect these crises in the early stages will depend on their personal qualities, their real influence within the company, their knowledge of the company and their experience in the industry. So, one cannot infer universal conclusions in this case either. Edwards and Fischer (1994) show that in almost half of the cases, when a company encounters serious difficulties, banks withdraw their financing, which gives the impression that the bank's commitment to the company is not always long term.

On the other hand, traditional bank prudence, particularly in a financial system that is slow to assimilate innovations, such as the German system, would probably suggest the opposite. Banks would wish to take an active part in a company's board meetings, not only when they are shareholders or through the proxy votes of other shareholders, but also when there is a degree of certainty about the company's ability to cope with the challenges it faces. In this sense, a bank tends to be, by definition, risk averse, both in lending money and in investing directly in a company's capital.

Finally, the benefits to be gained from active management by a bank during a period of business crisis are, in principle, also limited. A bank may prefer to wind up the company and recoup part of its loans rather than opt for a rescue plan that will probably commit it even deeper in the future. Obviously, such an argument is highly conditional: for example, everything will hinge on the size of the bank's investment in the company or the harm that might be done to the bank's reputation. However, these same conditions indicate that it is not possible to draw general conclusions on the supposed advantages enjoyed by the banks when rescuing companies.

A completely separate area is the social responsibility that banks might bear as a result of their control of an industrial company. In such cases, this responsibility is a consequence of their status as controlling shareholder rather than of their status as financial intermediary. As we will see later, when a company has a controlling shareholder that is clearly interested in the company's management, the concentration of capital in a few hands seems to offer certain efficiency advantages[4] and, in fact, concentration of shareholders is greater in German companies than in US or British companies.

These controlling shareholders' interest in the company seems to offer an incentive to follow the company's progress closely. In other words, the cost of monitoring the company is borne by these controlling shareholders.

On the other hand, in a financial system such as the British or the American, where the number of shareholders is much greater, the small shareholders are probably less interested in closely following the company's progress. This is the typical 'free-rider' problem: when there is a larger shareholder, the small shareholders think that the large one will do this monitoring for them.

Returning to the German case, we can see that this concentration of shareholders does not consist of bank shareholders, but of private individuals or other industrial companies who invest in other companies' equity. The case of the Daimler-Benz group is significant in this sense.

Therefore, these shareholders, irrespective of whether or not they are financial intermediaries, share a particular interest in these companies' progress and, at times of crisis, may play an important role in satisfactorily resolving it. However, the role of financial intermediaries is more discrete in this context and, consequently, they cannot really be credited with having a decisive weight in the management of business crises.

Cable (1985) suggests that the presence of banks on German companies' supervisory boards has, over the course of history, helped improve their performance and long-term viability. We have already discussed the first part of this conclusion in previous pages. The presence of the German banks in companies has a limited influence.

Therefore, it seems logical to state that, in accordance with the argument we have just proposed, the presence of major shareholders in a company's equity may help improve the supervisory boards' control and monitoring functions, as the large shareholder will have a clear personal incentive to do so: if that shareholder did not do it, it is unlikely that another smaller shareholder would take on this responsibility.

Furthermore, a controlling shareholder can also obtain significant savings in the transaction costs incurred in the management process. These costs include, in particular, the ones related to investments in specific assets that are of little value to other companies, the costs of co-ordinating the interests of a large number of small shareholders or the costs associated with information collection.

[4] In spite of the arguments proposed against this by Demsetz and Lehn (1985), other authors show the existence of a positive relationship between shareholders' concentration and return. See Berglof (1990).

5. SOME CONCLUSIONS

The German financial system is a universal banking system with a high bank concentration, less sophisticated financial markets than in the United States, a small stock market compared with the German GNP, capital markets that do not perform the function of monitoring companies, and an extensive network of relationships between the large banks and the large companies.

The opinion that the presence of German banks in German industrial companies is important and positive for the country as a whole is based on a series of assumptions. First, it is assumed that the presence of banks in company financing (either as shareholders or as lenders) or through directors on the companies' supervisory boards, is very significant, more than in other economies, such as those of Britain or North America.

Second, there are economies of scale in information collection, company monitoring, and supervision (Diamond, 1984). These circumstances offer clear advantages for a bank that acts as financial intermediary and shareholder in a non-financial company. The presence of a major shareholder which is also a financial intermediary avoids, at least in part, the problems arising from the lack of effort that a large number of small shareholders would make in supervising and monitoring a company. The so-called free-rider problem disappears immediately.

Third, financing costs for a company that has bank representatives on its supervisory board may be lower. There are two reasons for this. Banks have access to complete information on what is going on in the company and, consequently, in many cases, the risk premium will be lower than when this presence does not exist. Furthermore, the presence of bank representatives on the supervisory board reduces the cost of such companies' financial crises and provides a good argument for other banks to lend money to the company. The second argument is particularly important for debt and capital issues.

In previous pages, we have made a few caveats to the validity of these arguments. These may be summarized as follows. First, the number of companies with supervisory boards in Germany is small: approximately 30 per cent of the total number of companies. The bank presence on supervisory boards is confined, to all practical purposes, to the three largest German banks (Deutsche Bank, Dresdner, and Commerzbank). The presence of a bank as shareholder of a company does not exclude the possibility of other banks also being shareholders of the same company.

Second, the three top German banks generally have minority capital holdings. These large banks are not the largest lenders to most of the companies in which they buy shares: generally, the bank loan market shows a low concentration.

On the other hand, basic financial intermediation theory states that when the information a bank has on a company is limited and the return on the investment is uncertain, the bank will grant a loan to the company rather than invest in its equity. When the information is more abundant and the company's risk is limited, the bank may find it more interesting to invest in the company's equity. However, the evidence obtained from companies with supervisory boards is that only 15 per cent of their total funds is composed of shareholders' equity. The rest is made up of external resources.

Third, German companies generally use bank debt to a lesser degree than Japanese, Spanish, or British companies. They rely much more on self-generated resources.

Fourth, generally speaking, restructuring and reorganizing costs are not lower in Germany than in Britain or the United States, where business restructuring usually takes the form of hostile take-over bids. Furthermore, the evidence of recent decades shows that very rarely do German banks intervene in company restructuring. Therefore, it can hardly be said that they play a crucial role in such processes.

Fifth, as a general rule, there is no direct relationship between the number of votes a bank has or represents on a supervisory board and its influence in the company's decisions. If such an influence exists, the reason for this is ultimately to be found in the fact that, as a major shareholder of the company, a bank is particularly interested in its progress, although one could say the same of other major non-financial shareholders.

Consequently, the supposed advantages of the presence of banks in German companies is related primarily to their status as controlling shareholders. However, this status can also be taken on or shared by other non-financial shareholders. A controlling shareholder has a greater incentive in the company's supervision and may gain significant savings in the costs associated with investments in specific assets and the co-ordination of decisions. At the same time, the controlling shareholder will try to avoid any opportunistic, short-term behaviour. Therefore, the presence of a controlling shareholder seems to be a distinctive feature of a good system of government for companies. However, we must add two qualifying observations to this general opinion.

First, when the controlling shareholder is a bank, it runs a greater risk due to the concentration of investments in a single company and some monitoring problems. If the company should run into difficulties, for reasons, for example, related to the industry it operates in, the bank's solvency and profitability might be seriously damaged.

There are numerous examples of bank crises occurring as a result of disastrous industrial investments. The 1992–3 recession in Europe has caused resounding bank crises such as those of Banesto and Crédit Lyonnais and has affected, to a certain extent, large banks such as Deutsche Bank.

The second observation is of a social nature. The concentration of economic power in a few hands—large shareholders who control large corporations—may offer efficiency advantages but raises potential monopoly problems.

On the other hand, the German financial system is also witnessing a significant growth of capital markets. This development is having two effects. First, non-financial companies now have access to some alternative sources of finance other than banks. Second, banks are creating subsidiaries to operate on capital markets and thus carve off for themselves a chunk of the emerging financial business.

We can conclude from this second fact that banks are not going to lose their core role in the German financial system and that, although the nature of the relationship between the banks and the large companies may change, it will not fade away.

7

The Japanese Main Bank System and its Influence on Industry

1. INTRODUCTION

The structure of Japan's banking system was shaped in the 1950s, during the period of national reconstruction. However, the developments that gave rise to the Japanese financial model after the Meiji Restoration, in the second half of the nineteenth century, are still present today.

Among these developments, there were two which had a particularly strong influence on the subsequent development of the Japanese financial system. First was the crucial influence of the Central Bank, whose formal sphere of action was confined to a few functions specified by law; however, unofficially it permeated all areas of the financial system. In particular and among other tasks, the role of the Central Bank before the Second World War consisted of developing specialized institutions that provided financing for specific purposes: agriculture, industry, housing, and exports. In the process, the Central Bank adopted part of the banking model followed in France, where the existence of specialized financial institutions is also an important feature.

The second development, following directly from the first one, is the specialization of activities between the different financial organizations, both in terms of the time frame of the operations undertaken (short term versus long term) and in terms of the operations or industry financed by the banks.[1]

Figure 7.1 provides an overview of the structure of the Japanese financial system. Among organizations governed by private law it is usually advisable to differentiate between banks and non-bank firms, mainly insurance companies. In this chapter, we refer solely to private banks.

One of the most striking features of the Japanese banks in the 1970s and 1980s was the speed with which they shot up into the ranks of the world's largest banks. Table 7.1 lists the world's largest banks between 1969 and 1994 by volume of assets. Table 7.2 lists the world's largest banks by volume of international issues. Again, one is struck by the high percentage of Japanese banks in these lists.

Table 7.3 provides a comparison between Japanese commercial banks and

[1] For a detailed discussion, see Cargill and Royama (1988), Suzuki (1980, 1987), Patrick and Park (1994), Yamamura and Yasuba (1987).

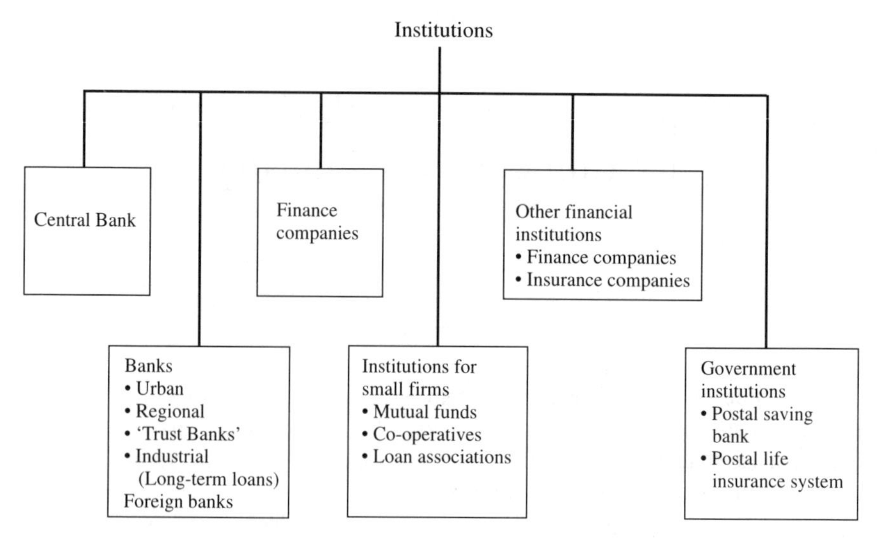

FIG. 7.1 *The Japanese financial system: institutions*

TABLE 7.1 *Japanese banks: world ranking* (1969–1994) (total assets)

	1969	1979	1981	1982	1985	1988	1990	1991	1994
Dai-Ichi Kangyo Bank		10	8	8	2	1	1	1	3
Sumitomo Bank	17	16	11	13	4	2	3	2	4
Mitsubishi Bank	16	17	14	12	5	4	2	3	1*
Mitsui (Sakura) Bank	29	36	24	23	18	13	4	4	5
Fuji Bank	13	14	13	10	3	3	6	5	2
Sanwa Bank	18	18	17	16	7	5	5	6	6
Norinchukin Bank	—	19	20	25	11	7	14	8	7
Industrial Bank of Japan	28	22	25	21	13	6	9	10	8
Tokai Bank	36	34	27	29	17	9	13	14	12
Bank of Tokyo	26	43	22	18	24	18	17	19	1*

* In 1995, after the merger between the Bank of Tokyo and Mitsubishi Bank.
Source: *The Banker*.

those of other Western countries, using certain efficiency indicators, between 1988 and 1990. These figures provide ample evidence of the Japanese banks' financial strength, which were severely tested after 1991 with the advent of the Japanese financial crisis, from which the Japanese banking system, weighed down by a series of highly doubtful investments, had still not recovered at the end of 1995. Tables 7.4 and 7.5 compare the productivity of the Japanese banks with some Western banks. One particularly striking point is the volume of bank assets per employee, which is about nine times larger in Japan than in other Western banks.

TABLE 7.2 *International bond issues* (1984–1994)

		1984	1985	1986	1987	1988	1989	1990	1991
Nomura International Group	Japan	6	5	4	1	1	1	1	1
Crédit Suisse/CSFB Group	Switzerland/USA	5	3	7	2	2	6	2	2
Daiwa Securities	Japan	8	10	8	3	4	2	5	3
Deutsche Bank	Germany	4	6	3	5	3	5	4	4
Goldman Sachs	USA	17	19	16	18	16	15	13	5
Paribas	France	14	16	11	12	9	11	11	6
Merrill Lynch	USA	9	7	5	22	8	9	12	7
Union Bank of Switzerland	Switzerland	3	2	1	7	5	14	3	8
Morgan Stanley	USA	7	8	6	9	17	10	20	9
Swiss Bank Corp.	Switzerland	2	1	2	10	14	22	7	10
Yamaichi Securities	Japan	16	17	17	6	7	3	10	11
Nikko Securities	Japan	15	18	12	4	6	4	9	12
Salomon Brothers	USA	1	4	9	13	15	12	8	13
J. P. Morgan	USA	7	9	10	8	11	7	6	14
S. G. Warburg Group	United Kingdom	10	11	13	11	10	17	16	15
Crédit Lyonnais	France	27	21	23	48	30	16	19	16
Industrial Bank of Japan	Japan	33	24	21	14	13	13	14	17
Crédit Commercial de France	France	50	32	39	34	28	24	15	18
Dresdner Bank	Germany	13	15	18	17	18	21	31	19
Hambros Bank	United Kingdom	—	—	—	25	20	19	22	20

Source: *Institutional Investor*.

TABLE 7.3 *Financial ratios for the banking industry* (1988–1990)[a]

	Return on shareholders' equity (%)	Return on assets (%)	Operating expenses over assets (%)	Debt/equity
1988				
France	15.29	7.42	1.64	45.3
Germany	17.93	6.89	2.36	20.3
Italy	10.60	7.69	2.77	15.8
Japan	25.18	5.28	0.68	39.1
Spain	13.82	9.61	3.25	7.8
Switzerland	10.24	5.99	1.45	15.3
United Kingdom	24.77	11.04	3.29	16.3
USA	21.28	9.94	3.23	16.9
1989				
France	15.05	8.08	1.56	44.6
Germany	16.88	7.66	2.22	18.4
Italy	12.49	7.01	2.16	17.3
Japan	15.69	5.65	0.54	36.1
Spain	16.84	10.53	3.11	9.0
Switzerland	10.21	7.39	1.54	14.4
United Kingdom	2.10	11.65	3.19	19.4
USA	11.00	10.49	3.28	17.4
1990				
France	11.48	8.21	1.47	38.0
Germany	14.92	7.93	2.09	18.3
Italy	13.5	8.31	2.57	15.3
Japan	11.40	6.90	0.60	33.1
Spain	16.33	11.38	3.12	9.0
Switzerland	8.26	8.06	1.54	14.8
United Kingdom	13.76	13.20	3.32	20.4
USA	10.09	10.47	3.48	16.4
Average (1988–1990)				
France	13.94	7.90	1.56	42.6
Germany	16.58	7.49	2.22	19.0
Italy	12.23	7.67	2.50	16.0
Japan	17.42	5.94	0.60	36.1
Spain	15.66	10.51	3.16	8.6
Switzerland	9.57	7.15	1.51	14.8
United Kingdom	13.54	11.96	3.27	18.7
USA	14.12	10.30	3.33	16.9

[a] For a group of the largest commercial banks.

Source: OECD (1992).

TABLE 7.4 *Japanese banking system: assets and productivity* (1991)

Institution	'Keiretsu'	Assets (US$ m.)	Employees	Assets per employee (US$ m.)
Long-Term Credit Bank of Japan	—	230,775	3,448	66.9
Industrial Bank of Japan	IBJ	320,498	4,900	65.4
Nippon Credit Bank	—	131,337	2,449	53.6
Sanwa Bank	Sanwa	436,750	13,913	31.4
Mitsubishi Bank	Mitsubishi	423,243	13,899	30.5
Fuji Bank	Fuyo	435,970	15,200	28.7
Sumitomo Bank	Sumitomo	446,472	16,669	26.8
Dai-Ichi Kangyo Bank	DKB	458,962	18,640	24.6
Tokai Bank	Tokai	269,523	11,748	22.9
Mitsubishi T&B	Mitsubishi	139,950	6,667	21.0
Sakura Bank	Mitsui	435,846	22,919	19.0
Sumitomo T&B	Sumitomo	126,856	7,451	17.0
Mitsui T&B	Mitsui	109,395	6,582	16.6

Note: Exchange rate: US$1 = 140.6 yen.
Source: Bank of Tokyo Annual Report.

TABLE 7.5 *Other financial firms: assets and productivity* (1991)

Institution	Country	Assets (US$ m.)	Employees	Assets per employee (US$ m.)
J. P. Morgan	USA	102,416	13,323	7.7
Bankers Trust	USA	63,684	12,171	5.2
Banque Nationale de Paris	France	289,747	59,676	4.9
Société Générale	France	204,485	45,776	4.5
Crédit Lyonnais	France	285,238	68,486	4.2
ABN–Amro Bank	Netherlands	242,686	58,329	4.2
Deutsche Bank	Germany	296,226	71,400	4.1
Crédit Agricole	France	302,983	74,450	4.1
Chemical Banking	USA	137,623	41,951	3.3

Source: Disclosure/Worldscope Global Database; Value Line.

2. PRIVATE FINANCIAL FIRMS IN JAPAN

2.1. Commercial banks

Japanese commercial banks focus primarily on short-term operations (both in their lending activities and in attracting deposits) and perform the traditional function of providing and guaranteeing the country's system of payments (Suzuki, 1987). Exceptionally, some banks also carry out medium and long-term financing operations. It is customary to distinguish between three types of commercial bank: urban banks, regional banks, and foreign banks. Table 7.6 shows the share of the various banks in the banking system's assets and liabilities.

Urban banks locate their headquarters in a large city, and have a vast network of branches that covers the entire country. This group is composed of 13 banks and it is estimated that their market share, both in bank loans and in bank deposits, accounts for about 20 per cent of the total financial system in 1992. Table 7.7 shows the distribution of the urban banks' total liabilities and the weight of each item in these banks' balance sheets.

Of the total of 13 urban banks, four belong to larger financial groups which offer a wide range of financial services. These are Mitsubishi,[2] Mitsui, Sumitomo, and Fuyo. For a complete list of the urban banks, see Table 7.8.

However, the distribution of the urban banks' business between types of company is not homogeneous. Their business is primarily with large companies and although, in recent years, they have tried to attract medium-sized companies, large corporations continue to occupy a very significant part of the urban banks' business. For example, at the end of 1990, about 50 per cent of their lending activity was aimed at large companies (Federation of Bankers Associations of Japan, 1990 Annual Report).

The urban banks are exponents of one of the distinctive features of the Japanese financial system: the so-called main bank (Aoki and Patrick, 1994). This bank is, first of all, the bank with which a company has the closest business relationship. But the concept of a main bank means much more than this and includes the relationships and practices between a company and its principal bank which range from the provision of financial services to share swapping and include the presence of the bank's representatives on the company's board of directors.

The concept of a main bank, which is similar in many ways to that of the 'hausbank' in Germany, refers to a system of running companies which has had a profound influence in Japan. A company's main bank is usually one of its major shareholders, as well as being the bank with which the company carries out the largest share of its financial transactions. Thus, the business groups or 'keiretsu' are groups clustered around a main bank at their core. However, other companies with a main bank are not incorporated in a 'keiretsu'. We will come back to this point in Section 4 of this chapter.

The second type of commercial bank is the regional bank, which operates within a particular region. This category includes 64 organizations specializing primarily in providing financial services to local small and medium-sized companies and local governments. The foreign banks comprise the third type of commercial bank. In order to gain entry to the Japanese market, a foreign

[2] This bank merged with the Bank of Tokyo in 1995, becoming the largest bank in the world by volume of assets.

Table 7.6 *Japanese banks: assets and liabilities* (bn. yen)

	Loans to non-financial companies		Financial assets		Deposits		Debentures		Equity capital	
		%		%		%		%		%
All banks										
1980	179,590	100.0	49,696	100.0	215,869	100.0	20,685	100.0	10,758	100.0
1984	266,053	100.0	66,459	100.0	293,603	100.0	29,643	100.0	11,323	100.0
1988	419,993	100.0	108,075	100.0	423,813	100.0	43,304	100.0	18,426	100.0
1989	466,667	100.0	125,097	100.0	481,943	100.0	45,875	100.0	25,467	100.0
Urban banks										
1980	66,631	37.1	16,827	33.9	85,418	39.5	1,395	6.7	4,463	41.5
1984	96,439	36.2	20,135	30.3	114,815	39.1	2,286	7.7	4,809	42.5
1988	177,183	42.2	37,102	34.3	172,817	40.8	4,148	9.6	8,930	48.5
1989	195,523	41.9	44,287	35.4	195,456	40.7	4,233	9.2	11,995	47.1
Regional banks										
1980	43,640	24.3	13,937	28.0	58,788	27.2	—	—	4,114	38.2
1984	65,431	24.6	18,315	27.6	83,731	28.5	—	—	4,226	37.3
1988	94,368	22.5	26,694	24.7	120,522	28.4	467	1.1	4,735	25.7
1989	106,759	22.9	30,291	24.2	135,969	28.2	355	0.8	5,975	23.5
Foreign banks										
1989	4,672	2.6	165	0.3	1,249	0.6	1,077	5.2	—	—
1984	6,849	2.6	391	0.6	1,712	0.6	263	0.9	—	—
1988	6,475	1.5	1,140	1.1	1,463	0.3	976	2.2	—	—
1989	6,966	1.5	1,366	1.1	2,163	0.4	328	0.7	—	—

Source: Economic Statistics Annual 1989, March 1990; Bank of Japan.

TABLE 7.7 *Japanese urban banks: liability structure* (% of total liabilities)

Year	Deposit	CD*	Bank bonds (%)	Interbank	Other bank loans
1950	55.5	—	—	0.2	8.5
1955	75.3	—	—	2.3	0.9
1960	73.9	—	—	3.1	5.7
1965	66.3	—	0.2	4.9	6.0
1970	65.9	—	0.3	5.5	5.8
1975	65.4	—	0.9	2.9	1.8
1980	69.5	0.1	1.1	3.7	1.5
1985	59.2	0.3	1.3	3.5	1.6
1986	62.4	0.3	0.4	5.0	2.4
1987	63.2	0.3	1.4	4.9	2.1
1988	61.3	0.3	1.5	4.4	1.9

* Certificates of deposit.

Source: Bank of Japan; Economic Statistics Annual.

bank must be licensed by the Japanese Ministry of Finance. Normally, its main business activities are foreign exchange operations and financing international operations undertaken by Japanese companies in their home countries, or operations undertaken by companies from their home countries in Japan. Until very recently, the steps required by the Japanese Ministry of Finance for a foreign bank to obtain a licence to operate in Japan have been numerous and complex.

2.2. *Specialized financial institutions*

Foremost among the specialized institutions are the long-term lending institutions. Within this group, in turn, we must distinguish between long-term loans banks and trust banks.

The long-term lending banks, created by a law passed in 1952, specialize in granting long-term financing. This sets them clearly apart from the ordinary banks, both by the type of operation and by the restricted geographical penetration. Furthermore, their sources of finance are not the deposits made by private individuals but long-term certificates of deposit (CDs). They can take deposits, but only from buyers of these certificates.

Trust banks perform functions that are relatively similar to those of the long-term lending banks, with the difference that the law also allows them to carry out custodianship and security trading activities. They can also take deposits.

The firms operating on the foreign exchange markets comprise the second group of specialized organizations. The main reason for their existence is that the Japanese economy—previously highly dependent on the rest of the world—needs to have organizations specializing in obtaining foreign exchange. Legislation

TABLE 7.8 *Some Japanese financial companies within 'keiretsu'*

'Keiretsu'	Bank/company	
	Name	Status
Mitsubishi Group		
Banks	Mitsubishi Bank	Urban bank no. 4
	Mitsubishi Trust	Trust bank no. 1
	Nippon Trust	Trust bank no. 7
	Hachijuni Bank	
	Shinwa Bank	
Insurance	Tokyo Marine & Fire	Non-life insurance no. 1
	Meiji Mutual Life	Life insurance no. 1
	Misshin Fire & Marine	
Leasing	Diamond Lease	
Consumer finance	Diamond Credit	Portfolio management no. 3
Investment banks	Nikko Securities	
	Ryoko Securities	
Real estate	Mitsubishi Estate	
Mitsui Group		
Banks	Mitsui Bank	Urban bank no. 7
	Mitsui Trust	Trust bank no. 3
Insurance	Taisho Marine & Fire	Non-life insurance no. 3
	Mitsui Mutual Life	
Leasing	Mitsui Leasing & Development	
Real estate	Mitsui Real Estate Development	
Sumitomo Group		
Banks	Sumitomo Bank	Urban bank no. 2
	Sumitomo Trust	Trust bank no. 2
	Kansai Bank	
	Mie Bank	
Insurance	Sumitomo Marine & Fire	Non-life insurance no. 4
	Sumitomo Life	Life insurance no. 3
Leasing	Sumisho Lease	
	SB General Leasing	
Investment bank	Daiwa Securities	Portfolio management no. 2
Real estate	Meiko Securities	
	Sumitomo Realty & Development	
Fuyo Group		
Banks	Fuji Bank	Urban bank no. 3
	Yasuda Trust	Trust bank no. 4
	Chiba Kogyo Bank	
	Ogaki Kyontsu Bank	
	Shikoku Bank	
	Higo Bank	
	Higo Family Bank	
Insurance	Yasuda Fire & Marine	Non-life insurance no. 1
	Yasuda Mutual Life	
	Nichido Fire & Marine	
Leasing	Fuyo General Lease	
	Fuyo General Development	
Investment banks	Yamaichi Securities	Portfolio management no. 1
	Daito Securities	
Real estate	Tokyo Tatemono	

Source: *The Economist*, 25 March 1989, p. 92.

provides that these firms may issue debt for terms up to three years, up to a limit equal to or less than ten times the bank's net worth.

The third group of banks consists of organizations specializing in financing small and medium-sized companies. These are the 'Sogo'. Created in 1951, these organizations were vital in turning around foundering mutual societies. However, in recent years, the restrictions on their scope of geographical and operational activity have been lifted. The only type of restriction still applied refers to the type of customer. These must be companies having fewer than 300 employees and billing less than 800 million yen.

The second group of organizations within the special category that engage in financing small companies are the 'Shinkin'. Their main difference from the 'Sogo' is that they are non-profit making, and are similar to co-operative societies in Europe. However, their customers are also small companies with fewer than 300 employees and billing less than 400 million yen. There is also a national confederation, known as the 'Zenshinren', which mainly acts as banker for the 'Shinkin' member banks.

Our description of the various specialized financial institutions in Japan shows that this specialization has not come about as a result of evolution or chance but of a direct government intervention in the Japanese financial system (Packer, 1994). The purpose of this intervention has been to set up a series of financial mechanisms for channelling the resources needed by companies. However, in its attempt to give a specific form to this objective, the Japanese government has established a relationship between banks and non-financial companies that leads to a system of corporate management and control that is different from that existing in other industrialized countries.

2.3. Other private financial firms

The two most important non-bank financial institutions in Japan are insurance companies and securities firms. Both types of institution carry out the activities that are typical of their main field of business. However, there are a number of distinctive features that it is worth mentioning.

The first is the strong presence of insurance companies in the Japanese industry. Kester (1991) estimated that about 20 per cent of the shares of Japanese listed companies were held by insurance companies in 1990. This percentage is much higher than in any other industrialized country.

Second, stock market trading is separated from banking activity by the 1948 Japanese Banking Act. This segment of financial activity did not take off until 1960, when economic growth in Japan started to gain speed.

During the 1980s, these institutions amassed an enormous economic power, not only in Japan but also on the international stock markets. Out of a total of more than 200 firms, a large part of the sector's business was concentrated in just four firms: Nomura, Daiwa, Nikko, and Yamaichi.

3. THE REGULATION OF THE JAPANESE FINANCIAL SYSTEM AND ITS IMPACT

The extent of bank specialization and the high degree of regulation by the financial authorities are two of the dominant features of the Japanese financial system. In our discussion in Section 2, we stressed that this situation is not a result of chance. The post-war Japanese financial system is the result of an explicit design which has had major effects on the Japanese economy.

The regulation of the Japanese financial system, in general, and the bank system, in particular, are among the most dense and extensive of the industrial world, clearly greater than that in the EU member countries and much more meticulous than that in the United States.

The Japanese regulatory system can be classified under two main concepts: the behaviour of the banks and the structure of the banking industry and, in particular, the limits of the links permitted between commercial banking and investment banking activities (Suzuki, 1987). There is a third concept referring to bank solvency and statutory levels of net worth. The rules included in this category of regulatory measures were proposed by the Bank for International Settlements (BIS) in 1988 and subsequently accepted by the Central Bank of Japan.

The first restriction on bank behaviour is that concerning the limits on interest rates. The interest rates on the Japanese banks' assets and liabilities were traditionally set by the Central Bank of Japan. Under the Temporary Control of Interest Rates Act, the Bank of Japan has been able to set and modify interest rate ceilings on all assets and liabilities operations.

However, these regulations have been phased out over the last few years. Competition from other financial and non-financial organizations and from the capital markets has meant that a policy of maintaining artificially low interest rates, such as that advocated by the Bank of Japan, is no longer viable. Long-term loans, certificates of deposit and other money market instruments, and time deposits were deregulated during the second half of the 1980s. In October 1994, the Bank of Japan completed full liberalization of interest rates. If the experience of other countries is of any value, almost complete price deregulation is inevitable. In the short term, this deregulation process has exacerbated the Japanese bank system's crisis as the banks have adopted more aggressive sales policies, with the subsequent shrinkage of profits.

The traditional *modus operandi* of the Japanese banks and the slowness with which the deregulation process has been implemented may prevent a cut-throat war to increase market share by raising interest rates on deposits and lowering interest rates on loans, as has happened in Britain, Germany, and Spain. However, the trend within the system is towards a complete liberalization of the prices of financial services.

The second limitation on the behaviour of financial firms refers to their lending policies and, in particular, to the concentration of risks. Banks are not allowed to grant loans to a single company—including subsidiaries and affiliates, if any—to a total amount exceeding 20 per cent of the bank's net worth. This percentage is increased to 30 per cent for banks specializing in long-term loans and 40 per cent for banks specializing in currency operations.

The regulation also states that, in the event that a bank provides guarantees, or open letters of credit, to a customer that has received loans from that bank, the total risk—including these operations—cannot exceed 30 per cent of the bank's total resources.

The legislation also provides for limits on bank holdings in other companies. The Japanese Anti-Trust Act limits a bank's direct interest in a company's equity to 5 per cent. Until 1987, the maximum limit was 10 per cent. This provision allows the formation of groups of companies around a main bank, even though the bank's interest in the companies' equity is not very high.

One final regulation affecting Japanese banks refers to their dividend policy. The dividends paid cannot exceed 40 per cent of net income after tax. This policy is aimed at increasing the banks' capitalization.

The second body of regulatory measures relates to the industry's structure and configuration. The first chapter establishes the separation between commercial and investment banking activities. This separation is stated in Article 65 of the Financial Assets Act and is somewhat more restrictive than the US Glass–Steagall Act.

In practice, this regulation has led to specialization and the creation of compartments within the Japanese banking system, based on the type of operation carried out by each financial organization and the term of such operations.

During the 1960s and 1970s, Japanese banks were able, without regulation, to carry out activities such as issuing and trading in commercial paper, trading in public debt, placing other companies' debt issues, providing financial consulting services through subsidiary banks, and trading in debt for their own investment portfolios. However, the dramatic changes that have taken place in the international financial system now strictly limit their freedom to do so. Consequently, the Central Bank of Japan was studying measures at the end of 1995 aimed at achieving a greater degree of liberalization of bank activities, leading eventually to the disappearance of the barriers separating the different types of bank.

In addition, banks may hold up to 50 per cent of the equity capital of a subsidiary operating on the stock market. For its part, a securities firm may hold up to 50 per cent of a bank's equity capital. Likewise, industrial companies may control bank ownership. This would regularize the situation of companies such as Toyota, which has created a subsidiary that grants loans to dealers or buyers of Toyota cars.

Another structural restriction refers to the presence of foreign banks in Japan.

For many years, the Japanese banking industry was, to all practical effects, out of bounds to possible foreign investors. In 1970, there were 16 foreign banks operating in Japan; these banks mainly operated in the currency market and in financing export credit for Japanese companies.

The increasing importance of the Japanese economy in the world has led to increasing pressure being brought to bear on the Japanese authorities to allow a greater presence of foreign banks and authorize them to carry out a wider range of activities. However, these remained limited, by definition, to operations on the foreign exchange market and the public debt market on behalf of third parties. The structural and legal difficulties in opening branches prevented foreign banks from developing a commercial banking system, forcing them to depend on the resources obtained on the interbank market.

In 1984, the Japanese government authorized foreign banks to buy and sell Japanese public debt. The size of this market in Japan opened the doors to an important segment for foreign banking.

In 1985, foreign banks were authorized to create branches specializing in portfolio management. The growing importance of the Tokyo Stock Exchange and the large current account surpluses were turning the Japanese financial markets into the world's second largest financial power. It was becoming increasingly interesting for foreign banks—particularly American banks—to enter these markets. However, subsequent experience has not been particularly positive, due to the increasing competition in this market segment and the stock market slump in recent years.

Another category of regulatory measures refers to minimum capital requirements. These requirements were proposed by the BIS in July 1988 and accepted by the central banks of the countries belonging to the so-called Group of 10 and, afterwards, by most industrialized countries.

These regulations mean that, after 1993, banks must fulfil a ratio between net worth and risk-bearing assets of 8 per cent. The net worth in this case corresponds to the so-called tiers 1 and 2. Tier 1 capital had to meet a ratio of 4 per cent of total resources. Tier 1 (core capital) includes equity capital, retained earnings, preference shares, and minority holdings, less goodwill, if any. Tier 2 (complementary capital) includes any type of shares with special rights, subordinated debt, and 45 per cent of reserves from unrealized capital gains on financial assets.

The chief problem faced by Japanese banks in recent years has been to bring themselves into line with these requirements, which are exceptionally strict, considering that at the end of 1992, the ratio between net worth and risk-bearing assets was only 2.7 per cent. In fact, the provision of 45 per cent of reserves from unrealized capital gains on financial assets was a clause that the Bank of Japan managed to insert in the Basle agreement to make the transition easier for Japanese banks.

This brief outline portrays a highly regulated, hierarchical, specialized financial system, in which banks also play an important part in the management of companies, as we will describe in the rest of the chapter. It is therefore a model with a high level of public interventionism.

4. BANKING AND NON-FINANCIAL COMPANIES IN JAPAN

The relationship between banking and industry in Japan has brought about a spectacular growth not only of the country's industrial base but also of the Japanese banks themselves. The historical evidence shows that the mutual relationships between banks and companies have been beneficial for both sides (Sheard, 1994).

The birth of the modern Japanese firm dates back to the second half of the nineteenth century. Even at that time, we can find certain characteristic features of the modern industrial corporation, such as the relationship between the company and the members of the family owning the company's shares, the relationship between customers and suppliers, and the presence of banking in the business activities of industrial companies. In many cases, this bank involvement occurred because a number of large corporations had created their own financial organization, so that the company's growth and management would not be limited by financial aspects.

After the Second World War, the Japanese economy commenced a period of reconstruction during which the members of the families owning the companies were displaced from management functions by professionals appointed by the banks (Kester, 1991). This relationship between banks and industrial companies consolidated itself for a cultural reason: the preference of Japanese employers for establishing implicit contracts—such as those deriving from the presence of suppliers on a company's board of directors—rather than maintain a pure market relationship. Finally, the financial specialization in long-term loans and the possibility for a bank to purchase shares in non-financial companies were the final touches to an institutional framework that has brought about the development of the rule of close relationships between banks and companies.

This relationship between banks and companies deepened in the 1960s in response to the goal sought by many Japanese industrial companies: growth of sales and market share in the global markets. Normally, the shortage of long-term financial resources is one of the major factors limiting a company's growth. The coalition between banks and companies helped ease this problem in Japan.

Obviously, this relationship increased the volume of risk the banks were exposed to. In fact, some of them—particularly, the medium-sized banks—started to experience difficulties. However, economic growth, the strong personal relationships, and the continual presence of the Central Bank of Japan in the day-to-day functioning of the financial system helped in the prompt, panic-free solution of these problems and prevented them from spreading to other organizations in the financial system.

The archetype of this relationship between banks and companies was the 'keiretsu' or industrial conglomerate headed by one of the large industrial banks or, failing this, one of the large trading companies. Table 7.9 shows the relationships between the members of the Mitsubishi Group, at whose core is the Mitsubishi Bank. The 'keiretsu' groups can also include other financial organizations, such as insurance companies or securities firms.

In section 2 of this chapter, we stressed the importance of the main bank in the Japanese financial system. Obviously, the 'keiretsu' is a particular structure within which a main bank operates. However, the concept and practice of the main bank in Japan goes beyond the sphere of the 'keiretsu' to include a large number of companies that are not included in a 'keiretsu'. Consequently, most of the advantages and disadvantages associated with the existence of a main bank are directly applicable to the 'keiretsu'.

At present, there are 16 'keiretsu' in Japan. Table 7.10 lists them. The rationale for the existence of a 'keiretsu' is to be sought not only in reciprocal equity holdings. The history of bank-industry relationships in Japan described above suggests a plausible explanation for their development. In addition to historical, legal, and cultural reasons for the advent of the main bank concept however, it is also a response to the need for economic efficiency (Kester, 1991).

Foremost among the motivations associated with this need is the effectiveness of the implicit contracts made between members of a conglomerate in Japan. The cost of designing, executing, and monitoring contracts, which entail important transactions, is usually high (Williamson, 1985).

One procedure for softening the impact of the transaction costs caused by the existence of market relationships between the contracting companies is to internalize these relationships and turn these contracts into implicit contracts. This is precisely what the principal bank or the 'keiretsu' succeeds in doing: the transactions take place within the group, and there is a very clear management hierarchy that indicates what is best for the group as a whole and not just for each of the member companies.

In this sense, the existence of implicit contracts between shareholders and managers in Japanese companies is in direct contrast to what happens in the West, particularly with hostile take-over bids. Shleifer and Summers (1988) comment that Japanese managers want to maintain good relationships with the various groups within a company. A manager who spends many years in a company will have received help on many occasions during his professional career and, consequently, his commitment to the firm is increased. This is one of the many implicit contracts in Japanese firms.

What are the incentives that the managers of the group's companies receive to continue these relationships with each other? These incentives are generally of two types. First, what we call the cultural factors: trust in the group's leading company, both in its decisions for the satisfactory progress of the conglomerate and in the belief that this leading company would come to the help of any of the other companies if it should fall into difficulties. Likewise, the

TABLE 7.9 *Mitsubishi Group: cross-holdings (%)*

Companies	Companies										
	M Main Bank	M. Trust & Banking	Meiji Mutual Life Ins.	Tokyo Marine & Fire Ins.	M. Corp.	M. Heavy Inds.	Kirin Brewery	M. Rayon	M. Paper Mills	M. Paper Ind.	M. Gas Chem.
M. Main Bank		3.1		5.0	5.4	4.6	4.4	5.9	5.0	4.6	4.8
M.Trust & Banking				2.5	4.1	4.0	2.7	4.9	4.3	3.4	5.1
Meiji Mutual Life Insurance	6.1	6.1		4.7	5.6	3.8	4.5	7.1	5.6	7.7	4.4
Tokyo Marine & Fire Insurance	4.7	2.0			6.5	2.6			3.4	2.6	2.1
M. Corp.	2.2	3.5		2.3		2.1			3.4		
SUBTOTAL	13.0	14.7		14.5	21.6	17.1	11.6	17.9	21.7	18.3	16.4
M. Heavy Industries	3.5	3.0		1.9	3.8			1.9	1.8		
Kirin Brewery											
M. Rayon											
M. Paper Mills											
M. Chemical Ind.											
M. Gas Chemical											
M. Oil											
M. Plastic Ind.											
M. Petrochemical											
Asahi Glass	1.5	2.5		1.8					2.5		2.8
M. Mining & Cement											
M. Steel											
M. Metal											
M. Kakoki											
M. Electric	1.5	1.8									
Nippon Kogaku											
M. Estate		1.9									
Nippon Yusen		1.3			2.1						
M. Warehouse											
TOTAL	19.5	25.2		18.2	27.5	17.1	11.6	19.8	26.0	18.3	19.2

Source: Kester (1991), Suzuki (1987), and Annual Reports.

existence of long-term employment relationships—the dismissal of executives was unheard of until very recently—also serves to consolidate this tendency.

The second type is related to economic efficiency. The main bank or the 'keiretsu' not only enables transaction costs to be reduced but also provides a flow of information on the situation of different companies and their markets, which eliminates part of the uncertainty that any company is subject to in its dealings with customers and suppliers.

This information flow is particularly important in the case of the banks. Indeed, in times of economic difficulty, banks usually step in, infusing new blood into the company's management team and, when necessary, providing capital.

However, the information that banks have on companies is useful not only in extreme situations but also in day-to-day operations. In fact, Japanese banks use this information in four different ways:[3] to study the company, to design

[3] This flow of information also provides the additional benefit of enabling the company to nurture a reputation for solvency or quality management in the eyes of the bank.

M. Oil	M. Plastic Ind.	M. Petro-chem.	Asahi Glass	M. Mining & Cement	M. Steel	M. Metal	M. Kakoki	M. Elec.	Nippon Kogaku	M. Est.	Nippon Yusen	M. Warehouse
5.0	2.6	5.9	5.4	5.0	5.0	4.2	5.8	2.9	6.5	4.4	3.7	4.9
3.3	1.8	2.9	3.8	4.9	3.7	5.8	3.3	2.1	6.5	5.1	3.0	5.7
2.8	2.6	5.3	5.8	9.1	5.8	6.0	5.5	4.5	5.1	4.4	4.6	7.7
5.0		5.7	5.1	1.9	3.1		2.5		2.7	3.7	5.6	6.2
20.0		3.5		1.8	3.9		5.4					
36.1	7.0	23.3	20.1	22.7	21.5	16.0	22.5	9.5	20.8	17.6	16.9	24.5
2.0				2.1	6.9		5.4	1.7			5.4	
												2.2
	48.1	6.0										
		6.8		1.5					2.6	1.8		1.9
			2.0	2.2								4.0
2.0												
40.1	55.1	36.1	22.1	28.5	28.4	16.0	27.9	11.2	23.4	19.4	22.3	32.6

the most suitable financing instrument, for ongoing supervision of the company, and, finally, to solve possible situations of insolvency (Corbett, 1987; Sheard, 1994).

The process of collecting information starts with the study of the company—normally, carried out on an ongoing basis. The company usually offers information at regular intervals to the banks it operates with. In addition to using the data provided by the company itself, these banks also use information prepared by security firms or rating agencies. The presence of former bank executives on the company's board of directors enriches the assessment the bank may make of the company with qualitative inputs.

This process of collecting information and assessing the company's needs—and its economic and financial risk—enables financing instruments to be designed and tailored to the company's situation and needs, in terms of interest rates, terms, and guarantees required by the bank.

The degree of subsequent monitoring of companies by banks is also quite

TABLE 7.10 *Japan: business groups*

Old Zaibatsus	Groups around banks	Groups around industrial companies
Mitsubishi	DKB	Nippon Steel
Mitsui	Sanwa	Hitachi
Sumitomo	IBJ	Nissan
Fuyo	Tokai	Toyota
		Matsushita
		Toshiba-IHI
		Tokyu
		Seibu

substantial. Monitoring consists of the routine scrutiny of financial statements, frequent visits by bank executives to the companies, and information provided by the banks' formal and informal representatives on the companies' boards of directors.

These control mechanisms reduce the risk of asymmetric information that is typical of the relationship between a bank and a company: the latter may have information that the bank does not, as a result of which the bank's assessment of the company may be too risky or too conservative. The informal communication mechanisms enable drastic decisions to be made in emergencies, while almost always avoiding the need to close the company. In fact, it could be considered that the principal bank in Japan plays a role similar to that of the LBO in the United States.

The monitoring process thus reduces the likelihood of a company going bankrupt, as becomes immediately clear when one compares the number of bankruptcies in Japan with those in any other industrialized country. In Japan, the figure for large companies is much lower (Corbett, 1987).

The distribution of bankruptcies is concentrated in those companies that are not under the umbrella of a bank. Bankruptcies are extremely rare in companies that are directly or indirectly controlled by a bank. The visible hand of the bank softens what would be the implacable verdict of the market. Furthermore, the percentage of bankruptcies among small, normally indebted companies is usually higher in Japan than in other industrialized countries.[4]

Within the context of the economic efficiency that can be achieved by a 'keiretsu', it is important not to forget the goal of economic growth and increasing market share. These have been the classic goals of Japanese companies, not earnings per share, price/earnings ratio (PER), or the annual dividend.

When the goal is growth, implicit contracts between banks and companies—and between customers and suppliers—act as lubricants in the company's efforts to achieve this goal. As the group's main shareholder is normally a bank, this

[4] Corbett (1987) supports these arguments with abundant empirical data.

bank is usually concerned not so much about a company's short-term profit as about the profit of the group as a whole in the medium term. Implicitly, Japanese bankers give the impression that they favour above all other things the option of gaining market share as a platform for earning greater profits in the future.

A second advantage of the existence of a main bank in terms of efficiency arises from the fact that the company's ownership is concentrated in a few hands, one of which is the main bank. As we saw in Chapters 4 and 6, the existence of a main shareholder in a company offers a number of important advantages: control of the board of directors, streamlined strategic decision-making, and simplicity in solving insolvency problems. In cases of insolvency, there is also the fact that the creditor banks and the largest shareholders share the same interests (Hoshi, Kashyap, and Loveman, 1994).

The existence of an implicit contract between banks and companies also has an economic impact on the banking business. A main bank within a company or a 'keiretsu' enjoys a certain amount of monopoly power *vis-à-vis* the company. This position is strengthened by the minimal price competition allowed by Japanese financial regulation.

As a result of this situation, Japanese banks have tended to charge higher interest rates than those that would prevail in a competitive situation (Corbett, 1987; Meerschwam, 1991) and, in turn, these higher rates are accepted by companies for the reasons we have just discussed. However, the liberalization of interest rates and the increasing rivalry between banks mean that the situation now is rapidly changing and companies are looking for the best conditions.

On the other hand, when the company's situation is unfavourable, banks tend to lower the margins charged to the company and, at the same time, guarantee the continued flow of financing to the company. This is in fact a further consequence of the existence of implicit contracts.

The growth goal reinforces part of the internal dynamics of the relationship between the main bank and the company in two different ways. First, a growing company tends to soften the differences in points of view between the various shareholders. Growth is like an oil that stanches the wounds caused by possible discrepancies in the way things are done within the industrial group.

Second, growth is a favourite goal of many executives, both inside and outside Japan. So long as the return is not negative, a spectacular growth in sales or market share usually hides other weaknesses of the management team.

In addition to these features of the main bank, the 'keiretsu' has a number of other features that help improve our understanding of the relationship between banks and non-financial companies in Japan. First is the nature of the managers' contracts with the companies belonging to a 'keiretsu'. These are long-term contracts in which both parties (the manager and the company) make a lasting investment in their relationship with the other party.

It is not easy to replace a senior manager in a 'keiretsu' company and the experience acquired in the group's *modus operandi* is one of a manager's prime assets. Consequently, the structure of the 'keiretsu' and the purpose of the company's growth tend to reinforce the continuity of the management teams, which are only broken by age or bankruptcy.

'Keiretsus' are living proof of Chandler's thesis, expressed in his book *The Visible Hand* (1977), according to which the true revolution of the twentieth century has been the professionalization of management tasks, placing the government of organizations in the hands of professional managers. The visible hand of management has replaced Adam Smith's invisible hand of the market.

Indeed, in the Japanese company, the management teams govern relationships not only within the company but also within a wider and more influential circle of economic institutions: those that make up the 'keiretsu'. Thus, market relationships in Japan are more limited in scope than in other countries with a market-based economic system. In this context, the influence of the main economic agents within a 'keiretsu'—normally, the banks—is, to all practical purposes, as great as that which can be developed by the market mechanism itself. This is the case particularly when the market leads one of the companies into a situation of financial crisis, or when uncertainty about a product or production process prevents the market from taking high-risk decisions.

In practice, these considerations on the relationship between banks and companies are important for qualifying the relationship reflected in the accounting statements, which consists of bank holdings in industrial companies. Table 7.11 provides information on the ownership structure of listed Japanese companies. Observe that the accounting figures corroborate the opinion expressed in previous pages. Indeed, at the close of 1987, the banks held 20.5 per cent of the listed Japanese companies shareholders' equity. If to the banks' holdings we add the holdings of the insurance companies—many of them created with bank capital—and other financial institutions, more than 40 per cent of the shareholders' equity of the listed companies in 1987 was held by the financial system. This percentage is unmatched by any of the other countries included in this study.

Thus, the formal relationship based on ownership relationships between banking and industry is strengthened by the more informal, but institutionalized relationship deriving from the nature of the principal bank system in Japan. The relationship observed between banking and industry in Germany is taken to a striking extreme in Japan.

If instead of considering the size of the banks' equity holdings, we analyse Japanese companies' financial structure, we will gain a number of new insights into the picture we have just painted (Tables 7.12 and 7.13).

Between 1983 and 1992, the following changes took place in the financial structure of Japanese industrial companies. First, there was an increase in the relative weight of equity capital. Second, there was a drop in short-term debt by almost 10 points and an increase in long-term debt by almost 4 points. Third, there was a slight decrease in bank debt out of total debt which, even so, continues to be very high, particularly in comparison with the United States or France, as shown in Figure 7.2.

TABLE 7.11 *Japan: ownership of listed companies* (1980–1987)

	1980	1981	1982	1983	1984	1985	1986	1987
Government	0.2	0.2	0.2	0.2	0.2	0.2	0.8	0.9
Financial institutions	38.8	38.8	38.7	38.9	38.9	39.6	42.2	43.5
Banks	17.1	17.3	17.3	17.6	17.9	18.3	19.6	20.5
Investment funds	1.9	1.5	1.3	1.2	1.0	1.1	1.3	1.8
Trusts	0.5	0.4	0.4	0.4	0.4	0.5	0.7	0.9
Insurances (life)	12.3	12.5	12.6	12.6	12.7	12.7	13.5	13.3
Insurance companies (non-life)	4.9	4.9	4.9	4.9	4.8	4.8	4.5	4.4
Others	2.1	2.2	2.2	2.2	2.1	2.2	2.6	2.6
Corporations	26.1	26.0	26.3	26.0	25.9	25.9	24.1	24.5
Investment companies	2.0	1.7	1.7	1.8	1.9	1.9	2.0	2.5
Private individuals	30.4	29.2	28.4	28.0	26.8	26.3	25.2	23.9
Foreigners	2.5	4.1	4.7	5.1	6.3	6.1	5.7	4.7
TOTAL	100.0	100.0	100.0	100.0	100.0	100.0	100.0	100.0

Source: Tokyo Stock Exchange.

It therefore appears that, after 1987, companies mainly relied on resources obtained from the fixed income market and retained earnings. Bank debt has fallen significantly (Campbell and Hamao, 1994; Kerster, 1991). Does this mean a rupture with the Japanese company's traditional sources of finance or the 'keiretsu' system? Rupture is probably too drastic a term to describe the slow but sure change that is taking place in Japanese finances.

The figures given in Table 7.12 show a phenomenon that has affected financial markets in the entire world: financial disintermediation and the decreased importance of bank debt within the spectrum of financing alternatives available to companies (Canals, 1993). In this sense, Japan has been no exception.

The advent of this phenomenon in Japan, however, has been accompanied by a number of unique features. Perhaps the most important of these is the strong growth of Japanese companies' reserves, which has enabled them, as we have seen, to do without part of their bank financing. Japanese industrial success, fuelled in part by the financial system itself, now seems to be turning against the banks.

On the other hand, the development of a stable, liquid commercial paper market in Japan has led companies to operate on it directly, dispensing with bank intermediation. Normally, the lower prices obtained on the capital market have been a highly powerful incentive to accelerate this process.

Also, although not as intense as that of the EU member countries, the deregulation process in Japan has brought about an increase in rivalry among banks.

The Japanese financial crisis in the first half of the 1990s has seriously damaged the solvency of some banks, for a number of reasons, such as loans to failing companies, or capital losses on stock market investments or real estate

TABLE 7.12 *Japan: financial structure of non-financial companies* (1983–1992)

	1983	1984	1985	1986	1987	1988	1989	1990	1991	1992
Shareholders' equity	24.3	25.2	26.4	27.6	28.7	24.5	30.7	31.1	31.6	32.0
Long-term debt	18.6	16.9	17.3	18.5	18.4	18.5	19.6	20.1	21.4	22.1
Of which, with credit institutions	14.5	12.6	12.4	12.9	12.2	11.8	11.7	11.8	12.8	13.8
Short-term debt	52.2	53.1	51.5	49.3	48.1	47.3	45.4	44.7	42.9	41.9
Of which, with credit institutions	15.2	15.6	15.9	16.3	15.1	13.8	11.9	11.4	11.1	11.9
Provisions	4.9	4.8	4.8	4.6	4.8	4.6	4.3	4.1	4.1	4.1

Source: BACH (European Commission; General Directorate II).

TABLE 7.13 *Sources of finance for non-financial companies in Japan**

Year	Total	Equity	Debentures		Loans		Commercial paper	Foreign debt
			National	International	Banks	Public banks		
1975	16,855	1,161	1,287	325	12,827	1,923	—	–670
1976	17,163	934	661	298	13,248	1,639	—	380
1977	13,259	1,079	647	144	10,256	1,646	—	–514
1978	12,933	1,148	747	142	8,724	1,340	—	830
1979	13,596	1,368	901	396	8,338	1,962	—	628
1980	18,313	1,440	563	214	13,359	1,939	—	7,602
1981	21,159	2,112	1,050	299	16,289	2,578	—	–1,175
1982	23,122	2,045	632	892	17,279	2,280	—	7
1983	22,664	1,564	298	1,286	17,903	1,585	—	27
1984	25,411	2,229	857	1,420	19,953	1,329	—	–379
1985	29,772	2,017	681	2,346	22,997	1,010	—	739
1986	33,415	2,205	1,579	2,587	26,285	553	—	202
1987	42,675	4,124	2,364	3,760	25,772	1,955	—	2,999
1988	54,193	5,225	1,607	4,282	30,112	3,863	7,587	1,513
1989	72,971	10,124	1,463	9,513	37,797	6,515	3,780	3,777
1990	66,740	4,438	3,130	3,768	39,031	6,739	2,696	6,934
1991	38,319	1,277	3,633	6,516	23,938	6,365	3,362	–95

* Billion yen.

Source: Bank of Japan.

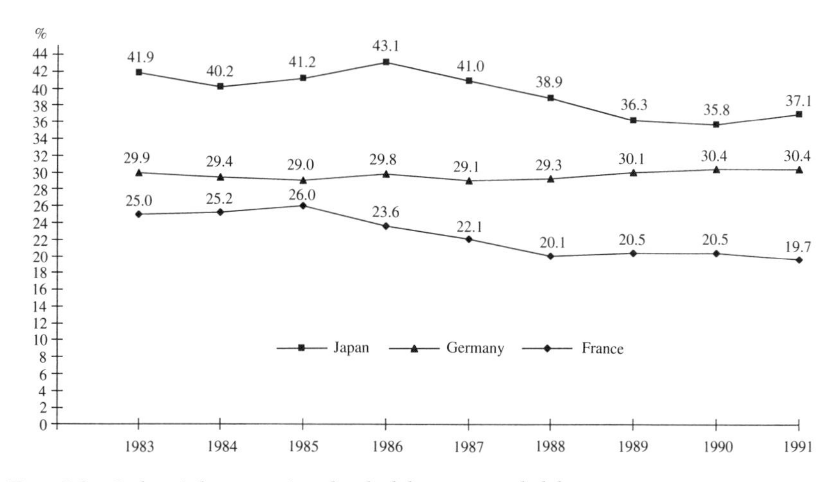

FIG. 7.2 *Industrial companies: bank debt over total debt*

projects. The Japanese banks' need to restructure has forced them in recent years to sell shareholdings in non-financial companies. This will no doubt have led to a fall in the Japanese banks' equity holdings in companies. Unfortunately, there are still no current estimates of the size of this reduction. While this fall does not suggest the disappearance of the traditional system of relationships between banks and companies in Japan, it does point to its weakening.

Again, in Japan as in other countries, the traditional relationships based on long-standing personal contacts between bank and company have been replaced—at least in part—by price-based relationships (Canals, 1993; Kester, 1991; Meerschwam, 1991).

5. THE FUTURE OF THE JAPANESE FINANCIAL MODEL

In Japan, deregulation has led to excess capacity in the banking industry, as has in part happened in the United States and the EU. Excess capacity has at least two major consequences. The first is a price war, which, in Japan, has not yet been declared openly, due to the implicit controls maintained by the financial authority. However, the increased rivalry between banks has exacerbated the crisis suffered by the bank industry in the 1990s. The second consequence is that banks are applying more stringent criteria when assessing their customers' profitability, with the result that the complacency of the past, justified by a stable, long-term relationship, has started to crumble.

These changes are in addition to the previously discussed phenomenon of the growing independence of companies from the group's main bank and, in general, of large companies from the banks, which, in turn, means a loss of bargaining power in their dealings with companies and, in the final analysis, a lower return.

On the other hand, the growing independence of companies from banks has led to the appearance of the market for corporate control—albeit still weak—implemented through hostile take-overs. Obviously, its volume is nowhere near that of the United States or, on another scale, the EU. It is therefore an incipient phenomenon.

Does this mean that bank-industry relationships in Japan will change to resemble more closely those of the West and, in particular, those of the Anglo-Saxon world? Is this the end of a model of bank-industry relations which, judging from the results obtained by Japanese companies, has been fairly successful for the country? (See Aoki, 1984.)

Although there are authors who voice opposing opinions, the reasons stated above enable us to indicate that it is very unlikely that Japan will follow a rapid transition towards a model that is highly similar to the Western model. The main reason is that the network of implicit contracts between banks and industrial companies is so densely interwoven that, even though some threads may break, and the Japanese banking system at the end of 1995 is in the throes of a deep crisis, the fabric as a whole is still very consistent. It is difficult to imagine that a company with a strong relationship with a main bank could cut ties with it. It would be more reasonable to think that both will try to find a new balance in their relationship which takes into account the changes that have taken place in the financial system.

Thus, over the next few years, we expect that bank-company relations in Japan will follow a pattern similar to that of the last thirty years, although mitigated by the appearance of bank disintermediation and increased banking rivalry.

In the medium term, we can expect that bank-industry relations in Japan will not have the strength they have had in the past, although they will continue to be stronger than in any other country in the Western world. These relations will be supplemented by the availability to companies of financial markets that offer more sophisticated products and, in some cases, at prices below those of the banks.

8

The Spanish Financial Model

1. INTRODUCTION

The relationship between banks and non-financial companies in Spain has a considerable historical tradition, densely populated with failures and some occasional successes during the early stages of industrialization in the nineteenth century. However, to understand the present status of bank-industry relations in Spain, one has to go back to the creation of industrial banks by the largest bank groups, within the framework of the legislation approved in 1962. This legislation signified a strong commitment by the Spanish government to the industrialization and modernization of the Spanish economy, best exemplified by the Development Plans.

The main purpose of industrial banks was to provide medium and long-term credit to industrial companies and to have an active presence in their equity capital. These new specialized banks, such as Bankunión, Bankinter, and Banco Urquijo, came into being during the 1960s.

However, the 1970s recession and the profound business restructuring that came in its wake showed the weakness of these financial institutions basically specializing in providing medium and long-term financing to non-financial companies.

Parallel with the development of specialized institutions, the large bank groups created or increased their portfolio of direct holdings in industrial companies of a certain size. Thus, for example, Banco Central and Banesto had large interests in the energy sector, Banco Bilbao in the food and electrical industries, and Banco Hispano Americano in the construction industry. Other large banks such as Santander or Vizcaya had smaller industrial portfolios, while Banco Popular was the only large large bank that had not acquired major holdings in non-financial companies.

Thus, the consolidation of the Spanish banking system in the 1970s fitted in perfectly with the universal bank model existing in Germany or France. In fact, banks specializing in providing finance to industry progressively disappeared or were taken over by larger banks.

The experience of the late 1970s and early 1980s shows that universal banks in Spain were much more successful than the so-called industrial banks. In fact, the latter's specialization disappeared and today there are no industrial banks in the strict sense of the term in Spain.

Any discussion of the relationship between banks and non-financial companies in Spain must include an analysis of the universal banks that possess large holdings in the equity capital of a fair number of non-financial companies. These banks are BBV, La Caixa, Banco Central Hispano (BCH), and, until the Bank of Spain intervened in December 1993, Banesto.[1]

The ultimate reason for the presence of Spanish banks in non-financial companies has not always been clear. In the 1960s, it was a process that, to a certain extent, was encouraged by the Spanish authorities, although it cannot be said that this government intervention was decisive. During the 1970s crisis, banks were more sceptical about industrial holdings. The larger the investment in non-financial companies, whether in loans or in capital, the more vulnerable were the banks' results to the business cycle.

In the second half of the 1980s, with the economy in full swing and in response to the liberalization and deregulation of the Spanish banking system, the large bank groups, with the exception of Popular and Santander, readdressed the creation of business groups with a bank at their core. Following this policy, BBV, Banesto, and BCH included as part of their banking strategy the acquisition of holdings in industrial companies. The economic recession of the early 1990s and the intervention in Banesto by the Bank of Spain have taken some of the steam out of this process.

However, the aspect of Spanish bank holdings in industry that must be stressed is that banks have considered them to be one of their strategic options in the face of the challenge of deregulation, the entry of foreign banks into Spain, and the creation of the single financial market. The acquisition of such holdings was the path chosen by BBV, BCH, and Banesto, whereas Santander—until 1995—or Popular have opted to concentrate on financial business and, within this, on banking business. Whether to acquire equity holdings in industrial companies is part of a series of decisions that banks have had to make in many countries: other decisions concern specialization, internationalization, and mergers with other financial institutions.

Before we discuss in some detail the involvement of Spanish banking in industry, the next two sections will offer an overview of the Spanish banking system and the most important changes that have taken place in recent years.

2. AN OVERVIEW OF THE SPANISH BANKING SYSTEM

The Spanish banking system, one of the backbones of the financial system, is composed of two types of organization: commercial banks and savings banks (see Figure 8.1).

[1] When Banco Santander, which bought Banesto in the Bank of Spain's auction in April 1994, took over Banesto's management, it set as its strategic goal the sale of all of the bank's holdings in non-financial companies.

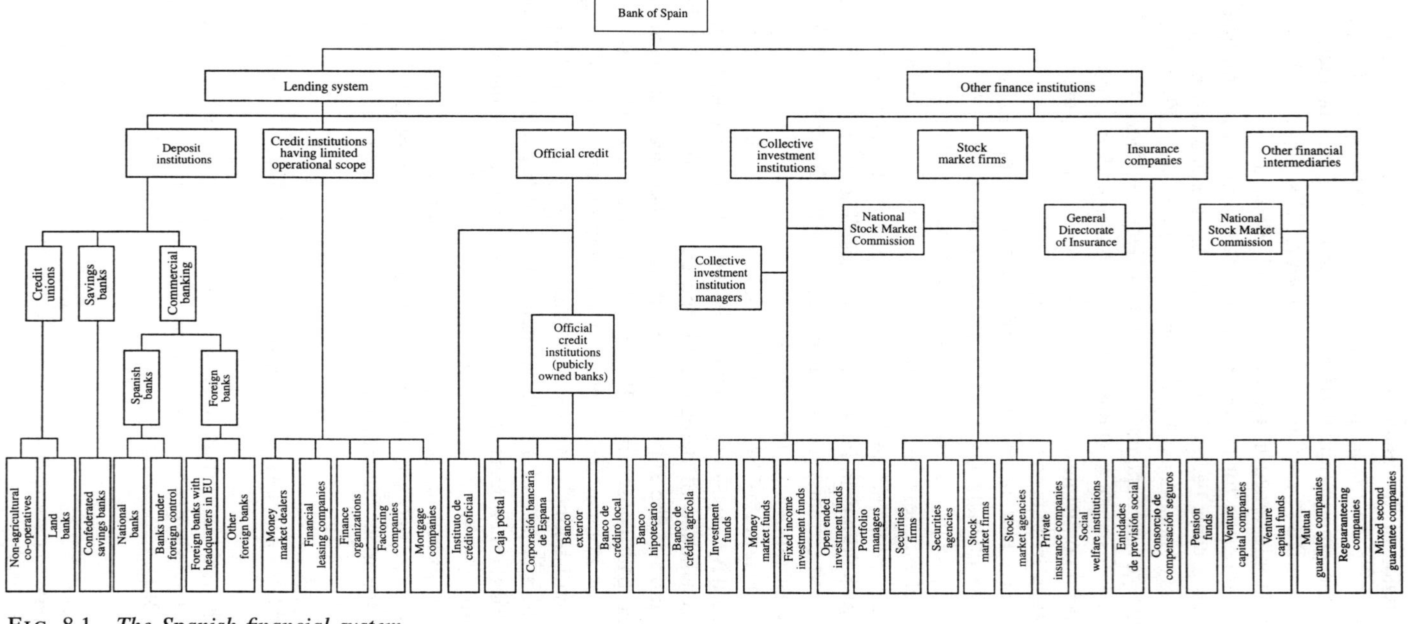

FIG. 8.1 *The Spanish financial system*

TABLE 8.1 *Spanish banking system: market share* (1988–1995) (bn. pesetas)

	1988	1989	1990	1991	1992	1993	1994	1995 (Oct.)
Assets								
Banks	34,059	38,743	42,639	49,688	53,535	66,713	70,399	73,211
Savings banks	19,218	22,947	25,448	26,825	30,788	33,650	36,940	38,614
Credit								
Banks	14,146	16,618	18,221	21,695	22,381	22,150	23,958	24,546
Savings banks	7,227	8,918	9,957	11,220	13,026	14,101	15,684	16,652
Deposits								
Banks	12,438	13,634	15,746	17,603	17,892	19,054	19,658	20,538
Savings banks	11,001	12,205	13,824	14,757	17,539	19,858	21,921	22,416

Source: Bank of Spain.

Table 8.1 provides information on the relative importance of each of these institutions within the banking system, measured in terms of their market share in receiving deposits and granting loans. It can be seen that the savings banks have eroded considerably the traditional dominance of the commercial banks in both dimensions.

The evolution of the commercial banks' profitability, measured by profit before tax over total mean assets, is shown in Table 8.2 for the period 1970–1994.

It can be seen that, after 1973, the banks' profitability falls to a minimum of 0.57 per cent of mean assets in 1982, after which it starts to rise again to a peak of 1.58 per cent in 1989. Since then, this ratio has been steadily falling.

The results of the savings banks are shown in Table 8.3 for the period 1978–1994. These results fluctuate more than those of banks although, since 1989, they have improved consistently to a peak ratio of 1.05 per cent over mean assets in 1992. Figure 8.2 offers a comparison of the banks' and savings banks' return on assets until 1992 and Figure 8.3 shows the changes in the market share in deposits of both groups of institutions.

Finally, Table 8.4 shows the specific structure of the banks' income statement for the period 1989–1994 and Table 8.5 shows the savings banks' income statement for the same period.

These changes in the banks' income statements reflect structural changes in the industry's structure and rivalry, which we will discuss in the next section. The most important observations are the fall in the financial margin (steeper in the private banks than in the savings banks), the increase in revenues from services (larger in the private banks than in the savings banks), and an attempt to contain operating expenses, in which the savings banks have been more successful.

TABLE 8.2 *Spain: evolution of banks' performance* (1970–1994)

Year	Pretax profit (bn. pesetas)	Total assets (bn. pesetas)	Profit after tax (% assets)
1970	18	1,461	1.21
1971	21	1,794	1.18
1972	28	2,279	1.22
1973	38	2,899	1.30
1974	46	3,578	1.29
1975	54	4,324	1.26
1976	65	5,348	1.22
1977	68	6,630	1.03
1978	67	7,703	0.87
1979	76	9,145	0.83
1980	84	11,160	0.75
1981	104	13,730	0.76
1982	97	17,022	0.57
1983	125	19,740	0.64
1984	139	23,334	0.60
1985	192	26,219	0.73
1986	229	27,803	0.83
1987	305	29,981	1.02
1988	443	30,763	1.44
1989	622	39,338	1.58
1990	670	43,311	1.55
1991	745	52,322	1.48
1992	620	56,052	1.11
1993	590	66,864	0.78
1994	471	72,481	0.65

Source: Bank of Spain (several years) and Termes (1994).

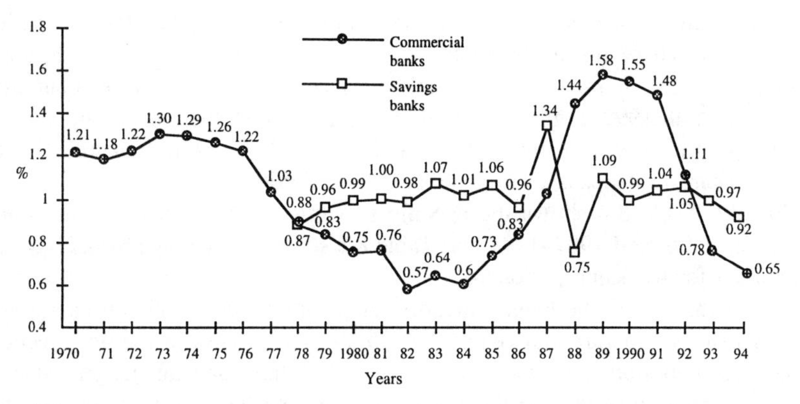

FIG. 8.2 *Return on total assets of commercial and savings banks (before tax)*

TABLE 8.3 *Spain: evolution of savings banks' performance* (1978–1994)

Year	Pretax profit (bn. pesetas)	Assets (bn. pesetas)	Profit after tax (% assets)
1978	28	3,151	0.88
1979	37	3,812	0.96
1980	45	4,545	0.99
1981	63	6,400	1.00
1982	62	6,351	0.98
1983	81	7,582	1.07
1984	95	9,350	1.01
1985	117	10,996	1.06
1986	118	12,269	0.96
1987	182	13,623	1.34
1988	111	14,896	0.75
1989	100	18,237	1.09
1990	212	21,478	0.99
1991	255	24,543	1.04
1992	285	27,263	1.05
1993	302	31,236	0.97
1994	318	34,422	0.92

Source: Termes (1994) and Bank of Spain.

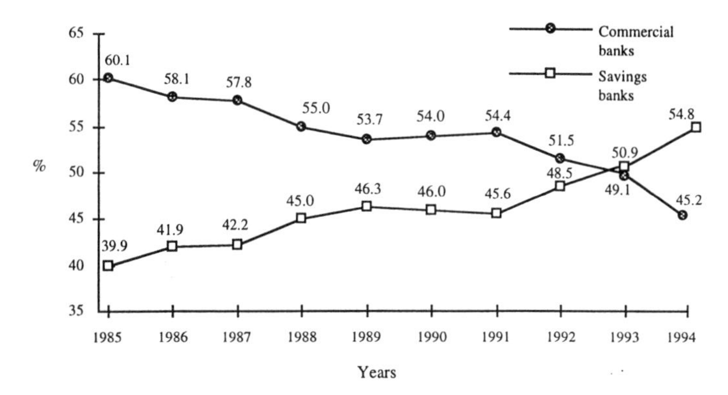

FIG. 8.3 *Evolution of market share in deposits*

3. THE FORCES OF CHANGE IN THE SPANISH BANKING INDUSTRY

In this section, we will briefly discuss the main forces that have brought about dramatic changes in the Spanish banking industry in the past few years. This process of change started with the bank liberalization measures approved by the government in 1977, in particular, the greater degree of freedom granted to financial institutions, the discontinuation of the specialization of functions between

TABLE 8.4 *Spanish banks: income statement* (1989–1994)

	1989		1990		1991		1992		1993		1994
	Billion pesetas	Percentage assets	Billion pesetas	Percentage assets	Billion pesetas	Percentage assets	Billion pesetas	Percentage assets	Billion pesetas	Percentage assets	Percentage assets
Financial revenues	4,453	11.32	5,330	12.31	5,831	11.89	5,984	11.38	7,082	11.24	8.74
Less financial costs	2,861	7.27	3,597	8.31	3,973	8.10	4,199	7.99	5,186	8.23	6.11
Financial margin	1,592	4.05	1,733	4.00	1,858	3.79	1,785	3.39	1,896	3.01	2.63
Less credit writedowns	163	0.41	155	0.36	265	0.54	345	0.66	455	0.72	
Net financial margin	1,429	3.64	1,578	3.64	1,593	3.25	1,440	2.73	1,441	2.29	2.63
Plus services revenues	271	0.69	314	0.73	341	0.70	468	0.90	558	0.89	
Total product	1,700	4.33	1,892	4.37	1,934	3.95	1,908	3.63	1,999	3.17	3.10
Less operating expenses[a]	1,173	2.98	1,347	3.12	1,406	2.87	1,454	2.77	1,631	2.59	2.41
Ordinary result	527	1.35	545	1.25	528	1.08	454	0.86	368	0.58	0.69
Plus extraordinary results[b]	95	0.23	125	0.30	197	0.40	130	0.25	126	0.20	
Profit before tax	622	1.58	670	1.55	725	1.48	584	1.11	494	0.78	0.65

[a] Personnel plus overheads and tax plus depreciation plus other writedowns and provisions.
[b] Sale of securities and properties plus other extraordinary results.

Source: Termes (1994) and Bank of Spain.

TABLE 8.5 *Spanish savings banks: income statement* (1989–1994)

	1989		1990		1991		1992		1993		1994
	Billion pesetas	Percentage assets	Billion pesetas	Percentage assets	Billion pesetas	Percentage assets	Billion pesetas	Percentage assets	Billion pesetas	Percentage assets	Percentage assets
Financial products	1,917	10.51	2,382	11.09	2,731	11.12	3,004	11.01	3,457	11.06	9.00
Less financial costs	1,121	6.15	1,510	7.03	1,748	7.12	1,901	6.97	2,246	7.19	5.31
Financial margin	796	4.36	872	4.06	983	4.00	1,103	4.04	1,211	3.87	
Less credit writedowns	32	0.18	56	0.26	123	0.50	176	0.64	279	0.89	
Net financial margin	764	4.18	816	3.80	860	3.50	927	3.40	932	2.98	3.69
Plus services revenues	45	0.25	58	0.27	72	0.29	125	0.46	183	0.59	0.52
Total product	809	4.43	874	4.07	932	3.79	1,052	3.86	1,115	3.57	4.21
Less operating expenses[a]	666	3.65	707	3.29	728	2.97	843	3.09	870	2.78	2.93
Ordinary result	143	0.78	167	0.78	204	0.82	209	0.77	245	0.79	1.28
Plus extraordinary results[b]	56	0.31	45	0.21	51	0.22	76	0.28	58	0.18	
Profit before tax	199	1.09	212	0.99	255	1.04	285	1.05	303	0.97	0.92

[a] Personnel plus overheads and tax plus depreciation plus other writedowns and provisions.
[b] Sale of securities and properties plus other extraordinary results plus other debits and credits.

Source: Bank of Spain.

commercial banks, savings banks, and other financial intermediaries, and the authorization of the entry of foreign banks in Spain.

These initial measures were followed by others in successive years, such as the progressive liberalization of interest rates on certain asset and deposit operations, the creation of specialized financial intermediaries, the elimination of operating differences between savings banks and universal banks, and the alignment of Spanish bank regulations with the Second Banking Directive of the EU. This Directive confirmed the principle of universal banking in the EU countries and the creation of a single banking market in Europe which, among other aspects, included the free entry of banks and insurance companies of one EU country into other countries.

The consequences of these dramatic changes in the space of little more than a decade have shaped a bank industry that is very different from that which existed in the early 1980s (Gual, 1993; Gual and Vives, 1990). There are fewer banks in 1995 than in 1977, banks have increased their mean size in a short period of time, specialized competitors have entered, and the principle of universal banking has come to dominate. The result of these changes has been an increase in rivalry in the industry, a major restructuring to reduce costs, and an effort by the financial organizations to offer new services to offset the fall in financial margin.

In the following sections, we will briefly discuss some of the changes that have led to this major mutation of the Spanish banking system.

3.1. Deregulation and the entry of foreign banks

The deregulation of Spanish banks has two sides to it, as in other European countries: the strictly national angle and that deriving from the Second Banking Directive of the EU. The deregulation of the industry has had the following main features.

First, there has been total freedom to set interest rates on deposits and loans, and the charges for other services, in any operation performed by a bank. The control of interest rates in Spain until the mid-1980s was based on the idea that rivalry in interest rates could generate a greater financial vulnerability among the banks that competed on price. The stability of the financial system seemed to be at stake and the authorities' reaction was to control prices to prevent an undesired outcome.

As we have seen in other countries, interest rate controls were harmful both for customers and for the banks. In fact, the bank's customers had to pay higher prices and the banks did not have much incentive to improve their efficiency and reduce costs. On the other hand, the relationship between interest rate controls and financial stability is less direct than is at first apparent. Therefore, it was logical that the Bank of Spain should cease to control interest rates, although it was some time before the banks undid the existing implicit price oligopoly.

This finally happened in September 1989 when Banco Santander launched the 'supercuenta', a high-interest-bearing current account.

The second component of the deregulation exercise in Spain was the progressive liberalization of the savings banks' activities, including the possibility of geographical expansion. In practice, this liberalization has brought about an almost complete functional equality between commercial banks and savings banks. With these measures, financial authorities wish not only to bring legislation on savings banks into line with that of the rest of the EU but also to stimulate rivalry within the bank industry.

The third component of the deregulation was the elimination of the obligatory investment ratios imposed on the banks in the late 1970s and early 1980s and the progressive reduction of the cash ratio to present levels. This measure has been very important for the banks, as the obligatory investment required by these coefficients significantly reduced their profitability. The reason was that these investments had a lower return than the investments freely made by the banks.

A fourth key factor has been the growing presence of foreign banks in Spain. Foreign penetration of the Spanish bank industry started in 1977, in the early stages of liberalization of the industry. However, this presence was consolidated in the second half of the 1980s.

Foreign banks have followed varying paths: some have grown internally, for example, Citibank and BNP; others have bought Spanish banks, such as Barclays, which bought Banco de Valladolid; a third group of banks have decided not to operate on the Spanish market as universal banks, but to limit their activity to large companies, for example, Amro–ABN or Bank of America.

It should be pointed out that the mere presence of foreign banks in Spain has not led to increased rivalry. Foreign banks have achieved modest market shares, less than 10 per cent both in loans and in deposits, although their penetration of the lending market has been higher (Table 8.6).

However, their presence has contributed to the more general use of many financial innovations that the Spanish banks have had to imitate in order to avoid being left behind. Thus, although foreign banks have not been the primary cause of increased rivalry, at least in quantitative terms, they have brought about a change of mentality and have opened the door of financial innovation to many Spanish banks.

Finally, we must mention the recent reform of the Spanish stock market, which has sought to increase the importance of the stock markets, both for companies seeking finance and for savers who wish to invest in securities. This reform has created an additional source of competition for the banks: financial disintermediation.

In Spain, large companies are becoming less dependent on bank financing, and this change has led to a reduction of the banks' loans business. Savers now have new opportunities for placing their savings, either directly on the stock market or through the investment funds. Therefore, as has happened in other

TABLE 8.6 *Spain: market share of foreign banks in deposits* (1989–1993)

Item	Foreign banks	Commercial banks	Savings banks	Total commercial and savings banks
1989				
Creditors	1,453	22,529	16,775	39,304
Percentage of banks	6.45			
Non-residents	177	2,600	379	2,979
Percentage of banks	6.82			
1990				
Creditors	1,453	25,099	18,257	43,356
Percentage of banks	5.79			
Non-residents	162	2,992	441	3,433
Percentage of banks	5.43			
1991				
Creditors	1,484	26,539	20,497	47,036
Percentage of banks	5.59			
Non-residents	154	3,164	498	3,662
Percentage of banks	4.87			
1992				
Debits	1,449	28,236	21,853	50,089
Percentage of banks	5.13			
1993				
Debits	1,785	30,401	24,014	54,415
Percentage of banks	5.87			

Source: Gual (1994).

countries, the Spanish banks have found themselves surrounded by new competitors. To prevent themselves from being pushed out of the market, they have taken major positions as intermediaries on the stock markets.

3.2. Price wars, alternative products, and the fall in the industry's profitability

The end of interest rate controls opened the door to a different type of rivalry in the Spanish banking industry. From 1974, the year in which the strong geographical expansion of Spanish banking began, the traditional bank's differentiation strategy basically consisted of geographical closeness to the customer. In the absence of intense financial innovation or the freedom to set the prices of financial operations, the only tool banks had to compete with was geographical location.[2]

[2] See Salop (1979) for a classical model of spatial or geographical competition. Fuentelsaz and Salas (1993) apply this model to account for the spatial competition of Spanish banking. Their results help explain why the Spanish banking system has a higher number of branches, with respect to the demand, than other EU countries.

When the Bank of Spain ceased to control the interest rates charged by the banks, the possibility of price competition emerged. This new type of competition for Spanish banking took place within the context of the creation of the single financial market in Europe. In other words, competition would become fiercer, both because of increased rivalry between Spanish banks and because of the greater penetration of foreign banks. However, it was some time before Spanish banks finally decided to break the status quo, as they were all aware that a price war would have negative effects on the industry's profitability.

After a few half-hearted attempts by Barclays (1985) and Banco Vizcaya (1987), it was Banco Santander that finally pushed the industry out into the cold winds of price competition with the launching of its 'supercuenta' in September 1989. Its sales aggressiveness left no room for doubt: this time, the price war was in earnest. After some dithering and doubting, all of the large banks, except Banco Central, which avoided these high-interest accounts, and Banco Popular, which tried to settle with its customers the remuneration they wished to receive on their accounts, all of the large and medium-sized banks entered the fray.

A number of points can be made about this mounting competition, which would be repeated with the investment funds war in 1991 and the 1993 mortgage war. First was the general fall of the bank's financial margin, as can be seen in Table 8.4.

Second, there were advantages to being the first mover in this type of action. Indeed, the results show that Banco Santander, the first to embark on the deposit war on a massive scale, was the one that was least harmed, in relative terms, by the squeezing of its financial margin.

The reason is that Banco Santander was also the bank that achieved the largest increase in market share in bank deposits after September 1989. The bank launching such an offensive runs the risk of seeing its income statement deteriorate sooner. However, if it manages to offset this fall in unit financial margin with an increase in the volume of deposits and, also, an increase in commissions from the possible increase in cross-sales of other financial products, the total result may improve, as was the case with Santander.

On the other hand, when one enters the war late and with poor planning and one does not have the people and the technological resources to compete, the results can be disastrous. The Banesto crisis is paradigmatic and, although it cannot be ascribed solely to the price war to attract deposits or the enormous growth in lending activity, it is true that the squeezed financial margin and the increase in bad debts due to an excessive growth of loans contributed decisively.

One final aspect of this increased rivalry in the financial services industry is the appearance of alternative products to those offered by the universal banks. By this, we mean the investment funds and, in general, other ways of placing savings. Alternative products to bank loans have also appeared or been developed, such as the stock market. However, in Spain, the process has not had such profound effects on the banks' asset side as on their liability side.

In general, an industry's economic performance is the result of a series of factors that underlie the supply and demand for that industry's products or services. In the banking industry, supply and demand refer to financial services, either on the asset side or on the liability side.

Let us look at bank deposits. The demand for bank deposits by families and private individuals has decreased because alternative financial services have appeared—such as investment funds, insurance, and stock market investments—that have undermined the banks' dominance. On the other hand, the supply of products offered by financial institutions to attract savings has been growing continuously, in part because there are more institutions trying to get a piece of the cake—for example, some foreign banks—causing the 'me-too' effect; or simply, because the existing institutions are trying to increase their market share.

The result of both phenomena—imitation and substitution—has a clear consequence: a drop in financial margins. Therefore, the banks' decreased profitability in recent years is due not only to the price war to attract deposits and loans but also to the substitution of a number of financial products offered directly by the banks by other products in which traditional banking initially does not play a decisive role.

Hence, the banks have an interest in creating investment funds or in acquiring an interest in a securities firm, so that the total savings managed by them does not decrease, even though the deposits in the individual banks do.

The consequences of these phenomena on the banks' profitability can be seen in Table 8.2. This shows how the Spanish banks' return, measured as net result over total mean assets, fell steadily from 1.30 per cent in 1973 to 0.57 per cent in 1982. Profitability then increased to a peak of 1.58 per cent in 1989, falling again to 0.65 per cent in 1993. It is significant—although we do not wish to establish in this case either a single direct causal relationship—that the banks' overall profitability started to fall a few months after the beginning of the high-interest-bearing accounts war.

Table 8.4 shows in somewhat greater detail the composition of the banks' income statements between 1989 and 1994. Note that, between these years, the financial margin (difference between interest income and interest expenses) fell from 4.05 per cent of assets in 1989 to 2.63 per cent of assets in 1994.

Operating expenses, for their part, fell slowly, from 2.98 per cent in 1989 to 2.41 per cent in 1994. This information also underlines the banks' difficulty in reducing overhead. Finally, the Spanish banks started a slow—and as yet insufficient—effort to offset the fall in financial margin by increasing revenues from commissions. This item increased from 0.69 per cent in 1989 to 0.89 per cent in 1993.

Figure 8.3 shows a particular aspect of the banks' competitiveness: the market share of commercial banks and savings banks in the deposit market. Note that the commercial banks' share in deposits fell steadily from 1985, from 60.1 per cent in 1985 to 51.3 per cent in 1993. The same thing happened with lending, where the banks' market share fell significantly. On the other hand, the savings banks' market share in both markets grew consistently during this period.

The second consequence of this phenomenon is the present existence of excess capacity. The reason is very simple: the supply of financial services has increased and the demand has not grown at the same rate. Indeed, for certain traditional products such as deposits, the demand has levelled off.

We can say that an industry has excess capacity when the supply in the industry increases and the demand does not grow at the same rate. Excess capacity causes price wars, squeezed margins, and, finally, forces some companies to withdraw from the industry.

This is a phenomenon common to many industries (see Canals, 1995a): chemicals, textiles, iron and steel, shipbuilding, airlines, etc. The solutions to excess capacity are clear: encourage certain companies to withdraw from the industry, reduce the capacity freely installed, or increase the degree of concentration through mergers and take-overs.

The special nature of the banking industry prevents the monetary authorities from allowing a massive closure of banks. Consequently, this solution is not feasible. Voluntary reductions in capacity are usually the exception rather than the rule: when a company is operating in an industry, it is very unwilling to leave it, for both objective and subjective reasons.

It is therefore reasonable to assume that the natural rationalization process for the banking industry is, in addition to a possible freeze or reduction in the branch network—a measure that all the banks have followed in one way or another—that of mergers and take-overs. This will be the subject of the next section.

3.3. Mergers and take-overs

The main reason used in the Spanish banking industry during the second half of the 1980s to justify mergers between banks was the supposed economies of scale associated with such actions. It was assumed that the large Spanish banks were still not large enough to compete in the single financial market of 1993 and the best way to be prepared for the new situation was through a mergers policy. J. Revell's report prepared in 1987 for Banco Vizcaya confirmed, using academic argument, the importance of this decision.

It seems that this report played some role in the government's subsequent belligerent support for an active merger and take-over policy in the Spanish bank industry. The academic argument was needed to justify a policy of doubtful effectiveness: the statements stressing the desirability of mergers between private companies and, what was more, establishing how these organizations should pair were taken up by the government.

Again, the political desire that Spain should have large banks seemed to be a pretext to win for the Spanish economy a decisive role in the construction of the new Europe. What the politicians forgot was that size is almost never a sign of efficiency or competitiveness and that, in the single financial market, the organizations that were going to survive were not the large organizations but the efficient ones.

The academic argument expressed in the Revell report, and actively used to defend the mergers policy, was the supposed economies of scale in commercial banking. The results of empirical studies performed on this subject had never obtained conclusive results in favour of the existence of significant economies of scale. Rather, the most authoritative studies indicated that economies of scale were obtained, both at branch and bank level, with volumes of deposits that were more than surpassed by all large and medium-sized Spanish banks.

Despite the lack of solid arguments, some banks started to take the road towards mergers and take-overs in 1987, with the unsuccessful take-over bid by Banco Bilbao for Banesto and the subsequent merger between Banco Bilbao and Banco Vizcaya.

The second merger that was announced but never consummated was between Banco Central and Banesto. It was later called off. In 1991, the merger between Banco Central and Banco Hispano Americano was announced, giving birth to Banco Central Hispano.

In this same year, Argentaria, Corporación Bancaria de España, was born. This was a holding company that grouped the state-owned credit institutions. Finally, after intervening in Banesto in 1993, the Bank of Spain auctioned the bank in April 1994 and it was bought by Santander. At the end of this process, the Spanish banking system is now more concentrated, with larger-sized organizations.

However, the problems and difficulties raised by this process of concentration in the banking industry are very clear. First, it is by no means definite that the resulting organizations are always more competitive. In fact, the income statements of the large merged banks have worsened in relative terms compared with banks that have not merged (Santander and Popular), although this comparison should be treated with caution, as the causal relationship is not immediate.

Second, mergers have not always urgently considered the need to rationalize the branch network or cut overheads, both of which are necessary prerequisite actions for a merger's success. Mergers have brought to light the difficulties in reducing expenses, eliminating branches, and, in short, rationalizing the large banks' structure.

Third, mergers have raised significant strategic, organizational, and human problems. The most important strategic problems concern the effort and time spent by the merged banks on managing and implementing the merger, instead of paying attention to a business that was changing at breakneck pace.

The most important organizational and human problems are the considerable difficulties that banks have found in the course of the merger process in putting people from the two banks in the right jobs and properly handling the balance of power within the new organization. The frequent reorganizations of some of the merged banks are a good indicator of this problem.

Generally speaking, mergers and take-overs may make good strategic sense but they are extremely difficult to manage. In such circumstances, human problems are paramount and, sometimes, certain management behaviours are the most powerful blocks preventing the organization from progressing along the desired path.

4. BANKS AS SHAREHOLDERS IN INDUSTRIAL COMPANIES IN SPAIN

The universal banking model—with a number of special qualifications as we have seen—is that which has been followed by Spanish banks in recent decades. After a few years of a certain amount of bank specialization (the 1960s and 1970s) during which some institutions appeared with a clear purpose of assisting in the long-term financing of industry, the universal bank model finally became consolidated in Spain.

Part of this consolidation has consisted of the creation of industrial portfolios belonging to a number of financial groups which, on occasion, have undertaken ambitious business operations.

The financial authorities' attitude to this process has followed two lines. Legally, industrial holdings have been authorized without any particular restrictions other than those of the EU. The only restriction has consisted of the special weight given to these holdings. Thus, in order to calculate the minimum net worth, the ratio applicable to the shares is 16 per cent, rising to 35 per cent if the shares in question correspond to banks. The percentage applicable to other risk assets is 7.5 per cent.

These rules are aimed at harmonizing Spanish regulations with EU legislation on bank holdings in the equity capital of other industrial companies. In particular, the EU's Second Banking Directive provides that a financial institution's qualified holding in a non-financial company may not exceed 15 per cent of the former's net worth. The Directive defines a qualified holding as being a direct or indirect holding of at least 10 per cent of the company's equity or voting rights. Furthermore, a bank's total investment in the equity of non-financial companies may not exceed 60 per cent of its net worth. If this limit should be exceeded—a possibility provided for in the Directive—the holdings should be fully backed by equity not included in the calculation of the corresponding bank organization's coefficient of solvency.

However, in recent years, a phenomenon has been sporadically observed that partly contradicts this approach. We refer here to the declarations by the financial authorities warning against the dangers of an excessive concentration of investment risks in the shares of industrial companies. This comes as somewhat of a surprise, particularly considering the liberal nature of the regulation. These statements may possibly have been made to voice the Spanish financial authorities' concern about the difficulties that a bank group with a large portfolio of industrial shares might experience, as Banesto did.

Obviously, bank holdings in an industrial firm can offer significant advantages in the medium term, provided that both the bank and the industrial company are well managed and their finances are in order. Otherwise, the danger of risk contagion is very high and, in the past, this has been the cause of serious bank crises.

Table 8.7 shows the weight of non-bank shares held by banks in Spain and other countries, between 1982 and 1988. This table offers an overview of the weight of banks in industry. It should be remembered that this table is only a snapshot and does not give any detailed indication of what the figures show. In particular, it should be remembered that bank holdings in industry reflect very many factors; some are of a historical or cultural nature, as we have discussed in previous chapters in relation to Germany and Japan; others are related to the legislators' attitude to the industrialization phenomenon or the concentration of power. Finally, one should not forget the major role played by the government in some countries' industrialization processes, creating financial organizations that have played an active part in the creation of industrial groups.

Another important caveat to be remembered in the analysis of these figures is the fiscal and accounting diversity existing in different countries, particularly regarding the posting of capital gains. This is particularly important in Germany, for example, where assets are only revalued exceptionally and, consequently, shares' nominal value is usually less than their market value.

In Japan, the phenomenon has two sides. The shares of listed companies usually include the corresponding stock market value, irrespective of whether the capital gains have been realized or not. For non-listed shares, the situation is the opposite. In any case, we find ourselves with a very tricky accounting problem. Nevertheless, the figures offered are illustrative.

Among the observations we can make, the first concerns the growth trend (at least until 1988) of bank holdings in the capital of both bank and non-bank companies—measured in terms of GNP. This confirms the universal nature of banking in most industrialized countries—with the exception of the United States and, to some extent, Great Britain. It also shows the strategic importance given by some bank institutions to their holdings in other companies.

The second observation refers to Spain. If we exclude Japan, Spanish banks' holdings in the equity of other non-bank companies are the highest—in relative terms—of all the countries considered. This reflects the special presence of Spanish banking in industry, which has increased somewhat after 1990, generally with the purpose of attaining a significant presence in certain industries considered to be strategic either for the bank's lending business or from the viewpoint of the country as a whole.

In relation to Spain, we can be a little more precise. Indeed, Figure 8.4 shows the evolution between 1976 and 1993 of the shares of non-financial companies held by Spanish banks. Bank presence in industry is measured using two

TABLE 8.7 *Banking system: share portfolio* (1982–1988) (% GDP)

	1982		1983		1984		1985		1986		1987		1988	
	(a)	(b)	(a)	(b)	(a)	(b)	(a)	(b)	(a)	(b)	(a)	(b)	(a)	(b)
Germany	1.97	0.97	2.20	1.03	2.26	1.10	2.44	1.22	2.76	1.36	2.94	1.54	—	—
Spain	2.37	1.92	2.61	1.82	2.98	2.15	2.79	1.86	2.77	1.88	2.84	1.83	3.83	2.57
United States	0.10	—	0.13	—	0.11	—	0.13	—	0.17	—	0.16	—	—	—
Japan	3.20	3.20	3.42	3.42	3.58	3.58	3.71	3.71	3.93	3.93	4.60	4.60	5.57	5.57
Great Britain	1.13	0.19	1.38	0.20	1.40	0.25	1.99	0.31	3.67	0.81	2.92	0.64	—	—
Italy	4.09	0.30	5.00	0.55	3.00	0.49	—	—	6.96	1.22	4.37	0.84	—	—

(a) Total share portfolio.
(b) Non-bank share portfolio.

Source: Chuliá (1990).

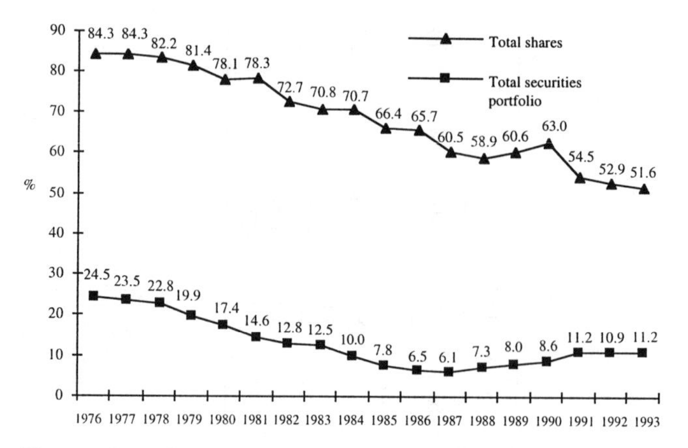

FIG. 8.4 *Shares of non-financial companies in the balance sheet of the banking system*

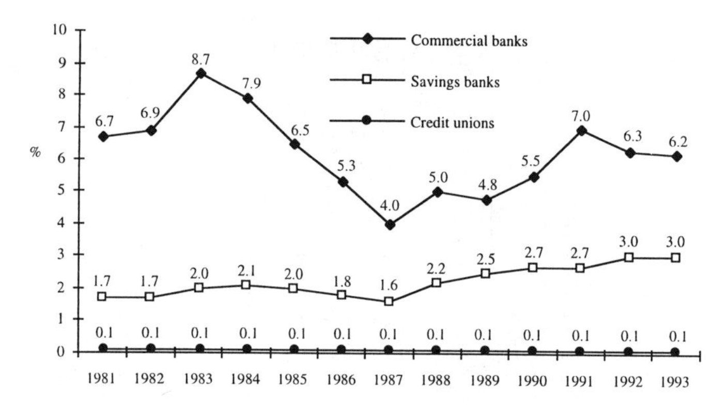

FIG. 8.5 *Outstanding stock issued by non-financial companies: distribution by holding sectors (% of total)*

indexes: the weight of the shares of non-financial companies in the total value of the shares (variable income) and in the total value of the banks' securities portfolio (including variable and fixed income). These graphs show the significant drop in the non-bank shares portfolio with respect to the volume of the securities portfolio between 1976 and 1988, a slight increase between 1987 and 1991, and a levelling off since 1991 (Ochoa, 1995).

Figure 8.5, in turn, shows the percentage of shares issued by Spanish non-financial companies and owned by the banking system, between 1981 and 1993. This figure shows the more active role played by commercial banks as compared with savings banks. The percentages held by banks in 1992 and 1993 are similar to those for 1981 and 1982.

These figures can be compared with those of other countries. Table 8.8 offers

TABLE 8.8 *Banking system: non-bank share portfolio* (1982–1988) (% total share portfolio)

	1982	1983	1984	1985	1986	1987	1988
Germany	49.4	46.8	48.8	50.0	49.4	52.4	—
Spain	81.0	69.6	72.2	66.7	68.0	64.3	67.1
Japan	100.0	100.0	100.0	100.0	100.0	100.0	100.0
Great Britain	16.9	14.6	17.5	15.5	22.0	22.0	—
Italy	7.3	11.0	16.3	—	17.5	19.3	—

Source: Chuliá (1990).

an international overview and shows the volume of non-bank shares in the total securities portfolio held by certain countries' banking systems between 1970 and 1987. This table confirms the observations previously made about the general growth of these holdings. However, in the Spanish banking system, these holdings have been reduced, because among other reasons, the Spanish banks alienated sizeable packages of industrial shares between 1981 and 1985 in order to improve their balance sheet figures.

One critical consideration with regard to bank holdings in industry is the significant percentage of shares held in unlisted companies (Table 8.9). This raises a possible illiquidity risk, which would be greater than that of listed companies. In such cases, the ultimate reason for bank investment in these companies' equity must be a higher expected return. However, experience shows that these holdings often exist for historical reasons—a bankruptcy that ends with the transfer of ownership of the shares to the creditor bank—or for opportunity reasons—a sale on special conditions or a company considered important among the other industrial companies within the bank group's sphere of influence. The only caveat to be made in such cases is that the bank could become, *de facto*, the shareholder responsible for the company's performance, irrespective of the existence of other shareholders. Were this to happen, it might give rise to additional risks in the bank's management of the financial organization. Hence, in practice, the universal banking model requires a greater amount of prudence than the specialized banking model, which rarely considers long-term relationships with industry.

A final observation concerning the above table refers to the distinction between a nominal interest in an industrial company's equity and an effective interest. Chuliá (1990) shows that, in the context of the Spanish banking system, with large bank holdings in the capital of other banks, the banks' effective interest in industry would be even greater if banks did not have cross-holdings and were independent of each other. This means that the weight of the banks in Spanish industry, in terms of control of ownership, is greater than the nominal percentage obtained by merely counting shares.

TABLE 8.9 *Banking system: variable income portfolio* (1982–1989) (% of balance sheet)

	1982	1983	1984	1985	1986	1987	1988	1989	Mean of period
Commercial banks									
Bank shares	0.42	0.53	0.49	0.54	0.49	0.55	0.69	0.63	0.55
Other listed shares	0.41	0.53	0.42	0.42	0.54	0.56	1.21	1.08	0.69
Non-listed shares	1.17	1.37	1.17	1.01	0.99	0.92	1.05	1.01	1.08
Foreign securities	0.25	0.41	0.36	0.36	0.34	0.38	0.41	0.46	0.38
TOTAL	2.25	2.83	2.44	2.33	2.37	2.42	3.36	3.19	2.71
Savings banks									
Bank shares	0.12	0.07	0.07	0.06	0.10	0.11	0.06	0.05	0.08
Other listed shares	0.48	0.44	0.38	0.39	0.59	0.81	0.68	0.65	0.55
Non-listed shares	0.59	0.73	0.68	0.64	0.67	0.57	0.70	0.73	0.66
Foreign securities	0.00	0.00	0.00	0.00	0.04	0.05	0.07	0.09	0.04
TOTAL	1.20	1.25	1.13	1.10	1.42	1.54	1.51	1.52	1.33

Source: Chuliá (1990).

It should not be forgotten that the interrelationships between banks and non-financial companies are not confined to holdings by the former in the equity of the latter. Another aspect of this interrelation is the loan investment. Table 8.10 shows the higher weight of total bank debt in total debt in several countries' industrial companies (Spain, Italy, and Japan), versus a low weight in the United States and France. However, this table shows the fall in the weight of bank debt in total debt in Spain, offset by an increase in issues on the financial markets.

Table 8.11 shows the evolution of Spanish industrial companies' financial structure between 1983 and 1993. We would like to emphasize the following points, among others: first, the considerable increase in the weight of the net worth, which accounted for 45.1 per cent of the liabilities in 1989; second, the drop by almost five points of short and long-term debt; third, the dramatic decrease in short and long-term bank debt, confirming the observation made about Table 8.10.

The trend in Spanish bank ownership of non-financial companies changed drastically after 1991, with the sharpening of bank competition and the entry of the Spanish economy into a period of stagnation which subsequently led to the 1992–4 recession. In a way, it was a repetition of the phenomenon experienced by industrial banks in the 1970s: the economic recession forced the demise of many of them. Table 8.12 shows the distribution by industries of investments in non-financial companies by some large Spanish banks between 1990 and 1993. In the following sections, we will discuss the industrial strategy followed by some Spanish banks.

4.1. The Banco Bilbao Vizcaya (BBV) Group

Having overcome the initial difficulties of the merger process, the BBV turned again to the redesign and growth of its industrial group in the early 1990s. Table 8.13 shows the evolution of BBV's most important holdings in non-financial companies between 1990 and 1993. We can see that these holdings have tended to increase and the bank has only sold shares when it has seen clear opportunities for capital gains or exceptional difficulties in the way of a good strategic positioning of the company in the medium term.

Unlike other Spanish banks which, in recent years, have disposed of their investments in non-financial companies, the BBV Group has increased such investments, following a mature industrial vocation within the bank. Likewise, the generally positive results of its business investments place BBV as an exception in the European banking industry. Indeed, it is one of the few bank groups that did not suffer difficulties during the recession of the 1970s and early 1980s and which has not experienced serious problems in the 1992–4 recession. This fact is noteworthy and BBV's record is one of the few success stories of non-financial bank diversification either in Spain or in the rest of the EU countries.

In a reorganization starting in April 1995, the BBV Group was structured

TABLE 8.10 *Industrial companies: bank debt over total debt* (1985–1993) (%)

	1985	1986	1987	1988	1989	1990	1991	1992	1993
Spain	47.9	42.4	38.7	31.9	31.7	34.7	35.6	36.1	33.1
Germany	29.0	29.8	29.1	29.3	30.1	30.4	30.4	30.7	—
France	26.0	23.6	22.1	20.1	20.5	20.5	19.7	17.4	16.2
United States	14.3	15.8	16.2	18.0	18.0	18.3	16.9	15.8	14.5
Japan	41.2	43.1	41.0	38.9	36.3	35.8	37.1	40.1	42.5

Source: BACH (European Commission).

TABLE 8.11 *Spain: financial structure of non-financial companies* (1983–1993)

	1993	1983	1984	1985	1986	1987	1988	1989	1990	1991	1992
Net worth	28.1	31.5	33.9	35.2	39.1	43.2	45.1	42.3	39.3	36.1	31.5
Long-term debt	21.0	19.4	18.0	16.9	14.6	13.6	11.6	11.4	13.0	14.9	16.4
Of which, with credit institutions	15.4	13.1	11.5	10.3	8.3	7.0	6.1	6.1	7.2	7.8	8.8
Short-term debt	50.3	48.5	46.9	46.4	44.8	41.3	40.6	42.5	43.6	44.6	45.1
Of which, with credit institutions	22.4	20.6	19.7	16.6	14.7	10.5	10.4	12.6	13.7	13.7	11.4
Provisions	0.5	0.7	1.1	1.5	1.4	1.9	2.7	3.8	4.4	4.4	7.0

Source: BACH (European Commission: General Directorate II).

TABLE 8.12 *Spain: number of companies with bank shareholders, by industry*

	La Caixa				Banesto			BBV				BCH		
	1990	1991	1992	1993	1990	1991	1992	1990	1991	1992	1993	1991	1992	1993
Carparks and motorways	6	5	3	5	0	0	0	1	1	1	1	2	1	1
Iron and steel	0	0	0	0	3	2	2	1	0	0	0	2	1	1
Mining	0	0	0	0	3	4	3	0	0	0	0	3	3	2
Insurance	5	6	6	6	2	3	2	3	4	3	4	10	4	4
Chemicals and oil	0	0	0	0	4	3	1	1	1	1	0	6	5	6
Paper and textiles	1	1	0	0	3	2	2	0	0	1	1	1	0	0
Transportation and communication	1	1	0	0	0	1	2	2	2	2	2	6	4	4
Cement, construction, and property	2	2	5	7	16	9	5	16	19	17	19	20	10	10
Agriculture and food	0	0	0	0	3	2	2	11	15	5	5	9	6	7
Water, gas, and electricity	3	2	2	2	1	0	0	4	3	3	2	2	3	3
Services	4	4	5	8	8	15	14	2	3	2	2	13	11	11
Others	5	5	2	2	0	0	0	14	15	10	8	25	11	13
TOTAL	27	26	23	30	43	41	33	55	63	45	44	99	59	62

TABLE 8.13 *BBV: Some industrial holdings*

Company	Industry	Percentage equity				Gross result				Equity[a]
		1990	1991	1992	1993	1989	1990	1991	1992	
Aguas de Barcelona	Services	8.44	—	—	—	2,204	—	—	—	14,539
Altos Hornos de Vizcaya	Iron and steel	14.42	—	—	—	4,410	—	—	—	16,247
Amper	Holding company	5.49	—	—	—	1,640	—	—	—	6,977
Autopista Vasco-Aragonesa	Motorways	41.33	27.89	27.57	27.45	844	1,452	2,078	1,832	26,039
Canal Plus	Communication	15.00	15.00	15.26	15.79	—	−3,696	−6,626	−3,106	30,000
Cubiertas y MZOV	Construction	3.70	—	—	—	3,216	—	—	—	4,512
Delicass comercial	Trading company	100.00	100.00	100.00	100.00	−89	−338	—	−214	400
Euroseguros	Insurance	100.00	100.00	100.00	100.00	3,244	4,017	2,522	2,599	11,300
Hambros PLC	Advertising	5.98	—	—	—	13,325	—	—	—	6,001
Helados y congelados	Food	75.10	51.52	51.52	69.52	1,405	1,790	1,633	−110	4,201
Hidroeléctrica del Cantábrico	Electricity	6.53	6.41	6.47	—	5,340	6,385	5,623	—	37,732
Industrial Asturiana Santa Bárbara	Real estate	34.73	17.37	—	—	152	−494	—	—	5,878
Koipe	Food	5.26	5.23	5.23	10.13	1,401	1,456	—	1,652	4,307
Promotora de Iniciativas de Desarrollo	Services	—	50.00	—	—	—	315	—	—	44,200
Repsol	Oil	4.21	4.02	4.17	—	62,600	43,044	70,170	—	150,000
Sevillana de Electricidad	Electricity	9.57	9.19	10.05	10.26	10,981	14,532	13,212	13,531	148,201

[a] Company's equity at the start of the last year in which BBV had a holding.

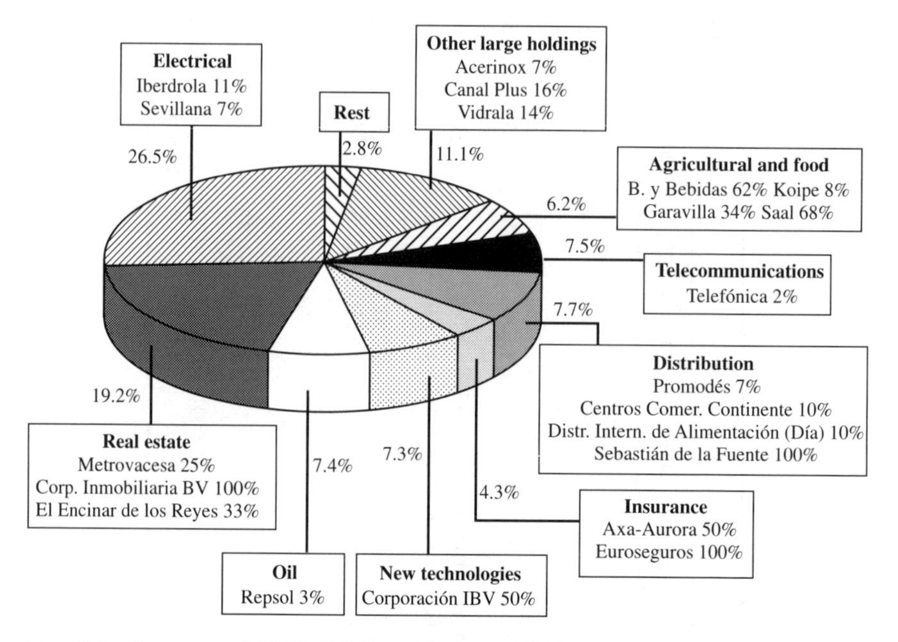

FIG. 8.6 *Structure of BBV's holdings by sector (1994)*

around five main business areas: retail banking, wholesale banking and diversification, markets, private banking, and BBV's banking subsidiaries, Banca Catalana and Banco de Comercio. The BBV Group's industrial, real estate, and insurance holdings are grouped within the wholesale banking and diversification unit.

This group of companies, with a market value at the beginning of 1995 exceeding 300 billion pesetas—excluding the bank business—emerged as one of Spain's largest non-financial company groups. In 1994, these companies accounted for 2.8 per cent of the Group's consolidated assets and contributed almost 10 per cent of the Group's gross profits. It can be inferred from these figures that this business group's return on assets in 1994 exceeded the return of the strictly banking business.

The latter figure shows the strategic importance of BBV's business holdings and their contribution to the Group's results. Likewise, the book value of the group's assets suggests the existence of significant latent capital gains (estimated at the close of 1994 at about 100 billion pesetas) resulting from the long-term nature of the investments made by BBV in businesses with healthy future prospects.

The BBV Group's business holdings were concentrated, at the end of 1995, in the following industries: energy, real estate, telecommunications, distribution, agriculture and food, and miscellaneous services (see Figure 8.6).

In the energy sector, the most important holdings were in Sevillana de Electricidad, Iberdrola, and Repsol. At the end of 1994, the investments in these companies accounted for more than one-third of the bank's industrial investments. The evolution of BBV's interest in Repsol could change if the State were to implement a new privatization plan after 1995.

Metrovacesa and Corporación Inmobiliaria BV constitute the major part of BBV's presence in the real estate market, although some real estate projects have been started by creating a bank-owned subsidiary. The investments in these two companies amounted to about 150 billion pesetas at the end of 1994, which, in practice, made the BBV Group the largest property company in Spain. The bank's real estate projects are focused on three targets: shopping centres, business parks, and residential areas.

In the telecommunications industry, of particular note is the bank's entry into Telefónica at the beginning of 1995, acquiring a 2.5 per cent interest. Argentaria, La Caixa, and BBV became the hard core of Telefónica shareholders. This holding in Telefónica has opened the door for BBV to invest in the future in other businesses in the telecommunications industry, such as digital mobile telephony (GSM) or the multimedia business.

In the distribution business, BBV's presence is very important in Promodes, the French parent company and owner of the Continente group and the Día discount chain. Its interest in Promodes amounted to 7 per cent of its share cpaital, making it the second largest shareholder at the end of 1994. One of BBV's goals is to follow Promodes in its international strategy. It also intends to promote the Día chain in the discount store segment, which is expected to grow significantly in the next few years.

In the food industry, the largest holdings are in Bodegas y Bebidas, Garavilla, and Koipe. Over the last few years, BBV has been studying numerous offers to enter companies in the food industry, with the purpose of acquiring a holding in some of the leading companies.

In the area of miscellaneous services, we would point to the importance of the insurance business through Euroseguros, a fully owned BBV subsidiary, and the Axa-Aurora holding company, of which BBV owns a 50 per cent interest.

The investment criteria used by the BBV Group to assess its holdings in industrial or services companies have been profitability, liquidity, and the business's perspective in the medium term. One basic management aspect has been the recognition of the different nature of each of the industries that BBV has invested in, seeking out good managers in each of the companies and setting growth and profitability goals adapted to each industry. In recent years, BBV has sold low-liquidity holdings in mature industries and has preferred to acquire relatively small interests in companies with profitable and more liquid shares such as Telefónica or Repsol.

BBV has tried to maintain a relatively balanced portfolio between different industries, taking into account their cyclical nature. The bank has also used a clear criterion with regard to the companies in which it has invested: not to monopolize the banking business generated by these companies. Thus, decisions on the financing of companies in which BBV has holdings are made with complete autonomy by the relevant department.

The excellent results obtained so far by the BBV Group's non-bank companies unit are very different, as we have pointed out previously, from the results achieved by other bank groups during recent years, in Spain and in the rest of the EU.

The investment and management models followed by BBV to organize its business holdings have been quite sophisticated, in many respects. The high level set by BBV in its business investments will not be easy to beat in the future. The increasing competition that the companies will face in their respective industries and the complexity of managing such a large group of companies will, perhaps, be the greatest challenges faced by the BBV Group in the management of its holdings over the next few years.

4.2. Other bank-company groups

Another financial organization that implemented a similar strategy is La Caixa, a Spanish savings bank, which has become a major shareholder in large industrial companies such as Gas Natural, Repsol, and Telefónica. La Caixa is following a course similar to BBV. After consolidating the merger process between Caja de Barcelona and Caixa de Pensions, the new organization that emerged from the merger initiated an ambitious industrial diversification project. Table 8.14 shows the evolution of its largest shareholdings in non-financial companies between 1988 and 1994. To this list we would have to add the purchase of a 2.5 per cent interest in Telefónica in February 1995, which has placed La Caixa in an excellent position in the telecommunications business, along with BBV, Argentaria, and Banco Santander. The main difference between La Caixa and BBV is that La Caixa's industrial holdings portfolio has not had such an ordered organizational model as that of BBV. This is probably due to the lack of prior experience in La Caixa in the management of industrial companies.

BCH has implemented a second type of industrial strategy, whose primary feature is not growth but the consolidation and restructuring of its holdings around a few critical sectors. Table 8.15 shows the evolution of its holdings in a number of companies. Figure 8.7 shows the concentration of industrial investment in six critical sectors: oil, property, motorways, food, construction, and water, gas, and electricity.

BCH's holdings in these industries have given rise to six strategic business units within the bank's structure. Instead of adopting the model used by BBV or Banesto, consisting of creating an industrial corporation, BCH has chosen an organizational model with an apparently simpler design, although its day-to-day management is becoming more complex.

We can see from these figures how BCH's holdings have evolved in accordance with each company's fit with the bank's objectives. Since 1993, BCH has

TABLE 8.14 *La Caixa: some non-financial holdings*

Company	Industry	Percentage of equity							Gross results						Equity[a]
		1988	1989	1990	1991	1992	1993	1994	1988	1989	1990	1991	1992	1993	
Acesa	Motorways	28.2	30.3	48.7	25.1	35.7	39.3	4.1	8,695	11,619	17,172	17,263	16,282	16,565	102,185
Aguas de Barcelona	Services	—	—	12.9	10.4	28.3	26.7	−26.8	—	—	2,204	5,602	6,730	5,363	20,635
Aucat	Motorways	—	—	25	25	25	25	25	—	—	0	—	—	−177	6,841
Autopista Terrassa-Manresa	Motorways	—	—	—	10	10	12.0	10	—	—	—	—	—	—	9,900
Gas Natural[b]	Gas distribution	14.9	23.6	30.4	25.5	25.5	25.5	25.5	3,118	4,061	6,491	7,964	12,024	14,560	22,389
Iberpistas	Motorways	—	—	5.8	5.8	—	—	6	—	—	325	526	—	—	22,568
Inmobiliaria Colonial	Real estate	—	—	—	—	96.8	99.8	99.8	—	—	—	—	455	1,325	23,855
Telefónica	Communications	—	—	2.8	2	0.4	0.4	0.7	—	—	93,073	93,188	—	—	462,482
Túnel del Cadí	Operation of Cadí Tunnel	31.4	28.4	55.1	54.8	53.9	53.4	53.4	?	368	0	?	?	—	9,505
Port Aventura	Tourism and leisure							33.1							15,810

[a] Company's equity at the start of the last year in which La Caixa had a holding.
[b] Until 1991, holding in Catalana de Gas shown. After 1992, holding in Gas Natural.

TABLE 8.15 *BCH: some industrial holdings*

Company	Industry	Percentage of equity			Results			Equity[a]	1990[b]	
		1991	1992	1993	Gross 1990	Net 1991	Net 1992			
Aceites y Proteinas, SA	Food	42.93	29.13	29.26	–374	67	–1,436	4,234	C	20.1
Altos hornos de Vizcaya	Metals	4.55	—	—	–3,850	—	—	16,247	C	5.1
Autopistas del Mare Notrum	Motorways	47.27	45.74	42.43	6,672	6,672	6,672	66,725	C	46.6
Bami	Real estate	25.34	24.24	15.04	73	?	–2,079	5,191	H	4.7
Central Hispano Generali, Hess	Holding company	—	50.00	25.00	—	?	–3,144	85,510	—	—
Cepsa	Oil	31.81	34.47	35.28	7,195	13,151	11,410	116,107	C	27.0
Compañía Sevillana de Electricidad	Electricity	3.22	3.27	3.14	?	14,418	13,557	148,201	—	
Conservera Campofrío	Food	22.04	23.49	21.25	3,018	3,506	1,833	5,009	C	24.0
Corporación Alimentaria Ibérica	Food	11.05	14.50	14.51	852	–826	–2,970	4,075	H	14.6
Dragados y Construcciones	Construction	22.40	22.62	23.06	7,503	12,719	11,115	29,724	C	23.6
Ercros	Chemicals	3.63	—	—	645	—	—	41,610	H	3.7
Eritisa	Chemicals	—	—	25.00	—	—	–2,456	5,500	—	—
Grupo Duro Felguera	Metals	9.73	10.04	10.04	2,301	1,100	–1,574	6,073	H	9.3
Pescanova	Food	3.22	3.15	3.78	?	3,006	1,492	5,358	—	—
Sociedad Española de Carburos Metálicos	Chemicals	10.18	10.50	10.94	1,623	1,704	1,711	13,012	C	10.8
Sociedad General Azucarera de España	Food	45.51	47.58	49.24	1,920	2,148	1,509	4,119	C	24.8
Tubacex	Manufacturing	4.43	—	—	648	—	—	10,013	H	4.4
Unión Eléctrica Fenosa	Electricity	—	3.69	3.66	—	14,466	13,807	145,069	—	—
Vallehermoso	Real estate	28.18	32.27	29.77	5,859	6,494	7,763	18,438	H	25.6

[a] Company's equity at the start of the last year in which BCH had a holding.
[b] 'C' signifies the former Banco Central, 'H' the former Banco Hispeno.

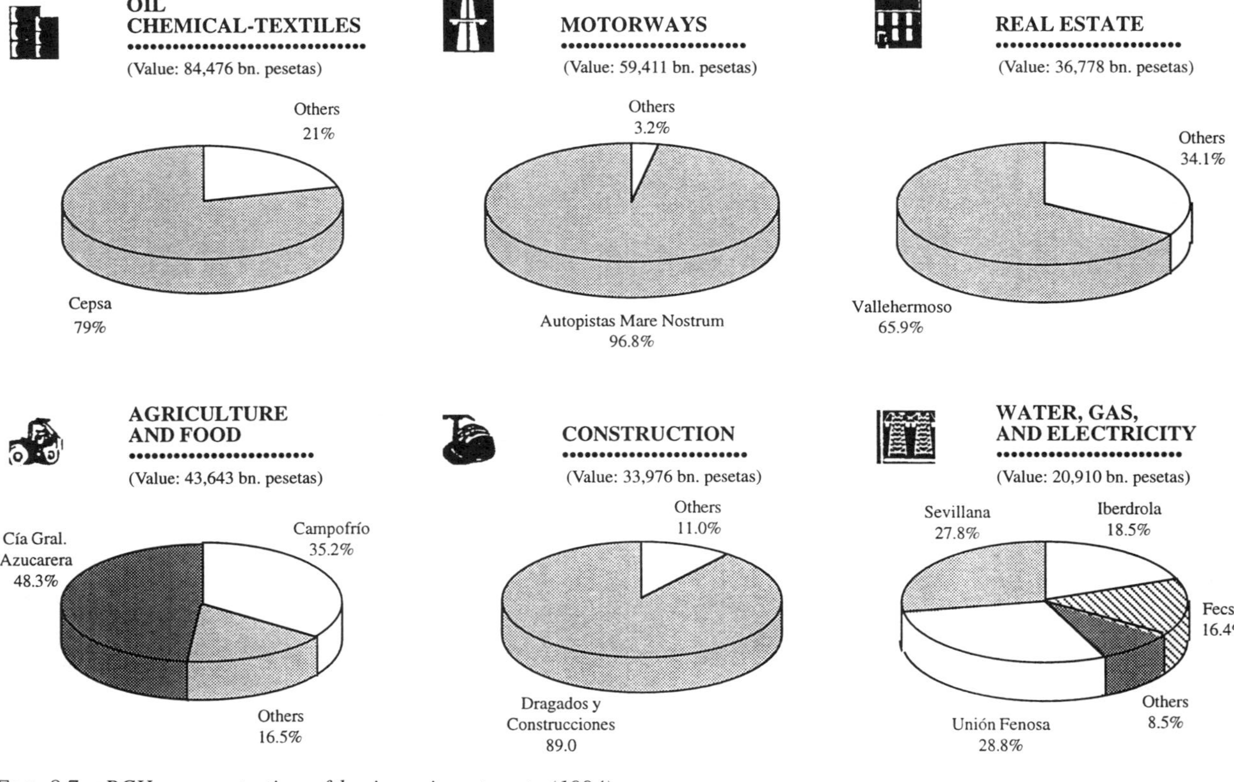

FIG. 8.7 *BCH: concentration of business investments (1994)*

pursued a profitability goal in its companies, at the same time as it has been seeking to maintain control of important companies in their respective sectors, such as Cepsa in oil, Dragados and Vallehermoso in construction, and Campofrío and Azucarera in food.

The third model of industrial portfolio is that implemented by Banesto since 1990, with the creation of Corporación Industrial Banesto. The corporation's goal was to achieve not only large capital gains accompanied by not insignificant tax exemptions but also the integrated management of the bank's industrial group. Table 2.5 (in chapter 2) shows the evolution of Banesto's largest holdings in industrial companies. The growth of lending by the bank to these companies to an extent far exceeding that of the other bank groups considered and the growing economic difficulties of quite a large number of these companies served to worsen Banesto's solvency problems and precipitated the intervention by the Bank of Spain in December 1993.

Subsequently, the entry of a new management group under the main shareholder, Banco Santander, has led to the gradual sale of the corporation's main assets. The new shareholders' philosophy is that Banesto should be, primarily, a commercial bank and should not indulge in industrial fancies.

5. SOME FINAL CONSIDERATIONS ON BANK-COMPANY RELATIONSHIPS IN SPAIN

One cannot understand bank involvement in the financing of non-financial companies in the 1980s and 1990s without taking into account two considerations that determine the context of the banking system in Spain: a growing rivalry in the industry and a recessive business cycle until 1984 and, again, between 1991 and 1993.

Generally speaking, we can say that the relationship between banks and non-financial companies in Spain is more similar to the German or Japanese model than to the Anglo-Saxon model. The reason is the significant weight of bank financing in companies' financial resources and the fact that some banks are major shareholders in large companies. However, the Spanish model has a number of features that distinguish it from the German model: Spanish companies' long-term bank debt is a small part of total bank debt; in Germany, a number of banks may be shareholders in the same non-financial company; finally, the role and structure of the companies' management bodies are different.

The three types of relationship between banks and non-financial companies existing in Spain that we have discussed in the previous section shape in turn the reasons behind the construction of an industrial group. Experience advises in favour of distinguishing between banks that invest in companies in emerging sectors and banks that mainly invest in companies that are well positioned in traditional industrial sectors.

BBV and La Caixa can be considered to be bank organizations that invest in emerging companies for two reasons: for financial reasons and the desire to finance business projects that are interesting from a variety of points of view.

BCH, for its part, seeks to maintain industrial holdings in strategic but more classical sectors of the economy, such as food, construction, and energy. The return on these investments is focused not so much on these sectors' growth—which is not expected to be very high in the next few years—but on the companies' good competitive positioning within their respective sectors. It seems that this was also going to be the model followed by Banesto. However, the crisis of the bank and the companies in which it had invested brought the corporation to an early death.

6. A COMPARISON OF THE BANK MODELS AND THE RELATIONSHIPS BETWEEN BANKS AND NON-FINANCIAL COMPANIES IN GERMANY, JAPAN, AND SPAIN

In this and the two previous chapters, we have analysed the elements that shape the banking system and the relationships between banks and non-financial companies in Germany, Japan, and Spain. The common denominator of all three is clear: all have universal banks which maintain a significant presence in the financing of non-financial companies and less sophisticated capital markets than those that the United States or Great Britain can offer.

However, the existence of this common denominator is insufficient to classify the three countries as having the same bank model or an identical relationship between banks and non-financial companies. Consequently, we cannot talk of a single model of universal banks but rather of a very general model with some features specific to each country.

Table 8.16 summarizes some of the figures on the financial structure of non-financial companies that we have discussed in the appropriate chapters. The use of these figures will enable us to carry out a rapid comparison between the various banking systems and their relationships with non-financial companies. We also include the figures for the United States in this table, which will allow us to compare with the alternative financial model, based on the capital markets, and whose paradigm is the United States. In this final synthesis, we will not discuss again the structural elements of the banking system in each of the countries considered—that we have done in the appropriate chapter—but we will confine ourselves to comparing the relationships between banks and companies.

We can draw the following conclusions. First, the level of bank debt in non-financial companies' total liabilities shows a high scatter. In the United States, it was only 9.3 per cent of the liabilities, while in Japan it was 27 per cent, and it was 17.1 per cent in Spain. Therefore, we can conclude that the weight of bank financing in non-financial companies is low in the United States and high in Japan and—although somewhat less so—in Spain.

Second, the companies' long-term debt with banks is between 6 per cent and

TABLE 8.16 *Non-financial companies: financial ratios*

	Germany (1992)	Japan (1993)	Spain (1994)	United States (1993)
Total bank debt/Total liabilities	15.4	26.9	17.1	9.3
Long-term bank debt/Total liabilities	7.6	15.1	6.1	6.6
Short-term bank debt/Total liabilities	7.6	11.8	11.0	2.7
Net worth/Total liabilities	24.0	32.4	34.9	36.3
Provisions/Total liabilities	25.9	4.2	5.5	—
Net worth + Provisions/Total liabilities	49.9	36.6	40.4	36.3
Long-term debt/Total liabilities	12.8	23.2	13.0	29.9
Short-term debt/Total liabilities	37.4	40.2	46.6	33.8
Total debt/Total liabilities	50.2	63.4	59.6	63.7

Source: BACH (European Commission).

8 per cent of total liabilities in Germany, Spain, and the United States, while it is 15 per cent in Japan. Therefore, long-term bank debt is more important for Japanese companies than for companies in the other countries studied. These data also reflect an interesting aspect of the relationship between banks and non-financial companies in Japan: the existence of a more extensive and longer-lasting relationship than in the other countries having universal banks, such as Germany or Spain.

Third, short-term bank debt for financing companies is particularly high in Spain (11.0 per cent) and Japan (11.8 per cent), while it is almost negligible in American companies. These figures reflect at least two important facts. First, the importance of short-term bank debt in Spanish and Japanese companies. The difference between companies in these two countries is that while in Japan almost 60 per cent of companies' bank debt is long term, in Spain this percentage falls to one-third. The second fact we wish to stress is the minor role played by short-term bank financing in North American companies. If we also consider that the long-term bank financing received by North American companies—analysed in Chapter 3—comes from bank-syndicated loans, we can conclude that the role of the banks in financing companies in the United States is much less prominent and, when it does take on a certain weight, it is due to bank operations on the capital markets on behalf of non-financial companies. Therefore, financial disintermediation on the commercial banks' asset side in the United States is almost total.

This table also offers a number of observations about corporate financing in these countries. First, the importance of shareholders' equity in the financing of Spanish (40.4 per cent of total liabilities) and German companies (49.9 per cent of total liabilities, if we include the large provisions charged to generated resources). In the case of the Spanish companies, this figure reveals a not particularly encouraging conclusion: Spanish companies must mostly rely on generated resources, as the banks—generally speaking—are not prepared to finance long-term business projects and the capital markets are not sophisticated enough to provide adequate financing to non-financial companies.

Second, the companies' level of total debt ranges between 50.2 per cent in Germany (lowest value) to 63.7 per cent in the United States (highest value), with Japan very close behind (63.4 per cent). These figures show the lower dependence of the German companies on external financing and the higher dependence of the Japanese companies. It is interesting to note again the existence of differences between two countries with a system of universal banks, a significant bank involvement in companies, and a very similar 'main bank' model. However, the differences are significant: companies prefer to rely on generated resources rather than increase their debt level, even if it is with banks in the same group.

Third, long-term debt is 29.9 per cent in the United States, 23.2 per cent in Japan, and considerably lower in the other countries, particularly Germany (12.8 per cent) and Spain (13.0 per cent). The comparison between Germany and Spain is interesting. German companies do not have much long-term debt but their volume of shareholders' equity and accumulated generated resources is higher than in Spanish companies.

Fourth, Spain is the country whose companies have the highest percentage of short-term debt in their balance sheets (46.6 per cent), while the United States has the lowest percentage (33.8 per cent). In addition to confirming what we have said about Spain, the figures for the American companies show that they are not as geared towards the short term as is sometimes said.

The comparisons we have made between the financial models of Germany, Japan, Spain, and the United States indicate two unequivocal conclusions. First, the financial models in countries having a universal banking model are not identical but have many unique features. These features, in turn, are the result of historical, regulatory, and business factors that allow each model to take on its own special character.

The second conclusion is that the American financial model, although different from the European or Japanese universal bank models, shares with them a number of similar features. With the Japanese model, it shares the high indebtedness of non-financial companies. With the German model, it shares the low percentage of bank financing, particularly in short-term bank financing, which is almost non-existent in the United States.

9

The Internationalization of Banking

1. INTRODUCTION

The globalization of the financial system has been accompanied by a parallel trend: the internationalization of banking that, in turn, has helped consolidate the globalization of the finance industry as a whole.[1]

The internationalization of banks is a complex phenomenon, for reasons that are in part similar to and in part different from those that account for the international expansion of industrial or other services companies. However, it shares one common factor with them. While, in certain industries that are tending towards globalization, companies are forced to be present in many different geographical markets in order to remain competitive, it does not seem that the same trend is happening in the banking industry.

This is because of a simple empirical fact. In the automobile, consumer electronics, computers, or household appliance industries (to mention just a few), the leading companies (General Motors, Toyota, Philips, Sony, or Whirlpool) are clearly global companies, while this is not so in the bank industry. Thus, the banks with the widest international diversification of activities are not to be found among the world's largest banks, as can be seen in Table 9.1. Or, looked at another way, the world's most profitable banks, in terms of the resources they handle, are predominantly national banks, such as Banc One, Banco Popular, and Wachovia.

Obviously, this does not prove—nor is it our intention to seek—any final conclusion; rather, it raises a paradox. This paradox is related to the fact that the internationalization of banks is somewhat more complex than the internationalization of companies in other sectors of the economy.

However, in the present situation of an almost complete deregulation of the industry, a broad freedom of capital movements, and global financial markets, banks of a certain size are considering their international expansion (or expansion of their international activities).

The internationalization of financial firms has generally followed three broad lines in the last 15 years. The first is the creation of a network of branches in foreign countries. The two banks most active in this respect have been Citibank and Barclays.

[1] Walter (1988) offers an overview of the factors that have determined the internationalization of financial services.

TABLE 9.1 *European banks: international activity (1993)*

Bank	Country	Assets abroad (%)	Total assets (US$ bn.)
Standard Chartered Bank	United Kingdom	63.7	43
Union Bank	Switzerland	57.7	181
Swiss Bank Corporation	Switzerland	53.1	149
Crédit Suisse	Switzerland	52.4	116
Paribas	France	45.9	184
Banque Indosuez	France	45.0	68
National Westminster Bank	United Kingdom	44.3	233
Banque Nationale de Paris	France	43.8	290
Banca Commerciale	Italy	38.7	93
Crédit Lyonnais	France	36.5	285

Source: *Euromoney* and *The Banker*.

The second line has consisted of buying a bank abroad. In recent years, this has been going on with some intensity in the EU, as can be seen in Figure 9.1. Thus, Deutsche Bank bought the Bank of America's subsidiary in Italy (1986), Morgan Grenfell (1989), and Banco de Madrid (1993). Crédit Lyonnais bought Banque de Commerce (Belgium, 1989), Banco Comercial Español (1990), and Banca Jover (1992). San Paolo bought Banco de Ibiza in 1990.

These acquisitions are usually expensive. Thus, Deutsche Bank offered 42 billion pesetas for Banco de Madrid, about 2.3 times its book value. For its part, Crédit Lyonnais paid 50 billion pesetas for Banco Comercial Español and about 100 billion pesetas for Banca Jover (which was 3.3 times its book value).

A rather less onerous form of internationalization than buying a bank outright is to take a minority holding in its equity, in some cases within the context of an alliance. This is a formula that has been extensively used by some banks to penetrate markets such as Spain. Thus, we observe the presence of Rabobank in Banco Popular, J. P. Morgan in Banesto, Commerzbank in BCH, and Royal Bank of Scotland in Banco Santander.

In this chapter, we will try to examine the internationalization of banking from the perspective of the developments that have taken place in the bank industry in recent years. In order to understand better the distinctive features of this industry, we will compare these developments with those that have taken place in other sectors of the economy.

1.1. The internationalization of banks: Banco Santander

Bank internationalization has followed very different paths depending on the banks' home country, the specific segment of the banking business occupied, and, finally, the history, the resources available and the final decisions made by banks, taking into account the opportunities and threats they have been able

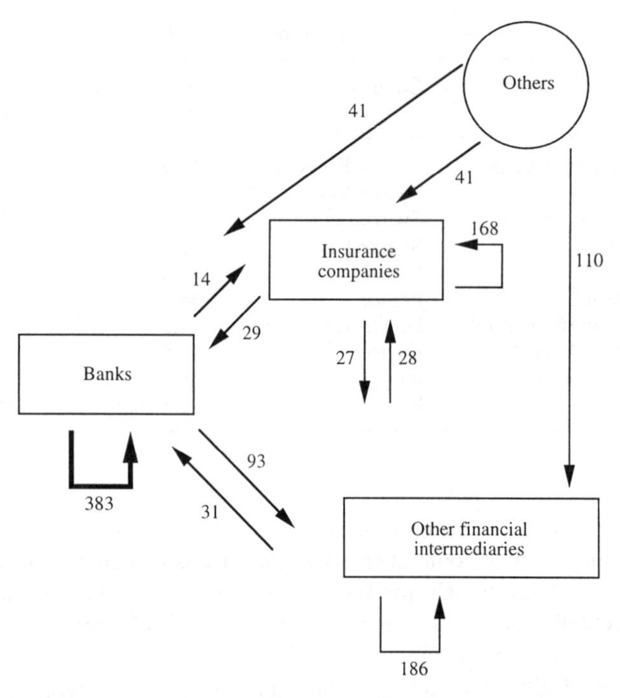

FIG. 9.1 *Bank acquisitions (no. of operations, 1990)*

to identify. The same bank has used different internationalization procedures at different times, depending on these and other criteria.

The case of Banco Santander illustrates the multiple dimensions that the banks' internationalization process may follow. In the early 1980s, Banco Santander had branches in six foreign countries and representatives in another eight.

Until 1987, Banco Santander's international growth was modest and the means used were mostly the traditional ones. However, in that year, Banco Santander changed the pace and procedure by deciding to purchase two financial organizations in Germany: CC-Bank and Visa Card Services. The first of these specialized in consumer loans (financing the purchase of motor vehicles and consumer durables).

In 1988, an important event took place in the European banking industry: Banco Santander established an alliance with Royal Bank of Scotland. This was one of the first alliances brought about by the single market in banking. This alliance not only intended to carry out a series of joint projects in computer applications and in the development of financial products but also included share swaps between the two banks. By the end of 1994, Banco Santander held 9.88 per cent of the British bank's equity.

That same year, Banco Santander established another important alliance, this time with Metropolitan Life, a renowned insurance company. The purpose of the alliance was to create the Sociedad de Seguros Santander-Met, which designs financial products to be distributed through the bank's network of branches.

In 1990 Banco Santander acquired a controlling interest in Banco de Comercio e Industria de Portugal. The Portuguese bank market was already being considered a natural extension of the Spanish market.

Banco Santander decided to carry out in 1991 the most ambitious acquisition so far: the purchase of approximately 10 per cent of the equity of First Fidelity, a large commercial bank in the north-east of the United States. By the end of 1994 Banco Santander owned about 30 per cent of First Fidelity's equity. This purchase caused surprise in some American financial circles, because the financial services industry was one of the few industries in North America that had so far remained immune to foreign investment.

This operation was to have unexpected consequences. Four years later, in June 1995, First Union, one of the 10 largest banks in the USA, launched a friendly take-over bid for First Fidelity. By this means, Banco Santander indirectly became the largest shareholder of the sixth largest bank in the United States. Its estimated interest in the new bank was about 11 per cent in June 1995.

The significance of the expansion of Banco Santander in North America can be understood better with a few figures. In 1994, 7.4 per cent of the entire group's assets and 6.2 per cent of the net income were generated in the United States and Puerto Rico.

Banco Santander's presence in the latter country is notable and has been achieved through two banks: Banco Santander Puerto Rico, which is the country's second largest commercial bank, with assets totalling more than 600 billion pesetas by the end of 1994; and Santander National Bank, which is a small bank that operates in certain cities in the country.

In 1994, Banco Santander formed Santander Investment Securities in New York. This firm was the first Spanish financial organization to be authorized to operate as a broker on the United States stock market.

Banco Santander was licensed by the Mexican government to operate in Mexico in 1994, which led to its decision to open several branches of its subsidiary, Banco Santander de Negocios, in Mexico.

One interesting aspect is Banco Santander's strong penetration of the growing investment fund and pension fund business in new emerging markets, such as Chile and Argentina. In Chile, Grupo Santander Chile was the fourth largest bank in the country at the close of 1994, both in assets terms and in profits. The group was also a leader in asset management, through its subsidiary Bansander AFP.

There is one final international move that is worth pointing out: the creation of IBOS, an alliance between Banco Santander, Banco de Comercio e Industria, Royal Bank of Scotland, and Crédit Commerciale. Its purpose is to develop

TABLE 9.2 *Santander Group: return on investment*

	1994		1993		1992	
	Weight (%)	Rate (%)	Weight (%)	Rate (%)	Weight (%)	Rate (%)
Central banks and State debt	17.63	8.68	11.05	9.28	11.97	8.89
Credit institutions	21.98	7.48	23.68	10.89	18.45	10.89
Pesetas	10.60	7.57	10.04	10.50	8.15	10.83
Foreign currency	11.38	7.39	13.64	11.17	10.30	10.92
Loans	36.38	10.91	41.78	14.62	49.38	14.46
Pesetas	23.22	12.18	26.70	15.37	34.24	15.23
Foreign currency	13.16	9.86	15.08	13.29	15.14	12.73
Stock portfolio	15.18	8.15	15.73	8.80	12.77	9.80
Pesetas	2.19	9.81	2.66	9.17	3.28	9.92
Foreign currency	12.99	7.87	13.07	8.72	9.49	9.76
Tangible and intangible assets	2.64	—	2.24	—	2.44	—
Other assets	6.19	—	5.52	—	4.98	—
TOTALS	100.00	8.40	100.00	11.10	100.00	11.47

Source: Annual Report.

computer applications that will enable financial transactions to be carried out between the member banks' branches in real time. The founder banks were joined in 1994 by Unibank, Denmark's second largest bank group, bringing the number of branches connected in real time by this system to 4,500 in seven countries by the end of 1994.

Tables 9.2 and 9.3 show the course of the return on assets and the mean cost of resources, respectively, between 1992 and 1994. The importance of foreign currency operations is immediately apparent, both on total employment of funds and on resources obtained.

Although the figures dip on occasions between 1992 and 1994, foreign currency operations accounted for more than 37 per cent of the total employment of funds in 1994. Furthermore, Banco Santander obtained approximately 34 per cent of its total resources in foreign currency. These two figures show the importance of international business in Banco Santander.

Finally, Table 9.4 gives a breakdown of assets and liabilities in pesetas and foreign currency, on the one hand, and assets and liabilities attributable to businesses in Spain or abroad, on the other hand. This table does not include Banesto. A quick look suggests the importance of assets located in other countries, which accounted for more than 40 per cent of total assets at the end of 1994.

TABLE 9.3 *Santander Group: mean cost of resources*

	1994		1993		1992	
	Weight (%)	Rate (%)	Weight (%)	Rate (%)	Weight (%)	Rate (%)
Credit institutions	36.81	7.65	37.47	12.02	26.30	12.91
Pesetas	22.42	7.50	19.73	12.00	11.11	12.81
Foreign currency	14.39	7.89	17.74	12.03	15.19	12.98
Customer debits	44.12	5.73	46.32	7.04	55.96	7.46
Pesetas	28.72	5.46	27.14	7.06	35.28	7.65
Foreign currency	15.41	6.23	19.18	7.03	20.68	7.14
Borrowing and subordinated liabilities	6.45	7.94	3.10	7.93	3.41	9.90
Pesetas	2.46	8.95	0.95	9.90	1.28	10.95
Foreign currency	3.99	7.32	2.15	7.07	2.13	9.26
Other resources	12.62	0.64	13.11	0.64	14.33	2.00
TOTALS	100.00	5.94	100.00	8.10	100.00	8.09

Source: Annual Report.

2. THE GROWTH OF SERVICES IN INTERNATIONAL BUSINESSES

The growth of the services sector in the more advanced economies is unquestionable. The services industry accounts for a growing proportion of total production and employment in these economies. The process is similar to that which took place in the late eighteenth century and early nineteenth century during the first industrial revolution. What at that time was a replacement of agriculture by the flourishing manufacturing industry is now being repeated in the closing years of the twentieth century with the displacement of the industrial sector by the services industry.

In practice, it is not easy to define the separation between industry and services. Any definition is liable to cause controversy. For example, is the design of an automobile an industrial activity or a service? Does the definition change if the company designing a car is different from the car manufacturer itself? Let us look at another industry, such as consumer electronics. Are the advertising activities supporting the launch of new products an industrial activity or a services activity? Again, would the definition change if this activity were carried out internally by the company manufacturing and selling the electronic products?

The growth of the services industry has also entered the area of international business. Thus, in 1991, according to United Nations estimates, 50 per cent of direct investment abroad was channelled to companies in sectors classified as services. That same year, of the total stock of foreign investment, 40 per cent

TABLE 9.4 *Santander Group: balance sheets by currency and location* (excluding Banesto) (1994)

	Total consolidated balance sheet	By currency		By location	
		Pesetas	Foreign currency	Business in Spain	Business abroad
Assets					
Cash and deposits in central banks	129,675	74,976	54,699	77,804	51,871
Public debt	1,464,074	1,464,074	—	1,323,164	140,910
Credit institutions	1,995,306	809,407	1,185,899	878,327	1,116,979
Customer credits (net)	3,328,161	1,944,758	1,383,403	2,054,918	1,273,243
Stock portfolio	1,989,081	428,494	1,560,587	871,362	1,117,719
Tangible and intangible assets	218,159	135,126	83,033	135,126	83,033
Treasury stock	4,672	4,672	—	4,672	—
Other accounts	543,586	347,362	196,224	331,704	211,882
Results of previous years in consolidated companies	16,229	2,226	14,003	2,226	14,003
TOTAL	9,688,943	5,211,095	4,477,848	5,679,303	4,009,640
Liabilities					
Credit institutions	3,357,224	1,740,224	1,617,000	2,145,501	1,211,723
Customer debits	4,117,081	2,342,064	1,775,017	2,334,571	1,782,510
Debits represented by marketable securities (loans)	704,313	313,397	390,916	354,071	350,242
Provisions and funds for risks	100,420	90,937	9,483	91,399	9,021
Subordinated liabilities	160,734	9,632	151,102	22,041	138,693
Consolidated profit	84,632	47,423	37,209	57,383	27,249
Capital and reserves	506,546	235,805	270,741	235,805	270,741
Other accounts	657,993	233,719	424,274	398,590	259,403
TOTAL	9,688,943	5,013,201	4,675,742	5,639,361	4,049,582

Source: Annual Report.

corresponded to investment in the services industry. A similar trend is taking place in the trading of services, whose share in the total volume of international trade is growing consistently.

These data seriously challenge a hypothesis used until a few years ago according to which services required production and consumption in the same location. According to this, international trade of services would be non-existent.

A variety of reasons have been used to account for the difficulty in internationalizing services. We will mention a few here. First, there is the difficulty of controlling the service's quality at the time of offering it, which is made all the more difficult if there is a significant physical distance between the producer of the service and the consumer of the service. Second, the separation between the producer of the service and the customer would make it difficult to ascertain accurately the latter's preferences. Third, low entry barriers exist in many services activities, such as restaurants or distribution. Fourth, in some services industries there exists considerable regulation, including, among other things, tariff barriers and the prohibition of direct investment from foreign countries. Fifth, there are no economies of scale or scope, and this absence helps to make any entry barriers quite insignificant.

It is important to describe these reasons because their disappearance is the primary indicator of the growing internationalization of services that is currently taking place. There are many reasons for this change. First, the new information technologies enable the steady removal of time and space barriers, so that a service produced in one country can be consumed almost simultaneously in another country. This factor is particularly important in information-intensive services.

Second is the progressive deregulation of the domestic markets in industries such as air transport, finance, transport, and telecommunications. The creation of the EU has led to a dramatic transformation of the national markets in these industries, the appearance of foreign competitors, and the growth both of direct investment and of transnational trade.

The third reason is the appearance of significant entry barriers. Technological change and, in particular, the modern information technologies, have also brought about the emergence of significant economies of scale in some industries. Thus, in the airline industry, the computerized reservation systems (CRS) requires very sizeable investments in information technologies. In the distribution industry, the increasing concentration of the market in large retailers has given these a negotiating power *vis-à-vis* their suppliers that small retailers do not have. Finally, in the telecommunications industry, the size of the investment required to be able to offer new services (mobile telephony, cable, etc.) is becoming increasingly larger and only a few companies can afford it. In any case, there is not room for many companies in this industry, due to the impressive size of the investments required and the fixed costs involved.

Also, in part due to the above reasons, significant economies of scope have appeared in some services, as a result of intangible factors such as a company's reputation world-wide (as, for example, McKinsey or Boston Consulting Group in consultancy, Reuters in financial information, or British Airways in airlines); or the experience accumulated in solving certain problems, which is particularly applicable to consulting and auditing firms such as Arthur Andersen or Price Waterhouse, or tourism or leisure companies, such as the Hilton chain or Walt Disney, for example.

Thus, the traditional barriers that impeded any possible expansion of international trade in services have diminished considerably in recent years, mainly as a result of technological and regulatory changes and changes in the demand itself.

2.1. The multinational services company versus the multinational industrial company

The unique features of the services internationalization process also reveal the existence of major differences between multinational industrial companies and multinational services companies.

In the multinational company theory (mainly applied to industrial firms), we can distinguish between three main models for explaining internationalization processes. The first is that developed by Hymer (1960), according to which the multinational company is justified by the existence of certain competitive advantages of a monopolistic nature that the company possesses and which it wishes to apply in markets other than its home market. These competitive advantages may be of many types, such as access to certain natural resources, superior technology, or the ability to create new products using basic skills that are superior to those of competitors (Prahalad and Hamel, 1990).

Essentially, this theory is the company growth theory proposed by Penrose (1959) or Chandler (1990). Penrose explains this growth phenomenon as a process driven by the existence of basic resources within the organization whose internal exploitation by the company possessing them will always be more efficient than trade on the external market. This explanation provides a second line of argument on the growth of multinational companies, which we will discuss later.

Chandler (1990), for his part, explains the growth of the modern industrial company in the United States, Germany, and Great Britain as being attributable to three basic factors: investment in production facilities that generate significant economies of scale, internal company organization that facilitates efficient management, and, finally, investment in marketing and distribution that ensures that the company's products are present in the most suitable locations for purchase by the end customers. This investment in marketing and distribution may give rise to significant economies of scope in certain industries. For example, a company's brand image, suitably reinforced by advertising, may reduce the costs of entering a particular distribution channel for a new product launched by the company. In short, the existence of certain differential advantages—which may or may not be of a monopolistic nature, as Hymer points out—is the primary fuel feeding the growth of large industrial companies.

A second paradigm to explain the internationalization process of industrial companies explicitly adopts the transaction costs approach (Williamson, 1975; Hennart, 1982; Caves, 1982; Casson, 1983). According to this approach, a multinational company is an organization that internalizes international markets for certain intermediate products (Casson, 1983). Instead of being offered freely on an open market, these products are offered internally through the functioning of multinational companies (Rugman, 1981; Hennart, 1982). Thus, we can say that direct investment (multinational companies) replaces—at least to begin with—merchandise trade (exports). In other words, the multinational company's activities replace the market's activities.

From this perspective, the multinational company is a derivative of the multidivisional company. Even if the multinational company is a single-product company, it tends to have a multidivisional form.

The ultimate reason that determines whether a company internalizes operations instead of leaving them to the free functioning of the markets is transaction costs. When the purchase of a product on a market implies a difference between profit and cost that is above that which would be obtained by the company's internal mechanisms, exporting the product will be preferred to direct investment. When the transaction costs on the market are higher, the company will opt for direct investment and, therefore, the multinational company will emerge.

The third model used to account for the multinational company is the so-called eclectic paradigm of international production that has been extensively developed by Dunning (1981). This author distinguishes between three types of advantage that account for the internationalization of an organization's production process.

1. Ownership advantages. A company that has certain unique assets or resources is able to develop sustainable competitive advantages that will enable it to withstand the force of imitation by other competitors. Essentially, this argument is similar to that proposed by Hymer or Penrose, as we have discussed above.
2. Location advantages. Direct investment abroad has often been justified on the basis of two criteria: closeness to customers or access to local markets, and access to certain raw materials or more efficient or cheaper production conditions (Caves, 1982).
3. Advantages obtained from internalizing certain transactions within the company, instead of carrying them out on open markets. This is therefore the argument used by the transaction costs model.

This eclectic model, known as the OLI (Ownership, Internalization, Location) model, adds the location factor to the two previous models. This factor may be decisive in accounting for the internalization characteristic of certain companies, such as oil companies, car makers, or consumer products manufacturers.

To what extent do these models account for the internalization of services companies? More specifically, can we account for the growth of multinational service companies and, in particular, financial services companies, with these arguments? There is no doubt that the transaction costs argument or the existence of competitive advantages that are difficult to imitate are valid reasons in industrial and services companies. However, qualifications are necessary.

Using as our basis the experience of a number of services industries (financial services, distribution, telecommunications, business services, and airlines), we will introduce the basic elements that may account for the growth and development of multinational services companies.

The first group of arguments, which we will call company-specific factors, accounts for the internationalization of services companies in terms of specific advantages developed by these organizations that are difficult to imitate and, therefore, suffer imperfections when they are exchanged on the market. Within this category, we can include factors such as the existence of economies of scale and scope, professional reputation, brand image, or experience in offering the same service to very different groups of customers.

The second group of reasons is related to demand and customers for certain services. These are services in which one country's demand can only be satisfied by going to another country, as the service is not exportable and the end customer is unlikely to move, since there exists an abundant and competitive supply in the country in question. An example is companies that offer financial services or advertising companies.

The third type of argument is related to the deregulation of many services markets as a result of the General Agreement on Tariffs and Trade (GATT) agreements or the formation of large trading blocs. The obstacles that formerly hampered a company from establishing itself in a foreign country are disappearing. The reasons for expanding abroad are varied and include both those which we have previously called demand or customer-related factors (as would be the case of financial services) and company-related factors (as would be the case of telecommunications).

2.2. Differences between foreign direct investment in services and in industry

In the previous section, we discussed the nature of the multinational company in the services industry, outlining a number of important differences between it and the industrial multinational company. In this section, we will try to define these differences with even greater precision, referring particularly to the process of foreign direct investment in services.

In the industrial sector, direct investment abroad is justified by reasons such as access to production resources or cheaper production costs, proximity to certain markets, risk diversification in assets in different currencies, or the specialization of a company's output with operations in different countries (Dunning, 1981).

In a service company, access to a particular market continues to be a valid reason. However, the other reasons become less applicable, because of the specific nature of the services company. Thus, the diversification of assets in different currencies loses force as an argument, as services companies, generally speaking, do not imply large physical investments and, when this is the case —as in financial services—this factor is usually not decisive. A similar statement could be made about access to cheaper production costs or the attempt to specialize production by countries in accordance with their competitive advantages.

Study of a number of service companies in different sectors reveals that direct investment abroad is due to reasons other than access to a particular foreign market. Among other reasons, we would mention the following. First, there is the need to acquire and exploit globally a global knowledge. This is a very important reason for the leading consulting firms or investment banks, which transfer the best products or the best business practices from one country to another.

The second reason is that some service companies have managed to develop a significant amount of know-how in the provision of certain services—particularly, professional and business services—and a significant international reputation that lowers the cost, for them, of entering certain foreign markets.

A third reason, which is in part a direct result of the previous two, is the existence of certain advantages deriving from belonging to the same group (network), with the access this provides to a truly global professional experience. Furthermore, the existence of such a group implies a relationship with global customers in several countries whose demand cannot be satisfied by simply exporting the service from another country or temporarily moving the company to another country.

To summarize, direct investment abroad in the services industry shares some of the features of investment by industrial companies, although it also has certain unique features that account for the spectacular growth of this type of investment in recent years.

2.3. A model of international competitiveness in services

In a previous study (Canals, 1995a), we have presented a model to account for international competitiveness which includes three categories of factors.

1. Country factors, mainly, the population's educational level and the quality of the infrastructures.
2. Factors that are specific to the industry that the company operates in, such as the degree of rivalry in the industry, the degree of government regulation, and the structure and evolution of the demand.
3. Factors that are specific to the company: these factors consist of possible

differential capabilities that the company has been able to develop over time such as production and distribution efficiencies, the existence of economies of scale, advantages in R&D, or marketing experience.

This model is perfectly applicable to the case of competitiveness in services, with a few qualifications. As regards country factors, the critical factor is the population's educational level. Companies imply relationships between people. This aspect is even more important in services, where part of the quality perceived by the customer depends on the nature of this relationship between people. Aspects such as labour cost or the availability of natural resources are usually less important. One obvious exception is tourism, where the availability of cultural resources or certain geographical or climatic conditions are critical for attracting certain types of tourism.

Industry-specific factors are very important here. The nature and growth of the demand, the degree of rivalry between companies, or the existence of a certain level of government regulation are all decisive factors in accounting for a company's competitive position on the international markets.

Finally, company-specific factors—their differential capabilities—are also critical in all sectors. The world-wide experience of McKinsey or Boston Consulting Group in consulting, that of Goldman Sachs or Salomon Brothers in investment banking, or that of Arthur Andersen or Price Waterhouse in auditing and legal services are decisive factors in accounting for their position as leaders of their respective sectors.

Within this third group of factors, we could include competitive advantages such as consistency in the quality of the service (McDonald's), the company's reputation (J. Walter Thomson), the existence of economies of scale (AT&T), and brand image (American Express).

In short, international competitiveness in the services industry can also be accounted for by this triple group of factors—country, industry, and company—although their specific contents and interaction may be slightly different in the services companies.

3. THE INTERNATIONAL EXPANSION OF BANKING: THE US BANKS

For the large American banks—mainly the New York money centre banks (Citibank, Chase Manhattan, Chemical Banking, and, perhaps, the Bank of America on the west coast of the United States)—expansion abroad started in the 1960s and early 1970s, mainly in Western Europe. A few years later, in the second half of the 1970s, the rapid economic growth in Latin America exerted a strong pull on these banks, which invested in those countries, mainly acting as agents, leaders, or underwriters for long-term government or company-issued debt.

During the Latin American foreign debt crisis of the 1980s, prudence and lack of resources slowed down the American banks' expansion abroad. However, the single financial market in Europe, the emergence of very important regional financial centres in South-East Asia and Japan, and the economic recovery of Latin American countries such as Chile or Argentina have given new impetus to the international operations of North American banks since the end of the 1980s.

The cause of the first international expansion of US banks in the 1960s is highly illustrative of the internationalization process followed by banking, which differs from the processes followed not only by other industrial companies but also by the services companies.

Thus, one of the obvious reasons for American banks was the impossibility of extending their activities in the United States outside their home state. Therefore, their growth possibilities were limited. Expansion abroad was the only possible means of growth and was used by some of the large banks.

Let us take the case of Citibank. Citibank's first international operations were based on the Eurodollar market in London. Citibank started to operate on this market by lending and borrowing for its own account or for third parties. The operations carried out on this market led to a number of branches being opened in London. In the 1960s, London was the financial centre with the most liberal regulation in Europe for direct investment.

The bank then evolved naturally from operations on currency markets to operations with large companies which included major financing projects. Thus, a currency market department came into being, together with a corporate finance department.

The supposed synergies between these operations and those that are more typical of commercial banking—taking deposits from customers and lending to small and medium-sized companies and private individuals—are not always clear, but an emerging market such as that of the EC in the 1970s was an opportunity that the bank could not afford to let go by.

In those years, financial regulation of direct investment by foreign banks in most European countries was still highly restrictive. There were countries where this was not permitted. Spain, for example, partially lifted the restriction on the establishment of foreign banks in 1977, when it allowed foreign banks to operate with up to three branches in Spanish territory.

The experience of Citibank and Bank of America or other American banks is clear: operations on currency or capital markets could be profitable. In fact, American banks provided a degree of experience and sophistication that could not be matched by their European counterparts. This situation was due to the lower level of rivalry in Europe and a certain financial conservatism—caused partly by an insufficient development of the capital market and partly by overregulation.

Financial consultancy and co-ordination of securities issues on European markets were also profitable operations for a long time. American banks had an important advantage in this too: their extensive experience of the American market and the greater ease with which they could obtain the necessary capital on the different markets.

Quite different in nature were commercial banking operations. In this sector, the difficulties were—and still are—enormous. To begin with, American banks could not have very many branches in Europe—a necessary prerequisite for commercial banking—because of the restrictive national regulations. In addition, in those countries with more liberal regulations, American banks found that customers were usually fairly loyal to the national banks they had always worked with.

In order to attract these customers, they had to offer them certain savings products which were more appealing. This was their initial experience. In fact, innovations such as the generalized use of credit or debit cards, current accounts bearing market interest rates, or combined products consisting of a current account with a consumer credit line were introduced on the European market by American banks. However, these products offered ephemeral advantages that the national banks were fairly quick to imitate.

The extensive network of branches of national banks meant that a foreign bank's chances of achieving a certain size in commercial banking were minimal. On the other hand, American banks had to rely on the interbank market to obtain resources if they wished to enter the corporate finance business. The interest rate volatility prevailing in several European countries such as Spain or Italy led some of the banks engaging in such operations to come out with severely burnt fingers.

Therefore, American banks' commercial banking operations tended to fade away with a certain amount of ease. However, it must be acknowledged that their presence increased competition in this segment of the bank market and also led to the introduction of major financial innovations and, therefore, contributed to the modernization of the European banking system.

For this reason, American banks in Europe have tended to limit their presence to capital market operations and financial consultancy, as the commercial banking business has a different competitive dynamic that requires enormous resources. Firms such as Bank of America or Chemical recognized this fact and decided to operate in Europe as investment banks, designing financing operations, and, when it seems advisable to them, taking part in the operations as lenders.

Citibank, on the other hand, has adopted a different model, consisting of exploiting whatever opportunities it finds, whether these be in investment banking, capital markets, or commercial banking. Hence Citibank's strong presence in commercial banking in countries such as Spain or Germany.

In fact, this is a model that Citibank also successfully implemented in some Latin American countries. The reason for these positive results in Latin America may be the lack of a fierce and fast-reacting competition—unlike the situation in Europe, where financial organizations are more sophisticated, almost to the same degree in some respects as American banks. However, Citibank's global ambitions have no precedent or clear imitators in other American banks.

To summarize, the international experience of American banking enables the following conclusions to be drawn. First, the impetus for American banks' international expansion was the impossibility of further growth within the United States, due to the regulatory apparatus that prevented banks from carrying out financial activities outside their home state.

Second, the commencement of the globalization of capital and currency markets in the mid-1960s opened up opportunities for the banks that were prepared to operate on these markets. These banks had to meet a number of conditions: large size, a well-known brand name, and a certain amount of experience in complex financial operations. The large American banks met these conditions. Thus, the first lever of international expansion was the desire to sidestep the limits imposed by rigid bank regulation in the United States; the second lever were the assets—financial resources—and the managerial and financial innovation skills that they could transfer to other markets and other banks—such as the European banks—that did not have them at the same level. This explanation concurs with some of the classic arguments used to account for the company growth theory (Penrose, 1959).

The third lever of expansion was the ability to offer a service to American companies established in Europe. In the 1960s, there was an explosion of direct investment by American multinational companies in Europe, such as Ford, General Motors, IBM, and General Electric. American banks were their natural providers of financial services and, therefore, if they did not want to lose these companies' financial operations in Europe, they had to be here with them. Consequently, the attempt to follow their customers was also an important factor in this expansion process.

Once American banks were in Europe they decided to broaden their spectrum of activities, entering commercial banking operations and also trying to attract local customers. The diversification of activities into commercial banking has proved to be fraught with problems, as a result of the strong competition existing in Europe. However, the expansion of the same investment banking activities to domestic customers has met with more success.

This is an interesting business case: the search for new customers to whom to offer the same service, or a service similar to what is already being offered, can sometimes be more interesting than penetrating other markets where one does not know how customers and competitors will react, or markets having a different competitive dynamic.

Figure 9.2 presents the reasons for the international expansion of American banks diagrammatically.

It should not be forgotten that part of the expansion of foreign banking in Europe in the late 1980s and early 1990s has been due to the significant liberalization, deregulation, and opening of the EU member countries' financial markets. Without this, the international expansion of American banking in Europe would not have reached the size it has today.

The almost complete freedom of capital movements that now exists in Europe creates the necessary conditions that favour the expansion of currency and

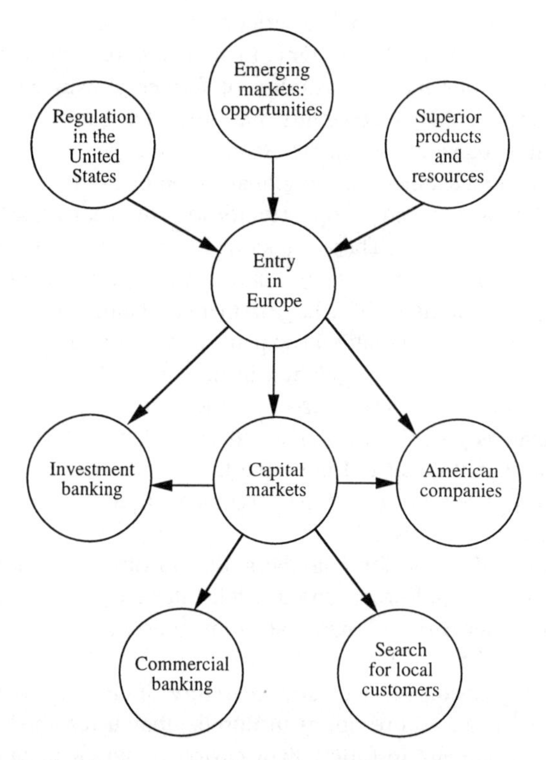

FIG. 9.2 *Reasons for the international expansion of American banks*

capital market operations. Therefore, the liberalization of a country's activities generally tends to attract investment in the financial sector, as is graphically illustrated by the cases of Spain, Great Britain, and France.

By means of a process of trial and error, American banks have had an international experience that stresses the importance of looking for market segments which meet at least one of the following two conditions:

(a) those that have products, services, or internal skills particularly suited to these markets;
(b) target market segments where rivalry is less intense and can be adequately modulated, as a result of the bank's ability to develop products superior to those of local competitors.

4. THE INTERNATIONALIZATION OF BANKING: THE JAPANESE BANKS IN EUROPE

The international importance of the Japanese banks in the first half of the 1990s is one of the outstanding developments of the international financial system. In

TABLE 9.5 *Japanese banks in the United States and the United Kingdom* (US$ bn.)

	United States			United Kingdom	
	Assets	Financial investments and loans	Deposits	Assets	% of IDE, Japanese banks
1980	60.8	1.4	10.1	97.6	46.8
1984	130.8	6.4	9.0	194.1	46.1
1988	306.7	23.2	27.6	444.6	39.7

Source: *Federal Reserve Bulletin* (1990).

1994, out of the world's ten largest banks in assets terms, eight were Japanese. In 1992, the world's four largest fixed-income issuers were four Japanese banks (Nikko, Nomura, Daiwa, and Yamaichi).

The financial clout of Japanese banks and the international expansion of their activities have contributed, among other factors, to increasing the importance of the yen as a commonly traded currency on the international markets. Table 9.5 shows the growth of the Japanese banks' activities in the United States and Britain.

The internationalization of Japanese banking activity has followed a slightly different path from that followed by American banks. The first cause of this internationalization process was neither the impossibility of domestic growth—this was limited but not less than the possibilities in the United States—nor the possession of superior financial products or skills.

The reason was simply to be able to offer a service to the Japanese companies that were starting to invest in Europe in the 1970s (Table 9.6). Not only did they wish to keep them as customers but they also wanted to develop long-term business with them, as many of them belonged to the same business group as the corresponding bank. Therefore, it was logical that they accompany the industrial company abroad. This explanation concurs both with what happened with American banks in Europe and with what happens, in general, in many sectors of the economy.

During the late 1960s and early 1970s, Japanese banks found two special qualities in the London market. First, a financial market with a highly liberal system, where they could operate to finance Japanese companies in Europe. This factor is crucial in explaining the success that Britain has traditionally had in attracting investments by Japanese companies.

The second reason is that the Japanese banks found in the Eurodollar market an opportunity to finance investments by Japanese companies, both inside and outside Japan. Therefore, access to abundant financial resources at a

TABLE 9.6 *Japanese industrial companies in Europe* (1989)

	No.	Industry
United Kingdom	132	Electronics; transportation equipment, automobiles
France	95	Electronics; food
Germany	89	Electronics; electrical equipment
Spain	55	Transport, automobiles; chemicals
Netherlands	34	Chemicals
Italy	28	Chemicals, electronics
Belgium	25	Chemicals
Eire	22	Electronics
Portugal	13	Textiles
Denmark	3	Chemicals, electronics
Greece	3	Steel
Luxembourg	2	Electronics, machinery
TOTAL	501	

Source: JETRO Survey.

reasonable cost provides another explanation for the entry of Japanese banks into Europe.

Some years later, Japan became a net capital exporter, as a result of high current account surpluses. Thus, these banks' presence in Europe ceased to have the rationale it originally had. However, this initial presence was useful to the Japanese banks in two respects. First, they had the opportunity to learn and acquire the necessary skills to be financial innovators in one of the most sophisticated financial markets of the world, London.

Second, this presence in London served to channel debt or capital on the Tokyo Stock Exchange in the 1980s by European and American companies. Therefore, the networks between banks and customers, created years before in Europe, subsequently gave rise to another type of operation that was perhaps more interesting for the Japanese banks. (See Figure 9.3 for a diagrammatic presentation of the reasons for the international expansion of Japanese banks.)

In fact, the current account surpluses generated during the 1980s made Japan the world's largest lender and catapulted Japanese banks to a pre-eminent position in international finance. Thus, in the 1980s, Japanese banks themselves started to finance projects by European companies, advise on financial operations, channel savings towards the stock markets, and manage security placements on the capital markets.

However, the Japanese banks' experience has not been the same in all countries. Perhaps it can be said that Britain is the country where the presence of the Japanese banks has been strongest. In other countries such as Germany or France, they have suffered a mild failure, in part due to these countries' less cosmopolitan financial practices or lesser degree of financial sophistication than in London.

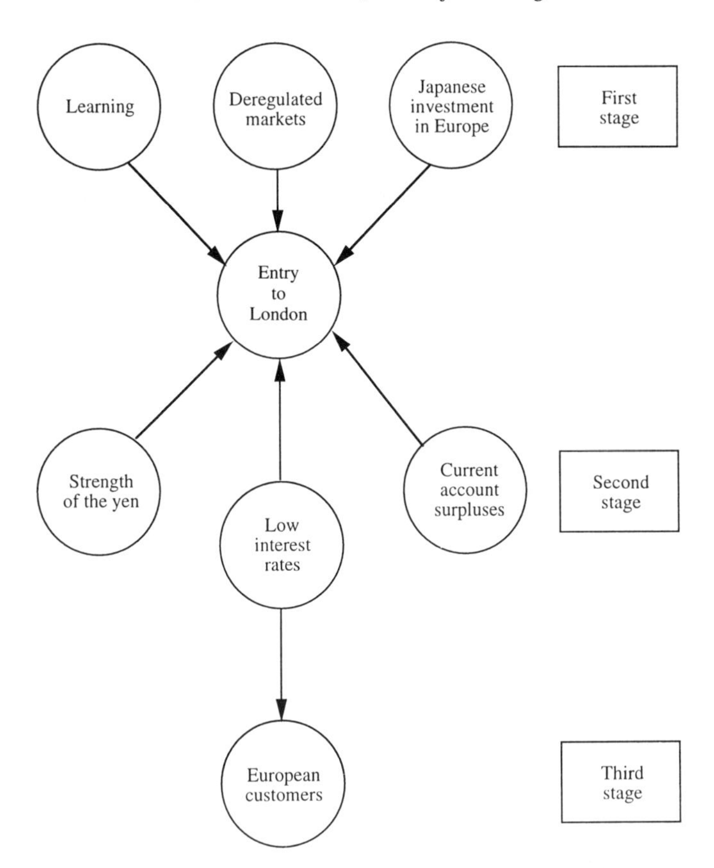

FIG. 9.3 *Reasons for the international expansion of Japanese banks*

We can also say that Japanese banks have been particularly successful in debt placement operations on the financial markets and in looking for resources for syndicated loans. However, their performance as financial consultants and their commercial banking activity have been minimal. When some banks have tried to operate in these segments of financial business, the results have been very mediocre.

Again, Japanese banks have found the same difficulties in the commercial banking sector as American banks found in Europe: the lack of a strong local presence and the intense rivalry offered by the local banks. However, this difficulty has been compounded, in the case of Japanese banks, by a corporate weakness: the lesser degree of sophistication of their financial innovation, compared with their American counterparts, which were at a clear advantage in this respect. Therefore, although it can be said that American banking has been a clear stimulus for the modernization of the financial markets and the banking industry in Europe, the same cannot be said of the Japanese banks, which have confined themselves to offering the same services as other banks, perhaps backed by the voluminous financial resources associated with Japan's strong current account surplus.

This consideration naturally leads us to ask what the Japanese banks' competitive advantages in Europe are. We certainly cannot say that Japanese banks' primary competitive advantage compared with European or American banks has been their ability to innovate in financial services or the superior skills of their financial analysts.

Japanese banks' main competitive advantage was—and still is—their access to abundant financial resources in Japan, deriving from the current account surplus and the low capital cost of the financial operations instrumented in Japan (Hawawini and Schill, 1994).

Although the question of capital cost in Japan has been the source of considerable controversy (Baldwin, 1986; Kester and Luehrman, 1992), depending on the indicators used to measure it, the short and long-term, nominal and real interest rates have, historically, been lower than the interest rates in the United States and Japan, as can be seen in Table 9.7.

The reason for these lower interest rates is to be found in three basic factors, all of them related to the accounting equality between the total savings available in a country and its total investment. First is an exceptionally high private savings rate (about 25 per cent of the families' available income in the 1980s). Second is a macroeconomic stability that has allowed very low inflation rates in Japan since the 1960s. Third, there is Japan's lower public deficit—as a ratio of the GDP—than most industrialized countries. These circumstances, as a whole, have favoured low real interest rates and, therefore, have made it very attractive for both Japanese and non-Japanese companies to place fixed- and variable-income issues in Japan.

The growing importance of the yen on the international financial markets is a further confirmation of this trend, particularly in the second half of the 1980s, when the appreciation of the yen against the dollar led to a flood of Japanese investment in the United States and Britain.

Finally, the experience of Japanese banks also reveals an important detail. The degree of internationalization of financial activity is related—more or less directly—to the volume of financial resources handled or traded, particularly on the syndicated loans market. In turn, this activity depends on the size of the bank's net worth.

Indeed, Japanese banks' strong penetration of Europe occurred in the second half of the 1980s, coinciding with a spectacular rise in the Nikkei, the Tokyo Stock Exchange's index, from 13,000 in 1985 to about 38,900 in 1989. This spectacular increase in stock prices was manna from heaven for the Japanese banks, for two reasons.

The first is that the proportion of Japanese banks' assets invested in the stock market is higher than that of German or English banks. In 1990, it was estimated that 11 per cent of the large Japanese banks' assets was invested in shares.

TABLE 9.7 *Long-term interest rates (%)*

	1981	1982	1983	1984	1985	1986	1987	1988	1989	1990	1991	1992	1993
United States	13.9	13.0	11.1	12.4	10.6	7.7	8.4	8.8	8.5	8.6	7.9	7.0	5.9
Japan	8.4	8.3	7.8	7.3	6.5	5.1	5.0	4.8	5.2	7.0	6.4	5.3	4.4
Germany	10.1	8.9	8.1	8.0	7.0	6.2	6.2	6.5	7.0	8.8	8.5	7.9	6.5
France	16.3	16.0	14.4	13.4	11.9	9.1	10.2	9.2	9.2	10.4	9.5	9.0	7.0
Italy	19.4	20.2	18.3	15.6	13.7	11.5	10.6	10.9	12.8	13.5	13.1	13.7	11.3
United Kingdom	14.9	13.1	11.3	11.3	11.1	10.1	9.6	9.7	10.2	11.8	10.1	9.1	7.6

Source: IMF.

Logically, during periods of strong growth of share prices, the opportunities for capital gains are enormous.

The second reason is the accounting rules followed by Japanese banks that enable an unrealized capital gain in shares to be posted as a profit and, therefore, be computed as generated resources which can be transferred to reserves and increase the bank's net worth. Although Japanese banks were not particularly active in stock trading in the second half of the 1980s, this accounting rule enabled them to boost their capital base considerably. Obviously, during that period, as a result of this increase in net worth, the large Japanese banks shot to the top of the world ranking by volume of resources.

The problems came later, on two fronts. First was the downward spiral of the Nikkei index in Japan since 1991, due to a more restrictive monetary policy which, coupled with a restrictive fiscal policy, has pushed up interest rates, triggering an economic recession and a drop in stock market investment. The Japanese recession has been all the more severe for those exporting companies which have seen how, since 1990, first the United States and then Europe also went into recession, thus diminishing the possibilities of exporting to those countries.

Therefore, in the same way that the unrealized capital gains increased the banks' net worth, the capital losses of the last three years have caused a contraction of net worth and, therefore, a reduction in the Japanese banks' lending activity, since they have had to withdraw from the international markets and concentrate on the domestic market, with rare exceptions.

The second problem is the banks' capital ratio approved by the Bank for International Settlements in Basle, in 1988, consisting, for each one, of 8 per cent of the bank's total assets, in accordance with a weighting by asset tiers. The Bank of Japan agreed to this regulation, together with the central banks of the EU countries and the United States.

This rule raised two problems for Japanese banks. First, their ratio was about 3 per cent in 1988, which was far below the figure required. The second problem was that the regulation did not allow the reserves obtained from unrealized capital gains to be considered as net worth. As a special measure, the Bank of Japan authorized up to 45 per cent of unrealized capital gains, but with the clear intention of progressively reducing this percentage to zero.

Faced with these challenges, Japanese banks have had to accept the harsh reality that they have only two options to bring themselves into line with this rule: increase capital or reduce the volume of assets. The first option has not been possible in recent years, due to the situation of the Japanese stock market. The second option could be applied to shares or loans. Selling shares in a bearish market would expose them to sure capital losses. Therefore, Japanese banks have cut back on their lending activities in Japan and on the international markets.

This decision has had two consequences. First, a credit crunch in Japan that has pushed up interest rates and exacerbated the recession. Second, a cutback in lending activity on the international markets, which is currently confined to leading or simply taking part in debenture and bond placements.

5. A MODEL OF BANK INTERNATIONALIZATION

5.1. Introduction

Having given, in the previous sections, some general aspects of internationalization as a strategic decision made by financial firms in a global economy, in this section we will present a conceptual explanation of the possible reasons for the internationalization of the banking industry, placing particular emphasis on the commercial banking business, although with some references to investment banking.

A recent study (Canals, 1993), based on the historical monitoring of the course of some European bank groups' international activity, describes two main types of force that account for the internationalization process. The first has to do with the forces of the economic environment in which the banking activity takes place and, in particular, with the globalization of financial markets and financial deregulation in the EU countries. The second type of force is related to intrinsic reasons within banks, some of them directly associated with the opportunities created by the globalization of financial markets.

In Chapter 1, we discussed the main mutations that have taken place in the EU countries' financial systems in recent years, at least as regards the deregulation and globalization of financial activities. Consequently, we will not repeat here our discussion of these forces. Obviously, both trends reinforce international banking activity. In this chapter, we discuss the internal reasons used by the banks that have undertaken or intensified their international activity.

5.2. The classic reasons for the internationalization of commercial banking

Some studies on the internationalization of banking activity have discussed the importance of certain forces inducing internationalization in the industry (see Figures 9.2 and 9.3). The first is closeness to customers and going where they go (Walter, 1988). According to this explanation, the banks internationalize operations in order to be able to offer their customers in a particular country a series of services of similar quality in other countries where they might also have operations.

Basically, the banking business is one in which closeness to the customer and the building of a stable relationship are critically important. The international expansion of Japanese banks to Europe and the United States, and of European banks within Europe and to the United States clearly seems to have occurred in response to these needs.

A second reason consists of considering internationalization as a reaction to other banks that decide to expand their international operations. This reaction—typical of industries where the number of competitors is small and where a certain oligopolistic tendency is observed—could perhaps be applicable to the bank industry. The case of the Spanish, French, and Italian banks in recent years could come into this category.

The third reason consists of increasing the business base by looking for new customers in foreign markets (Murray, 1984). Normally, this reason is applicable when the banks have a clear technical superiority over local banks, or when there is not too much rivalry in the local markets, for example as a result of strong regulatory control by the monetary authorities. This is an argument that fits with the entry of the North American banks to Latin America or the entry of the British or North American banks to Spain when the deregulation process started in 1977.

In this sense, foreign investment in the banking industry is usually a clear source of increased rivalry in the industry. This is because financial products and services can be quickly imitated by competitors with a minimum of skills and resources. Foreign banks become the motors of change in the industry and the introducers of financial innovations which, otherwise, would take much longer to arrive.

Capital cost is another factor that accounts for the banks' internationalization process (Aliber, 1984). Market globalization offers opportunities for arbitration and for gaining access to financial resources at the lowest possible cost in any market in the world and at any time. At the same time, new information technologies enable these resources to be invested in those countries where the return on the investment is highest. Obviously, an international bank has a greater capacity to react quickly and efficiently than a local bank.

The case of the Japanese banks is illustrative, as we have been able to show. During the 1980s, these banks had a lower capital cost than the banks of other countries and made use of this circumstance to accelerate their international expansion to European countries and the United States where the return on the financial resources invested was higher.

Finally, one more reason suggested for the internationalization of banking activities is the diversification of financial risk (Lessard, 1986). Investments in resources in different currencies and different geographical areas may be an effective means for preventing any significant fall in interest income at certain points of the business cycle. In short, a bank with a high level of internationalization can acquire a more diversified investment portfolio than a local bank.

In this section, we have presented a series of arguments that have been used in the past to account for the internationalization of banks. In the following section, we will offer a conceptual model that seeks to be more integrative.

5.3. An integrative model of commercial banks' international activity

The conceptual model we will present in the following pages is based on three hypotheses which we will describe below. The first hypothesis is that scale, customer service, and resource transfer are the main inducers of international banking activity.

The importance of scale

Banks' scale is one of the first factors that is noticeable when the international expansion of certain banks is analysed. The reason for this expansion is that the banks expect that with a larger size come certain economies of scale and scope that will enable a certain overhead structure to be absorbed or more revenues to be generated (Tschoegel, 1987). The main procedure used by banks to achieve this goal is to purchase other banks abroad.

The strategies followed by some European banks such as Deutsche Bank, Natwest, Barclays, or Crédit Lyonnais are good examples of this. They suggest that the achievement of economies of scale is a goal considered important by certain banks as a means enabling them to be competitive on the world market in subsequent years.

Deutsche Bank also illustrates the advantages that a European bank expects to obtain from a larger size: access to emerging national markets; presence in international markets; and the possibility of offering a global service to companies with a European rather than a national focus.

The ultimate roots of the possible economies of scale or scope in banking are not very clear and, as we discussed in Chapter 4, insufficient to justify the existence of significant cost savings. As we have seen, economies of scale are achieved with fairly low deposit volumes and consequently the argument of greater size is not conclusive.

On the other hand, it is clear that for a bank like Deutsche Bank, offering a service to European companies present on many markets and having access to international capital markets positions it in a more favourable situation than is possible for a national bank. It seems clear that an international bank is able to exploit fully the investment and financing opportunities that these markets offer.

In the previous section, we pointed out that an important reason for international activity is risk diversification and obtaining a suitably balanced investment portfolio. Obviously, this risk diversification provides not only more stable revenues but also lower costs in terms of losses due to changes in the price of financial assets and bad debts. In this sense internationalization, rather than size, ensures a better balance in the investment portfolio.

Another argument in favour of the importance of size is investment in modern information technologies. No one questions that any important bank must be in permanent contact with daily events on the international financial markets. This contact demands large investments in information technologies which could be amortised quickly if, in addition, the bank operates actively on the international financial markets, instead of confining itself to observing the course of events.

Note that in this argument, and in some of the previous arguments, we are referring to commercial banks that act on the international financial markets not only as financial intermediaries between savings and investment but also as agents that lend and borrow resources depending on the opportunities and prices available on the markets.

A final argument related to the importance of size is preventing the bank from becoming a target for a hostile take-over bid by another foreign bank. In this sense, the bigger the bank is, the more difficulties will be placed in the way of another bank trying to acquire a sizeable share of the target bank's equity against its will.

The experience of international expansion driven by the desire to achieve a larger size seems to be clear, but it is equally obvious that the international banks that have enlarged their international operations have paid a high price. Sometimes, this has consisted of ignorance of the national market and, at times, of losses on operations abroad. At other times, the basic problem has been the organizational complexity that an international bank—or an international organization in general—requires. Therefore, achieving a certain size seems to be a clear objective, although the costs associated with a positive action in this sense are also obvious. Finally, some banks—such as Crédit Lyonnais—have paid very high prices to buy a foreign bank. It is an investment that is not easily or quickly recouped.

Customer service

A second series of observations highlight the role of customer service as a reason for internationalization. In turn, this reason is closely linked with the imitation of the actions of rival banks, to prevent the customers of the first bank going to another bank for their international operations.

Here we can distinguish between two categories of situations. In the first, the strategy is that followed by banks such as Commerzbank, San Paolo, or Société Générale, which consists of offering services to their customers abroad with the same level of attention and quality as at home, particularly to multinational companies having the same home country as the bank.

The second situation refers to the entry of American and British banks to national markets with a lower degree of financial innovation, such as Spain, Portugal, or Italy, to offer products and services that the national banks do not offer. Some innovations such as cash management, money market operations, or variable-rate loans were introduced in some of these countries by foreign banks seeking to obtain a minimum market share in those countries. These innovations were immediately imitated by national banks which—with varying degrees of success—started to market these products.

Resource transfer

The third driver is the key role played by the transfer of resources or skills from the headquarters or a particular operating unit in one country to other countries. These resources may be physical resources (financial resources, technology, etc.) or intangible resources (such as the bank's image or management skills or techniques for successfully running a financial organization).

This is a factor that is behind the growth process of any company (Penrose, 1959) and, in particular, the growth of the multinational company (Caves, 1982). Therefore, it is not surprising that it is also applicable to banks.

Deutsche Bank's purchases in Great Britain (Morgan Grenfell), Spain (Banco de Madrid), or Italy (Bank of America's subsidiary) are clear examples that the German bank is not only pursuing access to these local markets, which it could perhaps obtain by other means, but intending to transfer to the subsidiaries in those countries the experience in bank management and financial innovation acquired in Germany and other countries.

The transfer of resources from one country to another raises an issue that has become increasingly important in recent years in the bank industry and other industries: the formation of alliances between banks in different countries.

Among other objectives, alliances between companies generally seek to share the resources contributed by each company to the alliance which other companies in the project might find difficult to obtain by other means. In the European bank industry, the alliances recorded in recent years have been alliances aimed at contributing financial product distribution capacity, financial innovation capacity, customer service capacity for a bank's customers when they operate in the other bank's territory, or financial resources to ensure control of the bank's capital. This latter reason seems to be the case in Spain.

The internationalization of the Spanish banking industry has been both active and passive. When we talk of passive internationalization, we are referring to two phenomena. First, there is the growing presence of foreign banks in Spain that compete in the different market segments with Spanish banks. Second, there is the significant presence of foreign banks as shareholders of Spanish banks (see Table 9.8).

Thus, at the end of 1993, more than 50 per cent of Banco Popular's equity capital was in foreign hands. Some of the more important shareholders were Allianz (3.3 per cent), Hypobank (1.66 per cent), and Rabobank (1.25 per cent).

Forty per cent of Banco Santander's capital in 1993 was held by foreign shareholders. Some of the largest were Royal Bank of Scotland (1.5 per cent), Nomura Securities (1.0 per cent), and Metropolitan Life (0.5 per cent). Banco Santander held 10 per cent of Royal Bank of Scotland and 22 per cent of First Fidelity.

At the end of 1994, BCH was the Spanish bank with the greatest presence of foreigners among its shareholders: Generali held 5.8 per cent, Commerzbank held 4.7 per cent, Banco Comercial Portugués held 3.1 per cent, Bouygues held 3.1 per cent, Elf Aquitaine held 2.1 per cent, UAP held 1.8 per cent, Bailliers held 1.4 per cent, and Fidis held 0.5 per cent, to mention only the largest shareholders. In total, these foreign shareholders held 28 per cent of the bank's equity at the end of 1994.

By the end of 1993, foreign shareholders held almost 24 per cent of BBV's

TABLE 9.8 *Spanish banks: foreign shareholders* (% of equity)

	1990	1991	1992	1993	1994
Popular	40.13	45.91	49.27	52.07	49.1
Santander	13.95	18.52	27.79	40.82	43.8
BCH	27.1	27.1	26.2	28.1	39.7
BBV	12.9	16.2	18.4	23.98	24.7

Source: *Expansión*.

equity, including Nippon Life, with a 2 per cent interest, General Electric Capital, with a 1.8 per cent interest, and Sumitomo Life, with a 0.5 per cent interest.

There is also a significant presence of foreign shareholders in Argentaria, particularly after its privatization. By the end of 1994, it was estimated that 24 per cent of its equity was in the hands of foreign investors, who had purchased their holdings mainly through investment banks such as Goldman Sachs or Salomon Brothers.

However, in the medium term, alliances between banks do not make much sense, unless the ultimate goal is merely to have a shareholding in another bank. The reason is that the advantages provided by alliances—share resources—are not very clear when the partners are banks. Rather, alliances can create serious competitive problems that arouse the partners' distrust and block any further progress. Perhaps this is the ultimate reason why so many cross-holdings never go beyond a mere financial investment.

One final point about these reasons for bank internationalization is that this scheme shows a certain degree of parallelism with the processes observed in other sectors of the economy. In particular, Bartlett and Ghoshal (1989) have tried to account for the internationalization processes of companies in the telecommunications, consumer electronics, and consumer goods industries using three key concepts: operational efficiency, responsiveness to customer needs, and global learning (see Table 9.9).

The relationship with the framework we have presented here is as follows (see Table 9.10). Operating efficiency is directly related to the scale that certain banks seem to pursue and with risk diversification and lower capital cost. Responsiveness to customer needs is similar to the attention that banks wish to offer to the domestic customer who operates internationally. Finally, the global learning that these authors posit leads one to think of the transfer of intangible resources that takes place in the bank industry between the parent bank and subsidiaries or between different operating units in different countries.

In the banking industry, as in the industries analysed by these authors, we observe that the most successful international strategies seek to combine all three of the forces mentioned. Strategies based on size usually lose sight of the importance of resource transfer. On the other hand, this transfer is difficult without a critical minimum size. Finally, a suitable size or a high capacity for

TABLE 9.9 *Some features of international organizations*

Features	Export company	Multinational company	Global company	Transnational company
Efficiency	Centralization of key tasks. Decentralization of distribution.	Decentralization and independence of national units.	Centralization. Global scale.	Interdependence and task specialization.
Adaptation	Adaptation of parent company's skills.	High sensitivity to local opportunities.	Implementation of the parent company's corporate strategies.	Differential contributions of national units to global operations.
Learning	Development of knowledge in the parent company and transfer to other countries.	Development of knowledge. Utilization of knowledge in each national unit.	Development and utilization of knowledge in the parent company.	Joint development and global utilization.

Source: Adapted from Barlett and Ghoshal (1989).

TABLE 9.10 *The main objectives of the internationalization process*

Objectives of internationalization and global company management[a]	Objectives of bank internationalization
Efficiency	Size Risk diversification Capital cost
Responsiveness	Adaptation to local financial markets
Learning	Capabilities transfer

[a] From Bartlett and Ghoshal (1989).

resource transfer will not have any impact at all if it is not accompanied by a high-quality service to the customer.

Internationalization procedures

Another hypothesis of the model presented here is as follows: in the cases of bank internationalization observed, there seems to exist a relationship between the reasons that favour internationalization and the specific means for achieving it. Thus, alliances are usually the appropriate procedure for the transfer of resources or skills, acquisitions are the ideal means for achieving a certain size, and internal development of branches is the best option for customer service.

Obviously, none of these specific decisions, associated with one of the abovementioned reasons, excludes the other two possible reasons. Thus, the acquisition of Banco de Madrid by Deutsche Bank includes both resource and skill transfer and the possibility of achieving a larger size. However, in other cases, the association between underlying reasons and specific procedures is usually much clearer.

Let us look at the different types of procedures used to drive the internationalization process that have been chosen by certain banks in recent years. First, internal growth through the creation of a network of branches was the path chosen by Citibank in Europe and, on a smaller scale, by Bank of America.

The advantages of this procedure are clear. Growth is slow, the commitment of resources is gradual, and it is easier to ensure cultural consistency between geographically separate units.

The problems that this procedure raises are also clear. First, this process is slower and consequently the risk of losing opportunities is greater. Second, the creation of branches requires an investment of important resources and, if the foreign bank intends to create a network of branches able to compete in some segment with a national bank, the investment effort is enormous. Finally, coordinating the network of branches in one country with the bank as a whole in other countries is not always a simple process. In fact, in practice, the situation may lead to confusion about the direction to take and mismatches between the parent company's needs and the bank's opportunities in a particular country.

The second procedure chosen by some banks to guarantee a greater international presence has been alliances. Table 9.11 lists some of the most important alliances that have been formed in recent years. The large number and the size of the banks involved in them gives an idea of their importance.

Among the alliances oberved, we can distinguish three main types. First are alliances aimed at improving the service to customers of the banks who operate in other countries. This has been one of the reasons for the alliance between Commerzbank and Banco Central Hispano.

The second category of alliances is aimed at sharing resources, such as the distribution capacity that a bank established in a particular country can offer to a foreign bank, or that a bank that is more innovative or is experienced in certain types of financial services can offer to another bank. This could be the case of the alliances between banks and insurance companies, such as Banco Popular and Allianz.

A third type of reason for alliances (in particular, equity alliances) consists of looking for friendly shareholders in the bank's share capital that could block or impede a possible hostile take-over bid by a third bank.

The third procedure used to drive international expansion is the merger of two banks or the acquisition of a bank in another country. In this case, the achievement of a minimum size and rapid penetration of another market are usually the two underlying criteria in the decision. The popularity of this procedure has been increasing in recent years. Table 9.11 provides some examples.

Bank take-overs, like company take-overs, generally offer a second important advantage, in addition to the advantage of speed. The bank that buys another bank knows what it is doing. The goal is clear, even though it is expensive to achieve. This is an important difference from alliances, where the existence of a balance of power and wills leads to a loss of definition in the unity of purpose.

However, in addition to these clear advantages, take-overs also raise a number of serious problems, as has been seen in the bank industry in recent years. First, the price of take-overs is usually very high. Thus, the price paid by Crédit Lyonnais for Banca Jover or by San Paolo for Banco Catalán de Crédito is surprisingly high and it is not easy to find economic or technical reasons to account for these investment decisions.

The second problem is that the purchase of a bank raises significant cultural problems. A bank is a services organization. The acquisition of services companies is associated with different types of problems from those associated with the acquisition of industrial companies: in the former, the customers are usually directly related to the services offered by a bank, for example, through certain people. In this sense, the production of services has an important human dimension—with the personal contact this implies—compared with the

TABLE 9.11 *Some alliances in the financial services industry in the European Union*

Alliance	Country	Year	Transaction
San Paolo Bank (Italy)	United Kingdom	1986	Purchase 6% of Hambros Bank
Deutsche Bank (Germany)	United Kingdom	1984	Purchase of Morgan Grenfell
San Paolo Bank (Italy)	France	1987	Purchase 1% of Compagnie Financière de Suez
Générale de Banque (Belgium)	France	1987	Purchase 1.5% of Compagnie Financière de Suez
Cariplo (Italy)	Spain	1988	Purchase 1% of Banco Santander
Commerzbank (Germany)	Spain	1984	Purchase 10% of Banco Hispano Americano
Banco de Bilbao (Spain)	United Kingdom	1987	Purchase 5% of Hambros Bank
Banco Santander (Spain)	United Kingdom	1988	Swap 5% with Royal Bank of Scotland
Bayerische Vereinsbank	Germany		Alliance with Lloyds Bank, Crédit Agricole, BBV, Banco Ambrosiano Veneto and Rabobana
Fortis (Holland)	Spain	1992	50% of Caixa de Pensions
Metropolitan Life (United Kingdom)	Spain	1987	50:50 alliance with Banco Santander
AGF (France)	Spain	1992	50:50 alliance with Banesto
Generali (Italy)	Spain	1992	Purchase 5% of Banco Central Hispano
UAP (France)	Spain	1990	Purchase 3% of Banco Central
Axa Assurances (France)	Spain		50:50 alliance with BBV
Allianz (Germany)	Spain		50:50 alliance with Banco Popular
BNP (France) and Dresdner (Germany)			Swap 10% of shares
Hongkong Bank (Hong Kong)	United Kingdom	1987	Purchase 15% of Midland Bank
Cariplo (Italy)	Spain	1988	Purchase 30% of Banco Jover and Banco Santander
Banco Santander (Spain)	Italy	1988	Purchase 30% of I.B.I. de Cariplo

production of consumer goods or machinery. Hence the greater chance for cultural shock or adaptation difficulties.

6. SOME CONCLUSIONS

In this chapter, we have analysed the globalization process of the financial system and the internationalization strategies followed by some financial organizations.

Bank internationalization occurs for certain reasons that are common to other sectors of the economy. However, there are also important differences from the international expansion of other companies. In particular, the commercial banking industry has a strong national component, both from the customers' viewpoint and from the viewpoint of the banks themselves. The development of commercial banking activity in Britain, for example, is different from its development in Spain. The internationalization process in investment banks is clearer and more intense.

Likewise, the reasons for bank internationalization in Europe are different from those that operate in the United States or Japan. In Europe, the dismantling of barriers to capital flows and the freedom to establish themselves in other countries have favoured significant direct investment flows by foreign banks.

We have presented an explanatory model that takes into account the diversity of circumstances that feature in the internationalization process. According to this model's hypotheses, bank internationalization is a strategy aimed at achieving several goals: a larger size, risk diversification, proximity to other financial markets, and the exploitation of a bank's successful resources and skills in different markets. Finally, we have pointed out that banks—particularly European banks—have made extensive use of alliances as a procedure to drive their internationalization.

10

New Organizational Patterns in Banking

1. WHY ARE NEW ORGANIZATIONAL FORMS NECESSARY IN BANKING?

The interrelationship between the various business units within a universal bank, or between banks and industrial companies within a group, which we have discussed in previous chapters, raises a number of strategic issues that require resolving: Is it in the universal banks' interest to diversify their activities both in financial and in non-financial activities? What is the financial and strategic risk of diversifying bank activities? Is it in the banks' interest to acquire equity holdings in industrial companies? Given the existence of equity holdings in industrial companies, is it in the banks' interest to play an active part in these companies' management?

However, to limit oneself to this type of question would be like discussing interminably the wisdom of following or not following a certain road, without ever deciding how to do it. Therefore, the interrelationships between different businesses within a bank group raise one crucial question: What is the best organizational design for a bank group with different businesses?

The organizational question is linked with a more general problem of universal banks, namely, the advantages that a universal bank may have in a certain business over a specialized bank. In principle, the cost advantages for certain financial services favour the specialized bank (Pierce, 1991), although some universal banks may enjoy certain economies of scope (Hellwig, 1991). The question, therefore, is: what does a particular business contribute to a universal bank and how can this contribution be maximized?

Perhaps a brief reflection on the universal banking crisis can help us understand better the nature of the organizational problem we are considering now. In our discussion, we will refer explicitly to the United States banks,[1] since it was in that country that the supposed advantages of diversified commercial banks over other financial organizations first started to be challenged a decade ago (Bryan, 1991, 1992; Pierce, 1991).

The banking crisis in the United States was heralded by a number of clear premonitory signs. At the end of 1992, the commercial banks' market share in

[1] In the United States, European-style universal banks do not exist. On the other hand, the large bank groups do not hold equity portfolios in non-financial companies, as is the case in a number of European countries.

financial intermediation was 31 per cent of total intermediated assets, compared with 45 per cent in 1970. About 25 per cent of the bank system's assets were in a situation of temporary or permanent insolvency. And the banks' operating margin had been steadily falling since 1980 (Bryan, 1992).

There are many reasons for this deterioration in the situation of the universal banks and they have been discussed in Chapter 1. Deregulation, globalization, and technological innovation dealt heavy blows to the actors in a protected system with limited rivalry.

The status quo in banking, in the United States and in Europe—with a few exceptions, such as Britain—consisted, until a few years ago, of protected national markets, heavy interventionism by the central banks in regulating interest rates and certain asset and liability operations, and (in Europe but not allowed in the United States) fierce competition for the control of new geographical or market segments through a densely knit network of branches.

As a result of this combination of factors, which limited the scope of rivalry between banks, these started to accumulate different business units within the same organization. Together with the traditional bank businesses of receiving deposits and granting loans to families and small and medium-sized companies, the banks started to operate in other emerging businesses that required slightly different skills, ranging from real estate to the stock market, the mortgage markets, or the money markets. Banks proceed to integrate different businesses.

Thus, banks started to lose focus of their businesses, that is, in defining who their customers were, what were the services they offered to these customers, and what was the relationship between the quality, price, and cost of each of these services.

Commercial banks thus started to move at an increasingly faster pace towards a new configuration as multibusiness companies, with the difficulties this entails for defining each service's cost and competitive advantage. In some of their businesses, some banks were losing money, as the consolidated figures for the United States at the end of the 1980s show.

In the setting of regulated interest rates, there was one type of customer that represented a strong source of income for banks: the large depositors and companies which used the banks to obtain financing on the capital markets. In both cases, the volume of funds and the customers' quality were reasonably clear indicators that these businesses were profitable for the banks.

However, the system first started to falter at the end of the 1970s with the advent of high-interest-bearing financial instruments for savers and the subsequent liberalization of interest rates on deposits. The market rates that these instruments offered were the main cause of the erosion of the commercial banks' high-volume customer base.

On the other hand, as a result of the growth of capital markets and the securitization phenomenon, it started to be more attractive—from some viewpoints—to borrow on the capital markets than from the banks. Not surprisingly, the banks' lending activity began to decline.

Banks thus found themselves caught in a pincer effect. On the one hand, they were losing loan customers to the capital markets. On the other hand, they were losing deposit customers to financial instruments that remunerated savings at market rates.

The US government introduced a number of measures to help the banks in their desperate plight. The most important of these was the 1982 Garn–St. Germain Depository Institutions Act. This Act accelerated deregulation of the prices of bank services, thus providing the banks with an exceptional opportunity to offer market rates to their customers. In addition, this Act allowed the commercial banks to take part in financing real estate projects, something which had been prohibited until then.

However, in neither case did this legislated deregulation have the desired effects (Bryan, 1992). On the one hand, price competition for deposits squeezed the banks' margins to an all-time low. On the other hand, the involvement in real estate projects opened the door for some banks to start treading a perilous path.

The combination of both effects led to a deterioration of the commercial banks' profitability and the deepest bank crisis in the United States since the 1930s. By way of example, total provisions for bad debts by American banks between 1948 and 1982 amounted to 28 billion dollars. Between 1982 and 1990, the provisions amounted to 75 billion dollars and, in 1991–2, to 60 billion dollars (Bryan, 1992).

In addition to the difficulties that these depressing results were creating for the unfortunate banks that were suffering them, there was another problem: the protection of deposits in banks with serious insolvency problems. To what extent should organizations such as the Deposit Guarantee Fund cover the risks incurred by a bank that actively invests in industrial companies or high-risk real estate projects?

There is no easy answer to these questions. The most advanced proposals developed in the United States—which the Bush administration even turned into a bill that was subsequently blocked by Congress—consisted of limiting the Deposit Guarantee Fund's official insurance—the FDIC—only to deposits that met certain conditions, such as maximum interest rates equivalent to the rates paid on short-term public debt instruments. In October 1995, the US Congress was considering three different proposals for liberalizing bank activities. Any one of these proposals—were they to be approved—would no doubt change the nature of the FDIC.

With these restrictions, a number of original proposals have been made to help universal banks adjust to this new situation. The proposals include the following aspects. First, banks must define their core businesses ('core banking'), which would include the traditional commercial banking activities: receiving deposits and remunerating them at market rates, and lending to small and medum-sized companies and private individuals. The deposit insurance would only cover these deposits and operations that could be included in this category of activities.

If universal banks were to be organized around this concept, it is estimated that in the United States the industry would undergo a number of dramatic changes (Bryan, 1992). Of the approximately three trillion dollars currently held in deposits, at the end of the process there would only be two trillion dollars. The remaining deposits would migrate towards higher yield, more volatile financial instruments. The industry would also become more concentrated, as the more profitable banks would take over the smaller, loss-making banks.

The money center banks would also undergo a certain amount of restructuring. These banks are so termed from the high proportion of money market operations within their range of banking activities. This group includes banks such as Citicorp and Chemical. These institutions have been engaging in increasingly sophisticated activities on the New York financial markets and in other international financial centres. In addition to being involved in these activities—basically related to corporate financing—the money center banks have also been very active in traditional commercial banking. In the future, these banks will progressively separate their commercial banking activities from the other operations on the money markets and corporate financing, in order to improve management in both areas and prevent the risks taken by the capital markets divisions from leading to a greater risk, to be borne by these banks' depositors.

The second aspect of the proposals to enable the universal banks to adjust to the new situation is this separation of activities. As a result of this separation—which is necessary in order to identify and differentiate each one's risks and improve management efficiency—some of these banks will compete even more fiercely with traditional investment banks such as Goldman Sachs or Bankers Trust, which specialize in financial consultancy, implementation of financial restructuring operations, and security issues.

Another aspect of the changes is that, if this restructuring of the banking industry actually happens, the more or less global nature of banking will no longer be so global. Indeed, only certain international financing operations, for which it is vital to have access to the international markets and economies of scale are clear, will be unequivocally global.

Instead, commercial banking will continue to be predominantly national in scope, as the national banks' network of branches raise formidable entry barriers to the penetration of foreign banks. The economies leading to globalization of commercial banking are not so apparent.

As a result of this drastic separation of activities between commercial banking and other activities within a bank group, the question arises of whether this separation will be attractive to the banks. The answer is yes, because commercial banking activities are reasonably profitable and the risk they entail is relatively small. Some regional banks in the United States and Europe report a return on capital between 18 per cent and 25 per cent and a price/earnings ratio between 10 and 15.

For their part, investment banking activities or the financing of real estate projects offer opportunities for substantially higher returns but, at the same time, their risk is much higher and they are much more sensitive to business cycles.

An additional advantage of separating activities is that it would reduce the risk borne by the depositors. Furthermore, the cost of a deposit insurance covering the risk of a bank becoming insolvent would be much lower, as the risk covered would be limited to typical commercial banking operations.

This might also have the effect of discouraging banks from including excessively risky operations in their strategies as the deposit insurance safety net would no longer cover operations that could not be strictly considered commercial banking. The TBTF ('too big to fail') rule would no longer apply and the more solvent, better managed banks would not have to bear unnecessarily the management shortcomings of less well-managed banks.

The message seems to be very clear. Separation of activities within a bank seems to be a response to two main factors. The first is reasons of efficiency in the management of each of the bank's businesses. The skills needed to operate on the capital markets are not the same as those required to operate as a good commercial bank. In turn, the skills required for proficient management of a diversified financial group are manifold and—judging from the European and American experience—in very short supply.

The second reason is related to the mechanisms for protecting investors. It seems reasonable that the cost of managing higher-risk activities should not be borne by lower-risk operations—commercial banking—or taxpayers. Consequently, the government, in co-operation with the banking system, would only guarantee with a deposit guarantee fund those activities that are carried out under the umbrella of the commercial banks.

The above considerations also have a clear message for the nature of the relationship between banks and non-financial companies. Traditionally, bank involvement in industrial companies has occasionally been a source of bank failures. Lack of experience in bank management, lack of caution in the assessment of risks, and the presence of banks in companies in highly cyclical industries have driven some banks into the red and, shortly after, into bankruptcy. On the strength of this argument, some authors have argued—and continue to argue—against the presence of banks in industry.

In previous chapters, we have shown that one cannot be so categorical. The vital issues are to determine whether these risks will be well managed and adequately to regulate the presence of banks in industrial companies. Again, it appears that commercial banking activities and the bank unit specializing in long-term finance for industrial companies should be completely separate, even to the point of being legally separate.

This separation would have the beneficial effects of improving the individual management of each of the business units and, also, reducing the commercial banks' risk. It would also bring about a greater bank involvement in the long-term financing of companies and this, as we have already discussed, could have beneficial effects on investment and economic growth.

Note that this approach is radically different from others used in the past. Indeed, with this strict separation of business units, one should measure the performance of each individual business unit and not that of the bank as a whole. This offers significant advantages as only those banks truly having the necessary capabilities to manage industrial companies will be able to justify to their shareholders and society as a whole the use of resources in this activity. It will never be possible to disguise the results with surpluses from commercial banking or other banking activities.

In a similar fashion, these business units must justify their competitive advantages in relation to other, more specialized bank organizations specifically geared to this type of activity, or in relation to the capital market itself. Basically, the idea is that each business unit within a bank group should be able to compete on an equal footing with specialized companies in each of the bank's activities, products, and customers.

Why is there so much discussion about specialization now, yet there was none before? First, we should point out that there has always been a certain degree of specialization in banking activities, with organizations such as pure commercial banks, investment banks, mortgage banks, and investment companies.

Perhaps the greatest difference we can see in the 1990s is that the financial needs of the banks' customers—private individuals and companies—have grown considerably, requiring a greater level of sophistication in the financial service they receive. On the other hand, the deregulation of financial activities and the evolution of information technologies have enabled totally new specialized organizations to spring into life.

These organizations have been started from scratch, without any need for dramatic strategic changes or traumatic restructurings. This combination of factors—increasing sophistication of customers' financial needs, deregulation, and technological innovation—has inexorably pushed the rivalry to extreme limits, with the universal banks being hard put to counter more flexible specialists that are experts in certain banking operations.

2. SOME ORGANIZATIONAL PROBLEMS IN UNIVERSAL BANKS

In Chapter 4, we said that a universal bank can be considered a nexus of contracts: those between the people who work in a bank and the different legal entities—if there is more than one—in which they carry out their professional activities; and those—whether legal or purely organizational—between the various business units of the universal bank. And, if a universal bank is structured as a holding company, these links relate each business unit to the holding company.

In this chapter, we will consider the relationships between the different business units operating under the same parent company; this parent company acts as a corporate headquarters. We will therefore leave out of our discussion the contractual relationships between the employees and the various business organizations with which the universal bank in question operates. What are the main organizational problems that are generated by these links?

Let us briefly recapitulate the problems discussed in more detail in Chapter 4. The first specific problem of universal banks is that of agency problems generated between the managers in the corporate headquarters and the managers in each of the business units. Agency problems arise when the owner or principal in an organization and the agent who must perform certain actions to implement the plans drawn up by the owner or highest officer are different people.

Obviously, agency problems are not the same as those that arise in a specialized bank with a simpler organization structure, where the agency problem is that the incentives of a universal bank's individual business unit managers may or may not be compatible with the group's overall goals. On the other hand, a universal bank's agency costs consist of the cost of designing explicit contracts between the corporate headquarters and the business units, the cost of supervising them, and the cost of ensuring fulfilment of the commitments that have been acquired.

Another problem facing universal banks is the moral hazard problem, related to the fact that the various agents involved have asymmetric information. The moral hazard problem arises when those who hold important information within the organization have interests that are different from those of the people who are responsible for making decisions with this information. Such a situation may lead to opportunistic behaviour in which the person holding the information manipulates it so that the decision made by another person benefits a particular business unit. Moral hazard problems can arise between business units and the corporate headquarters, for example, in financial operations requiring a high degree of decentralization for fast decision-making, such as that required for operations on the currency, derivatives or money markets.

Another organizational problem suffered by universal banks concerns the costs of co-ordinating the various business units. Generally speaking, co-ordination problems arise from the specialization of the various business units comprising a group. A business unit usually has partial and incomplete information about the rest of the organization and, consequently, it is vital to find formulas that enable this information to be shared and achieve efficient actions. One specific goal of this co-ordination in a universal bank is to crystallize the supposed synergies existing between the different business units in the form of lower costs or higher revenues for the group as a whole.

The management, planning, and compensation of professionals is of key importance in a universal bank, at two organizational levels. The first is that between employees in the same division. This is a common problem in any specialized bank and so we will not discuss it here.

However, there is also the problem of the coexistence of different compensation systems and different career paths followed by managers of the same rank and having the same qualifications in different units, for example, the commercial banking unit and the investment banking unit, respectively. These are two businesses with different features and requiring different skills. It is logical, therefore, that the motivation systems be different. However, these differences could generate resentment between the managers of different divisions, which might limit the possibilities for co-operation between different businesses in the same group.

There is another problem in universal banks which is typical of all complex organizations. It is that of the so-called influence costs. Influence costs belong to the more general problem of what are termed income-seeking activities, that is, those activities that are not productive and which seek to modify the distribution of revenues or costs among different groups of individuals. Within a universal bank, influence costs may be manifest in those activities or decisions which seek to transfer costs or revenues from certain business units to others within the group.

There are certain general criteria for limiting the impact of influence costs: decentralize as much as possible the decision-making process; try to limit the negative consequences of possible income redistributions, for example, by setting similar remuneration structures in all the corporate group's units; or establish, a priori, the policies affecting resource allocation within the group.

One procedure for limiting the impact of these design problems consists of having a holding company-type organization structure, in which each business becomes a unit with a high degree of autonomy but with certain performance measurement systems and reward and internal promotion mechanisms that facilitate co-operation between business units. The idea is to design systems that enable maximum benefit to be obtained from the possible synergies that may exist within a universal bank and, at the same time, limit the negative effect caused by the situations we have described above.

3. THE INTERRELATIONSHIP AND ORGANIZATION OF ACTIVITIES WITHIN A BANK GROUP

In order to gain a better understanding of a bank group's organization and specialization possibilities, it may be useful to present the sequence of activities that create value in a bank. Figure 10.1 shows a bank's value chain.

A commercial bank's activities consist of obtaining funds in the form of deposits or other financial assets and investing them in profitable assets. It is vital to separate these two activities and, in turn, break each of these activities down into specific subactivities.

The reason, as we have already hinted, is that the skills required to manage each of the products or businesses are different. Thus, although marketing activities for any financial product may have certain aspects in common, it is not the same thing to sell current accounts as it is to sell investment funds

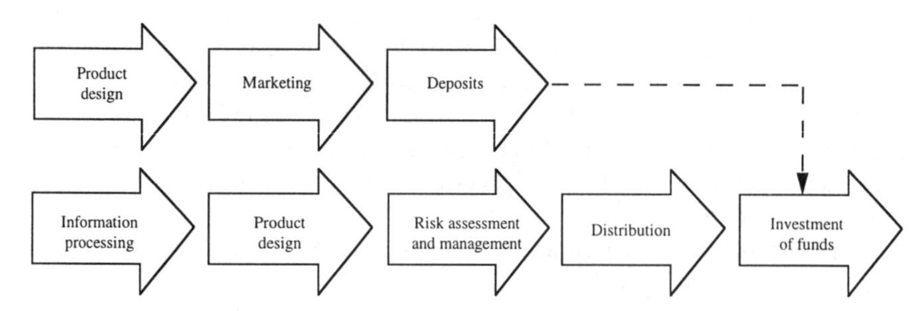

FIG. 10.1 *A bank's value chain*

or mortgages. Products are different and the skills required in each case are different.

In a universal bank, it is possible to distinguish between a large number of business units, these being understood to be that division of the organization that answers to a specific combination of product, customer, and geographical area. In some cases, the spatial dimension—geographical area—is not necessarily a defining characteristic of the business unit. Such would be the case of a global company in which geographical divisions and divisions by product lines or customers are combined in a matrix organization.

Using this criterion for defining the business unit, in a universal bank, we can distinguish between at least the following units: commercial banking (attracting savings and granting loans to families and small and medium-sized companies), wholesale banking, money markets, capital markets, the mortgage market, and private banking. In turn, the commercial banking unit could be subdivided into other business units when the volume of a certain type of operation (for example, loans to small companies) so warrants.

This classification into business units within a universal bank leads one to ask in which businesses the bank should be present, what is the bank's present or potential ability to compete in each of these possible segments of the banking business, and what is the best possible organization.

In order to evaluate its ability to compete in a particular segment of the banking business, a universal bank must ask itself at least two fundamental questions. The first is: What is the structural attractiveness of this segment, that is, what is its potential profitability? In the banking industry, the factors that determine this attractiveness are, at least, the following: the degree of rivalry between banks, the bargaining power of the bank's depositors, the bargaining power of the bank's borrowers, the appearance of new, alternative products and services—both those offered by banks and those offered by other companies with financial serivices, such as car manufacturers or department stores, the growth of demand, the entry barriers, and the degree of regulation or control by the financial authorities (Figure 10.2).

As can be seen in Figure 10.2, this set of factors directly affects the

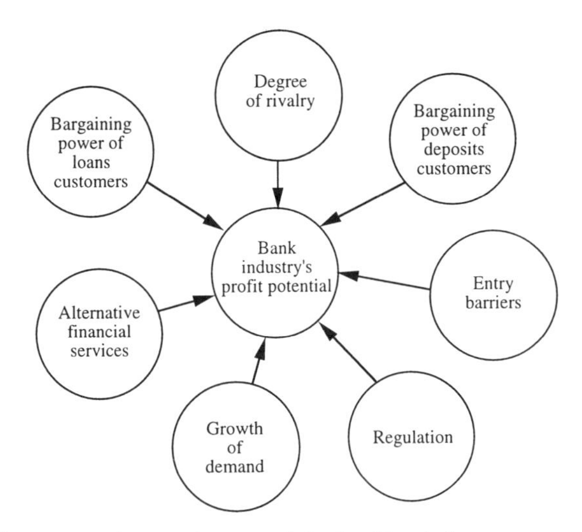

FIG. 10.2 *The structural attractiveness of the banking industry*

industry's structural attractiveness or that of a particular segment within the industry. Consequently, a universal bank must be continually assessing the potential appeal of the various segments in which it operates and how they develop over time. Each segment has a different attractiveness and, furthermore, this appeal changes over time. The case of the high-interest-bearing current accounts in Spain is a good example. When this product was launched massively on the market in September 1989, it seemed that it was going to be a 'hit' product for a long time. The subsequent launch of alternative products such as the investment funds partly eclipsed their dazzle. Therefore, a sector's or segment's appeal is a dimension that evolves with the passing of time.

The second fundamental question is: In what activities of the value chain does the bank have a core competence, an undoubted expertise, in comparison with other rival banks that are perhaps more specialized? If this competence is inferior to that of its competitors, the bank should reflect on whether it can acquire it by either internal development within a reasonable period of time or an alliance with another bank. If neither is possible, the bank would probably do well to forget about engaging in activities in which it cannot acquire the necessary skills to perform them satisfactorily.

While we are on this point, it is interesting to note that many business diversification decisions end up in failure (Ballarín, Canals, and Fernández, 1994), not so much because the financial estimates of the respective investment projects are incorrect but because the necessary skills and capacity to implement them (for example, the required technology or access to distribution channels) are lacking.

Therefore, it is always wise for a universal bank to reflect on the resources and capabilities for competing in a particular segment of the bank business or, to put it another way, what sustainable competitive advantage it can develop against other more specialized companies competing in the same segment. A thorough examination of the bank's resources and skills in each of the activities of the value chain may also bring to light exceptional opportunities for differentiation *vis-à-vis* other competing banks.

Let us consider, for instance, the quality of the marketing of savings products. It is a tremendously useful resource, not only for traditional bank operations on the liabilities side, such as opening new savings or deposit accounts, but also for developing similar new financial products and marketing them efficiently, combining these sales skills and utilizing them in operations on money markets or futures and options markets. Here, the bank's resource is not only the marketing of financial products for depositors but also the marketing of products aimed at remunerating savings.

This does not mean that the marketing activity should be centralized and be above the various business units. The specific answer to this question will depend on each business and each bank. However, each business unit should seek to exploit the differential skills and resources of other business units within the same universal bank.

One of the basic tasks of the bank group's management is to encourage and gain from the interrelationships between activities that can be shared between business products. Experience shows that this is the best way of identifying and realizing possible synergies between business units in the same business group (Porter, 1985).

In fact, a universal bank group's management must justify its very existence by the value it adds to each of the various business units' activities, whether this be as manager, co-ordinator, or consultant in each of the businesses. This additional cost should offset the additional cost incurred by having a corporate management for the entire group. One procedure for adding value consists of designing the necessary mechanisms for effectively utilizing all the possible interrelationships between the different business units.

Figure 10.3 shows some possible interrelationships which could exist between the commercial banking, corporate banking, and capital market divisions within a bank group. The most salient difference between this approach and other, more traditional approaches which justified the existence of universal banks in the past is that each business unit has a greater degree of operational autonomy and a greater need to co-ordinate with other units. Thus, each division becomes a profit centre so that one unit's surplus cannot be used to cover up another unit's losses. Likewise, the bank's corporate management is under the obligation to justify its existence by the value it adds to each of the business units.

One should not forget that the distribution capabilities required for an investment bank are very different from those of a commercial bank. For example, in an investment bank, distribution is tailored, as those banks develop very

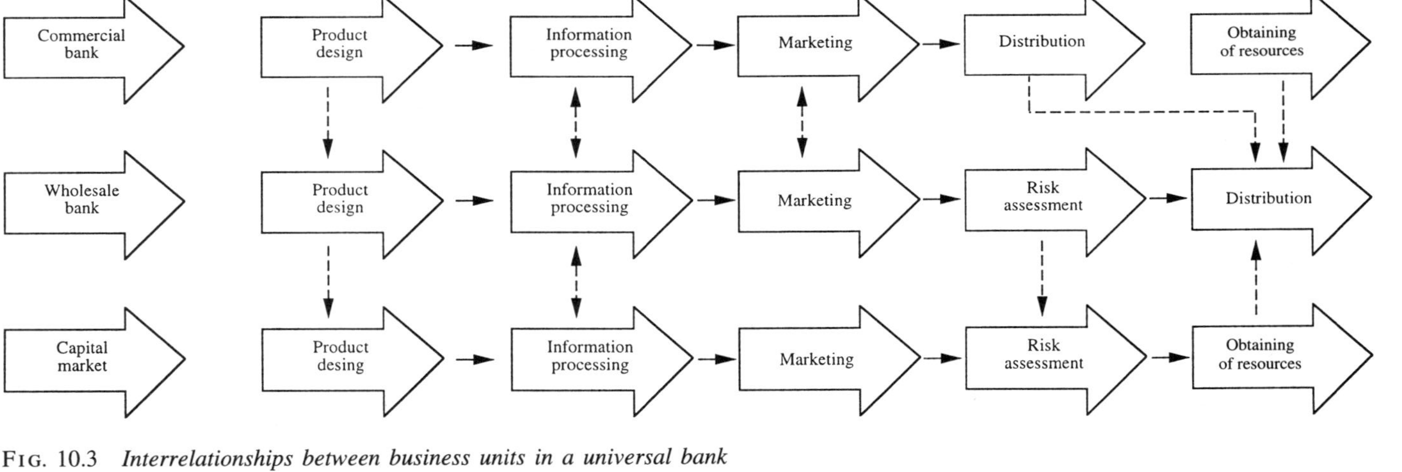

FIG. 10.3 *Interrelationships between business units in a universal bank*

personalized contacts with their customers due to the large size of the funds committed in the process (Eccles and Crane, 1988). A commercial bank, on the other hand, plans for a massive distribution of its products in order to reach the largest possible number of customers, without discriminating excessively between their different features. A similar statement could be made about marketing skills.

In the activities related to processing information about customers, the interrelationships arise from the possibility of sharing the technological resources available in the universal bank, rather than sharing the information. After all, the information required by each segment of the banking business is quite specific and it would perhaps not be sensible to have huge, unwieldy, and expensive databases.

The concept of a bank's value chain has enabled us to discuss how to go about examining in detail a universal bank's basic skills and resources, which now brings us full circle. In other words, we started by saying that the existence of a universal bank is only justified if this bank has a differential expertise or resources to carry out the various bank activities at least as effectively as a specialist. Otherwise, it could be in the best interests of everyone—employees, customers, and shareholders—to separate the various business units.

This consideration leads us to the role of a universal bank's corporate management. We will discuss this issue in the next section. However, we can say at this point that if the corporate management does not add value to each of the business units' activities, then these units would be in a better competitive position if they operated separately from the universal bank. Only when the corporate management adds value does it make sense for these units to be integrated within the universal bank.

At an earlier point, we said that one of the procedures by which a universal bank's corporate management adds value to the activities of its various business units is by maintaining and looking for interrelationships between them. This is one of the key mechanisms justifying a common management of business units.

Likewise, the bank group's corporate management may add value in other specific areas, such as an internal capital market that facilitates the availability of certain financial resources to exploit opportunities, the group's general brand image, the formulation and implementation of an international strategy matched to each of the group's units, the management of the various units' excess liquidity to ensure best use of this surplus on the international capital markets, or the management capabilities that can be contributed by the corporate headquarters, either directly or in a consultancy role.

However, although this approach to bank groups may seem very clear on paper, bank management has become extraordinarily complex in recent years, and this has enabled specialized finance companies to develop significant advantages over universal bank groups. The vital question in the next few years is how many universal banks will be able to maintain a high level of diversification of their activities without losing efficiency. In other words, in which activities, other than traditional commercial banking, will the universal banks continue to have a clear advantage over specialized banks and other specialized financial organizations?

Going back to the specific issue of bank holdings in other financial businesses or in industrial companies, the way this should be approached is clear: from the bank's viewpoint, what competitive advantage can this division or business unit have over specialized financial organizations such as investment banks, or over the capital market itself?

This question focuses our attention not only on the social or political desirability of this type of involvement but on what capabilities and advantages a universal bank can develop in these activities and how sustainable they will be over time. Again, the answer is not just that it is possible to carry out these activities; the business unit must be able to do so with the same efficiency as other companies.

In addition, the universal bank should ask itself whether or not operating under the group's flag, that is, having corporate management, contributes value to the specialized business unit. Logically, the added value should exceed the cost to the business unit of operating under the bank group's flag.

One of the clearest consequences of the increase in bank competition is the need for the divisions of a bank with several business units to be competitive in comparison with more specialized rivals. In organizational terms, this requirement means redefining the role of branch managers, who become customer service managers, liaising between customers and the bank's different departments or divisions.

In this way, a customer ceases to be a customer of a department or division and becomes a customer of the bank. This change of circumstances for the bank forces it to redefine its control systems and internal transfer prices so that each division or department fairly records the profit or loss generated by operations with a customer. In the next section, we will discuss in greater breadth the universal banks' organizational design requirements.

4. THE NECESSARY REORGANIZATION OF UNIVERSAL BANKS

The discussion presented in the previous section leads one to think that the combination of business units within the same bank group or universal bank is only justifiable when the market value of the group as a whole exceeds the sum of the individual values of each of the business units. In this case, the group clearly adds value to each business unit.

The criteria for evaluating a bank group's strategic approach and rationale are clear. However, there are no such clear criteria for designing the right

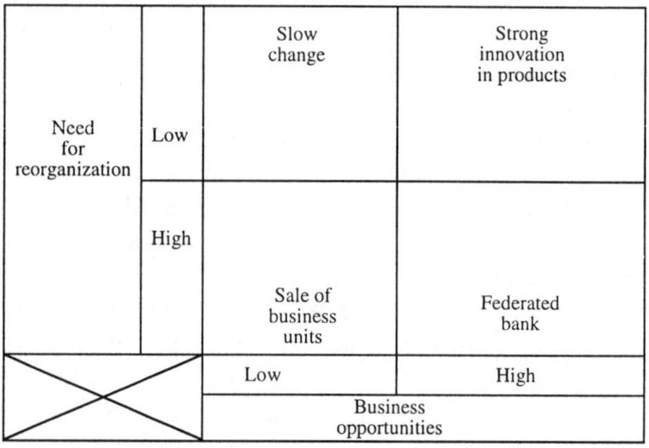

Need for reorganization			
	Low	Slow change	Strong innovation in products
	High	Sale of business units	Federated bank
		Low	High
		Business opportunities	

FIG. 10.4 *Changes in financial companies*

organizational form for the bank group so that a particular strategy will work in practice.[2]

Previously, we have mentioned certain proposals to reform universal banks in the United States, which have been reflected in new organizational forms proposed by certain authors (Bryan, 1991; Pierce, 1991). Thus, one has started to talk about the confederation of banking businesses, federated or confederated banking (Bryan, 1992). This model has been developed in response to the need to reorganize the traditional universal banks and the desirability of exploiting opportunities in emerging sectors within the financial services industry (see Figure 10.4). In the United States, this concept has also been used to try to separate the liabilities of the deposit guarantee fund covering commercial banking activities from the risk associated with other activities, such as operations on capital markets or real estate projects.

In the specific case of the universal banks, the term confederated banking—as in the recent case of Corporación Argentaria in Spain or Compagnie Bancaire in France—is used with the purpose of turning a traditional universal bank's different business units or divisions into genuine profit centres able to compete with the best of the specialists in each of the finance business's segments.

4.1. Organizational design for universal banks

The divisional model

The solutions to the organizational design problems of a universal bank are therefore varied, depending on the degree of autonomy given to the business

[2] Newman and Shriever (1993) have tried to measure the differences in operating efficiency of financial holding companies with respect to independent banks, using the transaction costs theory. However, the results obtained are not conclusive.

units and the role of the group's corporate management. A first solution consists of turning each business unit into a division within the group, with its own management team, reporting directly to the group's CEO or managing director. The group's management would retain certain tasks, such as the allocation of financial resources, the corporate brand image, and the purchase and administration of the information systems used by all of the business units.

Historically, such a divisional model first appeared in some large American companies early this century, as a possible solution to the problems that the functional structure was causing in companies that were becoming increasingly complex, such as General Motors, Sears, and DuPont. This organizational transformation had such a profound impact on these organizations' efficiency that it has been rated as one of the most important innovations of this century (Chandler, 1962).

These companies initiated a major decentralization process, forming divisional units. The company's corporate headquarters retained a few basic tasks, which largely consisted of the following: general management of the corporation, co-ordination between divisions, organization of the company as a whole, allocation of financial resources, performance appraisals, and the provision of central services shared by all the divisions.

This organizational transformation is currently in progress in many European bank groups. Thus, for example, the investment companies or insurance companies in banks such as Banco Central Hispano are divisions with a certain degree of autonomy within the bank group.

The same independence is being given in many banks to the management of information systems. These tasks are being grouped around a separate division that provides services to the rest of the group. In fact, if this division is not competitive enough, the bank groups will end up getting rid of it and subcontracting the task to an external company, as is already happening in the United States.

This divisional organization has the classic advantages associated with this type of organization structure in multiproduct industrial companies, such as, for example, consumer electronics or food companies.

The main advantage this divisional model offers to a universal bank is that it enables it to break down the banking services it offers into individual components, going from the complexity of the combination of businesses to the simplicity of considering each service in its own right. And this is the first step to take to be able to determine to what extent a particular banking business offers clear, sustainable advantages over its competitors.

However, in addition to these uncontested advantages in its operational functioning, the divisional model also has a number of disadvantages, such as the isolation of each divisional unit from others. This is particularly serious when the customers or markets targeted by these different divisions are the same or closely related.

Another critical aspect of the divisional firm—and one that is difficult to solve—is setting internal transfer prices for the services provided between divisional units or between these units and the corporate management (Milgrom and Roberts, 1992). This is a particularly important aspect in the case of universal banks, as they comprise an aggregation of businesses that share all of the bank's resources. From now on, it will be necessary to allocate assets and resources to each of the business units or to activities carried out by the universal bank's corporate management which are shared by all of the group's units, such as advertising the group's brand image or investing in information systems.

The confederated model

A second organizational model for bank groups consists not only of dividing the universal bank into separate business units but of turning these units into legally and financially independent companies controlled by the same bank group, for example, by creating a holding company or turning the bank group into a federation or confederation of companies with a corporate headquarters.

The creation of legally separate companies grouped under a corporate headquarters which co-ordinates and shares resources is becoming increasingly common in the banking industry. The main reason for this is that some of the new specialized financial services (for example, financial derivatives) can only be provided with the necessary quality by an organization that has been given a high degree of independence with respect to the rest of the bank organization, which normally revolves around the commercial bank structure and the network of branches.

A federated bank needs a number of basic cohesive elements that allow it to realize the benefits of decentralization without leading to dispersion. These elements, termed by some authors (Handy, 1992) federalist principles, seek to articulate the group's philosophy. Banc One is a good example of the federated bank and its organization rests on the following principles, among others:

1. The separation of power, jurisdiction, and rights between the corporate headquarters and each unit.
2. Subsidiarity, which, when applied to the bank, means that each unit should decide on all matters in which it is most efficient; in particular, decision-making power should be located in those places closest to the customer.
3. Independence between corporate headquarters and units, a principle that seeks to avoid domination of one side by the other and establish an equilibrium of power.

Although this type of federated form is still not common, many banks are drawing closer to it, creating, for example, units having a greater degree of independence.

At world-wide level, this phenomenon is present to a greater or lesser degree. Barclays has created two companies, Barclaycard and Mercantile Credit, in order to gain a stronger presence in the consumer credit segment. Banco Santander has created Santander Investments, specializing in corporate finance operations, derivative instruments, and the capital market. Banco Sabadell has created Sabadell Multibanca for high-income private customers. Banco Bilbao Vizcaya has done the same with Privanza. NatWest Bank has done the same thing with a mortgage company, NatWest Home Loans, which specializes in financing real estate projects and mortgages. Some of the specific tasks of this company include product development, assessment of the risk of customers and projects, and product distribution. The latter task is done in two ways: through the bank's network of branches and through direct marketing.

It is easy to see that none of these tasks, which are specific to the value chain of a mortgage loan unit, has a strong synergy with, for example, the large companies unit. Hence the complete separation of activities implies a substantial degree of organizational simplification.

This organization form may be justified if the group's growth is the result of mergers and take-overs. In this case, the cost of integrating two different organizations may advise in favour of maintaining the legal separateness. This is what happened with the take-over and subsequent integration of the Abbey Life insurance company by Lloyds Bank. The bank could have entered insurance distribution in several ways but its managers reached the conclusion that a take-over was a faster and less risky procedure than, for example, internal development. So as not to interfere excessively with the management of Abbey Life, this company has joined the Lloyds Bank group, but with complete management autonomy and a completely different board of directors.

However, for the same reason, it would not make much sense to follow, as a general rule, the criterion of legally independent companies, unless legal criteria or the universal bank's particular culture should so advise. The reason for not considering this formula as a universally applicable recipe is quite obvious: avoid the costs associated with the management of independent banks and try to capitalize as much as possible on the brand image offered by the universal bank. However, certain reasons that are specific to each bank (such as the strong culture that commercial banking may have in a universal bank) may advise in favour of creating legally independent companies.

Figure 10.5 shows a diagram of this type of confederated organization, whose configuration is very similar to that of a group of companies or a conglomerate, with the particular feature that all the divisions or member companies operate in the finance industry. Figure 10.6 shows an alternative structure.

Comparison of a bank organized in traditional units and a federated bank reveals considerable differences. Two in particular should be stressed, as they are the ones that really make the difference between the two types of structure. First, federated banking reduces the moral hazard problems associated with deposit insurance. Second, each unit in a federation is conceived on the basis of three criteria: focus on certain types of customer, definition of the resources to be shared, and the financial results for which it is responsible. The latter

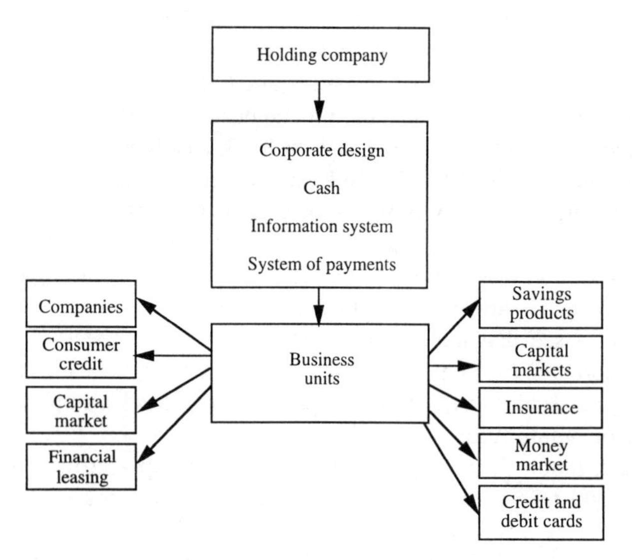

FIG. 10.5 *Confederated bank (1)*

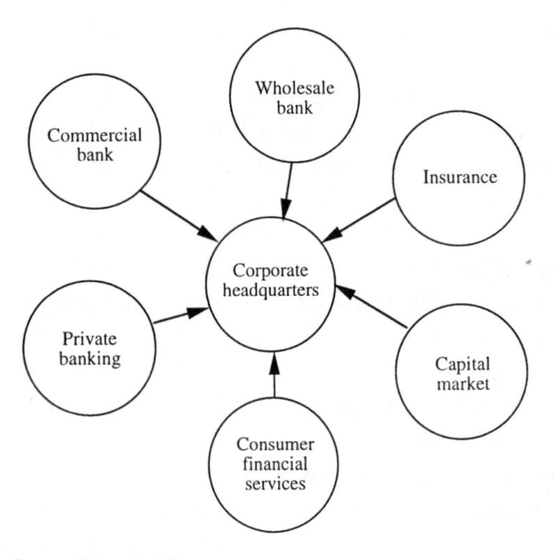

FIG. 10.6 *Confederated bank (2)*

aspect implicitly supposes the introduction of the market mechanism to stimulate efficiency within the organization.

If the organization of a bank group is based on the creation of divisions or if it goes a little further and creates legally separate companies, one critical question remains: what are the corporate headquarters' management styles and practices?

This subject has been extensively discussed in the literature on strategic

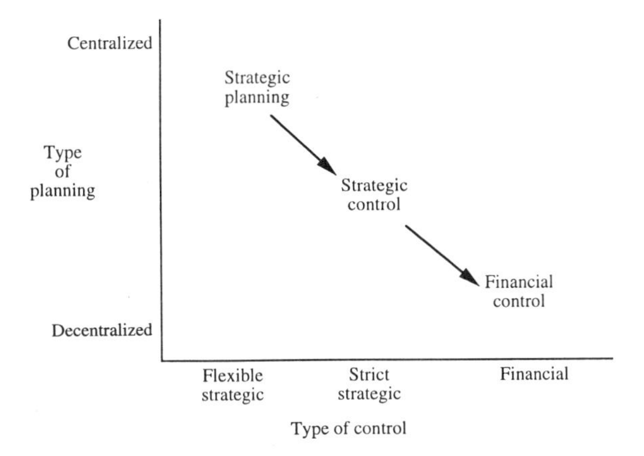

FIG. 10.7 *Relationships between the corporate centre and business units*

management (mainly Andrews, 1971; Goold and Campbell, 1987), although, unfortunately, there are no simple or straightforward answers. The reason is that each business group's history, the resources available to it, and the individual features of its members influence decisively the distribution of functions between the group's management and that of each divisional unit.

The relationships between corporate and business unit management

In Figure 10.7, we describe different configurations of the relationship between corporate management and a business unit's management, taking into account two basic variables: the type of planning used and the type of control established by corporate management.

The typologies described are clear. First, we have the model which we could classify as strategic management and planning. In this management model, two important processes are stressed: the search for and achievement of goals that are mutually agreed and shared between the different business units and the corporate management, and the use of flexible long-term planning to forecast scenarios for the group as a whole, anticipate problems, and establish action plans.

This management model is very flexible and requires a greater involvement on the part of the group's companies to set goals and action plans. It is a management model that is particularly useful when there are clear interrelationships between the different management units and it would be a waste if activities and resources were not co-ordinated in some way. The practical consequences of the management model are also immediate. First, each business unit's organization forms are varied although, normally, they include a matrix structure to facilitate ongoing communication between the business unit and corporate management.

Another aspect is the very extensive use made of strategic planning systems, which comprise this management model's backbone. This may create rigidities in each of the group's business units, although this will depend, in the final analysis, on the personal management styles of the people who hold the key positions in corporate management.

Something similar could be said of the preponderance of the corporate centre over the business units in the decisions made. In general, matrix structures end up tipping decision-making power towards the centre or towards the divisional units, depending on each unit's resources and personal management styles.

The second model is that known as the strategic control model. This model also stresses long-term planning, but with one important difference from the previous model: the planning processes are decentralized to each business unit and corporate management only intervenes to supervise and verify fulfilment. This model's main features are, therefore, different from those of strategic planning. First, the business units are profit centres that are very much separate from the rest of the group and, therefore, act with a considerable degree of autonomy.

Long-term planning in each business unit is a critical part of the process. Annual plans and budgets are important, although they play a secondary role in the planning process. Corporate management monitors the achievement of goals more closely than in the previous model. Finally, the goals are set individually for each of the group's business units, even though corporate management stresses the effects that these results—or the action plans—will have on the rest of the units in the group.

In this area, it is interesting to note an accounting practice that is becoming increasingly popular among large corporations: the overall results of the group's companies are separated from the total expenses generated by corporate management. By this means, it is possible to see more clearly what possible value corporate management can add to each of the group's companies.

The third model is that of financial control. In this case, the group of companies is a collection of business units that share barely any common elements, either in the businesses in which they engage or in the way they are managed within the group, as each one is completely self-sufficient.

This model is similar to the strategic control model but has a number of marked differences. First, the emphasis on financial results is usually decisive. A business unit's results are measured not by their contribution to the rest of the group but by the economic value they offer to shareholders.

Second, although planning may be used within each business unit, corporate management uses the annual budget as its primary monitoring tool. Short-term financial performance takes precedence over the long-term result. And if the business unit's performance is not adequate, corporate management will alienate it and look for another one.

At this point, one might wonder what advantage this group of companies offers—with purely financial links—over the capital market. The answer is not simple and depends on each particular group. There are cases—Hanson is one of the them—in which the corporate headquarters contributes management skills to turn around failing companies. In other cases, the presence of a stable investor as controlling shareholder enables the company to be monitored much more closely and a much deeper knowledge of it to be gained than could possibly be achieved by a capital market (which is not completely efficient). This presence would help solve, as we have already seen, the asymmetric information problems between banks and fund investors.

4.2. The confederated bank in practice: Argentaria

In order to understand better the challenges and opportunities of a federated bank, we will discuss below the case of Argentaria, which is interesting, among other reasons, because it deliberately chose this organization form.

Argentaria, Corporación Bancaria de España, came into being on 5 May 1991, with the purpose of co-ordinating and centralizing different State-owned bank organizations in Spain: Banco Exterior de España, Caja Postal, Banco de Crédito Industrial, Banco Hipotecario, and Banco de Crédito Agrícola. Argentaria adopted the federated banking model right from the start. This organization form was chosen to ensure maximum co-ordination between the different units while at the same time to give each one the maximum possible autonomy. The first stage (1991–3) was marked by a major restructuring of the group's members, aimed at improving each one's management and control and instilling a certain consistency in each member's businesses.

Argentaria came into being as a holding corporation that would group a number of financial organizations, following an alternative model to the merger. The holding company would seek to offer the services of a universal bank through a series of specialized organizations. This project, as it was designed, was aimed at facilitating each institution's autonomy and at the same time, ensuring the coherence of the group as a whole.

Consequently, its ultimate goal was very similar to that of other German or Spanish universal banks, although its beginnings were different. Other Spanish universal banks have separated some of their business units, while Argentaria has grouped under a corporate core previously existing organizations that until then acted independently.

Two specialization criteria have been applied to the different member banks: the product criterion (Banco Hipotecario de España, Banco de Negocios de Argentaria, the insurance division, and the investment management division), and the customer criterion (Banco de Crédito Local, Caja Postal, and Banco Exterior de España).

The firm's specialization is related to the perception held in Argentaria of the present and future of the banking business. The decline of traditional financial intermediation business has been paralleled by a spectacular growth in the volume of public debt trading on the markets. Debt trading has become a very important institutional business, although the margin is smaller. The commission charged on public debt is about 1.5 per cent whereas there is a much larger financial margin among the large banks.

The securitization process is developing slowly in Europe but it exists and its growth may start to pick up speed. If this should happen, investment funds may seek to obtain an ordered rating of the financial risks of different securitized instruments, which would stimulate the replacement of traditional bank products by new products.

Finally, the growth of the investment funds is changing direction. Banks are trying to stop being mere traders and to become genuine fund managers. In this business, the Banco de Negocios de Argentaria has become the largest Spanish operator on the stock market and the second largest operator on the capital market.

The convergence between investment banking and corporate banking observed in other countries has not yet happened in Spain. Investment banking (operations with financial instruments, fund management, etc.) continues to compete with the more traditional banking products. However, it is likely that this convergence between investment banking and corporate banking will end up happening.

Argentaria and other bank groups must learn to offer new services by combining complex products and managing their total risk. An example is a product referenced to the MIBOR (Madrid interbank offered rate) combined with a product that hedges interest rate risks. These profound changes that are taking place in the banking system are at the heart of Argentaria's concern to achieve growth both in the traditional businesses and in the new areas of banking business.

Organizational design criteria in Argentaria

The organizational structure of Argentaria was built around a corporate centre and a series of business units. Initially, the corporate centre carried out the following functions: strategic management of the group, allocation and joint use of resources, and co-ordination of the different business units.

Right from the inception of the group, business units were configured as customer-driven centres by means of the distribution of a very broad range of financial services. Each business unit has its own management bodies, in accordance with current company legislation. Likewise, a number of committees were formed to be responsible for implementing the projects and co-ordinating between the corporate headquarters and the different business units. One example of these efforts is the Domus Project (1992), in which Banco Hipotecario and Caja Postal took part and which sought to achieve a number of goals.

The first was to tie in the customers obtained mainly from the subrogation of Banco Hipotecario loans, by offering commercial banking products. Banco Hipotecario's customers would benefit from the expansion of the range of products and services available at their bank.

Second, extend the co-operation between Banco Hipotecario and Caja Postal to the sales networks. Thus, Caja Postal's sales force attends to Banco Hipotecario's customers in the latter's branches, marketing retail banking products. For its part, Banco Hipotecario has installed points of sale in selected Caja Postal branches, thereby placing an additional sales force at its disposal.

Another basic idea of organizational design consists of exploiting the advantages of a back office co-ordinated and shared by all of the group's units. This back office consists of the data processing department and the administrative operations centres department. In particular, in the data processing department, there were six different applications in 1991; in 1997, it is expected that there will be a single application for all the members of the group.

Each bank is a business unit. The purpose of Argentaria's corporate management is to co-ordinate the different organizations' strategies, help share resources, reduce costs that can be shared or lowered, and promote cross-sales efforts (for example, a Banco Hipotecario customer is a potential Caja Postal customer).

Another important advantage of co-ordinating each unit's strategies refers to financing policies. The group's total volume enables it to obtain financing on the international markets at a lower cost. This financing procedure has enabled it to contain the rising cost of traditional bank liabilities that has been recorded in Spain in recent years.

One indicator of this design's efficiency is the ratio between total assets and employees: about 17 trillion pesetas in assets with only 16,000 employees in 1994. This ratio is considerably superior to that of other universal Spanish or foreign banks.

The model chosen by Argentaria has enabled it to achieve a size and diversity of activities that it would be difficult to achieve by a merger or take-over. The advantage of integrating a group of banks with complementary and, at the same time, specialized activities, should allow Argentaria to enjoy the advantages of size and diversity.

The role of the corporate centre

Right from its inception, Argentaria's corporate centre was organized in accordance with a single management model under an executive chairman. The organization was structured around 11 business units—specializing in different financial services—and four co-ordination units.

Argentaria's corporate headquarters has changed its functions as the group's conception, strategy, and organization have evolved. Initially, in the first stage of restructuring the banks, the corporate headquarters' role was limited to management control and setting the strategy for the group and for each business unit. Since early 1994, the corporate centre is responsible for the group's financial monitoring, supervises each member's strategy (although each member should determine its own strategy within the framework of Argentaria's goals), allocates resources (for example, information systems), and is responsible for financial control and, in particular, control of the group's financial risk (in interest rates, depending on the instruments and markets).

The business units have very specific goals which they try to achieve. Their strategy, budget, and action plans are supervised by the corporate headquarters, which outlines each member's plans. One result of this effort is a single cash desk for the entire group (Markets project). This project seeks to equip the group with an integrated financial markets room, so that each bank in the group acts through this room.

Each business unit has an annual financial plan, which describes its main lines of commercial action and their financial impact for that period. Together with the committees, the financial plan is a key component in the corporate group's management.

The future of a confederated bank

Argentaria's competitive advantages—co-ordination and specialization of organizations—will be subjected to a severe test during the next few years, as rivalry in different segments of the banking business intensifies.

An analysis of Argentaria's competitive position shows a certain advantage in transformation costs which, as a percentage of total assets, are lower than in the rest of the industry. This advantage has been consolidated in recent years, thanks to a major cost containment effort.

Likewise, the consolidation of a large number of official credit institutions, with a less developed commercial mentality, under the Argentaria umbrella, will give rise to significant opportunities in the future. Although these institutions' management has improved considerably in recent years, obviously there are still areas or synergies to be exploited.

One of the challenges facing Argentaria is to achieve a large increase in financial margin. The recent volatility of the financial markets shows that it may be beneficial to operate on them at times but the results obtained are highly sensitive to the business cycle.

The businesses with best future prospects within Argentaria seem to be commercial banking, mortgage loans, and investment products. Corporate banking will continue to be important but the deteriorating margin plus disintermediation will lead to this unit losing part of its specific weight.

Another challenge facing Argentaria is the very feasibility of the confederated banking concept. The big advantage of this organizational model for a universal bank such as Argentaria is that it bypasses the problems caused by a merger. However, one of its main difficulties is the fact that several financial institutions specializing in different businesses coexist in Argentaria without being merged. Their autonomy—a valuable attribute—may clash with the universal bank's need to integrate and co-ordinate.

5. GROUP CORPORATE MANAGEMENT AND THE STRATEGY OF DIVERSIFIED FINANCIAL GROUPS

We have earlier defined three possible configurations of the relationship between a group's corporate headquarters and its business units. In this section, we will come back to this question from another angle. How can a group's corporate headquarters create value?

In order to better understand the role of the corporate headquarters in a universal bank, or in a bank with several business units, we need to reflect on two basic concepts: the group's corporate strategy, that is, the strategy for the business group as a whole and the advantages that the group's headquarters provides to each of its components.

In Chapter 5, we discussed some of the issues concerning the concept of corporate strategy and its applications to the management of universal banks and specialized financial groups. We would now like to return to this question, but from another angle. In general, a bank or financial group's strategy should include the following elements: the definition of the various businesses grouped under a corporate management, the competitive situation of each of these businesses, the consistency between each business's competitive dynamics, the consistency of each business unit with the matrix, the decisions to increase or reduce the business portfolio, the type of relationship the different business units have with each other and with the parent company, and, finally, the type of organization that best fits the nature of each business unit.

Many of these issues have already been discussed in Chapter 5. Now, in the context of a universal bank, we would like to examine in somewhat greater depth the type of relationship between the parent company or the corporate headquarters[3] and the different business units it groups. On the basis of this relationship, we will be able to define different types of function for the parent company with respect to the different business units.

Goold, Campbell, and Alexander (1994) have presented a conceptual framework, describing the type of resources and skills that the parent company can contribute to the different business units, that we can apply to universal banks.

Those authors distinguish between four different types of generic advantage obtained from a good management of the corporate group: decentralization and a high degree of autonomy of the different business units, search for interrelationships or synergies between the different business units, functional or interfunctional services shared between the corporate headquarters and the different business units, and, finally, corporate development guided by the parent company's management.

We will briefly discuss the main features of each of these possible contributions that the parent complany or corporate headquarters can make to the different business units. The first is decentralization and independent, autonomous management of the business units. Obviously, this autonomy is never complete. After appointing managers it trusts, the parent company will probably retain certain rights regarding the approval of operating and investment budgets and other critical decisions.

[3] We use the term parent company when a group's corporate headquarters has a legal status different from that of the business units.

However, the main advantage of this contribution is that each business unit acts as an independent competitor in its industry, with as much operating independence as any other competitor. In this case, the parent company's contribution is twofold: management autonomy or non-interference and recruitment of managers who are able to manage the business unit in accordance with this mentality.

One example of this type of organization is that which is found in certain financial groups between the commercial banking unit and the investment banking unit, or other different business units. Thus, S. G. Warburg created a separate company to manage investment funds, Mercury Asset Management, in which it had a 85 per cent interest. However, this company's operational management and strategic mindset were, for all practical purposes, independent from Warburg.

The second contribution made by the parent company to the business units consists of the series of relationships that it can establish with the business units and, at the same time, help them get maximum benefit from these relationships. The relationships that can be established are extremely varied: general policies, transfer prices, development of financial innovations to be shared, and centralized information systems.

An example of a close relationship between the parent company and the business units is Banc One. As we have already described in Chapter 1, this bank has grown spectacularly in the last 20 years by purchasing smaller regional banks. The policies followed by Banc One with any of its purchased banks is a clear example of relationships. We would like to stress the following. The first and most important is decentralization, at operational level and as regards responsibility for results. Each subsidiary bank has its own board of directors which is responsible for the bank's results.

However, subsidiaries share the same brand image, an operations processing (back office) and compensation system which is one of the most sophisticated of North American banking, a fairly standardized line of financial products and services which is transmitted from the corporate headquarters to the different subsidiaries, marketing and distribution policies for these services with shared resources, and, finally, a system called 'Management Information Computer System', which is an information system which enables each subsidiary to measure its performance against other Banc One subsidiaries targeting the same customers or products in other markets. By this means, each unit is able to ascertain its efficiency compared with the other units in the group.

Finally, the various units in Banc One share common goals that are focused on three indicators: the percentage of customers retained, the turnaround time to requests for services by customers, and, finally, the percentage of customers who say that they are very satisfied with the services offered by the bank. The bank also uses a profitability indicator, net profit over assets. When this indicator equals or surpasses 1.1 per cent, an incentives system for its subsidiaries' managers starts to operate.

The third type of contribution by the corporate centre is similar to the previous one, although it focuses more on the relationship between the corporate centre and the different business units than on seeking relationships between the business units themselves. This contribution consists of the influence the corporate headquarters has on the subsidiaries, either through a more or less active presence of the corporate group's managers in the different subsidiary units or through services that the group offers its subsidiaries. The parent's services may or may not match those described under the previous type of contribution. Perhaps the main difference between the two is in the involvement of corporate services in the subsidiaries' decisions. The degree of autonomy, consequently, is slightly less than in the second type of advantage.

Finally, the fourth type of advantage is related to corporate development, that is, to the development of the group by means of investment decisions, entering new businesses, or withdrawing from businesses that are no longer as interesting as in the past. It should be noted that this advantage is independent of whether, after the purchase of a new business, for example, the corporate group initiates some of the mechanisms described above. In fact, there are diversified companies that think that the corporate group has greater opportunities for discovering new businesses than each subsidiary separately. At the same time, the corporate centre will probably be able to use a volume of financial resources for undertaking these new businesses that the subsidiaries do not have.

All of these advantages or contributions of the corporate centre can be synthesized into a number of general principles that justify the existence of a corporate centre. First, the corporate headquarters must create value or prevent the destruction of value in the different business units. Second, in order to create value, the corporate headquarters' resources must be matched to the business units' needs and opportunities, in the knowledge that these can change over time.

Third, the corporate centre must show, with results, that it makes sense for a subsidiary to be in its group and not in another different business group, contributing a greater creation of value than that which could be contributed by an alternative business group. If the centre cannot demonstrate this, and the capital markets are efficient, the corporate group might end up losing ownership of this subsidiary.

Fourth, the corporate headquarters must be able to identify ways to increase the different business units' value in the future and contribute to this task and, in addition, do so with at least the same efficiency as other corporate groups.

Fifth, each business unit has different competitive dynamics. It is important that the corporate group concentrates on those units that compete in sectors in which it can contribute a differential value. The corporate group should alienate those business units where this creation of value is difficult due to the origin or nature of the group.

6. SOME CONCLUSIONS

None of the organizational solutions described above is ideal for restructuring universal banks and adapting them to the new competitive situation. Each one could be implemented with more or less success depending on the bank group's history, the dominant styles and cultures, the resources available, and the weight of each business unit.

In any case, we can say, on the basis of international experiences with universal banks and bank groups, that both the strategic control model and the strategic planning model offer clear advantages over the financial control model. Essentially, the different businesses of a bank group are related to the provision of financial services and, consequently, the interrelationships that can arise between them can become quite significant.

Perhaps we should exclude bank shareholdings in non-financial companies from this general statement. In these, the interrelationships are less clear and could justify an even greater degree of independence for the business unit controlling investments in the equity of non-bank companies.

Consequently, the problems of a universal bank or a confederated bank are very similar to those of a group of companies. In the final analysis, the crucial question is how to combine the independence the group's companies need with a suitable degree of co-ordination to achieve maximum efficiency within the group. The dilemma is not simple and only very high-quality corporate management will be able to overcome the maze of complexities involved in the modern management of a universal bank.

11

Universal banks, specialized banks and the regulation of financial services

1. INTRODUCTION

Public policies that regulate financial activity in industrialized countries have been varied, for historical, political and, economic reasons. However, all of them share in common two elements that derive in part from the 1933 Glass–Steagall Act, which was aimed at regulating the banking system in the United States.

These elements are the separation of activities between commercial banks and investment banks, and the creation of a deposit guarantee fund to protect depositors in the event that a financial organization should fail. To these two elements was added a third element: the control of interest rates on banks' lending and deposit-taking activities. It was thought that excessive price competition had been one of the causes of the bank crisis in the United States in the early 1930s. This regulatory structure, with individual variations, was applied in most industrialized countries until the end of the 1970s.

This regulatory structure, and the long period of economic stability and growth experienced by industrialized countries until the 1970s, no doubt contributed to preventing a repetition of the financial crises of the 1920s and 1930s during this period.

However, powerful forces of change were affecting the banking system, indirectly affecting this regulatory structure. Its validity started to be questioned. These forces were mainly fivefold. First, there was the liberalization of capital movements between countries. The freedom of capital movements is gradually erasing the limits to foreign investment in the financial sector, at the same time as it is increasing the competition that a country's banking industry is exposed to from international capital markets.

Second, there was the financial disintermediation process, caused by the possibility of companies of turning to capital markets for cheaper financing, thus bypassing the intermediary role played by banking. Banks have been losing business in the corporate segment, particularly among large and medium-sized companies. The traditional separation between commercial banks—specializing in a pure financial intermediation activity—and investment banks—specializing in financial consultancy and capital markets operations—imposed by this regulatory structure clearly benefited the latter at the expense of the former.

On the other hand, the growing weight of capital markets in industrialized countries has meant that they attract not only companies looking for financing but also savers willing to invest their funds in assets that offer a better combination of risk and return. Therefore, disintermediation has affected—and still affects—not only the banks' lending operations but also their deposit operations.

The third phenomenon is financial innovation, initially driven by the need to cope with the high inflation rates of the 1970s and sidestep the restrictions on certain operations imposed by the central banks. During the 1980s, innovation grew apace with the incipient globalization of finances, the progressive deregulation of the banking activity in industrialized countries, and the application of modern information technologies to the finance business.

The latter is the fourth force that has transformed modern financial systems. Information systems have triggered at least two far-reaching revolutions in the bank industry. The first is the dramatic change in the way commercial banking, investment banking, and capital market tasks are carried out. The second is that information systems have broken the space and time barriers, turning the world financial system into a truly global market.

Finally, there has been growing competition between financial organizations, caused by deregulation, liberalization of capital movements, the lifting of price controls on financial services, financial disintermediation, and the entry of new competitors into the financial services industry. The financial margin of banks in all industrialized countries has fallen dramatically. Banks have tried to offset this fall with an increase in the volume of activities, a clearer focus on the provision of financial services, and cost reductions. However, more than ever before, the banking industry is facing fierce competition in many countries.

In this context, and after almost 15 years of deregulation of the banking industry in Western Europe and the United States, the pull between the need for greater regulation to reduce the disastrous consequences of excessive competition and the desirability of deeper deregulation to enable the banks to stop losing further business to other finance companies is stronger than ever.

In this chapter, we will analyse the rationale of banking regulation in recent years, the development of the deregulation process, particularly in the European Union countries, and, finally, the possible solutions to enable an adequate supervision of the risk incurred by universal banks when they intervene in operations other than simple bank intermediation.[1]

2. WHY DOES THE BANKING INDUSTRY NEED SPECIAL REGULATION?

We plan to review the most important reasons that give rise to the need for adequate regulation of the lending system. All of these factors are related to

[1] Mayer and Neven (1994), Merton (1992), Tirole (1993) and Vives (1991, 1994) discuss major factors in the design and implementation of the regulation of a modern financial system.

the facts that financial markets are not complete and that market failures occur.

The first reason is that financial markets are affected by the asymmetric information problem between suppliers and customers of financial services. This phenomenon is two-way. On the one hand, when a bank acts as a lender it may not know the true risk it is taking on when it grants a loan to a customer.

On the other hand, a bank guarantees depositors a certain liquidity and return, but may conceal from its depositors information on its true financial situation. In this section, we wish to focus on the second aspect, as it refers directly to a bank's financial health, which is necessary to guarantee the financial system's stability in addition to the bank's solvency. In principle, this phenomenon occurs in other markets, for example, in secondhand car sales. However, in financial markets, it is also common and its consequences are more far-reaching.

Asymmetric information problems can be solved in different ways. First, the more secure financial firms offer less favourable conditions to their customers than the less secure firms. The recent case of Banesto, whose crisis was caused in part by a utopian offering to its loans and deposits customers the best possible conditions, is paradigmatic. However, when a financial firm offers better conditions, an adverse selection phenomenon may occur: all sorts of customers prefer to go to this firm because, at least in the short term, they obtain better conditions.

The second mechanism is the firm's credibility or the acquisition of a reputation for good management and solvency. This intangible resource acts as a guarantee to depositors and shareholders that the risk of the financial organization in question is low or, at least, not above the average of other financial organizations.

However, although these two mechanisms are useful in many industries[2]—from consumer goods to capital goods—they are not very practical in the financial services industry.[3] The first condition would prevent an organization that is more effective in its cost management from offering better conditions than another less effective organization. The second alternative, the development of a reputation, is difficult to achieve in the short term and, on occasions, bad decisions may send it plummeting downwards or, at least, damage it, as happened to J. P. Morgan in 1994 as a result of its involvement in Banesto's capital increases in 1992 and 1993.

The best indirect indicator of a financial organization's reputation is its volume of capital. Hence, the Bank for International Settlements (BIS) has established rules on the minimum value of a bank's capital. However, this is not the only indicator needed to guarantee a bank's financial health. A bank could fulfil this requirement but with extremely low-quality loans and an excessively

[2] See Shapiro (1983) on the role of the development of a reputation for being a supplier of quality goods. Kreps and Wilson (1982) model the interaction between consumers and suppliers in a game in which the former perceive a certain quality level in the products and react to it.

[3] Mayer and Neven (1994) discuss another perspective of the same phenomenon.

high level of risk, seriously compromising the bank's future. Hence there is a need to establish complementary mechanisms for regulating the bank industry.

We can therefore see that the asymmetric information and adverse selection problems are particularly acute in the financial sector and are not fully resolved by mechanisms such as reputation, unlike the situation in other industries.

In addition, with respect to this first phenomenon related to asymmetric information, banks have a number of additional features that lead them to a type of regulation different from that applicable to other industries. Among these, we will mention the following. First, there is the importance of banks' solvency to guarantee financial stability and the smooth functioning of the payments system. Bank crises cause financial panics and loss of control of systemic risk. Therefore, it is reasonable that the financial authorities take precautionary measures to prevent a country's payments system from collapsing.

The second factor is that a certain degree of contradiction could arise in the banking industry between growth and solvency. Normally, a bank grows either because it attracts more deposits, thanks to financial innovation or favourable conditions for savers, or because of a strong growth in loans, also for the above-stated reasons, although in this case customers are borrowers. In both cases, growth may lead to a decrease in the bank's financial margin and, therefore, to lower operating results. If this situation were to become consolidated, it could jeopardize the bank's solvency.

However, banks compete for capital with other non-financial firms on the stock market. In order to raise capital banks must offer return prospects comparable to those offered by other companies. These prospects may not be very favourable if there are no growth possibilities. Consequently, financial regulation has this dimension: to try to moderate the banks' drive towards excessively risky growth in an attempt to gain a greater short-term return for their shareholders.

Third, some of the deposits in banks and other financial organizations in many countries are insured by a deposit guarantee fund that guarantees depositors a part of their deposits in the event that the bank should fail. This guarantee may induce the bank to take on excessive risks, knowing that it has a safety net that will prevent it from going bankrupt if the risks are not sustainable.

Finally, banks usually have much lower ratios between equity and external resources than most companies in the other sectors. This situation implies that their risk is clearly greater, if their assets should lose value. For this reason, there must be either a higher capital requirement, which would be difficult and expensive in practice, or prudential regulation that prevents banks from taking on excessive risks.

After this discussion of some of the reasons for regulation in the financial system, a few observations recommending caution in the use of the public authorities' regulatory power are necessary.

First, innovation is one of the cornerstones of success of any type of organization. Financial innovation is, therefore, critical for financial firms. If an artificially rigid regulatory system prevents the development of a healthy degree of innovation, public authorities would be hampering the financial organizations from competing adequately in a global financial system. In a way, the situation would be the same as between countries with different fiscal systems or with more or less favourable attitudes towards foreign investment: the regulatory system would become a competitive advantage or disadvantage, depending on the country.

An analogy may help us to understand better the relationship between innovation and regulation.[4] The services of a high speed train need a special rail infrastructure. The high speed train is, in itself, a major innovation but it cannot travel on a rail network built for lower speed trains. The special infrastructure is what allows a high speed train to provide the transportation services that are expected of it, without any serious risk of accident for reasons associated with the speed it can reach.

In this sense, financial innovations of recent years bear a remote relation to high speed trains. If the regulatory system were to prevent their use and spread or, simply, did not try to limit the possible harmful effects caused by, for example, the greater risks involved, it would be poorly serving savers and investors and the financial system as a whole. Consequently, in a financial system driven continually by innovation, the role of financial regulation is becoming increasingly important.

The second observation is related to the first. The risk of excessive interventionism in the regulation of financial activities has always existed and becomes more acute during times of financial panic, as happened in the United States with the 1929 stock market crash or, decades later, with the October 1987 crash. A similar situation has happened in the currency markets, first with the crisis of the European Monetary System between 1992 and 1993 and then with the sharp fall of the dollar on the international markets in 1995.

If it is clear that it would be harmful for the financial system to over-regulate financial innovation, hampering new financial products from becoming more or less widely used financial assets or impeding banks from reducing their cost structure might be even worse. By this means, the flow of funds from savings to investment might be more limited or more costly and financial and non-financial companies' ability to compete might be impaired.

However, the need for regulation cannot hide one reality: a financial authority's ability to control the behaviour of banks is limited. It may stipulate certain behaviours, or a certain equity level, or set limits to some operations. However, this body of measures—or other measures—does not rule out two possible extreme results. The first is the existence of banks which act with a lack of professionalism or prudence, even in a regulated financial system. The recent cases of Crédit Lyonnais and Banesto are examples.

The second extreme is that the regulatory system may impose excessively

[4] This example is taken from Merton (1992).

difficult and unnecessary conditions that prevent the entry of certain financial organizations into new businesses. In such a situation, financial organizations may take on excessive risks in the businesses in which they can operate. The Latin American external debt crisis and its impact on US banking and the Savings and Loans crisis in the United States are good examples of this second situation.

This observation naturally leads us to a third comment on the regulatory system. In general, the banking system's regulatory system has adopted an institutional outlook in the United States and Europe. In other words, the regulatory measures have sought to establish clearly what the various financial institutions can do in their activities and, primarily, the limits they can reach.

However, on the basis of the perspective we discussed in Chapter 1, this approach to regulation—typical of an institutional interpretation of the financial system—may perhaps be the best. This is because a better understanding of the transformation of the financial system of industrialized countries comes from a functional view of this system. In other words, the idea is to see the activities or functions that the various financial intermediaries perform—or could perform—rather than confining oneself to observing what types of financial intermediary exist.

Consequently, it seems logical that the regulation of the financial system should also adopt this functional outlook, which would make it much more flexible in its reactions to major changes in the industry or virtually continual financial innovations. At the same time, this functional view would probably contribute a much greater realism to the possibilities of adequately regulating the activities of the various financial intermediaries and would not confine itself to merely establishing restrictions about what can or cannot be done.

Thus, it would not be necessary for financial intermediaries to look for loopholes which, in addition to having an undeniable cost, can sometimes affect the financial organization's solvency. The example of the high country risk taken on by the American banks during the Latin American external debt crisis of the 1980s is a clear example.

3. A STRUCTURE FOR THE REGULATION OF THE BANKING INDUSTRY

In the following pages we will refer to the regulation of the banking activity, without extending our considerations to include activities carried out by other financial institutions such as insurance companies, stock market firms, or special finance companies. The approach to these organizations' regulation is different from that of the banks and outside the scope of this book.

As we have already seen, any model of regulation of the banking activity seeks ultimately to achieve three goals. First, ensure a country's financial

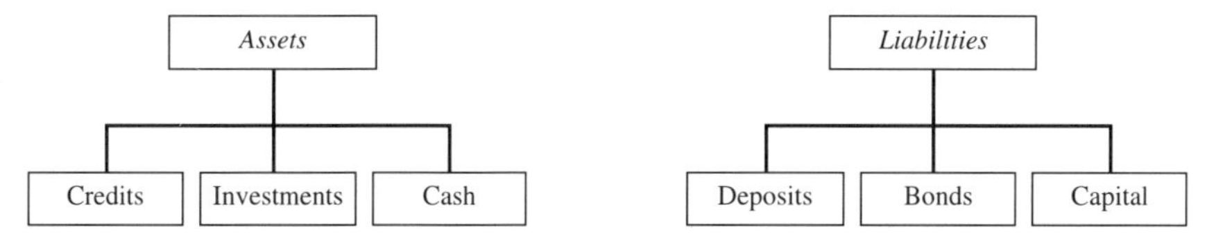

FIG. 11.1 *Risk in a bank*

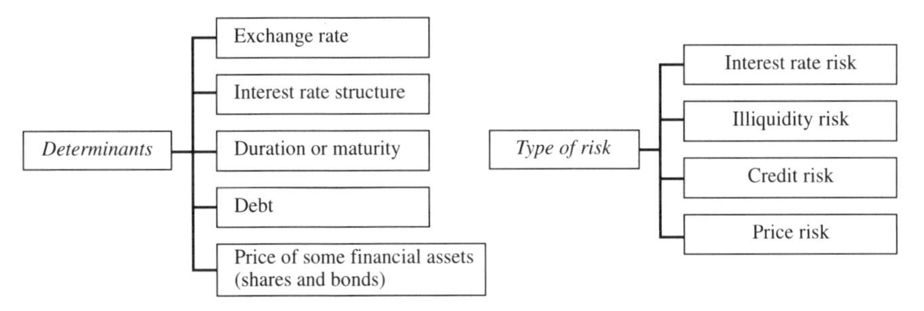

FIG. 11.2 *Determinants of bank risk*

stability—a stability which is dependent to a considerable extent on the confidence in the banking system. Second, ensure banks' solvency and profitability as a necessary measure for guaranteeing financial stability. This second goal is sometimes known as the prevention of systemic risk, that is, the risk of the failure of one bank having a negative effect on the rest of the financial organizations, which could damage the financial system as a whole, as well as non-financial companies. Third, protect the banks' depositors and investors from the losses deriving from malpractices in the activities performed by a bank or by excessive risk-taking (see Figure 11.1).

There is a final goal which is not directly related to regulation but to the promotion of competition in the different segments of the financial markets. We are referring to the policies designed to favour competition, preventing the formation of oligopolies *de facto* or the implementation of oligopolistic practices in the banking industry and promoting maximum efficiency in the allocation of financial resources.

The various types of regulatory measures can be classified in accordance with different criteria. A first criterion, widely used in industrial organization theory, distinguishes between regulatory measures affecting the behaviour of companies in a particular industry and regulatory measures affecting this industry's structure.[5] (See Figure 11.2.)

In the banking industry, regulatory measures affecting banks' behaviour are those which affect the interest rates and commissions charged for different financial operations, the free opening of bank branches, possible lending restrictions,

[5] See, for example, Gual and Neven (1993) and Vives (1991).

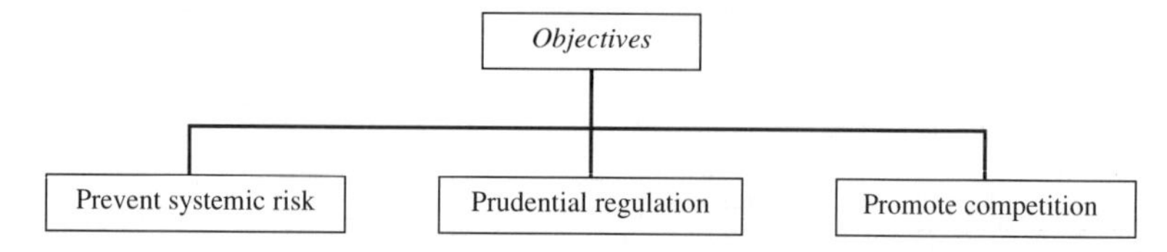

FIG. 11.3 *The regulation of the banking industry: objectives*

and the creation of special credit lines for certain sectors or agents of the economy.

The measures aimed at shaping the banking industry's structure are mainly of two types: those that force a certain separation of activities between banks (for example, between commercial banks, savings banks, and investment banks) and those that limit entry into the bank industry, in particular those that limit the entry of foreign investors.

A second classification of regulatory measures (see Figure 11.3) has three criteria.[6] First is the prevention of systemic risk in the banking system. Within this criterion, we would include measures aimed at configuring the industry's structure and those aimed at regulating banks' behaviour or activities.

Second are prudential supervisory measures that may be aimed both at preventing contagion risks in the bank system and at controlling the risks taken on by a bank organization or protecting the interests of the bank's depositors.

The third criterion is that relating to the promotion of competition within the banking industry. This criterion has, in turn, two parts: preventing the formation of oligopolies in certain segments of the banking business; and preventing a possibly excessive concentration of organizations within the bank industry. We will briefly discuss these criteria in the sections that follow.

3.1. The prevention of systemic risk

The threat of systemic risk has historically worried financial authorities, because a bank crisis can end up becoming a financial crisis that affects the entire country and not just the bank or the financial sector.

According to the regulators of the time, the American banking crisis of the 1930s was caused by two factors:[7] the high risk taken by some banks in the stock market and excessive rivalry in financial intermediation activities.

These reasons led to two types of regulatory measure. The first was a

[6] In a recent study (OECD, 1992), the OECD experts consider four archetypes of bank regulation: regulation of free competition on the financial markets, prudential regulation, regulation aimed at preventing risks to depositors, or investors, and, finally, regulation to promote competition. The main difference from the structure presented here is that the regulation aimed at protecting depositors' risk in our framework is implicitly included in prudential regulation.

[7] We have already said in Chapter 3 that these reasons are partial and insufficient to account for the 1930s bank crisis.

measure that has affected the banking industry structure in the United States even to our own days: the separation between commercial banking and investment banking activities.

The second type of regulation was a rule that started to be relaxed in the late 1970s in the United States and, slowly, during the 1980s in Western Europe: the control of the prices of financial services, both of interest rates and of commissions.

In the 1980s and early 1990s, two developments have been observed with respect to these regulatory measures, particularly in the member countries of the EU. First has been the progressive lifting of controls on the interest rates charged by bank organizations. The reason for this is very simple. In a globalized financial system undergoing an intense disintermediation process, banks would steadily lose their business base if they could not offer interest rates competitive with those of foreign organizations or other domestic financial competitors, such as, for example, public debt.

In addition to lifting controls on interest rates, the authorities have sought to promote competition and, therefore, have increased efficiency in the banking system. This lifting of controls has been associated with certain costs. In countries such as Germany or Spain, where price wars have been very intense, the liberalization of interest rates has led to a fall in the banks' financial margins and, in some cases, to a deterioration of their solvency. Banesto is a good example of the deterioration of bank solvency caused by an indiscriminate and reckless policy of offering high interest rates to attract deposits and excessively low interest rates to boost loan operations.

The second development is a reconsideration of the separation of bank intermediation activities from other activities associated with the provision of financial services, which has brought forth two responses. First is that of the EU which, through the Second Banking Directive, approved in 1989 by the European Commission, confirmed the validity of the universal banking model, with a number of caveats regarding the organization of stock trading activities or bank holdings in the equity of non-bank companies.

In Europe, the situation is slightly different. Within the general framework imposed by the EU, with a limit on investments in non-financial companies of 10 per cent of the bank's net worth and 40 per cent of a company's resources, some member countries have regulations of their own that relax or strengthen the EC's own regulations. Thus, for example, in France, banks can hold up to 15 per cent of non-financial companies' equity. The total holdings in non-financial companies by banks cannot exceed 60 per cent of the bank's capital.

In Belgium, banks can hold shares in non-financial companies up to a maximum equivalent to 5 per cent of the non-financial companies' voting rights, with a maximum of 5 per cent of the bank's assets concentrated in a single company and 35 per cent of a bank's total net assets for all investments by the bank in non-financial companies.

In Germany, the maximum limit for a bank's investment in other companies, financial or non-financial, is the value of the bank's own share capital. In principle, banks can invest without conditions in the shares of other companies. Non-financial companies have a prudential limit of 10 per cent of the equity of the target company. However, if the bank exceeds this percentage, the risk is calculated using the previous criterion. A second limitation is that the maximum allowable concentration of risk in a single customer is 50 per cent of the bank's share capital.

In Spain, the regulation is very liberal, within the framework of the EU regulation, due to the historical involvement of certain banks in the financing of industrial companies. There is an indirect restriction which is that the bank's solvency coefficient, for the purposes of the capital required, allocates a higher weighting to risks associated with non-financial companies.

Finally, at the other extreme, there is Italy. Banks are authorized to hold investments in other financial companies, up to 10 per cent of the bank's net worth and a maximum of 2 per cent of the share capital of the target company. However, bank holdings in industrial companies are totally forbidden by the Italian financial authorities, except when the bank's capital markets division leads a share issue of a non-financial company. In such a case, the bank can hold shares in the company, although only on a temporary basis.

The second response has come from the other side of the Atlantic. In the United States, since the early 1980s, bank officials, regulators, and academics have been arguing about the advantages and disadvantages of abolishing the separation of activities imposed by the 1933 Glass–Steagall Act and advancing towards a universal banking model in which commercial banks can offer all types of financial services, including long-term financing to non-financial companies, and allowing non-financial companies to own bank organizations.

This debate has been and continues to be very lively. The positions are diametrically opposed and range from those who think that this separation of activities has been beneficial for the American financial system as a whole (such as Corrigan, 1987), to those who advocate the opposite (Bryan, 1991; Saunders and Walter, 1994), with various stances in between.

In 1990, Nicholas Brady, at that time Secretary of State for the Treasury, presented a proposal to the US Congress that included a relative liberalization of commercial banking activities—mainly, the possibility of banks in one state expanding their activities to other states—and the possibility of non-financial companies (for example, General Electric) buying or owning commercial banks.

Logically, these liberalizing measures would have had two types of impact: a positive impact on rivalry and competition between different financial companies, both bank and non-bank; and, as a result of that, a negative impact in companies that could experience a fall in revenues or operating margin, from the increased competition.

The powerful lobbies organized around the US Congress and Senate blocked that legislative initiative, although the debate continues. However, the tone of the debate lost some of its strength, even though new proposals along the same lines were presented in spring 1995. The reason is that many commercial banks have found procedures for penetrating emerging financial businesses.

However, the possibility of taking a more active part in the financing of industrial or services companies or acquiring equity holdings is currently considered as being of secondary interest to the commercial banks, particularly after the recent financial crisis.

There remains the question of whether it would be good for a country to lift the restrictions on the entry of commercial banks into these activities. The debate on whether the typically American model of financial markets is better than the universal banking model, such as the German model, remains open, with both models having their advocates and detractors.[8]

Within the regulation on the separation of activities, the combination of commercial banking activities and insurance has raised considerable interest in recent years, particularly in Europe. There are two reasons for this. First, commercial banks can use their distribution network to sell all types of insurance, particularly life insurance, to their traditional customers. On the other hand, insurance companies have become significant competitors of commercial banks, offering financial products for placing savings that private customers find particularly appealing, such as retirement funds or single-premium insurance policies.

For this reason, banks and insurance companies have shown a mutual interest in exploring possibilities for co-operation. The regulation of these co-operative activities in Europe is minimal. A bank can have an insurance company as a subsidiary or an insurance company can be a shareholder of a bank. Finally, there are no major restrictions preventing banks from distributing insurance through their network of branches. In fact, there are 12 countries within the OECD where such operations can be carried out without the need for any type of prior approval from the regulatory authorities of that country (OECD, 1992).

This rather liberal legislation has led to two types of action. First, banks which had insurance companies have promoted them and have initiated the distribution of insurance products through their branch network. Second, banks without insurance businesses have swapped equity with insurance companies (as with Allianz and Banco Popular) or have simply come to agreements to distribute an insurance company's products through their branch network.

The regulation of the activities of organizations that combine banking and insurance raises the serious problem of the dual regulation to which they are subject. Thus, in Spain, regulation and supervision of the banks is the responsibility of the Bank of Spain, while that of the insurance companies is the responsibility of the General Directorate of Insurance. This situation raises a similar problem to that of the banks that have subsidiaries specializing in stock market trading. The banking activity is supervised by the Bank of Spain, while that of the securities firm is supervised by the National Stock Market Commission.

[8] See Chapter 2 for a discussion of the advantages and disadvantages of each financial model.

Both cases raise the need for co-ordination in the supervision of all the financial risks assumed directly or indirectly by a bank. Again, the situation created by the Banesto crisis in December 1993, which involved the Bank of Spain, the National Stock Market Commission, and the General Directorate of Insurance, graphically illustrates the need for co-ordination in the general supervision of the risk taken on by a bank that engages in activities that go beyond mere bank intermediation.

The last type of regulatory measure that affects the free behaviour of financial firms is that of the freedom of establishment and includes both the creation of a new bank in a country by domestic or foreign shareholders (normally a foreign bank) and the purchase of a national bank by a foreign investor (normally a foreign bank).

The legislation on the matter existing both in the USA and in the EU (in the latter case, particularly, after the Second Banking Directive of 1989) is very liberal. Restrictions are minimal, both on the creation of new banks and on the purchase of a national bank by a foreign investor, except for the normal precautions of supervision and guaranteeing a minimum capital for the project to be feasible. In this sense, the entry barriers that the bank industry would have faced in the early 1980s, particularly in the EU countries, have lowered dramatically.

3.2. Prudential regulation

Prudential regulation has a number of aspects. First, there is the establishment of suitable mechanisms for supervising and inspecting bank activities. These mechanisms are intended to review systematically bank's solvency and the evolution of the risk taken on.

Second is the supervision of the risk from the so-called off-balance-sheet operations: these are operations in financial derivatives, mainly futures and options on financial assets (primarily public debt and currencies).

The first type of mechanism functions more or less acceptably in most industrialized countries, whose central banks have created and developed supervisors with the necessary professional expertise and independence to perform their tasks.

However, the financial crises in the United States, with dozens of savings banks becoming bankrupt, or the recent bank crises in Europe, such as those of Banesto, Crédit Lyonnais, or that suffered recently by several German banks, have shown once again the difficulty of adequately supervising banks' risk and, in particular, universal banks' risk.

In fact, a universal bank poses enormous complexity not only for its managers, who have to give their attention to business units with different internal and competitive dynamics, but also for the regulators and the central banks' supervisors, who find themselves with more complex operations whose risk it is not always possible to determine or readily separate from other risks.

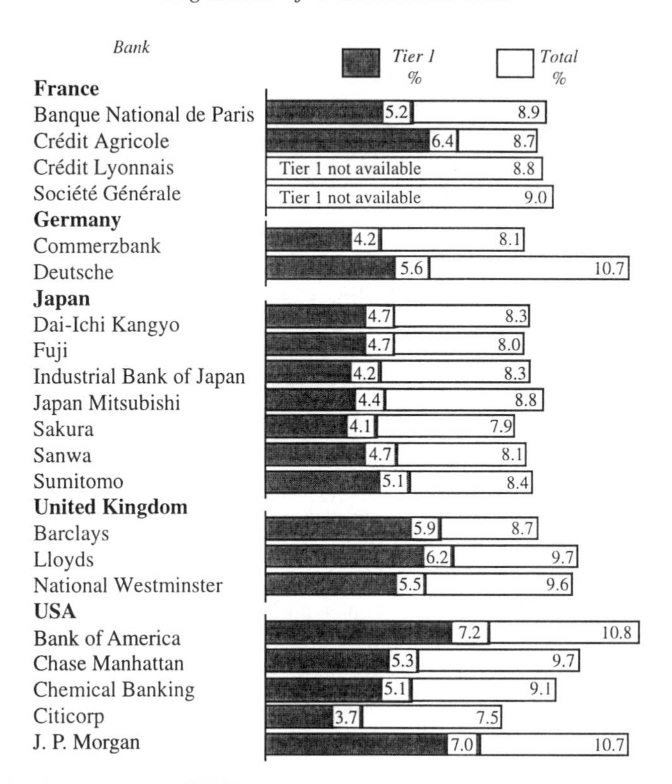

FIG. 11.4 *Capital ratios (1993)*

Hence, some authors have concluded that one of the most effective regulatory measures is a minimum capital requirement, as proposed by the Group of 10 in December 1987. Known as the BIS requirements, they were subsequently implemented by the EU. These rules distinguish between two types of capital. The first tier includes common shares, preference shares, and retained earnings; banks must have a ratio of at least 4 per cent of this tier over assets. The second tier includes fixed debt, subordinated debt, and hidden reserves. Banks must maintain a total ratio of at least 8 per cent. Figure 11.4 shows some banks' capital ratios at the end of 1993, distinguishing between tier 1 and tier 2.

In spite of the importance of this regulatory and supervisory instrument, the required capital ratio, there are two crucial issues that should not be overlooked. First, it is a ratio that is calculated on the basis of accounting information that may not adequately reflect the true situation. Second, it is a ratio that does not include the volume of investments in derivatives and other off-balance-sheet operations.

In fact, the major challenge facing prudential regulation over the next few years is to be found not in the supervision of universal banks but in the adequate monitoring and control of the volume and risk of universal or specialized banks' off-balance-sheet operations.

The growth in operations carried out by banks in financial derivatives in recent years has been enormous. The Annual Report of the BIS (1993) has estimated that the volume of these products generated by the banks grew 245 per cent between 1991 and 1993.

The advantages offered by these products are very significant. They can be used to modify the risk of fixed or variable-income securities (for example, their interest rate or exchange-rate risk) and, in general, to define the risk and price of the different components of a financial instrument. In particular, the intention is to separate the credit risk, the market risk, and the liquidity risk. It is important to stress that derivatives can be used to reduce an instrument's risk for an investor but they cannot reduce the systemic risk.

These products raise two problems for the central banks' inspection services. The first concerns the central bank's identification and knowledge of them. As these are off-balance-sheet operations, it is not easy to trace the various agents that could take part in them. There is, therefore, a very real possibility of opportunism by those acting on behalf of the banks, or of increased risk due to asymmetric information borne by the banks and the regulators, which cannot be ignored. The recent Barings scandal is a clear example.

Second, even if the supervisory services have all the necessary information, it is still not easy to assess these products' real risk. The assessment may be subject to different criteria; to a certain extent, the implicit risk that the inspection services determine will end up being dependent on these criteria.

It is therefore one of the most complex tasks that the industrialized countries' financial regulators have ever faced. The crisis of the European Monetary System in 1992 and 1993, caused in part by futures operations in currencies, the crisis in the debt market in summer 1994, also related to the operators' long or short positions in these markets, and the scandals that have affected Bankers Trust and Barings have helped draw attention to this problem.

In general, the proposals for supervision, made by some international financial agencies, such as the BIS, or opinion groups such as the Group of 30, are still modest. They include improving risk management and control by the banks, increasing the information disclosed, and a closer watch by the regulators on off-balance-sheeet activities.[9] On 5 December 1994, Bankers Trust, whose financial derivatives business has been growing steadily in recent years and which reported losses in 1994, reached an agreement with the New York Federal Reserve to inform more fully on these operations, which are particularly risky due to their high leverage. Basically, we are witnessing a revival in this context of the debate between regulation a priori and control a posteriori, typical of any type of regulatory measure applied to financial organizations.

The advocates of regulation a priori seek to place limitations that prevent the

[9] See Goldstein and Folkerts-Landau (1994).

excessive growth of risks in derivatives. The advocates of supervision a posteriori maintain that this will be ineffective and will lead to the appearance of new instruments, perhaps with greater risk and outside the control of the central banks. Now, the ball is with the financial institutions. There is one point on which there seems to be a certain amount of agreement: the separation of the exchange-rate risk from the risk of price changes due to fluctuations in the financial markets. The debate is open. It is more necessary than ever before to find a framework that provides clear rules of play for all parties (central banks and financial organizations). This framework should include not only more information for the regulatory authorities but also a better organization of the futures markets.

3.3. The promotion of efficiency in the banking system

The banking industry has been hounded by growing competition from other financial organizations and the capital markets. As a result, their volume of operations has stopped growing and, in some cases, the margin on these operations has decreased. Part of the blame for this deterioration of the banks' competitive position in the industrialized countries lies with the excessive regulation that shackled them until the end of the 1970s, limiting both their behaviour and the activities they could or could not perform.

On the other hand, the widespread belief in the existence of significant economies of scale or scope in banking activity has led to the question of whether some countries' banks are large enough to compete in a global financial system. The paradigm of this stance is that of the Spanish government since 1987, which has encouraged a process of bank concentration and, therefore, of mergers between banks and the purchase of one bank by another, in order to obtain a larger size.

For some, the policy of openly encouraging mergers has become a policy against competiton in the industry, in accordance with the tenets of Industrial Economics: rivalry in an industry is inversely proportional to the degree of concentration. However, in recent years, particularly after the formulation of the contestable markets concept and the evidence that a small number of rival companies is not synonymous with lack of rivalry, the advocates of bank mergers have found new life in their old arguments.

However, the policies promoting bank mergers must respect the regulation of mergers and acquisitions that promotes, rather than restricts, competition in an industry. In fact, the European regulation on mergers and take-overs and the Spanish regulation on the defence of competition are pointing in this direction (Ballarín, Canals, and Fernández, 1994).

At present, the risk is not so much whether there is promotion of competition in the banking industry, about which nobody in the industrialized countries, with a few exceptions, has any doubts. The root of the problem is how to implement a true promotion of competition without its leading to price wars and falls in bank returns that may cause a serious financial crisis. In the final analysis, this was one of the arguments of the 1930s crisis.

The solution to this dilemma is not to limit the banks' activities and way of competing—that would be like trying to put doors in a field—but for the central banks to be more effective in their supervisory activities. The dilemma between bank rivalry and solvency should not become a false dilemma between more rivalry or less rivalry but rather, rivalry with the necessary prudential supervision.

4. THE BANKING DEREGULATION PROCESS IN THE EUROPEAN UNION

The widespread phenomenon of financial deregulation in industrialized countries has been compounded in the EU with the creation of a single financial market.[10] This market requires two elements. The first is freedom to establish banks and in the provision of financial services in the EU countries. The second is the liberalization of capital flows between the EU countries. The Second Banking Directive is an attempt to respond to the first aspect, as we will see later; the second aspect is a response to the lifting of restrictions on capital flows, approved by the Council of Ministers of the EU in June 1988.

The road toward financial unification within the EU started in 1987, with the approval of the First Banking Directive, which applied to all credit institutions. This Directive established the minimum requirements for licensing and supervising credit institutions and was a first step towards what was called the principle of home country supervision.

This Directive required that member countries have a system for licensing new banks based on two main criteria: a minimum capital volume and an honest and experienced management team. The Directive also formulated the principles for future harmonization of the banks' liquidity and solvency ratios.

In practice, many EU member countries already had more stringent regulations than the minimum principles required by the First Directive. The result, therefore, is that there still persist major differences between the different member countries. Consequently, although EU banks have a basic right to establish themselves in another EU country, in practice the disparity of national regulations makes this enormously difficult.

In 1985, the European Commission adopted a new criterion for tackling the single financial market: the principle of mutual recognition, by which it was no longer necessary to harmonize the various national legislations. This principle was completed with the principle of home country control mentioned above.

[10] The work of Besanko and Thakor (1992) is interesting on this phenomenon. These authors attempt to measure the consequences of the deregulation process in the United States. Their results are clear: the well-being of depositors and borrowers increases at the expense of that of the shareholders.

This means that monitoring a bank's activity after its acceptance in a particular country should be the responsibility of that country's competent authority.

This principle is contained in the draft Second Directive, which was approved by the Council of Ministers in June 1989, by means of the so-called single banking licence issued by the home country's authority. This enables any bank to establish itself or to offer a wide range of financial services in another EC country on the sole basis of the initial licence. This is a very important step because it enables progress to be continued towards European financial integration without the need to increase the body of regulations.

This Directive seeks to harmonize classic accounting and bank regulation rules for the whole EC. It also lists a wide range of financial services whose supply is liberalized in all the EC countries, provided that they are authorized by the home country authorities. This text therefore reflects the move toward a universal banking system.

Furthermore, the Second Directive reserves the competence for supervising the banks' solvency and liquidity to the home country, while transferring to the host country regulation of the implementation of monetary policy and other practical rules of functioning. This is what is meant by the expression 'home country control and host country rules'.

The Second Directive also seeks to set guidelines in two specific areas related to the creation of banks. The first refers to the establishment of a minimum volume of capital, which is set at five million European Currency Units (ECU) for each bank; the branches of a bank that are opened in another country will not have to comply with this requirement. The EU has left to the BIS the matter of the ratio between total investment and equity. Compliance with the very demanding new regulation approved by the BIS may cause difficulties to certain Italian and French banks with a weak capital base.

The second area refers to the application of the principle of reciprocity to countries outside the EU. In accordance with a basic provision of the bank licence, a bank from a non-EU country may establish a subsidiary in an EU country and, from it, open branches in other countries. However, some of these countries could object, arguing that the bank's home country does not give the same treatment to its banks. In such cases, before a bank from a non-EU country establishes itself in a member country, the Commission will study whether the home country gives reciprocal treatment to each and every one of the member countries before granting the licence.

Another interesting aspect related to banks from non-EU countries is the discrimination that the legislation establishes between subsidiary organizations and branches of a foreign bank. Subsidiary organizations must satisfy the requirements of the EU country where they establish themselves but, from there, they can expand their activities to other EU countries as if they really were EU banks. On the other hand, branches of non-EU banks not having a separate legal form will be subject to the rules of each country. Among other things, this implies that each of the branches in different countries will have to comply with the minimum capital requirements, which will increase these banks' capital cost compared with that of banks operating through a subsidiary.

One final important aspect of the Second Directive is the limitation of risks. In accordance with this, banks may not own interests in industrial and commercial sectors in excess of 10 per cent of equity capital. Furthermore, banks may not lend more than 40 per cent of their equity capital to a single company or group of companies. This is a limitation that has not been particularly welcomed in universal banking countries such as Germany, where banks have close relationships with companies (and large holdings).

This move promoted by the Second Banking Directive has been accompanied by a complementary movement with respect to the liberalization of capital movements. This will no doubt have important consequences for the provision of financial services in Europe. This package of deregulation measures has led to increased rivalry in the different financial markets, a fall in the banks' financial margin, costs, and profitability, and a marked increase in the industry's concentration.

5. A SPECIAL CASE OF REGULATION: INDUSTRIAL GROUPS AND FINANCIAL CONGLOMERATES

In the previous sections, we have introduced the problems posed by the modern configuration of financial institutions and activities to financial authorities when regulating the behaviour of such organizations. One of the cases offering greatest complexity is that of financial groups and, within those, the bank-industry groups. We will explore this issue in this section.

In order to place it in the right historical context, we should remember that the two main models of organization of financial activity, the banks-based model and the financial markets-based model, came into being as a consequence of a series of social, political, and economic factors. In Germany, the main factors were tradition and the shape of the industrial revolution of the nineteenth century, when banks participated directly in financing large industrial corporations to reduce the country's supposed economic backwardness. In the United States, it was the Glass–Steagall Act that limited bank holdings in the capital of companies by prohibiting traditional commercial banks from taking part in share or other security transactions.

Therefore, it is important to take into account their historical origins when assessing the regulatory systems currently in force. Neither should we forget that the present re-examination of the regulatory system in the United States is the result of the financial disintermediation process that the banks have suffered themselves, to the benefit of the stock market and the agents that trade on it.

The supervision of bank-industry groups, both in the United States and in other countries where an attempt has been made to limit the absolute freedom of action, as in the EU, shows some regulatory policies' basic co-ordinates. First, a desire to ensure the banks' solvency and the security of the financial system as a whole. Generally speaking, an excessive concentration of risk in certain industrial companies—in the form of loans or equity holdings—or an excessive investment in securities could be the cause of serious problems in the future.

In fact, this suspicion seems to be confirmed by some recent cases in the EU. Consequently, in our opinion, the main issue is not whether this type of relationship between banks and non-financial companies can be acceptable but the volume and quality of the total risk borne by a bank with a particular company.

Furthermore, it is absolutely necessary to limit the risk in those countries which have a deposit insurance system that guarantees depositors a large part of their funds if the financial institution should go bankrupt. The idea underlying this reasoning is that a depositor must know the risk a bank takes on when it invests, or ceases to invest, in a group of non-financial companies.

Another consideration that the regulators have taken into account is the possible concentration of power in the hands of a bank-industrial companies group. Generally, this consideration could have been significant in the past, when the degree of rivalry in the bank industry or in some industrial sectors in Western Europe was limited.

The present situation of cut-throat competition in so many industries, including the banking industry, leads one to think that the risk of excessive accumulation of power or a possible monopolistic power on the part of the corresponding financial institutions is more limited. As we have pointed out in a previous section, viewed from the static efficiency in allocating resources, the degree of concentration of an industry may be an important indicator. In a context of dynamic efficiency and economies open to foreign competition, as is the case of European economies, this consideration becomes much less important.

That this is so is confirmed by the fact that governments themselves in several countries—precisely those authorities entrusted with defending competition—have not hesitated to support—with actions of dubious efficacy—merger or take-over processes aimed at increasing company size, believing that size is critical in order to be able to compete in the sector.

Therefore, with regard to the criteria of concentration of power or the existence of market power, the only conclusion we can draw is that regulation should not prevent the formation of strong financial groups—but without directly forcing the government to create them, as the likelihood of failure is not insignificant—provided that the degree of rivalry in the industry is not seriously damaged by such concentration.

Another criterion historically used by the financial sector's regulators is the issue—which has already been discussed in previous pages—of the possible conflict of interests between, for example, the stock market department and the corporate finance department of a universal bank. Regulating this potential conflict of interests is not an easy task because, basically, the problem is that of the free flow of information between a company's different departments.

In the following paragraphs, we will discuss a number of procedures that may help a financial firm to observe practices that avoid this. However, a financial group of this type not only introduces an appreciable degree of complexity into its management but also requires from its managers and employees a very high standard of honesty in their behaviour, as the opportunities for benefiting personally from insider information are enormous.

Generally speaking, financial authorities have two options for solving conflicts of interest in financial groups. First, prevent them by prohibiting the formation of these groups. This is the solution used in the United States. Second, control them through different regulatory measures aimed at limiting the possibilities for opportunistic behaviour as a result of knowing certain information. This is the case in Britain, where there are measures regulating the behaviour of commercial banks which have subsidiaries specializing in investment banking or securities trading.

This separation has been described as the 'Chinese wall' (for example, McVea, 1993). The purpose of this separation is to prevent or reduce the flow of information from one department to another in a financial organization and thus eliminate as far as possible any conflict of interest. In general, the attempts to build walls that restrict information flow are aimed at creating airtight compartments within financial groups. Obviously, these procedures never prevent the risk of informal transmission of this information, which is why we have stressed above the importance of a financial group's employees, like those of any other organization, being absolutely honest and upright in their behaviour.

The purpose of the creation of airtight compartments within financial groups is not only to control information flows between departments but also to create a reputation among customers that the information held by a particular division of a financial group is not obtained by other divisions in the same group. This reputation is very important for attracting customers. In this sense, the financial group itself—and not only the customer or society in general—will be interested in protecting the information that a department has and preventing it from flowing to other departments.

The creation of information-retaining walls may have a number of different facets. Generally speaking, there are a number of critical elements. The first is the identification of the departments where there exists a potential danger of information leaks. The aim is to establish prudential policies and criteria affecting (in the main) these departments' reporting practices, without having to subject all of the financial group's departments to a level of control that may prove to be confusing and, sometimes, unnecessary.

Second, there needs to be a series of criteria and procedures, drawn up on a very restrictive basis, on the type of information that can circulate between departments. These criteria are usually compiled in a reference manual with which the financial group's employees—or those of corresponding divisions—

should be familiar. These criteria or policies include access to computer files, reproduction of a department's reports or documents, or transfer of personnel from one department to another within the same group. Finally, it is important that these manuals specify who is formally responsible—in addition to the actual perpetrator of the transgression—in the event that the established criteria and policies are contravened. In this way, it is possible to claim legal and economic liability and the personnel made responsible for ensuring compliance with these rules will have a very clear incentive to be diligent.

The third element of a system of this type is the creation of a periodic supervision procedure that makes sure that the criteria are respected. This supervision can be carried out randomly and without prior notification to the departments concerned. In general, the existence of periodic supervision provides a significant incentive to ensure observance in practice of these prudential criteria.

Among the elements that an information-retaining procedure should include are periodic training courses for employees, questionnaires to be sent to customers so that they can indicate whether they have detected information-flow problems, steps to be taken if an undesired information flow is detected, and close co-ordination between the internal procedures and the monetary authority's inspection and supervision mechanisms.

However, no matter how sophisticated the system for preventing information flows is, one should be conservative about the possibilities of limiting the scope of this conflict of interests. No matter how perfect it is, no preventive system can ever limit informal contacts between employees. Therefore, the only guarantee for preventing abuses in the long term is promoting strictly ethical behaviour at all levels.

6. SOME CONCLUSIONS

In this chapter, we have discussed the challenges that financial innovation and the modern configuration of financial firms pose to financial authorities.

In general, commercial banks' need to enter new activities, due to the declining importance of traditional financial intermediation, has triggered a review of the ways of regulating the banks' activities. This review has affected—and still does affect—the separation between classic financial intermediation activity and other activities, mainly stock trading and bank holdings in other financial companies (for example, insurance) and non-financial companies (other industrial or services companies).

Among the major dilemmas raised by the new competitive situation in the financial sector, we have discussed the following. First is the dilemma between market efficiency and low industry concentration, on the one hand, and efficiency obtained from the economies of scale and scope achieved with larger organizations and a higher degree of concentration in the industry, on the other hand.

The second dilemma is that between price deregulation aimed at promoting a higher degree of rivalry between financial organizations and, therefore, a greater efficiency in resource allocation, and 're-regulation' aimed at preventing excessive competition in the industry that might endanger financial organizations' profitability and solvency and plunge the entire financial system into a crisis.

Third, there is the dilemma between the free formation of financial groups, including shareholdings in non-financial companies, in order to ensure stable, long-term financing of industrial companies, and the excessive concentration of risk in certain companies, the failure of which, should it occur, will have harmful effects on the bank's solvency.

Another dilemma that emerges with regard to financial groups is that of allowing the formation of groups with different divisions and possible conflicts of interest and then preventing the flow of confidential information between different divisions in a group that could be damaging to customers or third parties.

A final, more general dilemma is whether it is desirable to promote regulation and control a priori, limiting the banks' activities to a greater or lesser degree, or promote the ongoing supervision of financial organizations, in order to prevent the freedom of action leading to excessive risk-taking. This balance between regulation and freedom is always very delicate. However, it is the classic dilemma of public policies in the financial sector, a dilemma that financial innovation, globalization of the industry, and the new information technologies have only made more acute.

12

The Future of Banking: Some Final Ideas

1. INTRODUCTION

The analysis of the future of banking presented in this book has covered three different areas. First, we have examined the behaviour and performance of the banking industry in industrialized countries during the last few years. In this study, we have considered closely the impact that the deregulation process, the globalization of financial markets, disintermediation, the emergence of new competitors, and the development of information technology applications in banking have had on banks' strategies and performance. In this sense, both new competitors and capital markets offer financial services which, in the past, were offered only by banks. Therefore, the banking industry has gone from a situation of limited competition to one of increased rivalry.

The second area of analysis has been that of the financial model chosen explicitly or implicitly by each country. This model conditions the banks' strategy, the structure of the financial sector, and the financial structure of industrial firms. The existence of different models in different countries generates a series of forms of corporate government and behaviour patterns on the part of banks that must be considered in order to understand fully the transformation of the banking industry.

The third area of analysis has consisted of discussing the banks' strategic reactions to the changes discussed above, taking as our starting point each country's financial model. In particular, this book has sought to analyse banks' reaction to the financial disintermediation process, which has taken the form of four types of decision: transformation into a universal bank, diversification into non-bank and non-financial activities, internationalization of operations, and, finally, the adoption of new organization forms that enable them to respond to the rapid changes taking place in the market. We have also discussed the development of the banking system and its relationships with industrial firms in three countries: Germany, Spain, and Japan. Although the generalized universal banking model seems to dominate in these countries, each of these countries' financial system has certain unique features.

Banks have responded to this challenge in a number of different ways. Some have chosen to concentrate on the traditional banking business. Other banks have decisively opted to obtain control of part of the transactions taking place on the capital markets, avoiding the risk of substitution. One could even say that a bank that does not take an active role in the capital markets is severely limiting its options. Finally, some banks are following financial markets in their globalization process, seeking to internationalize their activities either using their own resources or in alliance with other banks. Whatever may happen to the banks that follow these strategies, one thing is sure: nothing is the same as it was in the banking industry.

The book's most important conclusions have been presented as the various chapters have developed. However, in this final chapter, we would like to underline some of these ideas, which we will present following the levels of analysis we have just described.

2. THE TRANSFORMATION OF BANKING AND THE THEORY OF FINANCIAL INTERMEDIATION

The starting point for this study has been the decreased profitability experienced by banks in industrialized countries in recent years and their loss of market share to other intermediaries or financial markets. Behind this fall in profitability lies not only the economic recession of the early 1990s but also a basic change in the nature of the banking business and an increase in rivalry.

The decline in the banks' results has led many managers and industry analysts to wonder about the banks' future. In the United States, some authors have dared to ask whether banking is dead. Behind this question is the concern that banks may have lost some of their differential skills *vis-à-vis* other companies or financial markets. This question cannot be adequately answered from the institutions' viewpoint (banks, investment companies, consumer finance institutions, financial markets, or capital markets, for example) but from the functional viewpoint.

The main function of a financial intermediary is to transform one financial asset into another. In general, this function is carried out by the different financial intermediaries that exist in an economy.

The functional viewpoint asks what are or should be the functions that a society expects from the financial system and financial intermediaries. Institutions may react more or less quickly to the change, or they may oppose it, while the functions of the financial intermediaries are basically similar, even though they can be carried out in more efficient ways. Indeed, the improvements that can be expected from a financial system are related to the efficiency with which financial intermediaries perform the functions that are expected of them.

As we have discussed in other chapters, the main functions that should be carried out by an efficient financial system are the following. First, the financial system must instrument and guarantee the adequate functioning of a system of payments. Second, a financial system must facilitate the allocation and efficient transfer of resources over time. Third, a financial system must offer guarantees that reduce the uncertainty about the real value of money and the different financial instruments and provide the investor with a reasonable and adequate control of risk. Fourth, the financial system must enable the issue of financial securities—debt or equity—that allow investment projects of non-financial companies to be financed. Finally, the financial system must provide information on the price of financial assets to the interested public.

The increasing competition in the banking industry is forcing banks to specialize in certain segments of the business. The functions performed by the new competitors and capital markets are similar to those performed previously by banks. What has changed is that some companies have been able to adapt more quickly and are more efficient than others in this dynamic game of innovation.

The financial innovation process is the response to this change in competitive conditions that banks are facing. The consequence is a re-examination not only of the banks' functions but also of which financial institutions can carry out these functions in the most efficient manner. The major challenge facing the banks is the need to become effective, competitive organizations with respect to other intermediaries and capital markets, and to enter the territories of both.

3. BANKS' STRATEGIC OPTIONS AND THE FINANCIAL MODELS

One of the conclusions we wish to stress is that the strategic options banks have open to them vary depending on their resources and their home country. Indeed, even within the EU, we can detect the existence of different opportunities and challenges, depending on the country being considered.

The reason for this variety of strategic options is related not only to each bank's starting position, resources, skills, and weaknesses, but also to the financial model within which it operates. By financial model, we mean the unique configuration adopted by the financial system in a certain country and, in particular, the relative weight that banks and capital markets have in it. At one extreme, we find countries with a financial model in which bank financing is predominant. At the other extreme, there are a few countries (with an alternative model) whose capital markets have a greater specific weight in financial activity.

Of the generic types of financial model, that based on financial markets shows little variation and is concentrated mainly in the United States and, to a lesser extent, in Great Britain. The model based on financial intermediaries (or the bank-based model) is much more varied.

Financial theory maintained, until a few years ago, that investment and financing decisions have no bearing on a company's market value. Implicitly, this was equivalent to attributing a superiority to capital markets over bank financing. However, the empirical evidence available and a number of additional developments indicate that this superiority is doubtful, among other reasons, because of the transaction costs entailed by the market.

These doubts about the efficiency of financial intermediation raise again the question of what is the best way of organizing an economy's financial system, both from the viewpoint of financial intermediaries and from the viewpoint of companies and society as a whole, to improve resource allocation in the long term.

In Chapter 2, we discussed in somewhat greater depth the different models of organization of the financial system. In contrast to the model organized around the capital markets, in the model organized around banks, financial markets have a more modest role in financing real investment projects.

However, these two models, with deep roots in different countries, are not static but are undergoing a process of change. This process tends to bring the two models closer together, rather than to differentiate or separate them.

Thus, on one hand, in countries such as Japan and Germany, where banks play a crucial role, capital markets are becoming increasingly important. This is due, in part, to the growing volume of bank activity on capital markets. On the other hand, in the United States, a paradigm of the financial market-based model, there is a growing pressure for banks to take on a greater role in corporate financing. Many factors are changing in the international financial system. And these changes seem to point towards an eclectic model in which both the banks and financial markets play an important role in corporate financing. In this model, the critical aspect will no longer be the financial intermediaries' legal status but the functions they perform, irrespective of their legal status.

In order to understand better the origin of this separation between banks and companies in the United States, in Chapter 3 we briefly reviewed the main arguments used in the United States—the country which enshrined in 1933 the separation between commercial banks and capital markets—regarding the desirability of disposing of the universal banking model and separating commercial banking from investment banking and the stock market.

The ultimate reason for this separation, confirmed by the 1933 Glass–Steagall Act, was the supposed relationship between financial trading carried out by some commercial banks and the deep banking crisis which brought about the disappearance of about 11,000 banks in the first years of the decade. This Act ratified a banking model in the United States that was separate from corporate financing and capital markets.

However, the arguments used against universal banks in the United States, constructed from partial data, are not unequivocal. In fact, banks that combined commercial banking with investment banking were, generally speaking, less sensitive to the banking crisis than the banks that confined their activities to pure commercial banking. Therefore, from the viewpoint of profitability or the number of banks that failed, the arguments are not in favour of the separation of activities.

One plausible historical interpretation of the genesis of this Act considers two factors. The first is the uncontested hypothesis that related bank failures to the involvement of some banks in stock market activities.

The second is the particular features of the lobbies in any democratic country and, particularly, in the United States. Using the argument we have just mentioned, investment banks tried to limit competition in their area of business, excluding commercial banks from it. Therefore, the ultimate reason for the separation was not technical—although technical arguments were used—but political, to defend private interests. In the final analysis, it is only possible to understand the aversion to the universal banking system in the United States by taking into account this specific historical context.

However, the possible return of the American banking system to the universal banking model can be viewed without panic, from the point of view both of society and of the financial system. The combination of different activities within the same bank organization does not necessarily imply a greater risk or conflicts of interest. The precautions to be taken, such as limiting deposit insurance to traditional commercial banking operations, seem to be completely reasonable.

In order to understand the different features of the universal banking model, we have studied three, apparently very similar countries: Germany, Japan, and Spain. Basically, they have similar features: banks play a very important role in the financial system, they usually adopt the form of universal banks, and, finally, they seem to play an important role in financing companies.

However, on the basis of the detailed analysis of these models, we have been able to conclude that there is not a single universal bank model and the role played by these banks in corporate financing is less important than it seems, particularly in Germany. The study of this country's financial model has been useful for improving our understanding of the consequences of the relationship between banks and non-financial companies.

By way of synthesis, the main conclusions reached concerning the German model are the following. First, bank presence on companies' supervisory boards is basically limited to the three largest German banks (Deutsche Bank, Dresdner, and Commerzbank). These banks generally possess small holdings in the equity of the companies they invest in. Furthermore, these banks are not always the largest lenders to the companies concerned.

Second, generally speaking, German companies finance themselves by a much lower proportion of bank debt than Japanese or Spanish companies. They rely much more on generated cash flows.

Third, the evidence of recent decades shows that only on very rare occasions do German banks intervene in the restructuring of companies. Therefore, it can hardly be said that their role in these processes is critical.

Fourth, there is no direct relationship between the number of votes a bank has on a supervisory board and its influence in the company's decisions. The ultimate reason for this possible influence is that, in its capacity as major shareholder of the company, the bank is particularly interested in the company's progress, although the same could be said of other non-financial shareholders that hold sizeable holdings. Consequently, the supposed advantages of the banks' presence in German companies are mainly related to their status as controlling shareholders. However, this status can also be assumed or shared by other non-financial shareholders.

The presence of a controlling shareholder is defined as a distinctive feature of a good system of government. However, when the controlling shareholder is a bank, it incurs a greater risk due to the concentration of investment in a particular company. Should the company fall into difficulties, for reasons related, for example, to the industry in which it operates, the bank's solvency and profitability might be damaged.

There is no shortage of bank crises caused by disastrous industrial shareholdings. The 1992–3 recession in Europe has caused major bank crises such as those of Banesto and Crédit Lyonnais, and has affected, to some extent, large banks such as Deutsche Bank. These crises have cast doubt on—or raised suspicions about—the apparent superiority of the German model. The business and financial crisis suffered by Japan since 1990 also raises doubts about this particular model of relationships between banks and companies.

In Table 12.1, we have synthesized the main functions and features of the financial system in four countries: Germany, Japan, Spain (which we have studied in detail in this text) and, as a contrast, the United States. Basically, we are seeking to compare three possible variants of the bank-based financial model (universal banks) with the American financial market-based model.

The most important conclusions we can draw from Table 12.1 is that it is dangerous to generalize about financial models. By way of example, the German model resembles the Japanese model as regards the importance of the role of banks in the financial system and the less developed state of financial markets. However, the German model is more similar to the American model as regards the relative importance of long-term debt in companies' total debt.

This observation indicates that changes in the banking industry affect banks differently depending on their home countries' financial model. Likewise, the interaction between the evolution of the financial model and the actions taken by banks in response to these changes seem to be leading towards an eclectic model with three features:

(a) the legal and practical acceptance of universal banks as the most flexible model;
(b) the growing presence of financial markets in their function of providing financing to companies, at the expense of banks;
(c) the emergence of bank dominance in financial markets.

In other words, banks seem to be gaining control, to a greater or lesser extent, of the markets' activity.

TABLE 12.1 *Banking industry: different perspectives*

Dimensions	Germany	Japan	Spain	USA
Universal banks	Yes	Yes	Yes	No
Degree of concentration in the banking industry	High	Medium	Medium	Low
Specialized banks	No	Yes	No	Yes
Bank shareholdings in companies	Yes	Yes	Yes	No
Bank-company cross-holdings	Yes	Yes	No	No
Bank debt of non-financial companies (over total debt, 1992)	30.3%	40.1%	36.1%	15.8%
Presence of banks on company boards	Yes	Yes	Yes	No
Degree of development of financial markets	Medium	Low	Medium	High
Importance of stock market in corporate finance	Low	Low	Low	High
Use of take-over bids for company control	Low	Low	Low	High
Role of banks in corporate restructuring	Medium	High	High	Low
Presence of controlling shareholders in companies	Yes	Yes	Yes	No
Degree of regulation of the banks' behaviour	Medium	High	Medium	Medium
Degree of regulation of the industry's structure	Medium	High	Medium	High
Existence of State-owned banks	Yes	Yes	Yes	No

4. STRATEGIC REACTIONS BY THE BANKS

Faced with deregulation and financial disintermediation, banks in the industrial countries are reacting to prevent further deterioration of their financial performance and to improve their competitive position. In order to achieve these goals, we have observed five strategies (which are perfectly compatible with each other) that numerous banks have tried to follow. These are as follows: their transformation into universal banks, the achievement of a larger scale (through internal growth or mergers and take-overs), diversification towards non-bank or non-financial activities, internationalization of activities, and the use of new organizational forms to respond sooner and better to industry changes. Let us examine the main conclusions on these alternative strategies.

First, the arguments used to discuss the advantages of universal banks over specialized banks—some of them extensively used in debates on the financial system or on public policy regarding the universal banks—are not fully conclusive in stating the superiority of one type of bank over another.

Perhaps we can condense this discussion into two points. First, it is extremely dangerous that the choice between the universal bank and the specialized bank system be made by financial authorities as there is no guarantee that they will make the right choice and, furthermore, as happened in the United States with the 1933 Glass–Steagall Act, the lobbies may tip the balance towards their private interests. Therefore, prudential regulation for both types of organization is needed, but it is dangerous to exclude activities beyond what is clearly necessary. The focus adopted in this area by the European Commission in the Second Banking Directive seems to be a step in the right direction.

The second conclusion is that, from the viewpoint of banks themselves, it cannot be said that universal banks are superior to specialized banks. In the final analysis, everything depends on the banks' personnel, resources, skills, and quality of management. We can observe—and we have discussed concrete cases—successful universal banks and specialized banks and, also, universal banks and specialized banks that have been resounding business failures.

One important factor that should be mentioned is that a specialized bank runs a larger substitution risk than a universal bank, because its business base is more limited and, therefore, more vulnerable to changes in the industry. On the other hand, a universal bank that offers different products and services—more or less interrelated—is able to balance its various businesses, depending on the internal resources available and the competitive dynamic in each financial market. In other words, a universal bank has more options for penetrating more quickly new segments within the financial services sector, as and when customers move towards these new segments.

To conclude the discussion on universal banks, we will underline one final aspect. Their greater difficulties in the 1990s have not been caused by a possible increase in the risk of their operations. The main problem has been the enormous complexity that universal banks must face by operating in businesses which, although they have as common denominator the provision of financial services, reveal considerable differences in their internal competitive dynamics and their defining features. Fundamentally, the most important challenge facing a commercial bank in the 1990s is the increasing complexity of their management, which is exacerbated by the competition from specialist banks in certain businesses.

The second strategic alternative is that of mergers. The road to universal banks has been confirmed by the supposed need of a large scale in banking. The rivalry in the financial services sector has started a race in which larger scale is identified with greater efficiency. Behind the strategies seeking a larger market share, there lies an implicit hypothesis that a larger market share is always matched by greater profitability, a relationship which experience has shown does not exist. Numerous small and medium-sized banks throughout the world are more profitable than many large banks.

In the American, Spanish or Italian banking industries, consolidation through mergers and take-overs has become very popular in recent years. Thus, in Spain, after the merger between Banco Bilbao and Banco de Vizcaya in 1988, there followed the announcement of the merger—which later fell through—between Banesto and Central, the merger between Caixa de Pensions and Caja de Barcelona, the merger between Banco Central and Banco Hispano Americano, the merger (under the corporate umbrella of Argentaria) of all the State-owned banks in Spain and, in 1994, the purchase of Banesto by Banco Santander, to mention only some of the operations that have taken place.

The experience of the Spanish banking industry offers quite a few lessons about the advantages and problems of bank mergers. Mergers between banks are complex processes, from the strategic, organizational, and cultural viewpoints. This means that bank mergers are neither good nor bad on an abstract level: they are good or bad on the basis of at least two criteria. First is the degree of compatibility between the two merging organizations, both from a market viewpoint and from the point of view of the banks' culture. Second, proper planning of the merger and its implementation are needed. Some mergers that are well focused, from a strategic viewpoint, may encounter numerous obstacles if the implementation process is not carried out adequately. The unsuccessful merger attempt between Banesto and Banco Central in 1990 and the more recent one between S. G. Warburg and Morgan Stanley in 1995 are good examples of the importance of these criteria.

Diversification of universal banks' activities towards other financial services and other businesses is the third strategic decision recently made by some banks. Among the advantages of diversification activities that we have discussed, using real-life cases, are the economies of scope between different financial services activities and the possibility of solving the capital markets' supposed information problems. One particularly interesting case on which a major debate is continuing is that in which a bank not only finances companies but also invests in their capital. This is a specific case, in which the bank promotes a group of industrial or services companies with the bank itself at its core.

In such a case, the circumstances the bank faces are slightly different from those of a universal bank. The bank intervenes directly in these companies' management and the bank's market value is influenced not only by the present value of the companies in which it has invested but also by these companies' future prospects. The case of the Corporación Industrial Banesto in Spain between 1990 and 1993 is a paradigmatic example.

Industrial corporations may help to give an industrial backbone to a country or to ensure the financing needed by certain large-scale business projects. However, such business projects are also associated with significant risks and difficulties, as has been shown by empirical evidence. Normally, these difficulties do not arise from the strategic approach of the companies in which the banks invest, but rather they are related to three types of problem: the internal management and control problems of diversified, complex organizations; limited rationality and asymmetric information problems; and competitive problems arising from the management of financial organizations competing in different industries, each one with its own competitive dynamics.

The internationalization of activities is the fourth critical decision made by some banks as regards the strategic course to follow. The globalization of the international financial system, driven by financial markets, also seems to be pushing banks in this direction.

The internationalization of banks is a response to factors somewhat different from those used in the international expansion of industrial companies or other services companies. Whereas, in certain industries tending towards globalization, companies try to be present in many geographical markets, it does not appear that the same thing is happening in the banking industry. There is a simple empirical explanation for this. In some industries (automobiles, consumer electronics, computers, or household appliances), the leading companies are clearly international companies, while in the banking industry this is not so. Thus, banks with a greater international diversification of activities are not the largest or the most profitable banks in the world, as we have already pointed out in Chapter 9.

The evidence acquired on bank internationalization shows three main types of behaviour. The first is the creation of a network of branches in foreign countries. The most active banks in this have been British and American banks such as Citibank and Barclays.

Another means has been through the purchase of a bank abroad. In recent years, this phenomenon has become very important in the EU. By way of example, Deutsche Bank bought Bank of America's subsidiary in Italy (1986), Morgan Grenfell (1989), and Banco de Madrid (1993). Crédit Lyonnais bought Banque de Commerce (Belgium, 1989), Banco Comercial Español (1990), and Banca Jover (1992) from Banco Santander. The prices paid for these purchases were very high. Thus, Deutsche Bank offered 42 billion pesetas for Banco de Madrid, which was about 2.3 times its book value. Crédit Lyonnais paid 50 billion pesetas for Banco Comercial Español and about 100 billion pesetas for Banca Jover (in the latter case, 3.3 times its book value).

A third procedure is acquiring a minority holding in another bank's equity, in some cases in the context of an alliance. This is a formula that has been widely used by some banks to penetrate markets such as the Germany or Spain. Thus, we can see the presence of Rabobank in Banco Popular, J. P. Morgan in Banesto, and Commerzbank in BCH.

It should also be pointed out that the reasons for bank internationalization in Europe are different from those in the United States or Japan. In Europe, the elimination of barriers to capital flows and the freedom to establish themselves in other countries have brought about significant direct investment moves from banks in one country to other countries.

Starting from this diversity of circumstances, in Chapter 9 we presented a model to account for this process. It is this model's hypothesis that bank internationalization is a process with four dimensions: the search for a larger scale, the proximity to other financial markets, the exploitation of one bank's successful resources and skills in other different markets, and the control and diversification of the financial risk.

The final critical question for banks, particularly for universal banks with a certain degree of diversification, is the choice of a new organizational design. In particular, we have looked at the multidivisional organizations and the model of the federated bank.

None of the organizational solutions (the divisional model, the matrix model, or the federated model) that we have described is ideal for restructuring banks and adapting them to the new competitive situation. Each solution can be implemented more or less successfully depending on the group's history, the dominant management styles and cultures, the resources available, and the weight of each of the business units.

In any case, we can observe, on the basis of the broad international evidence from banking, that certain organizational forms have clear advantages over the classic organization. Essentially, a bank group's different businesses are related to the provision of financial services and, consequently, the interrelationships between them can become quite significant. Perhaps we should exclude from this general statement bank shareholdings in non-financial companies. In these, the interrelationships are less clear, and this difference could justify an even greater degree of independence for the business unit supervising investments in the equity of non-bank companies.

One of the clearest effects of the new forms of bank organization is that managers in each unit have become responsible for maintaining customer relations. These managers are responsible not for directly solving customers' needs but for putting customers in contact with the specialist units within the bank. Consequently, customers go from being customers of a branch or department to being customers of the bank.

One problem caused by this new situation is that of incentives. Who is responsible for the profit or losses generated by a customer of several departments? The answer to this question can be viewed from many different angles but it must be objectively fair and consistent with the group's goals.

Finally, the problems associated with a federated bank are very similar to those of a group of companies. The critical question, in the final analysis, is how to combine the independence required by the group's companies with a suitable degree of co-ordination in order to ensure maximum effectiveness for the group. The dilemma is not simple and only an excellent management will be able to overcome the maze of complexities involved in a banking group.

References

Alchian, A., and Demsetz, H. (1972), 'Production, Information Costs and Economic Organization', *American Economic Review*, 62, 777–95.

Allen, F. (1993), 'Strategic Management and Financial Markets', *Strategic Management Journal*, Special Issue, 11–22.

—— (1994), 'Mercado de valores y asignación de recursos', in C. Mayer and X. Vives (eds.), *La Intermediación Financiera en la Construcción de Europa* (Bilbao: Fundación BBV).

—— and Gale, D. (1995), 'A Welfare Comparison of Intermediaries and Financial Markets', *European Economic Review*, 39, 179–209.

Aliber, J. W. (1988), 'Securitization in the Retail Banking World', *Journal of Retail Banking*, 10, 5–12.

Aliber, R. Z. (1984), 'International Banking: A Survey', *Journal of Money, Credit and Banking*, 16(4), 661–95.

Andrews, K. R. (1971), *The Concept of Corporate Strategy* (Homewood, IL.: Irwin).

Ang, J. S., and Richardson T. (1994), 'The Underwriting Experience of Commercial Bank Affiliates prior to the Glass–Steagall Act: A Re-examination of Evidence for Passage of the Act', *Journal of Banking and Finance*, 18, 351–95.

Ansoff, I. (1965), *Corporate Strategy* (New York: McGraw-Hill).

Aoki, M. (1984), 'Shareholders, Non-Unanimity on Investment Financing: Banks vs. Individual Investors', in M. Aoki (ed.), *The Economic Analysis of the Japanese Firm* (New York: North Holland).

—— (1988), *Information, Incentives and Bargaining in the Japanese Economy* (Cambridge: Cambridge University Press).

—— (1994), 'Monitoring Characteristics of the Main Bank System: An Analytical and Developmental View', in M. Aoki and H. Patrick (eds.), *The Japanese Main Bank System* (Oxford: Oxford University Press).

—— and Patrick, H. (eds.) (1994), *The Japanese Main Bank System* (Oxford: Oxford University Press).

Arrow, K. J. (1974), *Limits to Organization* (New York: Norton).

Baldwin, C. (1986), 'The Capital Factor: Competing for Capital in a Global Environment', in M. E. Porter (ed.): *Competition in Global Industries* (Boston: Harvard Business School Press).

Ballarín, E. (1985), *Estrategias Competitivas para la Banca* (Barcelona: Ed. Ariel).

—— Canals, J., and Fernández, P. (1994), *Fusiones y Adquisiciones: Un Enfoque Integrador* (Madrid: Alianza Editorial).

Baltensperger, E., (1980), 'Alternative Approaches to the Theory of the Banking Firm', *Journal of Monetary Economics*, 6.

Baltensperger, E., and Dermine, J. (1987), 'Banking Deregulation in Europe', *Economic Policy*, 4, 64–109.

Barney, J. (1991), 'Firm Resources and Sustained Competitive Advantage', *Journal of Management*, 17, 99–120.

Barro, R. J. (1991), 'Economic Growth in a Cross-Section of Countries', *Quarterly Journal of Economics*, 106, 407–44.

Bartlett, C. A., and Ghoshal, S. (1989), *Managing across Borders* (Boston: Harvard Business School Press).

Baumol, W., Panzar, J., and Willig, R. (1982), *Contestable Markets and the Theory of Market Structure* (New York: Harcourt Brace Jovanovich).

Baums, T. (1994), 'The German Banking System and its Impact on Corporate Finance and Governance', in M. Aoki and H. Patrick, (eds.), *The Japanese Main Bank System* (Oxford: Oxford University Press).

—— and Gruson, M. (1993), 'The German Banking System—System of the Future?', *Brooklyn Journal of International Law*, 19, 101–29.

Bengoechea, J., Arriaga, M., and Pizarro, J. (1992), *La Banca y el Cambio* (Madrid: Fundación BBV).

Benston, G. J. (1982), 'Why Did Congress Pass New Financial Service Laws in the 1930s? An Alternative Opinion', *Economic Review*, Federal Reserve Bank of Atlanta, 67, 7–10.

—— (1989), 'The Federal Safety Net and the Repeal of the Glass–Steagall Act's Separation of Commercial and Investment Banking', *Journal of Financial Services Research*, 2, 287–305.

—— (1990), *The Separation of Commercial and Investment Banking* (London: Macmillan and Department of Banking and Finance, City University Business School).

—— (1994), 'Universal Banking', *Journal of Economic Perspectives*, 8(2), 121–43.

—— Hanweck, G. A., and Humphrey, D. B. (1982), 'Scale Economies in Banking: A Restructuring and Reassessment', *Journal of Money, Credit, and Banking*, November, Part I, 435–56.

—— and Kaufman, G. G. (1988), *Risk and Solvency Regulation of Depository Institutions: Past Policies and Current Options*, Monograph 1988–1, Monograph Series in Finance and Economics (Salomon Brothers Center for the Study of Financial Institutions, Graduate School of Business Administration, New York University).

—— and Smith, C. (1977), 'A Transaction Cost Approach to the Theory of Financial Intermediation', *Journal of Finance*, May.

—— Berger, A., Hanweck, G., and Humphrey, D. (1983), 'Economics of Scale and Scope', Conference on Bank Structure and Competition, Federal Reserve Bank of Chicago.

Berger, A., Hanweck, G., and Humphrey, D. (1987), 'Competitive Viability in Banking: Scale, Scope and Product Mix Economics', *Research Paper*, Federal Reserve Bank, Washington, DC.

—— Hancock, D., and Humphrey, D. B. (1993), 'Bank Efficiency Derived from the Profit Function', *Journal of Banking and Finance*, 17, 317–348.

—— and Humphrey, D. B. (1990), 'The Dominance of Inefficiencies over Scale and Product Mix Economies in Banking, *Journal of Monetary Economics*, 28, 117–48.

Berger, P., and Ofek, E. (1995), 'Diversification's Effect on Firm Value', *Journal of Financial Economics*, 37(1), 39–66.

Bergés, A., and Sánchez del Villar, E. (1991), 'Las participaciones bursátiles de la banca en España', in A. Torrero (ed.), *Relaciones banca-industria* (Madrid: Espasa-Calpe).

—— and Soria, P. (1993), 'La empresa bancaria y la moderna teoría financiera', *Perspectivas del Sistema Financiero*, No. 42, 11–23.

Berglof, E. (1990), 'Capital Structure as a Mechanism of Control', in M. Aoki, B.

Gustafsson, and O. Williamson (eds.), *The Firm as a Nexus of Treaties* (London: Sage).

Berle, A. A., and Means, G. C. (1932), *The Modern Corporation and Private Property* (New York: Macmillan).

Bertero, E. (1994), 'The Banking System, Financial Markets, and Capital Structure: Some New Evidence from France', *Oxford Review of Economic Policy*, 10(4), 68–78.

Besanko, D., and Thakor, A. V. (1992), 'Banking Deregulation: Allocational Consequences of Relaxing Entry Barriers', *Journal of Banking and Finance*, 16, 909–32.

Bettis, R. A. (1981), 'Performance Differences in Related and Unrelated Diversified Firms', *Strategic Management Journal*, 2, 379–93.

Bhide, A. (1994), 'Efficient Markets, Deficient Governance', *Harvard Business Review*, November–December, 128–40.

Blanch, J., Garrido, A., and Sanromà, E. (1990), 'Las relaciones banca-industria y su incidencia sobre la eficiencia bancaria', *Economía Industrial*, March–April, 85–94.

Bolton, P., and Farrell, J. (1990), 'Decentralization, Duplication and Delay', *Journal of Political Economy*, 98(4), 803–26.

Brewer, E. III, Fortier, D., and Pavel, Ch. (1988), 'Bank Risk from Nonbank Activities', *Economic Perspectives*, Federal Reserve Bank of Chicago, July–August, 14–26.

Bryan, L. L. (1991), 'A Blueprint for Financial Reconstruction', *Harvard Business Review*, May–June, 73–86.

—— (1992), *Bankrupt* (New York: HarperCollins).

Bulow, J., Geanakoplos, J., and Klemperer, P. (1985), 'Multimarket Oligopoly: Strategic Substitutes and Complements', *Journal of Political Economy*, 93(3), 488–511.

Cable, J. R. (1985), 'Capital Market Information and Industrial Performance: The Role of West German Banks', *Economic Journal*, 95, 118–32.

Calomiris, C. W. (1993), 'Corporate Finance Benefits from Universal Banking: Germany and the United States, 1870–1914', mimeo.

Caminal, R., Gual, J., and Vives, X. (1990), 'Competition in Spanish Banking', in Jean Dermine (ed.), *European Banking in the 90s* (Oxford: Basil Blackwell).

Campbell, J. Y., and Hamao, Y. (1994), 'Changing Patterns of Corporate Financing and the Main Bank System in Japan', in M. Aoki and H. Patrick (eds.), *The Japanese Main Bank System* (Oxford: Oxford University Press).

Canals, J. (1990), *Estrategias del Sector Bancario Europeo* (Barcelona: Ariel).

—— (1991), *Competitividad Internacional y Estrategia de la Empresa* (Barcelona: Ariel).

—— (1993), *Competitive Strategies in European Banking* (Oxford: Oxford University Press).

—— (1994), *La Internacionalización de la Empresa* (Madrid: McGraw-Hill).

—— (1995a), 'Country, Industry and Firm-Specific Advantages in International Competition', in H. Thomas, D. O'Neal and J. Kelly (eds.), *Strategic Renaissance and Business Transformation* (New York: John Wiley).

—— (1995b), 'Bancos universales y bancos especializados: Los límites de la diversificación bancaria', *Papeles de Economía Española*, 65, 125–41.

Cargill, T. F., and Royama, S. (1988), *The Transition of Finance in Japan and the United States: A Comparative Perspective* (Stanford: Hoover Institution Press).

Casson, M. (ed.) (1983), *The Growth of International Business* (London: Allen & Unwin).

Caves, R. (1982), *Multinational Enterprise and Economic Analysis* (Cambridge: Cambridge University Press).

Chandler, A. (1962), *Strategy and Structure* (Cambridge, MA: MIT Press).

—— (1977), *The Visible Hand* (Cambridge, MA: Harvard University Press).

—— (1990), *Scale and Scope* (Cambridge, MA: Harvard University Press).

—— (1991), 'The Functions of the HQ Unit in the Multibusiness Firm', *Strategic Management Journal*, 12, 31–50.

Charkham, J. (1994), *Keeping Good Company* (Oxford: Oxford University Press).

Chuliá, C. (1990), 'Las participaciones del sistema bancario en las empresas no financieras', *Papeles de Economía Española*, 44, 73–87.

Christensen, H. K., and Montgomery, C. (1981), 'Corporate Economic Performance: Diversification Strategy versus Market Structure', *Strategic Management Journal*, 2, 327–43.

Clark, C. (1988), 'Economies of Scale and Scope at Depository Financial Institutions: A Review of the Literature', *Federal Reserve Bank of Kansas City Economic Review*, September–October.

Cleveland, M., and Huertas, T. (1985), *Citibank: 1812–1970* (Cambridge, MA: Harvard University Press).

Coase, R. H. (1937), 'The Nature of the Firm', *Economica*, 4, 386–405.

Collis, D. (1991a), 'Corporate Strategy: A Research Agenda', mimeo (Boston: Harvard Business School).

—— (1991b), 'A Resource-Based Analysis of Global Competition: The Case of the Bearings Industry', *Strategic Management Journal*, 12, 49–68.

Comment, R., and Jarrell, G. (1995), 'Corporate Focus and Stock Returns', *Journal of Financial Economics*, 37(1), 67–87.

Cooper, R., and John, A. (1988), 'Co-ordinating Co-ordination Failures in Keynesian Models', *Quarterly Journal of Economics*, 103(4), 441–64.

Corbett, J. (1987), 'International Perspectives on Financing: Evidence from Japan', *Oxford Review of Economic Policy*, 3(4), 30–55.

—— (1993), 'An Overview of the Japanese Financial System', in N. H. Dimsdale and M. Prevezer (eds.), *Capital Markets and Corporate Governance* (Oxford: Clarendon Press).

Corrigan, E. G. (1987), 'A Framework for Reform of the Financial System', *Quarterly Review*, Federal Reserve Bank of New York, Summer, 1–8.

—— (1989), 'A Perspective on the Globalization of Financial Markets and Institutions', *Quarterly Review*, The Federal Reserve Bank of New York, 12, 1–9.

Crane, D. B. *et al.* (1995), *The Global Financial System* (Boston: Harvard Business School Press).

—— and Hayes, S. L., III (1982), 'The New Competition in World Banking', *Harvard Business Review*, 60(4), 88–94.

——, —— (1983), 'The Evolution of International Banking Competition and its Implications for Regulation', *Journal of Banking Research*, 14(1), 39–53.

Cuervo, A. (1988), *La Crisis Bancaria en España 1977–1985* (Barcelona: Ed. Ariel).

—— (1991), 'Los grupos empresariales bancarios', *Papeles de Economía Española*, 49, 237–45.

Dale, R. (1993), *International Banking Deregulation* (Oxford: Blackwell).

Dasgupta, P., and Stiglitz, J. (1980), 'Uncertainty, Industrial Structure and the Speed of R&D', *Bell Journal of Economics*, 11(1), 1–28.

Davis, P., and Mayer, C. P. (1991), 'Corporate Finance in the Euromarkets and the Economics of Intermediation', *Discussion Paper No. 570*, Centre for Economic Policy Research.

Demsetz, H. (1983), 'The Structure of Ownership and the Theory of the Firm', *Journal of Law and Economics*, 26, 375–90.

—— and Lehn, K. (1985), 'The Structure of Corporate Ownership: Causes and Consequences', *Journal of Political Economy*, 93, 1.157–1.177.

Dewatripont, M., and Tirole, J. (1994), *The Prudential Regulation of Banks* (Cambridge, MA: MIT Press).

Diamond, D. W. (1984), 'Financial Intermediation and Delegated Monitoring', *Review of Economic Studies*, 51, 393–414.

—— (1991), 'Monitoring and Reputation: The Choice between Bank Loans and Directly Placed Debt', *Journal of Political Economy*, 99, 688–721.

Dimsdale, N., and Prevezer, M. (eds.) (1994), *Capital Markets and Corporate Governance* (Oxford: Clarendon Press).

Dodwell Marketing Consultants (1990), *Industrial Groupings in Japan* (Tokyo: Dodwell Marketing Consultants).

Donalson, G., and Lorsch, J. W. (1984), *Decision Making at the Top* (New York: Basic Books).

Dunning, J. J. (1981), *International Production and the Multinational Enterprise* (London: Allen & Unwin).

Eccles, R. G., and Crane, D. G. (1988), *Doing Deals: Investment Banks at Work* (Boston: Harvard Business School Press).

Edwards, F. (1993), 'Financial Markets in Transition—Or the Decline of Commercial Banking', in Federal Reserve Bank of Kansas City, *Changing Capital Markets* (Wyoming: Jackson Hole).

Edwards, J. S. S., and Fischer, K. (1994a), 'Banks, Finance and Investment in West Germany since 1970', *CEPR Discussion Paper*, No. 497.

——, —— (1994b), *Banks, Finance and Investment in Germany* (Cambridge: Cambridge University Press).

Fama, E. F. (1970), 'Efficient Capital Markets', *Journal of Finance*, May, 383–417.

—— (1980), 'Agency Problems and the Theory of the Firm', *Journal of Political Economy*, 88, 288–307.

—— (1985a), 'Contract Costs and Financing Decisions', *Working Paper*, University of Chicago.

—— (1985b), 'What's Different about Banks?', *Journal of Monetary Economics*, 15, 29–40.

Faulí-Oller, R., and Giralt, M. (1995), 'Competition and Co-operation within a Multi-divisional Firm', *Journal of Industrial Economics*, XLIII(1), 77–99.

Federal Reserve Bank of Kansas City (1993), *Changing Capital Markets* (Wyoming: Jackson Hole).

Fernández, Z. (1993), 'La banca federada. Aportaciones y límites de un nuevo modelo organizativo', *Perspectivas del Sistema Financiero*, 42, 24–32.

Fisher, I. (1931), *The Theory of Interest* (New York: A. M. Kelley, 1965 edition).

Frank, J., and Mayer, C. (1990), 'Capital Markets and Corporate Control: A Study of France, Germany and the UK', *Economic Policy*, April, 191–231.

Franke, H. H., and Hudson, M. (1984), *Banking and Finance in West Germany* (New York: St. Martin's Press).

Frankel, A. B., and Montgomery, J. D. (1991), 'Financial Structure: An International Perspective', *Brookings Papers on Economic Activity* 1: 257–97.

Fuentelsaz, L., and Salas, V. (1993), *Estudios sobre Banca al por Menor* (Madrid: Fundación BBV).

Furash, E. E. (1993), 'Banking's Critical Crossroads', *The Bankers Magazine*, March–April, 20–6.
Galve, C., and Salas, V. (1995), 'Propiedad y resultados de la empresa: Una revisión de la literatura teórica y empírica', *Economía Industrial*, 300, 171–96.
Gardener, E. P. M. (ed.) (1991), *The Future of Financial Systems and Services* (New York: St. Martin's Press).
Gardener, E. P. M., and Molyneux, P. (1989), *Changes in Western European Banking* (London: Unwin).
Gerlarch, M. (1987), 'Business Alliances and the Strategy of the Japanese Firms', *California Management Review*, Fall, 126–42.
—— (1992), *Alliance Capitalism: The Social Organization of Japanese Business* (Berkeley: University of California Press).
Gerschenkron, A. (1962), *Economic Backwardness in Historical Perspective* (Cambridge, MA: Harvard University Press).
—— (1968), 'The Modernization of Entrepreneurship', in A. Gerschenkron, *Continuity in History and Other Essays* (Cambridge, MA: Harvard University Press).
Gilligan, T., Smirlock, M., and Marshall, W. (1984), 'Scale and Scope Economies in the Multiproduct Banking Firm', *Journal of Monetary Economics*, 13, 383–405.
Gilson, R. J., and Roe, M. J. (1992), 'Comparative Corporate Governance: Focusing the United States–Japan Inquiry', Columbia Law School, Working paper.
Goldsmith, R. W. (1969), *Financial Structure and Development* (New Haven, CT: Yale University Press).
Goldstein, M., and Folkerts-Landau, D. (1994), *International Capital Markets* (Washington, DC: IMF).
Goold, M., and Campbell, A. (1987), *Strategies and Styles* (Oxford: Basil Blackwell).
——, ——, and Alexander, M. (1994), *Corporate Level Strategies* (New York: John Wiley & Sons).
Grima, J. D., and Von Löhneysen, E. (1991), 'Nuevas estructuras organizativas para bancos y cajas universales', *Papeles de Economía Española*, 49, 221–36.
Grossman, S. J., and Hart, O. D. (1980), 'Takeover Bids, the Free-Rider Problem, and the Theory of the Corporation', *Bell Journal of Economics*, 11, 42–64.
——, —— (1982), 'Corporate Financial Structure and Management Incentives', in J. J. McCall (ed.), *Economics of Information and Uncertainty* (Chicago: University of Chicago Press).
Grubel, H. G. (1977), 'A Theory of Multinational Banking', *Banca Nazionale del Lavoro Quarterly Review*, December, 349–64.
Gual, J. (1993), *La Competencia en el Sector Bancario Español* (Madrid: Fundación BBV).
—— (1994), *La Racionalización del Sector Bancario Español* (Madrid: Fundación BBV).
—— and Neven, D. (1993), 'Deregulation of the European Banking Industry', *European Economy*, 3, 153–83.
—— and Vives, X. (1990), *Desregulación y Competencia en el Sector Bancario Español* (Madrid: FEDEA).
Hamel, G. (1991), 'Competition for Competence and Inter-Partner Learning within International Strategic Alliances' *Strategic Management Journal*, 12, 53–104.
—— and Prahalad, C. K. (1994), *Competing for the Future* (Boston: Harvard Business School Press).
Hamilton, J. D. (1987), 'Monetary Factors in the Great Depression', *Journal of Monetary Economics*, 19, 145–69.

Handy, C. (1992), 'Balancing Corporate Power: A New Federalist Paper', *Harvard Business Review*, November–December, 59–72.

Harm, C. (1992a), 'The Financing of Small Firms in Germany', Working Paper 899, The World Bank.

—— (1992b), 'The Relationship between German Banks and Large German Firms', Working Paper, The World Bank.

Harris, C., and Vickers, J. (1985), 'Perfect Equilibrium in a Model of a Race', *Review of Economic Studies*, 52(1), 193–209.

Hart, O., and Moore, J. (1988), 'Incomplete Contracts and Renegotiation', *Econometrica*, 56(4), 755–86.

Hawawini, G., and Schill, M. (1994), 'The Japanese Presence in the European Financial Services Sector', in M. Mason and D. Encarnation (eds.), *Japanese Multinationals in Europe* (Oxford: Oxford University Press).

—— and Swary, I. (1990), *Mergers and Acquisitions in the US Banking Industry* (New York: Elsevier Science Publishers).

Hayes, S. L., III, Spence, A. M., and Marks, D. Van Praag (1983), *Competition in the Investment Banking Industry* (Cambridge, MA: Harvard University Press).

Heggestad, A. (1975), 'Riskiness of Investments in Nonbank Activities by Bank Holding Companies', *Journal of Economics and Business*, 27, 219–23.

Hellwig, M. F. (1989), 'Asymmetric Information, Financial Markets, and Financial Institutions', *European Economic Review*, 71, 155–70.

—— (1991), 'Banking, Financial Intermediation and Corporate Finance', in A. Giovannini and C. Mayer (eds.), *European Financial Integration* (Cambridge: Cambridge University Press).

Hennart, J. F. (1982), *A Theory of the Multinational Enterprise* (Ann Arbor, MI: University of Michigan).

Hill, C., and Shell, S. (1988), 'External Control, Corporate Strategy and Firm Performance in Research-Intensive Industries', *Strategic Management Journal*, 9, 577–90.

Holmstrom, B. (1979), 'Moral Hazard and Observability', *Bell Journal of Economics*, 10(1), 84–91.

—— and Tirole, J. (1989), 'The Theory of the Firm', in R. Schmalensee and R. D. Willig (eds.), *Handbook of Industrial Organisation* (Amsterdam: North-Holland).

Hoshi, T., Kashyap, A., and Loveman G. (1994), 'Financial System Reform in Poland: Lessons from Japan's Main Bank System', in M. Aoki and H. Patrick (eds.), *The Japanese Main Bank System* (Oxford: Oxford University Press).

——, ——, and Scharfstein, D. (1990), 'The Role of Banks in Reducing the Costs of Financial Distress in Japan', *Journal of Financial Economics*, 27, 67–88.

——, ——, —— (1991), 'Corporate Structure, Liquidity, and Investment: Evidence from Japanese Industrial Groups', *Quarterly Journal of Economics*, February, 33–60.

Hoskisson, R., and Turk, T. (1990), 'Corporate Restructuring: Governance and Control Limits of the Internal Capital Market', *Academy of Management Review*, 15(3), 459–77.

Hubbard, R. G. (ed.) (1990), *Asymmetric Information, Corporate Finance, and Investment* (Chicago: University of Chicago Press).

Hymer, S. (1960), 'The International Operations of National Firms: A Study of Direct Investment', doctoral dissertation, Massachusetts Institute of Technology, Cambridge, MA.

Immenga, U. (1978), 'Beteiligungen von Banken in anderen Wirtschaftszweigen' (Baden-Baden: Nomos Verlagsgesellschaft).

Isimbabi, M. J. (1994), 'The Stock Market Perception of Industry Risk and the Separation of Banking and Commerce', *Journal of Banking and Finance*, 18, 325–49.

Jacobs, M. (1991), *Short-Term America* (Boston: Harvard Business School Press).

Jensen, M. C. (1986), 'Agency Costs of Free Cash Flow, Corporate Finance and Takeovers', *American Economic Review, Papers and Proceedings*, 76(2), 323–9.

—— (1987), 'The Free Cash Flow Theory of Takeovers: A Financial Perspective on Mergers and Acquisitions and the Economy', in L. E. Browne and E. S. Rosengren (eds.), *The Merger Boom* (Boston: Federal Reserve Bank of Boston).

—— (1988), 'Takeovers: Their Causes and Consequences', *Journal of Economic Perspectives*, 2(1), 217–54.

—— (1989), 'The Eclipse of the Public Corporation', *Harvard Business Review*, September–October, 61–75.

—— (1993), 'The Modern Industrial Revolution, Exit and the Failure of Internal Control Systems', *Journal of Finance*, July, 831–80.

—— and Meckling, W. H. (1976), 'Theory of the Firm: Managerial Behavior, Agency Costs, and Ownership Structure', *Journal of Financial Economics*, 3, 305–60.

—— and Murphy, K. (1990), 'Performance Pay and Top Management Incentives', *Journal of Political Economy*, 98, 225–64.

John, K., John, T. A., and Saunders, A. (1994), 'Universal Banking and Firm Risk-Taking', *Journal of Banking and Finance*, 18, 307–23.

Jones, G., and Hill, C. (1988), 'Transaction Cost Analysis of Strategy–Structure Choice', *Strategic Management Journal*, 9, 159–172.

Kaplan, S., and Weisbach, M. (1992), 'The Success of Acquisitions: Evidence from Divestitures', *Journal of Finance*, XLVII(1), 107–38.

Kester, W. C. (1991), *Japanese Takeovers: The Global Contest for Corporate Control* (Boston: Harvard Business School Press).

—— (1992), 'Banks in the Board Room: The American versus Japanese and German Experiences', Managing the Financial Services Firm in a Global Environment, Harvard Business School, Research Colloquium.

—— and Luehrman, T. A. (1992), 'The Myth of Japan's Low-Cost Capital', *Harvard Business Review*, May–June, 130–8.

King, R. G., and Levine, R. (1994), 'Intermediación financiera y desarrollo económico', in C. Mayer and X. Vives (eds.) (1994), *La Intermediación Financiera en la Construcción de Europa* (Bilbao: Fundación BBV).

Klein, B., Crawford, R. G., and Alchian, A. (1978), 'Vertical Integration, Appropiable Rents and the Competitive Contract Process', *Journal of Law and Economics*, 297–326.

Kreps, D., and Wilson, R. (1982), 'Reputation and Imperfect Information', *Journal of Economic Theory*, 27, 253–79.

Lank, L., and Stulz, R. (1994), 'Tobin's Corporate Diversification and Firm Performance', *Journal of Political Economy*, 102(6), 1.248–1.280.

Lawrence, C. (1989), 'Banking Costs, Generalized Functional Forms and Estimation of Economics of Scale and Scope, *Journal of Money, Credit and Banking*, August, 368–80.

Lawrence, P., and Lorsch, J. (1967), *Strategy and Environment* (Boston: Harvard Business School Press).

Lerena, L. A. (1993), 'Las reestructuraciones bancarias: una perspectiva microeconómica', *Papeles de Economía Española*, 54, 57–76.

Lessard, D. R. (1986), 'Finance and Global Competition: Exploiting Financial Scope and Coping with Volatile Exchange Rates', in M. E. Porter (ed.), *Competition in Global Industries* (Boston: Harvard Business School Press).

—— and Perotti, E. (1988), 'Moving Toward 1992: Managing the Globalization of Business', Background Paper for MIT-IRI Symposium, Managing the Globalization of Business, Italy.

Lieberman, M. B., and Montgomery, D. B. (1988), 'First-Mover Advantages', *Strategic Management Journal*, 9(1), 41–58.

Litan, R. E. (1987), *What Should Banks Do?* (Washington, DC: The Brookings Institution).

Llewellyn, D. T. (1986), *Regulation and Supervision of Financial Institutions* (London: Chartered Institute of Bankers).

—— (1988), 'Financial Intermediation and Systems: Global Integration', in D. Fair and C. Boissieu (eds.), *International Monetary and Financial Integration: The European Dimension* (The Hague: Kluwer).

—— (1989), 'Structural Change in the British Financial System', in D. T. Llewellyn (ed.) (1989), *Reflections on Money* (London: Macmillan).

—— (1995), 'Universal Banking and the Public Interest: A British Perspective', mimeo.

Lodge, G., and Vogel, E. (1987), *Ideology and National Competitiveness* (Boston: Harvard Business School Press).

Lowestein, L. (1991), 'Why Managers Should (and Should Not) Have Respect for their Shareholders', *Journal of Corporation Law*, 17, 1–27.

Macho-Stadler, I., and Pérez-Castrillo, J. D. (1992), '¿Delegar o centralizar? Qué dice la Economía de la Información', *Cuadernos Económicos del ICE*, 52, 25–46.

McVea, H. (1993), *Financial Conglomerates and the Chinese Wall* (Oxford: Clarendon Press).

Manne, H. G. (1965), 'Mergers and the Market for Corporate Control', *Journal of Political Economy*, 73, 110–20.

Mañas, L. (1990), 'El sector bancario ante el mercado único: Reflexiones críticas', *Papeles de Economía Española*, 44, 2–19.

Mayer, C. (1988), 'New Issues in Corporate Finance', *European Economic Review*, 32, 1.167–1.189.

—— (1990a), 'Financial Systems, Corporate Finance, and Economic Development', in R. G. Hubbard (ed.) (1990), *Asymmetric Information, Corporate Finance, and Investment* (Chicago: University of Chicago Press).

—— (1990b), 'The Regulation of Financial Services: Lessons from the UK for 1992', in J. Dermine (ed.) (1990), *European Banking after 1992* (Oxford: Blackwell).

—— and Neven, D. (1994), 'The Design and Implementation of Financial Regulation', mimeo.

—— and Vives, X. (eds.) (1994), *La Intermediación Financiera en la Construcción de Europa* (Bilbao: Fundación BBV).

Meerschwam, D. M. (1991), *Breaking Financial Boundaries* (Boston: Harvard Business School Press).

Mester, L. (1992), 'Traditional and Non-Traditional Banking: An Information-Theoretic Approach', *Journal of Banking and Finance*, 16, 545–66.

Merton, R. C. (1992), 'Operation and Regulation in Financial Intermediation: A Functional Perspective', mimeo, Harvard Business School.

—— (1993), 'Operation and Regulation in Financial Intermediation: A Functional Perspective', in P. Englund (ed.) (1993), *Operation and Regulation of Financial Markets* (Estocolmo: The Economic Council).

—— (1995), 'Financial Innovation and the Management and Regulation of Financial Institutions', *Journal of Banking and Finance*, 19, 461–81.

—— and Bodie, Z. (1993), 'Deposit Insurance Reform: A Functional Approach', in A. Meltzer and C. Plosser (eds.) (1993), *Carnegie-Rochester Series on Public Policy*, 38.

——, —— (1995), 'A Conceptual Framework for Analyzing the Financial Environment', in D. Grane *et al., The Global Financial System* (Boston: Harvard Business School Press).

Milgrom, P. (1988), 'Employment Contracts, Influence Activities and Efficient Organization Design', *Journal of Political Economy*, 96(1), 42–60.

—— and Roberts, J. (1988), 'An Economic Approach to Influence Activities in Organizations', *American Journal of Sociology*, 94, Supplement, 154–79.

——, —— (1990), 'The Economics of Modern Manufacturing: Technology, Strategy and Organization', *American Economic Review*, 80(3), 511–28.

——, —— (1992), *Economics, Organization and Management* (Englewood Cliffs, NJ: Prentice-Hall).

Miller, M. H. (1988), 'The Modigliani–Miller Proposition after Thirty Years', *Journal of Economic Perspectives*, 2(4), 99–120.

—— (1994), 'Is American Corporate Governance Fatally Flawed?', *Journal of Applied Corporate Finance*, 6(4), 32–9.

Modigliani, F. (1988), 'MM—Past, Present and Future', *Journal of Economic Perspectives*, 2(4), 149–58.

—— and Miller, M. H. (1958), 'The Cost of Capital, Corporate Finance and the Theory of Investment', *American Economic Review*, 48, 261–97.

Montgomery, C. (1985), 'Product Market Diversification and Market Power', *Academy of Management Journal*, 28, 789–98.

—— (1994), 'Corporate Diversification', *Journal of Economic Perspectives*, 8(3), 163–78.

Morck, R., Shleifer, A., and Vishny, R. W. (1987), 'Characteristics of Hostile and Friendly Takeover Targets', mimeo.

Mullineux, A. (ed.) (1992), *European Banking* (Oxford: Basil Blackwell).

Murphy, K. J. (1985), 'Corporate Performance and Managerial Remuneration: An Empirical Analysis', *Journal of Accounting and Economics*, 7, 11–42.

Murray, J. D. (1984), 'Comment on International Banking: A Survey', *Credit and Banking*, 16(4), 690–5.

Neven, D. (1990), 'Structural Adjustment in European Banking', in J. Dermine (ed.) (1990), *European Banking in the 1990s* (Oxford: Basil Blackwell).

Newman, J. A., and Shriever, R. E. (1993), 'The Multibank Holding Company Effect on Cost Efficiency in Banking', *Journal of Banking and Finance*, 17, 709–32.

Noulas, A., Ray, S., and Miller, S. (1990), 'Returns to Scale and Input Substitution for Large U.S. Banks', *Journal of Money, Credit and Banking*, 22, 94–108.

Ochoa, J. L. (1995), 'Las participaciones bancarias en empresas no financieras en España: Antecedentes, crisis y posible evolución futura', in *El Papel del Ahorro e Inversión en el Desarrollo Económico*, Ekonomigerizan, 235–48.

OECD (1992), *Banks under Stress* (Paris: OECD).

Packer, F. (1994), 'The Role of Long-Term Credit Banks within the Main Bank System', in M. Aoki and H. Patrick (eds.) (1994), *The Japanese Main Bank System* (Oxford: Oxford University Press).

Patrick, H., and Park, Y. (eds.) (1994), *The Financial Development of Japan, Korea and Taiwan: Growth, Repression and Liberalization* (New York: Oxford University Press).

Pauly, M. (1968), 'The Economics of Moral Hazard', *American Economic Review*, 58(1), 31–58.

Pecchioli, R. M. (1983), *The Internationalization of Banking* (Paris: OECD).

Pérez-López, J. A. (1993), *Fundamentos de Dirección de Empresas* (Madrid: Ed. Rialp).

Penrose, E. (1959), *The Theory of the Growth of the Firm* (Oxford: Basil Blackwell).

Pierce, J. L. (1991), *The Future of Banking* (New York: The Twentieth Century Fund).

Porter, M. E. (1980), *Competitive Strategy* (New York: The Free Press).

—— (1985), *Competitive Advantage* (New York: The Free Press).

—— (1986), 'Competition in Global Industries: A Conceptual Framework', in M. E. Porter (ed.) (1986), *Competition in Global Industries* (Boston: Harvard Business School Press).

—— (1987), 'From Competitive Advantage to Corporate Strategy', *Harvard Business Review*, May–June, 43–59.

—— (1990), *The Competitive Advantage of Nations* (New York: Free Press).

—— (1992), *Capital Choices* (Washington, DC: Council of Competitiveness).

Pound, J. (1992), 'Beyond Takeovers: Politics Comes to Corporate Control', *Harvard Business Review*, 70, 83–93.

Prahalad, C. K., and Hamel, G. (1990), 'The Core Competence of the Corporation', *Harvard Business Review*, May–June, 71–91.

Prowse, S. D. (1990), 'Institutional Investment Patterns and Corporate Financial Behavior in the US and Japan', mimeo, Board of Governors of the Federal Reserve System, Washington, DC.

Puri, M. (1994), 'The Long-Term Default Performance of Bank Underwritten Security Issues', *Journal of Banking and Finance*, 18, 397–418.

Ramseyer, J. M. (1994), 'Explicit Reasons for Implicit Contracts: The Legal Logic to the Japanese Main Bank System', in M. Aoki and H. Patrick (eds.) (1994), *The Japanese Main Bank System* (Oxford: Oxford University Press).

Reinganum, J. F. (1982), 'A Dynamic Game of R&D: Patent Protection and Competitive Behavior', *Econometrica*, 50, 671–88.

—— (1989), 'The Timing of Innovation: Research, Development, and Diffusion', in R. Schmalensee and R. D. Willig (eds.) (1989), *Handbook of Industrial Organization* (Amsterdam: North-Holland).

Ricart, J. E. (1987), 'Una introducción a los modelos de agencia', *Revista Española de Economía*, 4(1), 43–62.

Roe, M. J. (1994), *Strong Managers, Weak Owners* (Princeton, NJ: Princeton University Press).

Rogers, D. (1993), *The Future of American Banking* (New York: McGraw-Hill).

Roll, R. (1986), 'The Hubris Hypothesis of Corporate Takeovers', *Journal of Financial Economics*, 323–39.

Rotemberg, J., and Saloner, G. (1994), 'Benefits of Narrow Business Strategies', *American Economic Review*, 84(5), 1.330–1.349.

Rugman, A. (1981), *Inside the Multinationals* (London: Croom Helm).

Rumelt, R. P. (1974), *Strategy, Structure, and Economic Performance* (Boston: Harvard Business School Press).

—— (1982), 'Diversification Strategy and Profitability', *Strategic Management Journal*, 3, 359–69.

Salas, V. (1992), 'Incentivos y supervisión en el control interno de la empresa: Implicaciones para la concentración de su accionariado', *Cuadernos Económicos del ICE*, 52, 127–46.

—— (1993), 'La financiación de la empresa española: Una perspectiva institucional', *Economía Industrial*, September–October, 7–18.

Salop, S. (1979), 'Strategic Entry Deterrence', *American Economic Review*, 69 (May), 335–8.

Sánchez Asiain, J. A. (1990), 'Relaciones banca-industria', *Papeles de Economía Española*, 44, 87–90.

Santomero, A. M. (1984), 'Modelling the Banking Firm: A Survey', *Journal of Money, Credit and Banking*, 16, 576–602.

—— (1989), 'The Changing Structure of Financial Institutions: A Review Essay', *Journal of Monetary Economics*, 24, 321–8.

Saunders, A. (1994), 'Banking and Commerce: An Overview of the Public Policy Issues', *Journal of Banking and Finance*, 18, 231–54.

—— and Walter, I. (1994), *Universal Banking in the United States: What Could We Gain? What Could We Lose?* (New York: Oxford University Press).

—— and Yourougou, P. (1990), 'Are Banks Special? The Separation of Banking from Commerce and Interest Rate Risk', *Journal of Economics and Business*, 42, 171–82.

Scherer, F. M., and Ross, D. (1990), *Industrial Market Structure and Economic Performance* (Boston: Houghton Mifflin).

Shapiro, C. (1983), 'Premiums for High Quality Products as Rents to Reputation', *Quarterly Journal of Economics*, 98, 659–80.

Sheard, P. (1989), 'The Main Bank System and Corporate Monitoring and Control in Japan', mimeo.

—— (1994), 'Main Banks and the Governance of Financial Distress', in M. Aoki and H. Patrick (eds.) (1994), *The Japanese Main Bank System* (Oxford: Oxford University Press).

Shleifer, A., and Summers, L. H. (1988), 'Breach of Trust in Hostile Takeovers', in A. J. Auerbach (ed.) (1988), *Corporate Takeovers: Causes and Consequences* (Chicago: University of Chicago Press).

—— and Vishny, R. (1986), 'Large Shareholders and Corporate Control', *Journal of Political Economy*, 94, 461–88.

Shull, B. (1994), 'Banking and Commerce in the United States', *Journal of Banking and Finance*, 18, 255–70.

Silk, A. J., and Berndt, E. (1994), 'Costs, Institutional Mobility Barriers and Market Structure: Advertising Agencies as Multiproduct Firms', *Journal of Economics and Management Strategy*, 3(3) 437–80.

Sirri, E. R., and Tufano, P. (1993), 'Competition and Change in the Mutual Fund Industry', in S. L. Hayes, III (ed.) (1993), *Financial Services* (Boston: Harvard Business School Press).

Steinherr, A. (1990), 'Financial Institutions in Europe under New Competitive Conditions', mimeo.

—— (1992), *The New European Financial Marketplace* (London: Longman).

—— and Huveneers, C. (1989), 'Universal Banks: The Prototype of Successful Banks in the Integrated European Market? A View Inspired by the German Experience', mimeo.

——, —— (1994), 'On the Performance of Differently Regulated Financial Institutions: Some Empirical Evidence', *Journal of Banking and Finance*, 18, 271–306.

Stiglitz, J. E. (1974), 'On the Irrelevance of Corporate Financial Policy', *American Economic Review*, 64, 851–66.

—— (1988), 'Why Financial Structure Matters', *Journal of Economic Perspectives*, 2(4), 121–6.

——, and Weiss, A. (1981), 'Credit Rationing in Markets with Imperfect Information', *American Economic Review*, 71(3), 393–410.

Suzuki, S., and Wright, R. (1985), 'Financial Structure and Bankruptcy Risk in Japanese Companies', *Journal of International Business Studies*, Spring, 97–110.

Suzuki, Y. (1980), *Money and Banking in Contemporary Japan* (New Haven, CT: Yale University Press).

—— (1986), *Money, Finance and Macroeconomic Performance in Japan* (New Haven, CT: Yale University Press).

—— (ed.) (1987), *The Japanese Financial System* (Oxford: Oxford University Press).

Swary, I., and Topf, B. (1993), *Global Financial Deregulation* (Oxford: Blackwell).

Teece, D. (1982), 'Towards an Economic Theory of the Multi-Product Firm', *Journal of Economic Behavior and Organization*, 3(1), 39–63.

Termes, R. (1994), 'El sistema financiero en la recuperación de la economía española', Real Academia de Ciencias Morales y Políticas, Conferencia.

Tilly, R. H. (1966), *Financial Institutions and Industrialization in the Rhineland 1815–1870* (Madison: University of Wisconsin Press).

—— (1986), 'German Banking 1850–1914', *Journal of European Economic History*, 15, 113–52.

—— and Fremdling, R. (1976), 'German Banks, German Growth and Econometric History', *Journal of Economic History*, 36, 416–27.

Tirole, J. (1993), 'On Banking and Intermediation', *European Economic Review*, 38, 469–87.

Torrero, A. (1991), *Relaciones Banca-Industria. La Experiencia Española* (Madrid: Espasa Calpe).

—— (1993), *La Crisis del Sistema Bancario: Lecciones de la Experiencia de Estados Unidos* (Madrid: Ed. Civitas).

Tschoegel, A. E. (1987), 'International Retail Banking as a Strategy: An Assessment', *Journal of International Business Studies*, 18(2), 67–88.

Tullock, T. (1967), 'The Welfare Costs of Tariffs, Monopolies and Theft', *Western Economic Journal*, 5, 224–32.

Vickers, J. (1985), 'Delegation and the Theory of the Firm', *Economic Journal*, 43, Supplement, 138–47.

Vives, X. (1988), 'Concentración bancaria y competitividad', *Papeles de Economía Española*, 36, 62–76.

—— (1990), 'La nueva competencia', *Papeles de Economía Española*, 44, 20–5.

—— (1991), 'Banking Competition and European Integration', in A. Giovannini and C. Mayer (eds.) (1991), *European Financial Intermediation* (Cambridge: Cambridge University Press).

—— (1994), 'Desregulación y reforma regulatoria en el sector bancario', *Papeles de Economía Española*, 58, 2–13.

Walter, I. (1988), *Global Competition in Financial Services* (Cambridge, MA: Ballinger).

—— (ed.) (1985), *Deregulating Wall Street* (New York: John Wiley).

Wenston, J. F. (1970), 'The Nature and Significance of Conglomerate Firms', *St. John's Law Review Special Edition*, 44, 68–80.

Wheelock, D. C. (1993), 'Government Policy and Banking Market Structure in the 1920s', *Journal of Economic History*, December.

—— (1995), 'Regulation, Market Structure and the Bank Failures of the Great Depression', *Review*, Federal Reserve Bank of St. Louis, March–April, 27–38.

White, E. N. (1983), *The Regulation and Reform of the American Banking System, 1900–1929* (Princeton, NJ: Princeton University Press).

—— (1984), 'A Reinterpretation of the Banking Crisis of 1930', *Journal of Economic History*, March, 119–38.

—— (1986), 'Before the Glass–Steagall Act: An Analysis of the Investment Banking Activities of National Banks', *Explorations in Economic History*, 23, 33–55.

—— (1992), 'Change and Turmoil in U.S. Banking: Causes, Consequences, and Lessons', mimeo.

Williamson, O. E. (1970), *Corporate Control and Business Behavior* (Englewood Cliffs, NJ: Prentice-Hall).

—— (1975), *Markets and Hierarchies* (New York: The Free Press).

—— (1985), *The Economic Institutions of Capitalism* (New York: The Free Press).

Willig, R. (1979), 'Multiproduct Technology and Market Structure', *American Economic Review*, 69(2), 346–51.

Wilson, J. D. (1986), *The Chase* (Boston: Harvard Business School Press).

Yamamura, K., and Yasuba, Y. (eds.) (1987), *The Political Economy of Japan* (Stanford: Stanford University Press).

Zimmer, S. A., and McCauley, R. N. (1991), 'Bank Cost of Capital and International Competition', *Quarterly Review*, Federal Reserve Bank of New York, Winter, 33–59.

Index